Mastering Deepfake Technology: Strategies for Ethical Management and Security

RIVER PUBLISHERS SERIES IN DIGITAL SECURITY AND FORENSICS

The "River Publishers Series in Security and Digital Forensics" is a series of comprehensive academic and professional books which focus on the theory and applications of Cyber Security, including Data Security, Mobile and Network Security, Cryptography and Digital Forensics. Topics in Prevention and Threat Management are also included in the scope of the book series, as are general business Standards in this domain.

Books published in the series include research monographs, edited volumes, handbooks and textbooks. The books provide professionals, researchers, educators, and advanced students in the field with an invaluable insight into the latest research and developments.

Topics covered in the series include:-

- Blockchain for secure transactions
- Cryptography
- Cyber Security
- Data and App Security
- Digital Forensics
- Hardware Security
- IoT Security
- Mobile Security
- Network Security
- Privacy
- Software Security
- Standardization
- Threat Management

For a list of other books in this series, visit www.riverpublishers.com

Mastering Deepfake Technology: Strategies for Ethical Management and Security

Editors

Sanjay Taneja
Professor, Department of Management Studies,
Graphic Era deemed to be University, India

Swati Gupta
Chitkara Business School, Chitkara University,
Punjab, India

Mohit Kukreti
University of Technology and Applied Sciences Ibri, Oman

Abhishek Singh Chauhan
Graphic Era deemed to be University, India

River Publishers
Routledge
Taylor & Francis Group
NEW YORK AND LONDON

Published 2025 by River Publishers
River Publishers
Broagervej 10, 9260 Gistrup, Denmark
www.riverpublishers.com

Distributed exclusively by Routledge
605 Third Avenue, New York, NY 10017, USA
4 Park Square, Milton Park, Abingdon, Oxon OX14 4RN

Mastering Deepfake Technology: Strategies for Ethical Management and Security / Sanjay Taneja, Swati Gupta, Mohit Kukreti, and Abhishek Singh Chauhan.

Routledge is an imprint of the Taylor & Francis Group, an informa business

ISBN 978-87-4380-113-9 (hardback)
ISBN 978-87-4380-185-6 (paperback)
ISBN 978-87-4380-115-3 (online)
ISBN 978-8-743-80114-6 (ebook master)

Contents

Preface

Sanjay Taneja, Graphic Era deemed to be University, India
(Drsanjaytaneja1@gmail.com)

Swati Gupta, Chitkara Business School, Chitkara University, Punjab, India
(swati.gupta@chitkara.edu.in)

Mohit Kukreti, University of Technology and Applied Sciences Ibri, Oman
(MOHIT.KUKRETI@utas.edu.om)

Abhishek Singh Chauhan, Graphic Era deemed to be University, India
(abhishek.singhchauhan3692@gmail.com)

This book, *Mastering Deepfake Technology: Strategies for Ethical Management and Security*, aims to act as a roadmap on how to manage best the issues that deep fakes bring into the corporate sphere. Today, managers must protect their organisations from possible deepfake attacks that will bring reputational loss, financial loss, and legal liabilities. It involves inputs for not only the technology but also the ethics behind the operation of the synthetic media. To the readers and practitioners interested in learning about or dealing with legal frameworks and privacy concerns about deepfakes, these chapters offer practical rubrics on how they can shield their organisations from deepfake threats, along with insights on the current laws that govern AI-generated media production and what they cannot do.

The problems that arise from deepfake technology are not just a matter of a technical nature – they involve managing, ethical, and anticipatory aspects. Inexperienced as most corporate leaders may be, traversing this uncharted territory calls for mastery of technological solutions and an understanding of the more profound social, political, and ethical context. This book has been written with that understanding in mind. Thus, it aims to offer guidance to those who can be addressed as AI/media/corporate responsibility managers to think before implementing and regulating deepfake technology.

The editors have been in consultation with an array of scholars and professionals to provide a balanced consideration of the pertinent questions about deepfakes. From engineers and legal experts to ethicists and corporate leaders, the contributors bring a wealth of perspectives to the table. This book promotes a multidisciplinary lens through which the intricate nature of deepfake technology is viewed. This is important because the implications of deepfakes go beyond just any type of subject area or domain. It is a technological issue, but also a social, legal, and managerial one.

Thus, for managers and leaders, it is high time they deepen their knowledge concerning deepfakes and act accordingly, given that the world is entering a period of enhanced utilisation of deepfake technologies. This book is the beginning of the discussion and exploration of how this technology will redefine business, governance, and society. Our aim for this book is for the readers to not only gain a clear perspective of the deepfake problem but also learn how to make better decisions and be more critical and thoughtful in our actions.

We thank all the authors for making this book possible and all the people who are joining us on this kind of learning. We believe that through education, dialogue, and thoughtful action, we can navigate the challenges posed by deep fake technology and turn them into opportunities for innovation and growth.

Foreword

In today's rapidly evolving digital landscape, the intersection of artificial intelligence and media production has given rise to one of the most contentious technologies of our time: deepfakes. What used to be a specific technological curiosity – deepfake – has become incredibly popular and, at the same time, raises numerous philosophical questions. While corporations, government agencies, and regular individuals are trying to assess the implications of these synthetic media, there is no better time to give priority to understanding the effect on businesses, politics, and privacy.

This book, *Mastering Deepfake Technology: Strategies for Ethical Management and Security*, offers a timely analysis of this inherently complex domain of deep fakes while coherently focusing on the role of management in it. The editors, Sanjay Taneja, Swati Gupta, Mohit Kukreti, and Abhishek Singh Chauhan, along with a cohort of expert contributors, dissect the legal, ethical, and operational implications that deep fake technologies introduce to the corporate sphere.

From the historical evolution of deepfakes to their use in political manipulation, the book thoroughly analyses the risks and opportunities presented by synthetic media. The book is quite useful to managers and decision-makers who will learn how to manage and address this issue: the strengths and weaknesses of algorithms, the available options for addressing algorithmic risks and building reliable protection systems for corporations, their reputation, and security.

In another respect, one of the book's most significant assets is the wide range of issues that it covers, from the technological foundations of deep fakes to broader societal concerns and practical guidance on what managers should do to manage potential risks. Alongside critique, the book addresses concrete examples to ground the reader and show, by now, what impact deep fakes have had on various industries and people.

As we venture deeper into an era where authenticity can be easily manipulated, corporate leadership's role in maintaining trust and safeguarding operations becomes paramount. This book serves as both a wake-up call and a guide for business leaders to stay ahead of a fast-evolving technological landscape that challenges traditional notions of media integrity.

So, I would like to express my gratitude to the authors and editors for attempting to address this critical issue. I am confident that this work will be the essential reference for any manager who wants to deal with the specificities of deep fake technologies in the future.

Regards,
Rajendra Rajaram,
Unisa School of Business and Leadership,
South Africa.
rajarr@unisa.ac.za

List of Contributors

Abuselidze, George, *The University of Georgia, Georgia*

Agrawal, Vikas, *Amrapali University Haldwani, India*

Ahsan, Mohammad, *Imam Abdulrahman Bin Faisal University Dammam, Saudi Arabia*

Bahl Walia, Sargam, *Graphic Era Hill University, Dehradun, India*

Bansal, Ankita, *Vivekananda Institute of Professional Studies, India*

Bhatnagar Mukul, *Graphic Era Deemed to be University, India*

Davim, J P, *Universidade de Aveiro, Portugal*

Dhiman, Babli, *Lovely Professional University, India*

Dixit, Pragti, *University School of Business, Chandigarh University, India*

Fulara Saurabh, *Graphic Era Hill University, Dehradun, India*

Ghai, Sachin, *Graphic Era Deemed to be University, India*

Gokhale, Nilesh P, *Sri Balaji University, India*

Gupta, Swati, *Chitkara Business School, Chitkara University, Punjab, India*

Iyer, Vishwanathan, *Sri Balaji University, India*

Johri, Amar, *Saudi Electronic University, Saudi Arabia*

Kaushal, Deepak, *Graphic Era (deemed to be) University, Dehradun, India*

Kaur, Arvinder, *Chandigarh University, India*

Kaur, Dilpreet, *Sri Balaji University, India*

Kaur, Harshdeep, *Punjabi University, India*

Kaur, Manjeet, *School of Management Studies and Commerce, RIMT University, Mandi Gobindgarh, India*

Kaur, Manpreet, *Lovely Professional University, India*

Khurana, Kajal, *Punjabi University, India*

K. Savale, Tushar, *Sri Balaji University, India*

Kukreti, M, *University of Technology and Applied Sciences, Ibri, Oman*

Kumar, Pawan, *Graphic Era (deemed to be) University, India*

M. Kamble, Sandeep, *Sri Balaji University, India*

Miglani, Mehul, *Chandigarh University, India*

Mistrean Larisa, *Academy of Economic Studies of Moldova, Moldova*

Mishra, K. K., *University School of Business, Chandigarh University, Punjab, India*

Mitali Soni, *Faculty of Management Studies, University of Delhi, India*

Negi, Naveen, *Graphic Era (deemed to be) University, Dehradun, India*

Ozen Ercan, *Usak University, Turkey*

Pant, Pawan, *University School of Business, Chandigarh University, India*

Pillay, Surendran, *University of KwaZulu-Natal, South Africa*

Prasher, Navjyoti, *University School of Business, Chandigarh University, Punjab, India*

Rajaram, Rajendra, *Unisa School of Business Leadership, University of South Africa, South Africa*

Rana Sudhir, *College of Healthcare Management and Economics, Gulf Medical University, UAE*

Reepu, Chandigarh University, *Punjab, India*

Shamsuddin, Zelhuda, *Universiti Sultan Zainal Abidin, Malaysia*

Sharma Rajat, *Graphic Era Deemed to be University, India*

Sharma, Pirtibha, *TMIMT, Teerthanker Mahaveer University, India*

Sharma, Umang, *Chandigarh Group of Colleges, India*

Sharma, Vivek, *Chandigarh University, India*

Shaukat, M. R., *University of Technology and Applied Sciences, Ibri, Oman*

Singh, Bupiinderpal, *Yorkville University, Canada*

Singh, Muskan, *Graphic Era Deemed to be University, India*

Singh, Raj Kumar, *SOM, Graphic Era Hill University, India*

Taneja Sanjay, *Universiti Sultan Zainal Abidin, Malaysia*

Taneja, Sanjay, *Graphic Era Deemed to be University, India*

Ullah, S., *University of Central Punjab, Pakistan*

Vardari, Luan, *University "Ukshin Hoti" Rruga e shkronjave Nr., Prizren, Kosova*

Zoidze, Gia, *Batumi Shota Rustaveli State University, Georgia*

List of Figures

List of Tables

List of Abbreviations

ADT	Awareness of deepfake technology
AI	Artificial intelligence
APIs	Application programming interfaces
AR	Augmented reality
ATM	Automated teller machine
AVE	Average variance extracted
BBC	British Broadcasting Corporation
C-DSS	Cloud-data security system
CNN	Cable news network
ECC	Elliptic curve cryptography
GAN	Generative adversarial networks
GDPR	General data protection regulation
HCI	Human-computer interaction
HTMT	Heterotrait-Monotrait
KYC	Know Your Customer
MLP	Multilayer perceptron
MPT	Modern Portfolio Theory
NFTs	Non-fungible tokens
NPAs	Non-performing assets
PJS	Perceived job security
PLS	Partial least squares
RBI	Reserve Bank of India
RDS	Responsible data science
SDGs	Sustainable development goals
TDR	Training on deepfake recognition
TiM	Trust in management
UIs	User interfaces
UX	User experience
VR	Virtual reality

Introduction to the Book

Dr. Sanjay Taneja

Graphic Era deemed to be University, India
Email: drsanjaytaneja1@gmail.com

The advancement of AI innovation has brought innovative experiences about technological advancement to reform several spheres of society. Of these, deepfake technology is one of the most revolutionary yet argued innovations brought up in recent years. This book, *Mastering Deepfake Technology: Strategies for Ethical Management and Security*, covers a dynamic and multifaceted arena of deepfake technology within the corporate environment.

In an era where fake news and synthetic media are gaining a foothold in everyday life and are more and more difficult to detect, the work addresses relevant issues related to deepfakes in corporate settings. Such applications present various difficulties and problems, including the ability and propensity to leverage media for political and reputational sabotage, privacy issues, and legal questions, as well as the acceptable use of such technologies. With businesses leaning more toward digital media and AI, organisations must understand the effects that deepfake technology has on their business to sustain the company's reputation and prevent future threats to the company's security.

Exploring historical and algorithmic angles and utilising further suggestions for corporate managers, legal practitioners, and students, the book is informative. It paints a picture of what could go wrong while providing a course of action when tackling these new phenomena. A few specific examples highlighted in the case studies demonstrate how deepfakes are being used in different practical situations to make corporate, political, and privacy-related decisions and what both the negative and positive possible applications of this technology are.

Through a detailed analysis of the technological, ethical, and managerial challenges posed by deepfakes, this book serves as an essential resource for anyone tasked with protecting organisational reputations and ensuring ethical corporate practices in the age of synthetic media. The editors and contributing authors offer a balanced perspective, helping readers understand the dangers and opportunities that deepfake technology presents in the business world.

1

The Role of Intellectual Capital in Combatting Deepfake Threats to Corporate Reputation and Trust

Rajat Sharma[1], Mukul Bhatnagar[2] and Ercan Ozen[3]

[1,2]Graphic Era Deemed to be University, India
[3]Usak University, Turkey

Email: sharmarajat126@gmail.com; mukulbhatnagar1993@gmail.com; ercan.ozen@usak.edu.tr

Abstract

This study explores the complex interrelations between human capital competency, knowledge sharing practices, corporate reputation, and stakeholder trust by employing Partial Least Squares Structural Equation Modelling (PLS-SEM) to analyze data gathered through structured questionnaires, revealing that while human capital competency – measured through indicators like employee preparedness, intellectual protection, and training – significantly bolsters corporate reputation, the effect of knowledge sharing practices, though highly correlated with internal communication quality and knowledge transfer efficiency, exhibits a negative relationship with corporate reputation, challenging traditional assumptions, and further showing that stakeholder trust is moderately influenced by human capital competency but not significantly impacted by knowledge sharing practices, thus addressing a critical research gap and offering managerial insights into optimising internal competencies for enhanced external perceptions and stakeholder engagement, with the findings validated through robust reliability and discriminant validity assessments including outer loadings, composite reliability, and HTMT, further supported by bootstrapping to confirm statistical significance across the model's hypothesised pathways.

1.1 Introduction

In an era where the confluence of human capital development and strategic knowledge dissemination has become paramount for corporate success (Jaiswal et al., 2024), this study delves into the intricate dynamics between Human Capital Competency – encompassing essential variables such as employee preparedness (Lotfi et al., 2024), intellectual protection, and collaborative learning – and knowledge sharing practices (Lotfi et al., 2024), examining their respective impacts on corporate reputation and stakeholder trust through a rigorous application of structural equation modelling and advanced statistical analyses (Jaiswal & Samuel, 2023), thereby offering profound insights into how organisations can optimise these internal constructs to not only enhance external perceptions but also foster deeper trust among stakeholders in an increasingly complex and reputationally sensitive business environment (Kushwah & Siddiqui, 2023).

1.2 Literature Review

The literature on human capital competency and knowledge sharing practices, deeply rooted in organisational theory and strategic management, has long posited the optimisation of

- employee preparedness (Choudhary et al., 2023),
- skill acquisition (Nagvanshi et al., 2023),
- intellectual protection (Das et al., 2023), and
- collaborative learning (Govil et al., 2023).

These are not only instrumental in driving internal efficiency but also serve as pivotal determinants of external corporate reputation and stakeholder trust, as underscored by seminal works exploring the multifaceted relationship between internal competencies and external perceptions (Tabassum et al., 2023); however, recent empirical studies leveraging advanced methodologies such as Partial Least Squares Structural Equation Modelling (Gupta & Bhatia, 2022), have revealed more nuanced and sometimes counterintuitive interactions – particularly in the context of knowledge transfer's indirect effects on corporate image – thus suggesting a complex interplay of factors where not all internal strengths directly translate into enhanced stakeholder perceptions (Ali et al., 2022), necessitating further examination of how knowledge dissemination processes might either positively or negatively influence organisational outcomes in varying contexts and industries (Gera et al., 2023).

1.3 Research Gaps

This study addresses a critical research gap by empirically investigating the nuanced and understudied impact of knowledge-sharing practices on corporate reputation and stakeholder trust (Paul et al., 2023), challenging the conventional assumption that all internal competencies inherently enhance external perceptions (Singh et al., 2023), thus contributing novel insights to the field of organisational management (Jaiswal et al., 2023).

1.4 Research Methodology

This research employs a quantitative methodology utilising Partial Least Squares Structural Equation Modelling (PLS-SEM) to analyse the relationships between human capital competency (Nanda & Kumar, 2022), knowledge-sharing practices, corporate reputation, and stakeholder trust, with data collected via structured questionnaires, testing hypotheses through bootstrapping and validating constructs with outer loadings, reliability metrics, and discriminant validity assessments (Tiwari et al., 2022). The questionnaire framed for the research is shown in Table 1.1.

1.5 Data Analysis

The PLS algorithm in the figure shows that human capital competency has a strong positive influence on corporate reputation (0.565) and a moderate effect on stakeholder trust (0.278). In contrast, knowledge-sharing practices have a minor impact on corporate reputation (0.093) and stakeholder trust (0.098).

The outer loadings in Table 1.2 demonstrate strong correlations between constructs and their respective indicators, with high values across all variables, particularly for knowledge sharing practices, human capital competency, corporate reputation, and stakeholder trust. This indicates robust construct measurement validity.

The outer loadings in Table 1.3 indicate strong correlations between the latent variables and their corresponding indicators. Knowledge-sharing practices, human capital competency, corporate reputation, and stakeholder trust all show high levels of association with their respective measures.

Table 1.1 Questionnaire.

Variable name	Question heading	Question statement	7-Point scale
Corporate Reputation(Thota et al., 2022)	Perception of ethical standards	The company upholds high ethical standards, even when facing deepfake threats.	1 –Strongly disagree to 7 –Strongly agree
	Handling deepfake incidents	The company effectively manages its reputation after a deepfake incident occurs.	1 –Strongly disagree to 7 –Strongly agree
	General public perception	The public's perception of the company remains positive despite potential deepfake risks.	1 –Strongly disagree to 7 –Strongly agree
Stakeholder Trust(Arora et al., 2024)	Trust in the company's resilience	I trust this company's ability to withstand the impact of deepfake-related challenges.	1 –Strongly disagree to 7 –Strongly agree
	Confidence in leadership	I feel confident that the company's leadership can protect intellectual capital from deepfakes.	1 –Strongly disagree to 7 –Strongly agree
	Trust in safeguarding assets	The company has the proper measures to protect its assets from deepfakes.	1 –Strongly Disagree to 7 –Strongly Agree
Human Capital Competency (Prakash et al., 2022)	Employee preparedness	Employees are well-prepared to detect and handle deepfake-related threats.	1 –Strongly disagree to 7 –Strongly agree
	Skill in intellectual protection	The company's employees have the skills to protect intellectual capital from digital threats like deepfakes.	1 –Strongly disagree to 7 –Strongly agree
	Employee training	The company provides regular training to improve employees' ability to combat deepfakes.	1 –Strongly disagree to 7 –Strongly agree
Knowledge Sharing Practices(Nathani & Kushwah, 2022)	Internal communication quality	Employees regularly share information about handling deepfake risks within the organisation.	1 –Strongly disagree to 7 –Strongly agree
	Knowledge transfer efficiency	The company's knowledge-sharing practices help enhance the organisation's ability to protect against deepfakes.	1 –Strongly disagree to 7 –Strongly agree
	Collaborative learning	Teams within the company collaborate effectively to share knowledge about intellectual capital protection.	1 –Strongly disagree to 7 –Strongly agree

Source: Authors'compilations

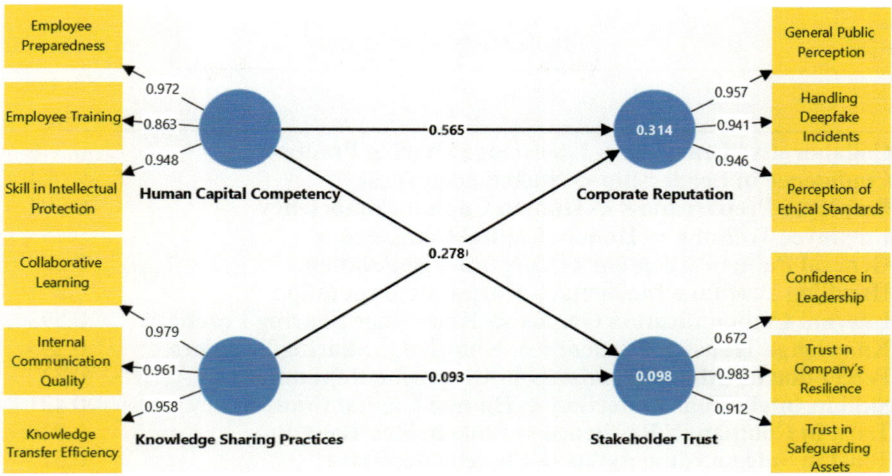

Figure 1.1 PLS algorithm. Source: Authors'compilations.

Table 1.2 Outer loadings.

	Outer loadings
Collaborative Learning <- Knowledge Sharing Practices	0.979
Confidence in Leadership <- Stakeholder Trust	0.672
Employee Preparedness <- Human Capital Competency	0.972
Employee Training <- Human Capital Competency	0.863
General Public Perception <- Corporate Reputation	0.957
Handling Deepfake Incidents <- Corporate Reputation	0.941
Internal Communication Quality <- Knowledge Sharing Practices	0.961
Knowledge Transfer Efficiency <- Knowledge Sharing Practices	0.958
Perception of Ethical Standards <- Corporate Reputation	0.946
Skill in Intellectual Protection <- Human Capital Competency	0.948
Trust in Company's Resilience <- Stakeholder Trust	0.983
Trust in Safeguarding Assets <- Stakeholder Trust	0.912

Source: Authors'compilations.

- Table 1.4 shows that all constructs have high reliability and validity, with Cronbach's alpha and composite reliability values exceeding the acceptable threshold of 0.7.
- The average variance extracted (AVE) values indicate a high level of variance explained by each construct's indicators, confirming strong construct validity.

Table 1.3 Outer weights.

	Outer weights
Collaborative Learning <- Knowledge Sharing Practices	0.348
Confidence in Leadership <- Stakeholder Trust	0.024
Employee Preparedness <- Human Capital Competency	0.394
Employee Training <- Human Capital Competency	0.253
General Public Perception <- Corporate Reputation	0.357
Handling Deepfake Incidents <- Corporate Reputation	0.361
Internal Communication Quality <- Knowledge Sharing Practices	0.393
Knowledge Transfer Efficiency <- Knowledge Sharing Practices	0.293
Perception of Ethical Standards <- Corporate Reputation	0.337
Skill in Intellectual Protection <- Human Capital Competency	0.421
Trust in Company's Resilience <- Stakeholder Trust	0.710
Trust in Safeguarding Assets <- Stakeholder Trust	0.313

Source: Authors'compilations.

Table 1.4 Construct reliability and validity.

	Cronbach's alpha	Composite reliability (rho_a)	Composite reliability (rho_c)	Average variance extracted (AVE)
Corporate reputation	0.943	0.945	0.964	0.898
Human capital competency	0.922	0.973	0.949	0.862
Knowledge sharing practices	0.965	0.984	0.977	0.934
Stakeholder trust	0.873	1.449	0.898	0.750

Source: Authors'compilations.

The HTMT values in Table 1.5, all below the 0.85 threshold, indicate good discriminant validity between the constructs, meaning they are distinct and not excessively correlated.

The bootstrapping results confirm that all relationships are statistically significant except for the path from knowledge sharing practices to corporate reputation, which is not substantial.

Human capital competency significantly impacts corporate reputation, while other paths show no significance or, in the case of knowledge sharing practices to corporate reputation, a significant adverse effect.

Table 1.5 HTMT.

	Corporate reputation	Human capital competency	Knowledge sharing practices	Stakeholder trust
Corporate reputation				
Human capital competency	0.519			
Knowledge sharing practices	0.124	0.257		
Stakeholder trust	0.251	0.229	0.137	

Source: Authors'compilations.

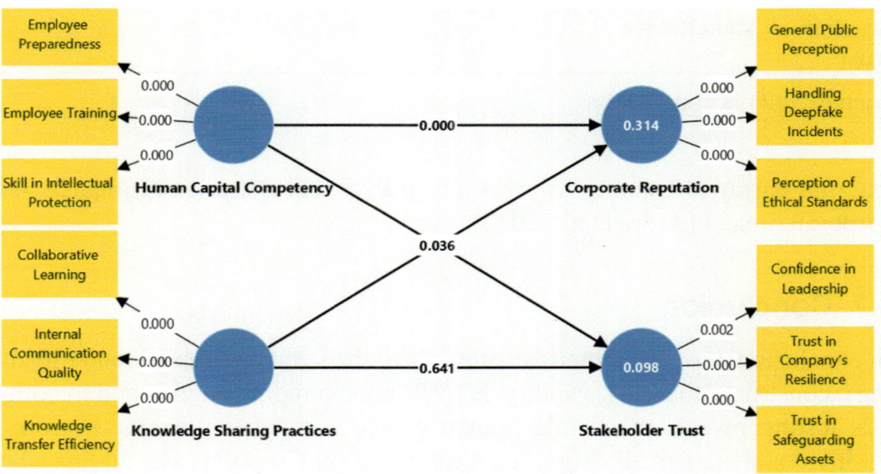

Figure 1.2 Bootstrapping. Source: Authors compilations.

1.6 Managerial Implications

The managerial implications of these findings suggest that organisations must prioritise the enhancement of Human Capital Competency – encompassing facets such as employee preparedness (Thomas et al., 2023), intellectual protection, and collaborative learning – as it demonstrates a profound, statistically significant influence on bolstering Corporate Reputation while simultaneously acknowledging that Knowledge Sharing Practices, although pivotal for internal cohesion (Garg et al., 2023), may not directly fortify external perceptions and stakeholder trust, thereby necessitating a more nuanced, strategic approach to interdepartmental knowledge dissemination and its

Table 1.6 Hypothesis testing.

	Original sample (O)	Sample mean (M)	Standard deviation (STDEV)	T statistics (|O/STDEV|)	P values
Human capital competency -> corporate reputation	0.565	0.577	0.111	5.103	0.000
Human capital competency -> stakeholder trust	0.278	0.292	0.155	1.791	0.073
Knowledge sharing practices -> corporate reputation	−0.259	−0.259	0.124	2.092	0.036
Knowledge sharing practices -> stakeholder trust	0.093	0.091	0.199	0.466	0.641

Source: Authors'compilations

external narrative framing to avert any inadvertent detrimental impacts on corporate image (Arora et al., 2023).

1.7 Conclusion

In conclusion, the comprehensive analysis of the structural model, outer loadings, construct reliability, validity, HTMT, bootstrapping results, and hypothesis testing reveals that while human capital competency exerts a strong, positive, and statistically significant influence on Corporate Reputation, the relationship between Knowledge Sharing Practices and Corporate Reputation is notably negative, albeit substantial, with the latter also failing to show significant impact on Stakeholder Trust, highlighting the critical need for organisations to meticulously balance their internal knowledge management strategies with their external reputation-building efforts, as well as fine-tuning the intricacies of stakeholder engagement to enhance both corporate image and trust, thereby necessitating a multidimensional approach to organisational competency and knowledge sharing that integrates robust employee training, collaborative learning, intellectual protection, and effective communication with strategic external communication and trust-building mechanisms.

References

Ali, S., Mathur, A. N., & Jaiswal, A. K. (2022). Antecedents to firm performance during re-internationalization. *Australian Journal of Management, 47*(3), 423–453. https://doi.org/10.1177/03128962211040134

Arora, M., Gupta, J., & Mittal, A. (2023). Adoption of food delivery apps during a crisis: exploring an extended technology adoption model. *Global Knowledge, Memory and Communication*. https://doi.org/10.1108/GKMC-01-2023-0005

Arora, M., Prakash, A., Mittal, A., & Singh, S. (2024). Examining the slow acceptance of HR analytics in the Indian engineering and construction industry: a SEM-ANN-based approach. *Engineering, Construction and Architectural Management*, *31*(5), 1973–1993. https://doi.org/10.1108/ECAM-09-2021-0795

Choudhary, S. L., Dixit, R. S., Das, D., Ranjith Singh, K., & Dinesh Babu, V. (2023). Smart Telemedicine Using IoT by Integrating 5G and Block-Chain Techniques. *Proceedings of International Conference on Contemporary Computing and Informatics, IC3I 2023*, 2002–2008. https://doi.org/10.1109/IC3I59117.2023.10397928

Das, S., Mishra, A. K., & Paul, S. (2023). Non-performing assets - an important parameter of measuring the financial soundness of banks. *International Journal of Services and Operations Management*, *45*(4), 514–529. https://doi.org/10.1504/IJSOM.2023.132860

Garg, S., Pooja, Chaoudhary, S. L., Dixit, R., & Govil, N. (2023). Implementing and Analyzing Behaviour of ML based Tamil Songs Recommendation System. *2nd International Conference on Sustainable Computing and Data Communication Systems, ICSCDS 2023 - Proceedings*, 381–386. https://doi.org/10.1109/ICSCDS56580.2023.10104744

Gera, N., Yadav, S., Dana, L.-P., & Mittal, A. (2023). Determinants for adoption of new products: an empirical study on smart phone customers in Delhi NCR. *International Journal of Business Information Systems*, *43*(2), 143–163. https://doi.org/10.1504/ijbis.2023.131347

Govil, N., Sharma, N., Thakral, D., Garg, S., Dixit, R., & Chaoudhary, S. L. (2023). A Proposed Architecture for Quality based Decision Making Approach for Software Re-engineering. *2023 4th International Conference on Electronics and Sustainable Communication Systems, ICESC 2023 - Proceedings*, 1114–1119. https://doi.org/10.1109/ICESC57686.2023.10193032

Gupta, P., & Bhatia, P. (2022). An empirical investigation of N-11 countries as successors of BRICS using panel data modeling. *International Journal of Emerging Markets*, *17*(8), 2024–2051. https://doi.org/10.1108/IJOEM-07-2020-0809

Jaiswal, A., Mishra, V., Bhatnagar, S., & Bandyopadhyay, N. (2024). Sentiment Analysis of Social Welfare Tweets for Supervised Learning About Brand Loyalty. *Indian Journal of Marketing*, *54*(2), 8–26. https://doi.org/10.17010/ijom/2024/v54/i2/173473

Jaiswal, A., Negi, P., & Singh, N. (2023). MCDM Computational Approaches for Green Supply Chain Management Strategies. *2023 6th International Conference on Information Systems and Computer Networks, ISCON 2023*. https://doi.org/10.1109/ISCON57294.2023.10112124

Jaiswal, A., & Samuel, C. (2023). A Literature Review Based Bibliometric Analysis of Supply Chain Analytics. *Lecture Notes in Mechanical Engineering*, 397–408. https://doi.org/10.1007/978-981-19-0561-2_35

Kushwah, S. V., & Siddiqui, A. A. (2023). Relationship Between Oil Price Movements and Stock Returns of Oil Firms in Oil Importing Economies. *Global Business Review*, *24*(5), 916–932. https://doi.org/10.1177/0972150920917018

Lotfi, R., Khanbaba, A., Ali, S. S., Afshar, M., Mehrjardi, M. S., & Omidi, S. (2024). Net-zero, resilience, and agile closed-loop supply chain network design considering robustness and renewable energy. *Environmental Science and Pollution Research*. https://doi.org/10.1007/s11356-024-32661-y

Nagvanshi, S., Gupta, N., & Kumar, V. (2023). Social Media Advertising in The Recent Years: A Bibliometric Analysis and Thematic Overview. In L. E.Y., C. S.-I., & Y. B. (Eds.), *Proceedings of the International Conference on Electronic Business (ICEB)* (Vol. 23, pp. 553–572). International Consortium for Electronic Business.

Nanda, P., & Kumar, V. (2022). Information Processing and Data Analytics for Decision Making: A Journey from Traditional to Modern Approaches. *Information Resources Management Journal*, *35*(2). https://doi.org/10.4018/IRMJ.291693

Nathani, N., & Kushwah, S. V. (2022). Volatility study in some of the emerging stock markets: a GARCH approach. *World Review of Science, Technology and Sustainable Development*, *18*(3–4), 364–378. https://doi.org/10.1504/WRSTSD.2022.123781

Paul, S. N., Upadhyay, R. K., & Garg, A. (2023). Antecedents of Investment Decision-Making in Mutual Fund: An Indian Perspective. *DLSU Business and Economics Review*, *32*(2), 161–173.

Prakash, A., Arora, M., Mittal, A., Kampani, S., & Dixit, S. (2022). Green manufacturing: Related literature over the past decade. *Materials Today: Proceedings*, *69*, 468 – 472. https://doi.org/10.1016/j.matpr.2022.09.142

Singh, N., Jaiswal, A., Singh, P., & Sharma, D. K. (2023). A/B Testing and Audience Creation for Effective Digital Marketing: Evidences from Facebook Analytics. *2023 6th International Conference on Information Systems and Computer Networks, ISCON 2023*. https://doi.org/10.1109/ISCON57294.2023.10112086

Tabassum, S., Yadav, M. P., Yadav, S., & Al-Qudah, A. A. (2023). Capturing Symmetrical and Asymmetrical Volatility in the Energy Market: Evidence of COVID Outbreak Tenure. *FIIB Business Review*. https://doi.org/10.1177/23197145231176113

Thomas, M., Gupta, M. V., Gokul Rajan, V., Rajalakshmi, R., Dixit, R. S., & Choudhary, S. L. (2023). Soft computing in computer network security protection system with machine learning based on level protection in the cloud environment. *Soft Computing*. https://doi.org/10.1007/s00500-023-08395-3

Thota, S., Dixit, R. S., Nurpeiis, M., Parida, D. K., Iissova, A., & Nigmetova, A. (2022). Robotics and Automatics in Terms of Utilizing Rules-based Business Processes. *4th International Conference on Inventive Research in Computing Applications, ICIRCA 2022 - Proceedings*, 261–266. https://doi.org/10.1109/ICIRCA54612.2022.9985682

Tiwari, A., Sharma, T., & Sharma, R. R. (2022). Exploring workplace dignity from managerial lens. *Management Research Review*, *45*(4), 545–562. https://doi.org/10.1108/MRR-08-2020-0544

2

The Face of Deception: Unmasking Deepfake Fraud in Financial Markets

Pawan Kumar[1], Arvinder Kaur[2], Surendran Pillay[3] and Sudhir Rana[4]

[1]Graphic Era (deemed to be) University, India
[2]Chandigarh University, India
[3]University of KwaZulu-Natal, South Africa
[4]College of Healthcare Management and Economics, Gulf Medical University, UAE

Email: pawan2006@gmail.com; arvinderkaurcs@gmail.com; pillays18@ukzn.ac.za; dr.sudhir@gmu.ac.ae

Abstract

This chapter meticulously examines the profound impact of deepfake fraud on global financial markets, highlighting how the proliferation of hyper-realistic, algorithmically generated synthetic media enables malicious actors to manipulate market dynamics through deceptive impersonations, disinformation campaigns, and fraudulent schemes that erode investor confidence, distort price discovery mechanisms, and destabilise the foundational trust in financial systems, ultimately exacerbating systemic risks and market volatility, while emphasising the critical role of advanced technological sophistication in deepfake detection tools, real-time threat intelligence, and comprehensive cybersecurity measures to mitigate these multifaceted threats and safeguard the integrity, stability, and resilience of global economic infrastructures in an increasingly digitised and deception-prone landscape .

2.1 Introduction

The unprecedented proliferation of deepfake technology, characterised by hyper-realistic synthetic media generated through advanced machine learning algorithms, poses an existential threat to the integrity and stability of global financial markets, as it enables nefarious actors to orchestrate sophisticated fraudulent schemes that manipulate market sentiments, erode investor confidence and destabilise the very bedrock of economic systems through deceptive impersonations of corporate executives, dissemination of false information, and artificial inflation of stock prices, thus compelling regulatory bodies and financial institutions to adopt cutting-edge countermeasures to mitigate these multifaceted risks (Chemerys, 2023).

"The burgeoning advancement of deepfake technology in financial markets has engendered a complex and insidious landscape where nefarious actors exploit synthetic media to craft meticulously deceptive narratives. This manipulation of audiovisual content distorts perceptual reality and precipitates a dangerous erosion of trust within global fiscal ecosystems. By engineering fraudulent representations of vital financial stakeholders and institutions, these actors catalyse cascading economic destabilisation, undermining regulatory frameworks and challenging the very bedrock of market integrity (Boccignone et al., 2022). The ramifications of such duplicitous machinations reverberate across the financial domain, instigating unprecedented vulnerabilities in an increasingly digitalised economy."

Concept of deepfake and financial market: "The confluence of deepfake technology and the financial market introduces a perilous frontier where hyper-realistic, algorithmically generated fabrications of corporate executives, financial analysts, and market-moving influencers can be weaponised to orchestrate sophisticated disinformation campaigns, ultimately subverting market dynamics, eroding investor confidence, and engendering systemic risks that threaten the stability and integrity of global financial infrastructures (Li, 2015)."

2.2 Variables of the Study

2.2.1 Dependent

Market stability refers to the consistency and stability in the market. The market observes fluctuations in trading activities, and its stability is affected by various factors.

2.2.2 Independent variables

Prevalence of deepfake incidents: This refers to the growing use of highly realistic AI-generated media that manipulates visuals or audio content, often for deceptive purposes, undermining trust in digital information.

Investors' confidence: Investor's confidence constitutes the intricate amalgamation of psychological certitude and behavioural predisposition of financial stakeholders, grounded in nuanced perceptions of market equilibrium, projected risk-adjusted returns, and macroeconomic stability, which collectively modulate their propensity to allocate capital amid fluctuating systemic dynamics, exogenous shocks (Rana, 2024; Raut et al., 2024), and latent uncertainties, thereby serving as a pivotal barometer of liquidity influx, market volatility, and the long-term sustainability of asset price equilibrium within increasingly interconnected global financial ecosystems characterised by complex adaptive behaviours and algorithmic interventions (Balasubramanian et al., 2022).

Technological sophistication tools of deepfake detention tools: Technological sophistication of deepfake detection tools refers to highly advanced, algorithmically driven systems that employ machine learning, neural networks, and forensic analysis to detect subtle, often invisible digital anomalies in AI-generated synthetic media, ensuring the precise identification and mitigation of increasingly deceptive deepfakes. These tools continuously evolve in response to advancing adversarial tactics, playing a critical role in safeguarding the authenticity of information and preventing disinformation in an ever-evolving, complex digital and media landscape (Dincer et al., 2023).

Cybersecurity measures in financial institutions: Cybersecurity measures in financial institutions encompass an intricate array of proactive and reactive defensive strategies, including multi-layered encryption protocols, advanced threat detection systems, real-time monitoring, regulatory compliance frameworks, and comprehensive incident response mechanisms, all designed to safeguard sensitive financial data, prevent unauthorised access, mitigate cyber threats, and ensure the continuity, resilience, and trustworthiness of financial operations amidst an increasingly volatile and digitally interconnected global landscape (Arunkumar et al., 2022).

2.3 Research Gap

The research gap lies in the lack of empirical exploration into the complex, multidimensional interrelations between the prevalence of profound fake incidents, investor confidence, technological sophistication of deepfake detection tools (Shukla et al., 2024), and cybersecurity measures within financial institutions, specifically regarding their collective and nuanced impact on market stability, as existing literature inadequately addresses the emergent risks and adaptive mechanisms required to mitigate the systemic vulnerabilities posed by increasingly sophisticated AI-driven disinformation and digital security threats in global financial ecosystems (Kharub et al., 2024).

Table 2.1 Research instruments.

Serial number	Name of the variable	Question statement	Scale description
1	Market Stability (Kapsis, 2020; J. E. Kim, 2020)	How stable do you believe the financial markets are in light of technological advancements?	1 = Strongly Disagree, 7 = Strongly Agree
2	Prevalence of Deepfake Incidents (Sardana et al., 2024; Sharma et al., 2024)	To what extent do you perceive deepfake incidents as a growing threat to financial markets?	1 = Not a Threat at All, 7 = Extremely High Threat
3	Investor Confidence (Jager-Waldau et al., 2021; Saadah & Panjaitan, 2016)	How confident are you in the reliability of information shared in financial markets amidst potential deepfake fraud?	1 = No Confidence, 7 = Very High Confidence
4	Technological Sophistication of Deepfake Detection Tools (Y. Kim et al., 2022)	How effective do you believe deepfake detection tools are in safeguarding financial market integrity?	1 = Not Effective, 7 = Extremely Effective
5	Cybersecurity Measures in Financial Institutions (Faura et al., 2023)	How well do you think financial institutions are equipped with cybersecurity measures to prevent deepfake-related fraud?	1 = Not Equipped at All, 7 = Very Well Equipped

Source: Data compiled by author.

2.4 Data Analysis

Table 2.1 describes the information about the questions and respondents based on scale.

Table 2.2 presents the distribution of respondents and reflects a diverse asymmetrical representation, with retail investors comprising an overwhelming majority at 60.83%, juxtaposed against the relatively modest participation of financial analysis, market experts, and technology experts in cybersecurity, who together account for 23.96%, while institutional investors, corporative executives, legal experts in financial crimes and journalists collectively contribute to a more minor albeit critical, 15.2% demonstrating a multifaceted cross-section of expertise that underscores the predominance of individual investors in this evaluative cohort of 217 participants.

Table 2.2 Respondents.

Respondents	**Number**	**%**
Financial Analysts and Market Experts	25	11.52%
Institutional Investors	6	2.76%
Corporate Executives and Financial Officers	5	2.30%
Technology Experts in Cybersecurity	27	12.44%
Retail Investors	132	60.83%
Legal Experts in Financial Crimes	10	4.61%
Journalists and Media Professionals	12	5.53%
TOTAL	217	100.00%

Source: Data compiled by author.

Table 2.3 provides an exhaustive statistical examination of several critical variables – namely "Prevalence of Deepfake Incidents", "Investor Confidence", "Technological Sophistication of Deepfake Detection Tools", "Cybersecurity Measures in Financial Institutions", and "Market Stability" – where each variable's mean and standard deviation are meticulously adjusted for bootstrapped bias and standard errors, with confidence intervals delineating the range of plausible values, thus offering a robust depiction of the central tendencies and dispersions within the dataset, ensuring statistical precision and reliability, and presenting a comprehensive quantitative portrait of the variability and relationships across these pivotal constructs in the financial ecosystem.

The graph (Figure 2.1) represents a multilayer perceptron (MLP) neural network architecture comprising an input layer with multiple nodes corresponding to distinct features, followed by a hidden layer where each neuron employs the hyperbolic tangent activation function, modulated by bias terms, and weighted synaptic connections (both positive and negative) to propagate transformed inputs through non-linear combinations; the output layer utilises the softmax activation function to deliver probabilistic classifications across the output nodes, indicating the system's ability to map complex, multi-dimensional input data into distinct output categories with precision across weighted interconnections.

The descriptive analysis reveals in Table 2.4 a nuanced interplay among the variables, where investor confidence exhibits a significant positive correlation with market stability, technological sophistication of deepfake detection tools, and cybersecurity measures, underscoring its central role in maintaining market equilibrium; conversely, the prevalence of deepfake incidents shows an insignificant relationship with market stability, while technological sophistication and cybersecurity measures demonstrate robust

Table 2.3 Descriptive statistics.

Descriptive statistics							
			Bootstrap				
					95% Confidence Interval		
		Statistic	Bias	Std. Error	Lower	Upper	
Prevalence_of_Deepfake_Incidents	Mean	5.1429	0.0013	0.1081	4.9217	5.3456	
	Std. Deviation	1.57023	–0.00626	0.06986	1.42168	1.69899	
	N	217	0	0	217	217	
Investor_Confidence	Mean	4.5622	–0.0020	0.0874	4.3825	4.7372	
	Std. Deviation	1.25722	–0.00181	0.06268	1.13454	1.37734	
	N	217	0	0	217	217	
Technological_Sophistication_of_ Deepfake_Detection_Tools	Mean	4.1751	–0.0015	0.1014	3.9770	4.3641	
	Std. Deviation	1.58603	–0.00156	0.06388	1.44808	1.70374	
	N	217	0	0	217	217	
Cybersecurity_Measures_in_ Financial_Institutions	Mean	4.5760	–0.0019	0.0866	4.4055	4.7327	
	Std. Deviation	1.31056	–0.00246	0.06384	1.17801	1.42991	
	N	217	0	0	217	217	
Market_Stability	Mean	4.0000	0.0012	0.1002	3.8112	4.2120	
	Std. Deviation	1.50308	–0.00372	0.06148	1.37437	1.61437	
	N	217	0	0	217	217	

a. Unless otherwise noted, bootstrap results are based on 1000 bootstrap samples
Source: Data compiled by author.

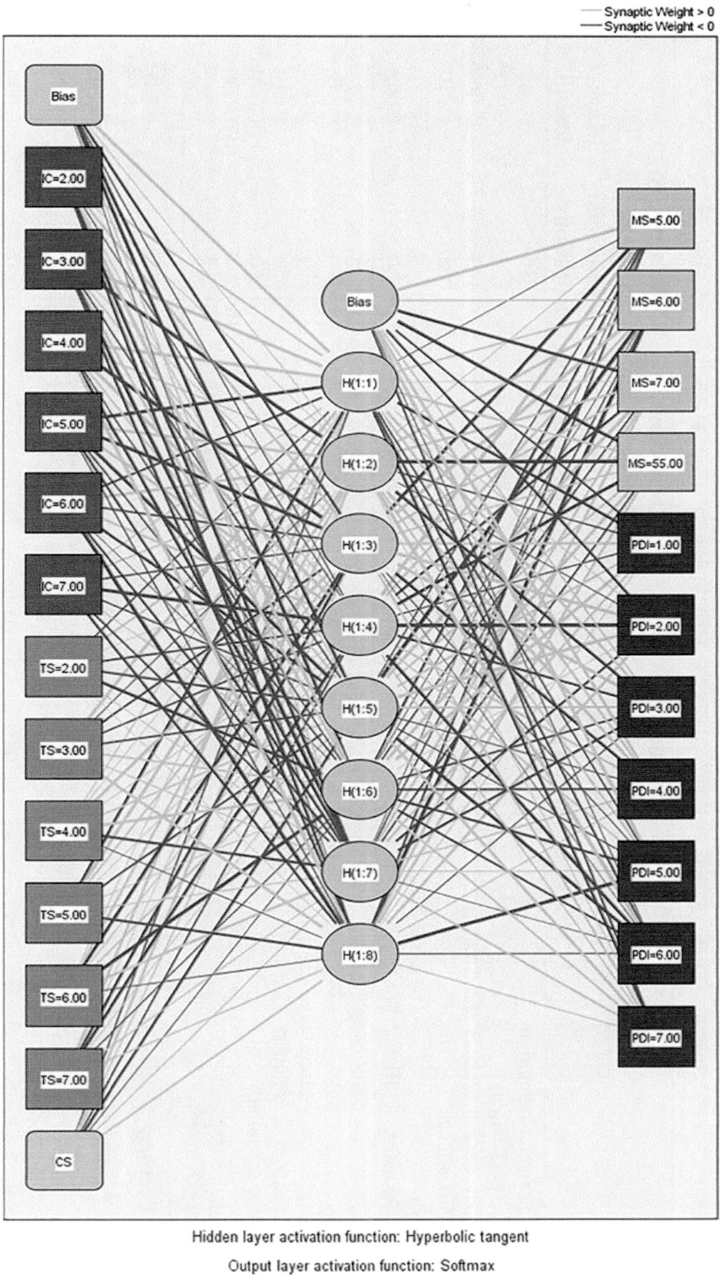

Figure 2.1 Neural network between variables. Source: Designed by author.

Table 2.4 Correlations.

Correlations				Prevalence_of_Deepfake_Incidents	Investor_Confidence	Technological_Sophistication_of_Deepfake_Detection_Tools	Cybersecurity_Measures_in_Financial_Institutions	Market_Stability
Prevalence_of_Deepfake_Incidents	Pearson Correlation			1	0.130	−0.088	0.016	−0.049
	Sig. (2-tailed)				0.055	0.196	0.814	0.472
	The sum of Squares and Cross-products			532.571	55.571	−47.429	7.143	−25.000
	Covariance			2.466	0.257	−0.220	0.033	−0.116
	N			217	217	217	217	217
	Bootstrap	Bias		0	−0.002	−0.001	0.000	−0.002
		Std. Error		0	0.070	0.070	0.072	0.074
		95% Confidence Interval	Lower	1	−0.006	−0.223	−0.123	−0.196
			Upper	1	0.262	0.054	0.156	0.097
Investor_Confidence	Pearson Correlation			0.130	1	0.475**	0.536**	0.416**
	Sig. (2-tailed)			0.055		0.000	0.000	0.000
	The sum of Squares and Cross-products			55.571	341.410	204.636	190.724	170.000
	Covariance			0.257	1.581	0.947	0.883	0.787
	N			217	217	217	217	217
	Bootstrap	Bias		−0.002	0	0.002	0.001	0.001
		Std. Error		0.070	0	0.052	0.056	0.062
		95% Confidence Interval	Lower	−0.006	1	0.373	0.426	0.290
			Upper	0.262	1	0.575	0.642	0.535
Technological_Sophistication_of_Deepfake_Detection_Tools	Pearson Correlation			−0.088	0.475**	1	0.528**	0.565**
	Sig. (2-tailed)			0.196	0.000		0.000	0.000
	The sum of Squares and Cross-products			−47.429	204.636	543.346	237.111	291.000
	Covariance			−0.220	0.947	2.515	1.098	1.347
	N			217	217	217	217	217

	Bootstrap	Bias		−0.001	0.002	0	0.002	0.001
		Std. Error		0.070	0.052	0	0.058	0.054
		95% Confidence	Lower	−0.223	0.373	1	0.405	0.457
		Interval	Upper	0.054	0.575	1	0.634	0.669
Cybersecurity_Measures_in_Financial_Institutions	Pearson Correlation			0.016	0.536**	0.528**	1	0.425**
	Sig. (2-tailed)			0.814	0.000	0.000		0.000
	The sum of Squares and Cross-products			7.143	190.724	237.111	370.995	181.000
	Covariance			0.033	0.883	1.098	1.718	0.838
	N			217	217	217	217	217
	Bootstrap	Bias		0.000	0.001	0.002	0	0.004
		Std. Error		0.072	0.056	0.058	0	0.061
		95% Confidence	Lower	−0.123	0.426	0.405	1	0.312
		Interval	Upper	0.156	0.642	0.634	1	0.544
Market_Stability	Pearson Correlation			−0.049	0.416**	0.565**	0.425**	1
	Sig. (2-tailed)			0.472	0.000	0.000	0.000	
	The sum of Squares and Cross-products			−25.000	170.000	291.000	181.000	488.000
	Covariance			−0.116	0.787	1.347	0.838	2.259
	N			217	217	217	217	217
	Bootstrap	Bias		−0.002	0.001	0.001	0.004	0
		Std. Error		0.074	0.062	0.054	0.061	0
		95% Confidence	Lower	−0.196	0.290	0.457	0.312	1
		Interval	Upper	0.097	0.535	0.669	0.544	1

Source: data compiled by author.

Table 2.5 Case processing summary.

	Cases					
	Included		Excluded		Total	
	N	Percent	N	Percent	N	Percent
Market_Stability * Prevalence_of_Deepfake_ Incidents	217	100.0%	0	0.0%	217	100.0%
Market_Stability * Investor_Confidence	217	100.0%	0	0.0%	217	100.0%
Market_Stability * Technological_ Sophistication_of_ deepfake_Detection_Tools	217	100.0%	0	0.0%	217	100.0%
Market_Stability * Cybersecurity_Measures_ in_Financial_Institutions	217	100.0%	0	0.0%	217	100.0%

Source: data compiled by author.

positive associations with market stability, suggesting their critical influence in bolstering financial resilience against the destabilizing effects of deepfake threats and cyber vulnerabilities.

The result of the case processing summary reveals in Table 2.5 and revealed comprehensive analysis wherein the entirety of the dataset was included for all examined pairwise interactions between market stability and the independent variables – prevalence of deepfake incidents, investor confidence, technological sophistication of deepfake detection tools, and cybersecurity measures in financial institutions – without any exclusions, ensuring that the statistical analysis remains unimpeded by missing data and thus provides a robust and complete evaluation of the interdependencies between these critical variables within the context of financial stability and technological influences.

Table 2.6 reveals that market stability fluctuates across varying levels of deepfake prevalence, with bootstrap-adjusted means and standard deviations highlighting a tendency towards higher market stability at increased prevalence levels, while bias-corrected confidence intervals ensure the robustness of these findings across extensive resampling iterations, confirming the statistical reliability and consistency of the observed relationships.

Table 2.7 presents an intricate statistical analysis of the correlation between "Market Stability" and varying degrees of "Investor Confidence",

Table 2.6 Market_Stability * Prevalence_of_Deepfake_Incidents

			Bootstrap[a]			
					95% Confidence Interval	
Prevalence_of_Deepfake_Incidents		Statistic	Bias	Std. Error	Lower	Upper
1.00	Mean	2.5714	−0.0349[b]	0.5805[b]	1.4000[b]	3.7012[b]
	N	7	0[b]	3[b]	2[b]	13[b]
	Std. Deviation	1.51186	−0.15475[d]	0.34609[d]	0.00000[d]	1.73205[d]
2.00	Mean	4.0000	−0.0256[c]	1.0059[c]	2.0000[c]	6.0000[c]
	N	5	0[c]	2[c]	1[c]	10[c]
	Std. Deviation	2.23607	−0.34945[e]	0.68431[e]	0.50000[e]	3.05505[e]
3.00	Mean	3.4706	0.0014	0.3656	2.7503	4.1762
	N	17	0	4	9	25
	Std. Deviation	1.54587	−0.05495	0.19644	1.08373	1.88083
4.00	Mean	4.7907	0.0015	0.1709	4.4445	5.1199
	N	43	0	6	32	55
	Std. Deviation	1.14555	−0.01622	0.16929	0.79708	1.43870
5.00	Mean	4.2264	−0.0093	0.1765	3.8801	4.5555
	N	53	0	6	41	66
	Std. Deviation	1.26554	−0.02057	0.11772	1.01348	1.46902
6.00	Mean	3.8485	−0.0028	0.2896	3.2581	4.4371
	N	33	0	5	23	43
	Std. Deviation	1.69781	−0.03529	0.16117	1.32938	1.96795
7.00	Mean	3.6271	−0.0012	0.1863	3.2667	4.0134
	N	59	0	7	46	73
	Std. Deviation	1.48438	−0.01074	0.12465	1.22114	1.72240
Total	Mean	4.0000	−0.0034	0.0993	3.8203	4.1750
	N	217	0	0	217	217
	Std. Deviation	1.50308	−0.00121	0.05890	1.38767	1.61293

a. Unless otherwise noted, bootstrap results are based on 1000 bootstrap samples
b. Based on 998 samples
c. Based on 990 samples
d. Based on 993 samples
e. Based on 965 samples
Source: data compiled by author.

Table 2.7 Market_Stability * Investor_Confidence

Market_Stability * Investor_Confidence							
Market_Stability							
			Bootstrap[a]				
					95% Confidence Interval	
Investor_Confidence		**Statistic**	**Bias**	**Std. Error**	**Lower**	**Upper**
1.00	Mean	1.6667	0.0061[b]	0.6195[b]	1.0000[b]	3.0000[b]
	N	3	0[b]	2[b]	1[b]	7[b]
	Std. Deviation	1.15470	–0.38286[c]	0.54237[c]	0.00000[c]	1.41421[c]
2.00	Mean	2.8750	0.0004	0.6406	1.6667	4.3333
	N	8	0	3	3	14
	Std. Deviation	1.72689	–0.16271[d]	0.41379[d]	0.70711[d]	2.33166[d]
3.00	Mean	3.2069	–0.0006	0.2494	2.7241	3.7388
	N	29	0	5	19	39
	Std. Deviation	1.34641	–0.02289	0.15080	1.01003	1.61716
4.00	Mean	3.7213	–0.0091	0.1848	3.3540	4.0727
	N	61	0	7	48	75
	Std. Deviation	1.39201	–0.01202	0.11160	1.16149	1.59897
5.00	Mean	4.2029	0.0016	0.1645	3.8573	4.5238
	N	69	0	7	56	83
	Std. Deviation	1.37819	–0.01303	0.13038	1.09828	1.61328
6.00	Mean	4.9412	–0.0078	0.2110	4.5129	5.3226
	N	34	0	6	24	45
	Std. Deviation	1.22947	–0.03291	0.19680	0.81720	1.58617
7.00	Mean	4.7692	0.0068	0.4333	3.8953	5.6146
	N	13	0	3	7	20
	Std. Deviation	1.53590	–0.07871	0.23619	0.95119	1.93629
Total	Mean	4.0000	–0.0034	0.0993	3.8203	4.1750
	N	217	0	0	217	217
	Std. Deviation	1.50308	–0.00121	0.05890	1.38767	1.61293

a. Unless otherwise noted, bootstrap results are based on 1000 bootstrap samples
b. Based on 959 samples
c. Based on 816 samples
d. Based on 998 samples
Source: data compiled by author.

revealing a nuanced interplay where each confidence level is characterised by distinct central tendencies and dispersions, meticulously adjusted for bias and standard errors via bootstrapping, with confidence intervals offering a comprehensive understanding of variability; the analysis underscores how shifts in investor confidence exert differential impacts on market stability, with higher confidence levels associated with more stable outcomes and lower levels introducing greater volatility, all while ensuring statistical rigor and precision through robust methodological framework.

Table 2.8 presents a sophisticated statistical analysis of the correlation between "Market Stability" and varying levels of "Cybersecurity Measures in Financial Institutions", wherein each level of cybersecurity is associated with distinct central tendencies and deviations, rigorously adjusted for bias and standard error using bootstrapping, with confidence intervals offering a comprehensive view of the variability; this analysis underscores the critical influence of cybersecurity robustness on market stability, revealing that higher levels of cybersecurity measures correspond to greater market resilience, while lower levels introduce heightened volatility, all achieved through a methodologically rigorous framework ensuring the precision and reliability of the findings.

2.5 Managerial Implication

The managerial and practical implications of this research underscore the urgent necessity for financial institutions to integrate advanced deepfake detection tools, robust cybersecurity frameworks, and dynamic real-time threat intelligence systems into their strategic operations (Mante & Khan, 2020; Rahi et al., 2023; Singh et al., 2023), not only to safeguard against the increasingly sophisticated nature of algorithmically driven disinformation and cyber fraud but also to preserve market integrity, maintain investor confidence, comply with regulatory demands, and ensure long-term stability, resilience, and sustainability in a financial ecosystem that is progressively more susceptible to destabilisation through emergent AI-driven vulnerabilities and complex technological threats (Kumar et al., 2024).

2.6 Conclusion

The overall analysis of the tables demonstrates that market stability is profoundly impacted by several interdependent factors including investor confidence the prevalence of deepfake incidents and the technological sophistication of deepfake detection tools and cybersecurity measures in financial

Table 2.8 Market_Stability Cybersecurity_Measures_in_Financial_Institutions

Market_Stability * Cybersecurity_Measures_in_Financial_Institutions						
Market_Stability						
			Bootstrap[a]			
					95% Confidence Interval	
Cybersecurity_Measures_in_Financial_Institutions		**Statistic**	**Bias**	**Std. Error**	**Lower**	**Upper**
1.00	Mean	2.2000	0.0083[b]	0.7867[b]	1.0000[b]	3.8712[b]
	N	5	0[b]	2[b]	2[b]	10[b]
	Std. Deviation	1.78885	−0.33151[d]	0.69081[d]	0.00000[d]	2.82843[d]
2.00	Mean	2.0000	−0.0076[c]	0.3206[c]	1.3750[c]	2.6667[c]
	N	8	0[c]	3[c]	3[c]	14[c]
	Std. Deviation	0.92582	−0.07655[e]	0.16851[e]	0.48795[e]	1.09545[e]
3.00	Mean	2.6897	0.0053	0.2342	2.2145	3.1706
	N	29	0	5	19	40
	Std. Deviation	1.28462	−0.02692	0.16953	0.93743	1.58810
4.00	Mean	4.1250	−0.0037	0.1658	3.7834	4.4575
	N	56	0	6	44	68
	Std. Deviation	1.25136	−0.01673	0.11662	1.01674	1.46746
5.00	Mean	4.4762	0.0001	0.1636	4.1251	4.7965
	N	63	0	7	49	76
	Std. Deviation	1.33026	−0.01238	0.12356	1.08410	1.55285
6.00	Mean	4.5217	0.0012	0.1994	4.1429	4.9037
	N	46	0	6	35	57
	Std. Deviation	1.34560	−0.02134	0.14400	1.03148	1.60870
7.00	Mean	4.2000	0.0012	0.4639	3.2500	5.0000
	N	10	0	3	4	17
	Std. Deviation	1.47573	−0.12863[c]	0.39644[c]	0.54772[c]	2.06828[c]
Total	Mean	4.0000	−0.0034	0.0993	3.8203	4.1750
	N	217	0	0	217	217
	Std. Deviation	1.50308	−0.00121	0.05890	1.38767	1.61293

a. Unless otherwise noted, bootstrap results are based on 1000 bootstrap samples
b. Based on 995 samples
c. Based on 999 samples
d. Based on 974 samples
e. Based on 997 samples
Source: data compiled by author.

institutions while deepfake incidents pose a destabilising risk by eroding trust and disseminating disinformation their negative effect is counterbalanced by strong investor confidence advanced cybersecurity protocols and robust detection mechanisms which act as protective barriers to safeguard market integrity investor confidence emerges as a critical psychological driver that sustains liquidity and price equilibrium whereas the deployment of sophisticated deepfake detection technologies and fortified cybersecurity frameworks ensures the preservation of information authenticity mitigates the risks posed by cyber fraud and enhances overall market resilience the statistical data underscores that the synergy between high investor confidence and the adoption of advanced technological tools is crucial to stabilising market dynamics protecting against financial disarray and ensuring smooth capital flows ultimately the key to maintaining long term market stability in a volatile and increasingly digitalised economy lies in the integration of both psychological and technological safeguards with advanced cybersecurity and deepfake detection systems forming the backbone of a resilient financial system.

References

Arunkumar, P. M., Sangeetha, Y., Raja, P. V., & Sangeetha, S. N. (2022). Deep Learning for Forgery Face Detection Using Fuzzy Fisher Capsule Dual Graph. *Information Technology and Control*, *51*(3), 563–574. https://doi.org/10.5755/j01.itc.51.3.31510

Balasubramanian, S. B., Kannan, J. R., Prabu, P., Venkatachalam, K., & Trojovsky, P. (2022). Deep fake detection using cascaded deep sparse auto-encoder for effective feature selection. *Peerj Computer Science*, *8*. https://doi.org/10.7717/peerj-cs.1040

Boccignone, G., Bursic, S., Cuculo, V., D'Amelio, A., Grossi, G., Lanzarotti, R., & Patania, S. (2022). DeepFakes Have No Heart: A Simple rPPG-Based Method to Reveal Fake Videos. In S. Sclaroff, C. Distante, M. Leo, G. M. Farinella, & F. Tombari (Eds.), *Image Analysis and Processing, ICIAP 2022, PT II* (Vol. 13232, pp. 186–195). Springer International Publishing AG. https://doi.org/10.1007/978-3-031-06430-2_16

Chemerys, H. Y. (2023). Truth & Trust in the Age of Deepfakes: Recognize & Overcome. *Українські Студії в Європейському Контексті: Зб. Наук. Пр. Київ: ГО "Інноваційні Обрії України*, *7*, 403–407.

Dincer, S., Ustubioglu, B., Tahaoglu, G., & Ulutas, G. (2023). Deep Fake Video Detection Based on Enhanced Capsule Network with Golden Ratio. *2023 31ST Signal Processing and Communications Applications Conference, SIU*. https://doi.org/10.1109/SIU59756.2023.10224003

Faura, G., Siewiersky, C., & Tal, I. (2023). A User-Centric Evaluation of Smart Contract Analysis Tools in Decentralised Finance (DeFi). In O. C., R. P., R. A., E. A., B. X., H. H., & J. M.G. (Eds.), *Springer Proceedings in Complexity* (pp. 453 – 476). Springer Science and Business Media B.V. https://doi.org/10.1007/978-981-19-6414-5_25

Jager-Waldau, A., Kakoulaki, G., & Taylor, N. (2021). The Role of Photovoltaics in the Response of the European Member States to the European Green Deal. *Conference Record of the IEEE Photovoltaic Specialists Conference*, 1106–1110. https://doi.org/10.1109/PVSC43889.2021.9518555

Kapsis, I. (2020). A Truly Future-Oriented Legal Framework for Fintech in the EU. *European Business Law Review*, *31*(3), 475–514.

Kharub, M., Gupta, H., Rana, S., & McDermott, O. (2024). Determination of driving power and dependency of wastes in the healthcare sector: a lean and ISM-Based approach. *International Journal of Quality and Reliability Management*, *41*(7), 1838–1864. https://doi.org/10.1108/IJQRM-11-2021-0380

Kim, J. E. (2020). Regulation trumps economics? Examining renewable energy policy, diffusion and investment in 80 developing countries. *Energy Research & Social Science*, *70*. https://doi.org/10.1016/j.erss.2020.101613

Kim, Y., Song, H., & Han, J. (2022). A Deepfake-Based Deep Learning Algorithm for Medical Data Manipulation Detection. *Journal of System and Management Sciences*, *12*(1), 13–26. https://doi.org/10.33168/JSMS.2022.0102

Kumar, A., Khan, E. R., & Deepika. (2024). A Review On Heart Disease Detection Using Machine Learning Techniques. *Proceedings - 2024 6th International Conference on Computational Intelligence and Communication Technologies, CCICT 2024*, 317–323. https://doi.org/10.1109/CCICT62777.2024.00059

Li, X. (2015). Accounting Problems and Countermeasures in SME. In Y. Wu & W. Deng (Eds.), *Proceedings of the Aasri International Conference on Industrial Electronics and Applications (IEA 2015)* (Vol. 2, pp. 656–658). ATLANTIS PRESS.

Mante, R. V, & Khan, R. (2020). A Survey on Video-based Evidence Analysis and Digital Forensic. *Proceedings of the 4th International Conference on Computing Methodologies and Communication, ICCMC 2020*, 118–121. https://doi.org/10.1109/ICCMC48092.2020.ICCMC-00024

Rahi, P., Singh, A. P., Badoni, P., Singh, I., & Khan, R. (2023). Use of Blockchain Technology in Electronic Voting Systems: An Overview from

Computer Security. *2023 International Conference on Communication, Security and Artificial Intelligence, ICCSAI 2023*, 758–762. https://doi.org/10.1109/ICCSAI59793.2023.10420927

Rana, S. (2024). Understanding Roles and Practices of a Responsible Scholar. *FIIB Business Review*, *13*(4), 387–390. https://doi.org/10.1177/23197145241247869

Raut, S. K., Alon, I., Rana, S., & Kathuria, S. (2024). Knowledge management and career readiness: a review and synthesis. *Journal of Knowledge Management*, *28*(7), 1821–1866. https://doi.org/10.1108/JKM-02-2023-0140

Saadah, S., & Panjaitan, Y. (2016). The green shoe option's effectiveness at stabilizing the IPO'S stock price on the Indonesian stock exchange (2000-2013). *Gadjah Mada International Journal of Business*, *18*(1), 71–82. https://doi.org/10.22146/gamaijb.9292

Sardana, F., Mishra, K. K., Singh, A., & Saini, N. (2024). Transforming social media marketing through deepfake technology. In *Navigating the World of Deepfake Technology*. IGI Global. https://doi.org/10.4018/979-8-3693-5298-4.ch022

Sharma, R., Sharma, M., Singh, M., & Bhatnagar, M. (2024). Facades and fortunes: Intellectual capital's influence on firm dynamics in the deepfake epoch. In *Navigating the World of Deepfake Technology*. IGI Global. https://doi.org/10.4018/979-8-3693-5298-4.ch009

Shukla, V., Kumar, J., Rana, S., & Prashar, S. (2024). Navigating the adoption landscape of blockchain in food delivery: a UTAUT perspective. *British Food Journal*, *126*(8), 3113–3133. https://doi.org/10.1108/BFJ-08-2023-0681

Singh, A. P., Khan, R., Rahi, P., Singh, I., & Basu, N. (2023). An Improved Login Authenticable Model Using Memory Gallery Apps. *2023 International Conference on Next Generation Electronics, NEleX 2023*. https://doi.org/10.1109/NEleX59773.2023.10421280

3

Deepfake News Technologies: Contemporary Challenges for Society's Sustainable Economic Development and Security

Gia Zoidze[1] and George Abuselidze[1,2]

[1]Batumi Shota Rustaveli State University, Georgia
[2]The University of Georgia, Georgia

Email: zoidzegia00@gmail.com; george.abuselidze@gmail.com

Abstract

The purpose of the study is to determine the role of online media in evaluating the attempt to change the political and socio-economic orientation of the broad masses and present the dangers accompanying the mentioned process. The subject of research is one of the main tools for influencing society – information. The object of study is online media, which includes web pages, online publications, and internet broadcasting. At least media means are considered the main pillars of the information war, and several printed publications, websites, television, and internet television are the primary sources of support. The media is the tool that most easily shapes the attitudes and moods of the audience. Online media's role and influence are growing increasingly in the modern world. It is an alternative way of receiving news and information through which the cycle of information movement is increasingly accelerated. The research will allow interested readers to see how and in what form deepfake news is spread on social networks in reality, what the impact is on the audience, and what the reaction from the public is.

3.1 Introduction

Modern technologies are humanity's most outstanding achievement, without which life would be unimaginable today. Our daily lives are directly connected with digital technologies and social networks. New technologies have brought changes in all areas. Nowadays, any field of activity runs on modern technologies [1, 2].

The Internet has made the computer even more necessary as it helps us solve today's problems more efficiently. A lot of information we get through modern technologies (computers, smartphones, tablets, etc.) provides us with opportunities to get education, answer various questions, and perform different activities.

Man has needed news since ancient times. Providing this service (giving information) was and is being carried out best by journalism as a result of its activity [3]. Although the channels and means of information dissemination have changed over time, news remains one of the main foundations of journalism.

Along with the development of technologies, journalism's work style and resources have changed. Modern technologies have made the internet one of the most popular places and means of "news" distribution today. In recent years, the number of online publications has increased, and cyberspace has become one of the primary resources for traditional media (nowadays, almost every media company has its own website and social network, where it provides information dissemination).

The internet has greatly facilitated the work of journalists, as cyberspace places many sources of information in one space, where it is easier to manoeuvre if we do not count the inconvenience that social media and the internet, in general, have also brought: a lot of information is spread around us, and it has become quite challenging to find and analyse relevant information from this stream of information [4]. On the other hand, the internet has become the most essential tool for mass communication, and naturally, this tool is very convenient for news journalism.

The digital world has also changed the way media works. It changed new values, journalistic ethics, working conditions and working standards of the "newsroom". If we look at it from the positive side, the digital world has made access to information more accessible, but the negative side also accompanies the technological development in journalism, namely, the fact that ethics in cyberspace are less respected and plagiarism is common [5, 6].

Along with the development of technological innovations and unlimited information possibilities, people have less and less time to read entire articles. At the same time, the demand for promptness has increased; if the story that happened earlier in the day was news on television, the story covered at the end of the day on social networks is already outdated [7]. With new technologies, the media can deliver information with an accuracy of seconds, so it is rare for anyone to read a weekly newspaper to get the news.

It should be noted that, on the one hand, simplified technological possibilities have made it difficult for journalists to work because it is challenging to be so operative and not make mistakes simultaneously. When working in this style, fact-checking requires quite a lot of effort.

It can be said that the internet has made the work of a journalist somewhat more manageable; however, at the same time, the shift of journalism to cyberspace has its disadvantages, and first of all, it is the abundance of information. If, on the one hand, it can be considered positive that both the methods of receiving and spreading information have been simplified, the ways and means of spreading false information have also been simplified. With a lot of information that can be found on the internet daily, it is pretty difficult to distinguish between real and fake news [8–10].

In the era of smartphones, when any internet user can become a reporter, the chances of disseminating unverified or incorrect information increase dramatically, given that professionals often find it difficult to distinguish between correct and inaccurate information, and even professional journalists usually make mistakes. It is easy to imagine how difficult it can be for an audience whose media literacy level is not ready to distinguish between real and fake news [11]. That is why, on the one hand, if we can quickly spread the news and this can be considered an essential achievement of democracy, there is also a danger that, through fake news, a necessary part of society can be easily manipulated.

The danger we see in the relationship between the media and social networks is the unverification of facts. The most essential condition of the press is to check the facts systematically. However, often due to operational requirements, some media directly report the facts from the social network or from the material prepared by the public relations service [12]. On the one hand, unverified misinformation is a reputational blow to a media outlet. Still, we have a far more significant consequence when the media becomes the mouthpiece of a particular fringe group and reports the news unverified.

The spread of fake news can not only have small and insignificant consequences, but it can increase on a large scale to the level of changing the political climate of one of the largest countries in the world, affecting the image of influential people, causing conflicts between countries, etc. Therefore, when talking about social media and cyberspace in general, it must be taken into account that this is a relatively simple and convenient tool that media representatives can use along with people working in other professions. It is an important weapon marginalised groups can use well in any situation. Cybersecurity has become a significant challenge since information is the most valuable thing today.

Spreading false information and manipulating public opinion is not only a modern phenomenon. Its roots can be traced back to the ancient Roman period, during Marcus Antonius's political activity. Antonius's political rival, Octavian, resorted to spreading false information against his rival (36 BC) and printed short messages to insult Antonius's dignity on coins. Gaius Octavius even won the information war and gained public support [13].

Since the twentieth century, one of the first scientists to formulate the essence of public opinion, define its role in governing the country and review how newspapers form and change public opinion was W. Lippmann. "Public Opinion" is his most famous work. W. Lippmann formulates the idea that the primary function of the press is "to create pictures in our minds of the outside world". It also describes cases where these images are distorted and incorrect. All this is based on the opinion that "the news is not true". The author says that the "images in our minds" create a "pseudo-reality" and do not reflect what is happening in the outside world. Those who make news, editors, and journalists are always limited in time, finances, and newspaper space [14].

Propaganda is a term associated with international communications. Propaganda has become more critical and often dangerous with the development of communication technologies. Propaganda aims to shape public opinion through the use of various manipulative methods. Propaganda is carried out in 3 critical ways:

1. Government leaders use it to shape public opinion.
2. It improves or worsens the country's reputation worldwide.
3. Non-governmental organisations used to change the political course [15].

In a 2018 paper, "Defining Fake News", authors E.C. Tandoc Jr, Z.W. Lim and R. Ling, from Nanyang Technological University in Singapore, classify "fake news" into several categories:

1. News satire – uses humour, makes fun of news programs and tries to imitate them.
2. News parody – Its characteristics are similar to satire, as both are based on humour; however, parody spreads entirely fictional news.

3. News fabrication – news published as authentic "news" is not based on facts.
4. Photo manipulation – The commandment of "fake news" also applies to visual material, such as the distortion of a photo or video by artificial intervention and the help of various programs.
5. Advertising and public relations (PR) – advertising materials and press releases, which are published in a news format, can often fall into the category of "fake news" because they serve to advertise a product, to sell it, and not to present reality without distortion.
6. Propaganda – refers to the type of news that tries to influence public opinion and serves the interests of an individual, political organisation or government [16].

C. Paul and M. Mathews, in the work "The Russian 'firehose of falsehood' propaganda model", say that after Russia invaded Georgia in 2008, the Russian propaganda "machine" underwent a significant evolution and was revealed in all its "magnificence" in 2014, during the annexation of the Crimean Peninsula by the Russian Federation. This model continues to work actively in various international conflicts, such as conflicts in Ukraine and Syria. Modern Russian propaganda has several main characteristics: it spreads quickly and continuously, is repeated over time, and lacks consistency and logic [17].

The authors of the work single out several features, which is why they believe that the Russian propaganda method works successfully. First, disinformation, fake news, propaganda, and rumours spread with great intensity and volume. For this, they use many different communication channels. "Fake news" includes textual and visual materials, videos, photos and audio recordings. All this is spread through radio, television, the press, the internet, and social networks.

The Russian propaganda model works very quickly. This is explained by the fact that "fake news" is not based on facts and truth, so its authors do not need to verify information or interview sources to publish a new story. In other words, they manage to spread disinformation using minimal time and resources, which is why they quickly overtake real, authentic media. They respond very promptly to all events in the country.

The Russian propaganda model does not reflect objective reality and does not take responsibility for it. However, some Russian media deliberately spread authentic information along with misinformation. The goal is to confuse the audience and create the impression that they are an actual media outlet. Sometimes, they attach evidence to a breaking news story that is false. Nevertheless, this method still works. Audiences are so lazy to fact-check that they readily believe information backed by evidence, regardless of whether the evidence is objective or fabricated [18].

The Russian government uses three tools effectively: military force, special services and propaganda. "Russian propaganda, first of all, does not serve the promotion of the Russian Federation; its primary task is to promote the anti-PR of those states that the Russian Federation considers to be an opponent." Within this task's framework, a solid narrative is spread to discredit the West, in which the West is presented as a society on the path of degradation, which is doomed. Against this background, Russian propaganda tries to establish the perception that the Russian Federation is the foremost defender of traditional values in the modern world [19].

Another reason the Russian propaganda model works is that it is inconsistent. It can manoeuvre. This means that if, say, a fake news story on television gets a bad response or is not believed by the audience, other channels can always modify, change, and deliver that "news" to the target market in a different way. Fake news purveyors have no obligation to be consistent.

In C. Ireton and J. Posetti's "Journalism, Fake News and Disinformation" [20], the authors outline some basic principles and core values that should guide journalists in an era where "fake news" has almost completely taken over the digital space. It is with the help of these values and principles that they will be able to gain the trust of society:

1. Accuracy – A journalist cannot always guarantee the truth, but accurately reporting the facts will help him avoid mistakes as much as possible. Accuracy should always remain one of the central values for a journalist.

2. Independence – Each journalist should represent an independent voice. This means that whether he acts officially or unofficially, represents any media organisation or himself, he must maintain maximum transparency and avoid conflict of interest.

3. Fairness – A journalist should cover the news, any information, sources, and their stories according to the principle of fairness. It should adequately describe the context and communicate information from different perspectives to the public.

4. Confidentiality – One of the most critical responsibilities of a journalist, especially an investigative journalist, is to maintain the confidentiality of the source. This ensures the source's safety and gains the public's trust. Citizens will trust such a journalist in the future and will help him obtain more information.

5. Humanity – Any material journalists publish can benefit individuals or society. Therefore, a journalist must maintain humanity, correctly assess the risks and how much the information may harm people or minority groups, and cover the news with this in mind.
6. Accountability – Accountability to the public is a characteristic of ethical and professional journalism. That is, journalists should listen to the audience's concerns and interests and correct errors if they exist or are detected.
7. Transparency helps journalists and they maintain the truth and report the facts correctly.

Although these are challenging times for journalism, there are ways journalists and citizen journalists can earn and maintain public trust. In addition, they can verify the spread of fake news as quickly as possible and then provide correct and accurate information to their audience. All this will contribute to the sustainable socio-economic development of the country and the strengthening of democratic principles.

3.2 Methodological Foundations

We conducted a study of fake news propaganda using content analysis. We used straightforward content, message, and meaning analysis to detect and analyse fake news propaganda messages. Content analysis is a research method that identifies, describes, and quantifies trends. Through this method, the correlation of data with context will be established.

We carried out this content analysis in several stages. First, we identified the research population and the number of media outlets. Then, we identified specific research questions and those variables, based on which we correlated the research question.

In the second stage, the unit of analysis, the so-called keywords, was selected. The content categories were identified in the third stage, according to which the categorisation was carried out. At the final stage, the obtained data were analysed, trends were outlined, and conclusions were drawn.

As it is already widely recognised, any news spreads the fastest through social media, including facts and "fake news". Hence, in this case, the main research question is: Can social media users identify fake news, and what methods do they use to combat it? Due to the relevance of the research, there was a need to study several issues: Do social media users believe that they can distinguish facts from fake news? Whether and in what ways do they check the reliability of the received information? What do they do after they realise that the information is false? What impact do they think fake news has on social media users?

Within the framework of the work, we formalised several research questions:

- Research Question 1: How should journalists maintain public trust in the age of global fake news?
- Research Question 2: How can they remain committed to society and serve the interests of citizens?
- Research Question 3: How do we protect the right of citizens to receive accurate and verified information?
- Research Question 4: How can a democratic society be protected from the threats of propaganda and false information?

Based on the research questions mentioned above, we conceptualised the variables. In particular:

- Information warfare – the American concept combines electronic, cyber, and psychological operations in one combat mechanism. It aims to demoralise and suppress the adversary by controlling or influencing information sources.
- Hybrid war is considered an attempt to weaken the opposing side and shake its positions using modern technologies, possibly with the solid technological capabilities of one side disrupting or damaging the information and communication networks of strategic objects of the other side. In this paper, hybrid war is considered an abstract form of war, including information war; however, it also has military and political implications.
- Propaganda is a component of information warfare that involves influencing the public or forming public opinion about a particular issue, person, or group. This can be both positive and negative. In this work, propaganda is viewed in a negative light as a mechanism for forming public opinion based on false and fake information, violence, xenophobia, and racism.
- Disinformation refers to spreading false and fake information through mass media. In this work, media agents present disinformation as a tool for influencing, misleading, and manipulating society.
- Media literacy – involves the audience's perception, understanding, interpretation and critical information analysis. However, in this paper,

media literacy is not considered unilaterally and is regarded as the main component of the information provider (journalist) and the receiver (audience). Therefore, the concept of media literacy is considered, on the one hand, as a tool for orienting a massive flow of information and filtering information and, on the other hand, a tool for creating and sharing new information/knowledge.

- Online media – refers to separate internet publications, traditional media websites, and social media. In this paper, online media refers to any means of information dissemination in the internet space.
- Media environment – an environment created taking into account the legislation regulating the activities of mass communication media. The concept also takes into account how often different political forces manage the media in accordance with their own interests while protecting or restricting the right to speech and expression.

3.3 Results and Discussion

3.3.1 The phenomenon of deepfake news

The problem of spreading deepfake news is urgent all over the world. This phenomenon is not new. However, technological progress has created a particularly fertile ground for the spread of "Deep Fake News" at lightning speed. Social media platforms like Facebook, Twitter, YouTube, and so on create ideal conditions for creating and spreading fake news. In our century, any individual can spread the news. Phones, social networks, and the internet are enough for that. The media plays a significant role in shaping public opinion.

Unscrupulous people are misusing the opportunities of the 21st century. To influence public opinion, they create and spread fake news. This phenomenon usually serves to change the political agenda, discredit any party or individual, change the political path of the state, threaten democratic processes, and serve other nefarious purposes.

To combat fake news, first of all, it is essential to understand in what ways and forms "fake news" is created and spread in social media, how it reaches the audience, and what is the target group's reaction to this type of information, whether readers can identify fake news and deal with it.

In the 21st century, "fake news" has gained new power and possibilities. The development of technology and the creation and accessibility of new media platforms have accelerated the spread of news.

Researchers still cannot agree on the exact definition of "fake news." The term is associated with lies, manipulation, misinformation, propaganda, conspiracy theories, and rumours [21]. According to the Oxford Dictionary, fake news was named the word of the year in 2016, when the US presidential election took its use to a new level [22].

According to Google Trends, the frequency of searches for the term "fake news" has increased dramatically since 2016, which means that public interest in this phenomenon has increased, especially in recent years. During this period, US President Donald Trump repeatedly referred to such huge media outlets as CNN and The New York Times as spreaders of fake news [23].

People shared the same amount of fake news before and after the 2016 US presidential election as real news. As Facebook later clarified, for two years, 100,000 US dollars were financed from Russia for advertisements directed against Hillary Clinton and intended to influence the American elections. According to a New York Times investigation, Russian operatives created fake Facebook and Twitter profiles on behalf of the American people and shared anti-Clinton messages. Already in 2016, various media revealed a so-called troll farm based in North Macedonia, where mostly teenagers were employed. More than 100 pro-Trump media websites were created to spread fake news [24].

The "case" of trolls and fake news has been repeated many times and has changed the course of world events. For example, we can cite the well-known case of "Brexit", when many pro-Brexit messages were spread on social networks [25].

Due to recent developments, Facebook has declared a fight against "fake news" using different methods. However, it has been repeatedly proven that this is not such an easy task, as the limit sometimes crosses the restriction of freedom of speech [26]. The social network has a "report" feature: when users believe a shared story is not true, they can "report" and indicate that the story is fake.

Facebook is constantly testing new features that will more quickly and effectively identify so-called "clickbait" (click-oriented links with screaming titles intended to mislead the user), and the algorithm will try to limit their distribution in the news feed as much as possible [27].

Despite the ongoing battle, deepfake newsis still circulating in large numbers, and social media users are not fully informed about how to distinguish fact-based information from fiction [28]. Therefore, in Table 1, we present the main challenges of fake news at the individual, organisational, and societal levels.

Table 3.1 Challenges of deepfake news at individual, organisational and societal levels.

	Reputational damage	Financial	Manipulation of decision-making
Individual level	• Intimidation/Abuse • Defamation	• Identify Theft • Phishing-type scams • Extortion	• Attracts politicians
Organisational level	• Brand damage • Undermining of trust in the organisation	• Stock-price manipulation • Insurance fraud	• Fabricated court • Faked education papers • Media manipulation • Attacks on political parties, advocacy groups, etc.
Societal level	• Damage to societal cohesion, norms of trust and truth, etc. • Domestic or foreign electoral manipulation • Deliberate stoking of tension/panic/conflict.		

Source: Authors compilations.

The problem of fake news coverage raises doubts and mistrust towards real journalism and journalistic principles. In our age, anyone with an intelligent cell phone, camera, or video camera can spread news at lightning speed. It requires no license, special education or equipment [30]. It is enough for him to be in the right place at the right time, take out his phone and take a picture of the incident. Depending on the importance of the information, this story may even spread virally, bringing the author world-class fame. This means that TV stations and newspapers no longer have an exclusive right to spread news, and ordinary citizens will do it faster.

Citizen journalism and citizen journalist are terms that usually attribute journalistic actions to ordinary citizens. They do not have special education and are not members of various media organisations but act individually and significantly contribute to informing the public [31, 32]. In citizen journalism, it is difficult to distinguish between honest and dishonest people, who are spreading the correct information and manipulating the facts, who are serving the country's interests honestly, and who are bribed with money. Given that a large part of the audience cannot distinguish between fake news and facts or does not know how to verify "fake news", there is a great danger that false information will be perceived as truth. This will negatively change the country's current processes and harm individual people or the interests of the democratic society.

3.3.2 The main "incentives" for spreading fake news

The digital world has brought both positives and negatives to journalism. Cyberspace allows the audience to choose what they want to see, read and hear. If a decade ago, the audience depended on the material selected by the editorial team and was forced to receive the material offered by a particular media outlet via radio, television or newspaper. Now, he himself controls where, when and what to watch, read and listen to, or what part of the material is provided by the media – in cyberspace, it is much easier for the user to manage this. Therefore, the problem we face in this direction is that people often do not view the material in full; for example, it is established that the majority of users on social networks only read the titles, the initial part of the relatively small text, and only in rare cases if they read the article to the end. That is why there is a frequent tendency for the materials placed on the internet to recognise the entire main content of the article in the title.

New technologies have changed all fields, and the media has been no exception. Public relations (PR) have coexisted with the press for decades. Public relations covered almost all areas, including business and politics. PR and journalism activities are significantly related to each other. At the same time, among them, along with many commonalities, are several principled differences [33, 34].

It is essential to see the connections and differences between journalism and PR to coordinate their coexistence without confusing each other. Nowadays, PR and journalism are two intertwined fields, neither of which representatives can carry out their activities perfectly without the other [35]. Both the media and PR have seen the possibility of internet space together with business, and therefore, an essential part of both activities is carried out in cyberspace.

The internet has covered the "newsroom" workspace just as the PR workspace is the internet. For both areas to work successfully in the internet space, it is essential to see their work styles and common and distinguishing features. Where is the line between journalism and PR, and where do they intersect? What is the impact of their coordinated work on society, and what are the principles and aspects of good cooperation between these two areas? How do PR and journalism work in cyberspace? What are the common and distinguishing characteristics of these two work areas in the online world?

Table 3.2 Disinformation in the corporate and public sectors [36].

Actors	Threats	Risks
State Actor Corporate Actors Opportunistic Actors	• Fake New stories (text, audio, video) • Fake social media accounts • Marketing on social Platforms • Marketing on search engines (SEO) • Deep fakes (text, audio, video) • Other	• Brand and reputation damage • Loss of social and customer trust • Finacial Losses

Source: Authors compilations.

We are interested in the motivations behind the spread of disinformation, fake news, conspiracy theories, rumours, propaganda and clickbait-oriented "content", what drives people who mislead the public and what drives so-called trolls (Table 3.2).

In his book "Fake News: False Fears or Real Concerns," T. McGonagle points out that disseminators are motivated by the desire for power and money and to be entertained [37].

L.J. Egelhofer and S. Lecheler [38] reiterate roughly the same point in their paper, "Fake News as a Two-Dimensional Phenomenon." According to the authors, fake news is created to deceive and mislead the public. Political, ideological and financial interests are behind them. However, we should not exclude the reason the so-called trolls are motivated by the desire to have fun. It should be emphasised here that the creation of fake news is premeditated and targeted, while its distribution may not be targeted, and the public may become complicit.

Some researchers see different types of motivation behind various types of "fake news" and divide them into categories, for example:

1. The motivation behind satire and parody is to make fun of people but not to harm anyone.

2. Misleading content aims to mislead people about a specific issue or an independent person.

3. Imposter content: when people deceive the audience by imitating accurate sources. Here, too, the motivation is to mislead the public.

4. Fabrication – Everything in such content is a lie. The spreader intends to mislead people and harm someone or something [39].

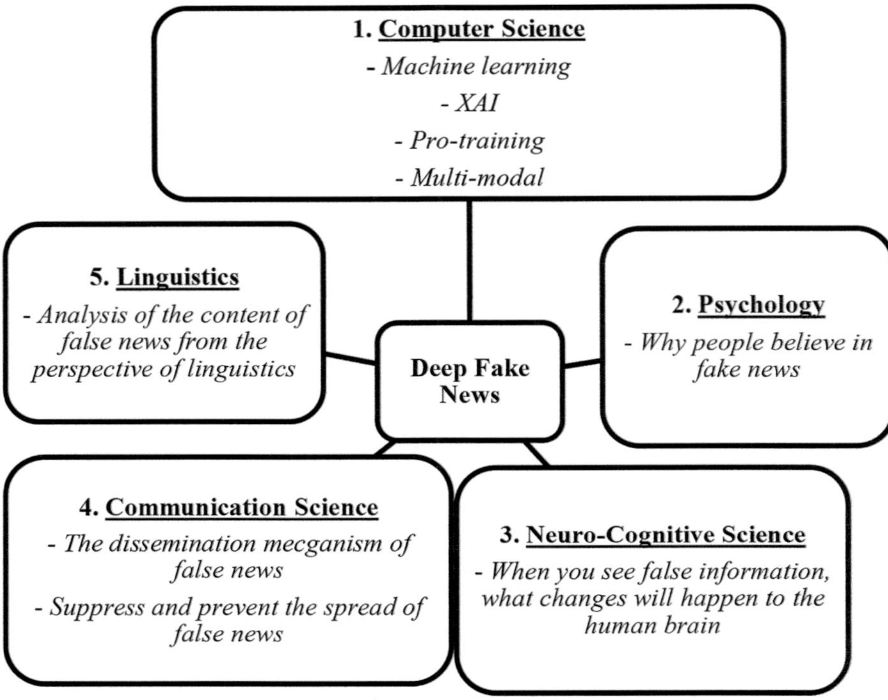

Figure 3.1 Interdisciplinary analysis of deepfake news. Source: Authors compilations.

Although internet trolls may be motivated by entertainment and public ridicule, their main interest is financial, behind which are political and ideological interests. A person can make a joke several times, but he cannot do it intensively and organise it because it requires financial and time resources [40].

For example, as the 2016 US presidential election approached, international media outlets and reporters began to identify more trolls hired to influence the US election. That's how they found the so-called troll factory in the territory of Macedonia, the former Yugoslav Republic, where mostly teenagers were employed. As a result of a journalistic investigation, it was determined that some "trolls" even earned more than 16,000 US dollars in a three-month pre-election campaign [24, 41]. This is quite a large amount. When it comes to financial rewards of this magnitude, the motivations of the fake news spreader become less murky.

Based on the above analysis, the interdisciplinary character of deepfake newswas revealed (Figure 3.1).

Overall, in our opinion, one of the ways to solve these challenges is to provide people with a resource that they can use to verify the information they receive. So far, fact-checking can't be done quickly and automatically because search algorithms are as flawed as the people who create them. It is necessary to think about how to increase the source's authority: it is essential to tag and structure quality content effectively. Google and Facebook have announced that they will significantly expand their anti-disinformation departments [43]. However, the mechanisms of these companies' fight against "fake news" and compliance with the laws now being developed in different countries are of concern to us.

3.4 Conclusion

The study's analysis shows that "fake news" has a large effect on society. The spread of disinformation affects the audience and creates its political mood, which, in many cases, is used by interested political forces or individuals for nefarious purposes. Also, the research established that the population actively uses television and social media to get information.

It becomes clear that the problem of the spread of false information cannot be regulated by law because the limit is placed on freedom of expression and speech, which is essential for the sustainable socio-economic development of the country, the formation of public security, and democratic values.

The above examples of fake news have shown us how disastrous the results can sometimes be and how mighty cyberspace and social media are for spreading fake news. Naturally, without a proper response, we may have more large-scale consequences. That is why cyberspace has become the main battlefield in the 21st century.

The research results are interesting for every citizen because the danger of being a victim of fake news is relatively high. The research will contribute to informing the public and developing media literacy. The results will be necessary for the government to plan a strategy against one of the country's main challenges – fake news. The study will also help non-governmental organisations develop recommendations and increase the international community's involvement in the fight against fake news.

References

[1] R. Adriani, The evolution of fake news and the abuse of emerging technologies. European Journal of Social Sciences, 2(1), 18–24, 2019.

[2] S. Veshapidze, R. Otinashvili, A. Gvarutsidze, G. Abuselidze, G. Zoidze, Modern technologies to overcome the challenges of globalisation. Entrepreneurship, 10(2), 22–32, 2022.

[3] M. Westerlund, The emergence of deepfake technology: A review. Technology Innovation Management Review, 9(11), 2019.
[4] J. A. Braun, J. L. Eklund, Fake news, real money: Ad tech plat-forms, profit-driven hoaxes, and the business of journalism. Digital Journalism, 7(1), 1–21, 2019.
[5] R. Otinashvili, S. Veshapidze, G. Zoidze, Impact of Economic Crime on the State's Sustainable Development. Three Seas Economic Journal, 4(1), 10–17, 2023.
[6] N. Datsii, G. Abuselidze, O. Zborovska, R. Zborovskyy, D. Mishchenko, N. Karpeko, Public administration of de-shadowing of the economic system in the conditions of globalisation. E3S Web of Conferences, 371, 05013, 2023.
[7] B. Martens, L. Aguiar, E. Gomez-Herrera, F. Mueller-Langer, The digital transformation of news media and the rise of disinformation and fake news. 2018.
[8] S. K. Kim, J. H. Huh, B. G. Kim, Artificial Intelligence Block-chain based Fake News Discrimination. IEEE Access, 2024.
[9] G. Abuselidze, L. Mamaladze, The impact of artificial intelligence on employment before and during pandemic: A comparative analysis. Journal of Physics: Conference Series, 1840, 012040, 2021.
[10] T. Chauhan, H. Palivela, Optimization and improvement of fake news detection using deep learning approaches for societal benefit. International Journal of Information Management Data Insights, 1(2), 100051, 2021.
[11] M. G. Arencibia, E. H. V. Corozo, D. M. Cardero, Fake News: An Analysis from Political Economy. Economics, 12(2), 72–82, 2023.
[12] X. Zhang, A. A. Ghorbani, An overview of online fake news: Characterization, detection, and discussion. Information Processing & Management, 57(2), 102025, 2020.
[13] N. Liv, D. Greenbaum, Deep fakes and memory malleability: False memories in the service of fake news. AJOB Neuroscience, 11(2), 96–104, 2020.
[14] W. Lippmann, Public opinion. Routledge, 2017.
[15] R. C. Vincent, K. Nordenstreng, M. Traber, Towards Equity in Global Communication. 1999.
[16] Jr, E. C. Tandoc, Z. W. Lim, R. Ling, Defining "fake news" A typology of scholarly definitions. Digital journalism, 6(2), 137–153, 2018.
[17] C. Paul, M. Matthews, The Russian "firehose of falsehood" propaganda model. Rand Corporation, 2(7), 1–10, 2016.
[18] N. Ruchansky, S. Seo, Y. Liu, Csi: A hybrid deep model for fake news detection. In Proceedings of the 2017 ACM on Conference on Information and Knowledge Management, pp. 797–806, 2017.

[19] G. Pennycook, D. G. Rand, The psychology of fake news. Trends in cognitive sciences, 25(5), 388–402, 2021.

[20] C. Ireton, J. Posetti, Journalism, fake news & disinformation: a handbook for journalism education and training. Unesco Publishing. 2018.

[21] A. Gelfert, Fake news: A definition. Informal logic, 38(1), 84–117, 2018.

[22] L. Buntić, M. Damić, D. Greganić, Impact of Fake News on the Global Economy. In Trade Perspectives 2020: The interdependence of COVID-19 pandemic and international trade, pp. 73–81, 2020.

[23] B. Kalsnes, Fake news. In Oxford Research Encyclopedia of Communication. 2018.

[24] J. Posetti, A. Matthews, A short guide to the history of 'fake news' and disinformation. International Center for Journalists, 7(2018), 2018–07, 2018.

[25] D. M. Lazer, M. A. Baum, Y. Benkler, A. J. Berinsky, K. M. Greenhill, F. Menczer, ... J. L. Zittrain, The science of fake news. Science, 359(6380), 1094–1096, 2018.

[26] X. Zhou, R. Zafarani, A survey of fake news: Fundamental theories, detection methods, and opportunities. ACM Computing Surveys (CSUR), 53(5), 1–40, 2020.

[27] A. Mosseri, Working to stop misinformation and false news. Facebook Newsroom, 7, 2017.

[28] A. Gupta, N. Kumar, P. Prabhat, R. Gupta, S. Tanwar, G. Sharma, ... R. Sharma, Combating fake news: Stakeholder interventions and potential solutions. Ieee Access, 10, 78268–78289, 2022.

[29] A. Collins, T. Ebrahimi, Risk governance and the rise of deep-fakes. 2021.

[30] G. Abuselidze, N. Levchenko, G. Zoidze, T. Zaytseva, G. Shyshkanova, Importance of Professional Diversification in Economy and Higher Education. Studies in Systems, Decision and Control, 537, 597–609, 2024.

[31] M. Adria, Y. Mao, (Eds.).: Handbook of research on citizen engagement and public participation in the new media era. Igi global. 2016.

[32] G. Abuselidze, G., Zoidze, Economic analysis of factors associated with education and employment. CEUR Workshop Proceedings, 3364, 24–37, 2023.

[33] K. Shu, A. Sliva, S. Wang, J. Tang, H. Liu, Fake news detection on social media: A data mining perspective. ACM SIGKDD explorations newsletter, 19(1), 22–36, 2017.

[34] F. Monti, F. Frasca, D. Eynard, D., Mannion, M. M. Bronstein, Fake news detection on social media using geometric deep learning. arXiv preprint arXiv:1902.06673. 2019.

[35] G. Zoidze, S. Veshapidze, The Modern Economy and Values. Cambridge Scholars Publishing. 2022.

[36] S. Joyce, M. Kashifuddin, J. Nocera, P. Upton, Disinformation attacks have arrived in the corporate sector. are you ready? 2019.

[37] T. McGonagle, "Fake news" False fears or real concerns? Netherlands Quarterly of Human Rights, 35(4), 203–209, 2017.

[38] J. L. Egelhofer, S. Lecheler, Fake news as a two-dimensional phenomenon: A framework and research agenda. Annals of the International Communication Association, 43(2), 97–116, 2019.

[39] A. Kruger, Ahead of the e-curve in fact checking and verification education: The University of Hong Kong's cyber news verification lab leads verification education in Asia. Asia Pacific Media Educator, 27(2), 264–281, 2017.

[40] V. Bakir, A. McStay, Fake news and the economy of emotions: Problems, causes, solutions. Digital journalism, 6(2), 154–175, 2018.

[41] E. Mwangi, Technology and fake news: shaping social, political, and economic perspectives. Political, and Economic Perspectives, 2023.

[42] L. Yuan, H. Jiang, H., Shen, L. Shi, N. Cheng, Sustainable Development of Information Dissemination: A Review of Current Fake News Detection Research and Practice. Systems, 11(9), 458, 2023.

[43] N. Giansiracusa, How algorithms create and prevent fake news. Berkeley, CA: Apress. 2021.

4

Workplace Resilience Against Deepfakes: Awareness, Trust, and Training

Harshdeep Kaur[1], Kajal Khurana[1] and Mehul Miglani[2]

[1]Punjabi University, India
[2]Chandigarh University, India

Email: harshdeepk54@gmail.com; mmiglani452@gmail.com; kajalkhurana07@gmail.com

Abstract

Deepfake technology, a relatively new threat, poses a challenge to maintaining security and trust. These sophisticated fakes, often created from advanced audio, video, or images, are dangerous as they can alter information, compromise functions, and demoralise employees and stakeholders. This research paper explores strategies to mitigate deepfake risks within organisational settings, with a strong emphasis on three critical areas: awareness, trust-building, and employee training. The application of PLS-SEM to this descriptive research underscores the need for prevention. Actions that increase awareness, provide comprehensive training on deepfake recognition, and most importantly, foster trust among employees, are crucial in ensuring the enhancement of integrity and swift identification of threats in organisations in the emerging era of computer technology.

4.1 Introduction

The advancement of technology in the last years has created tools for producing very realistic graphic images and videos with the help of advanced computer graphics and AI algorithms. This progress has made it impossible. Although these kinds of computer-generated images and videos have many real-life uses, the threats to privacy and security are also enormous.

An example of this is "deepfakes", a term that combines "deep learning" and "fake", which is the possibility of malicious intent of these technologies. Deepfakes, which articulates deep learning and fake content, is a procedure by which one's face in a video is replaced by another person's but is recorded saying something the targeted individual actually said. These methods are also known as face swapping or manipulation of the facial expressions and are the core to deepfake technology (Khoshru et al., 2020; Rajput et al., 2024; Shakya et al., 2018; Y. K. Sharma et al., 2018). The detection rates are presumably the same as in other cases, but the level of deception is much higher because vision plays an essential role in understanding human beings. It incorporates alterations in the message content and visual proves including making the impression that a person uttered or performed something they in fact did not (Kumar et al., 2018; Kunwar et al., 2021; J. Pant et al., 2021; Suravajhala et al., 2018). The established dominance of visual signals in human perception intensifies the impact of this type of deception.

As the digital world is shifting and evolving at a very high pace, deepfake technology has brought about a paradigm shift in terms of both prospects and threats. Depending on the AI's abilities, deepfakes and synthetic media produced by a neural network can genuinely change many fields by allowing for realistic simulations and new forms of creativity. However, they are also associated with certain potential threats to information protection and employment (M. Pant & Thakur, 2021; Rawat, Singh, Ray, & Szabo, 2020; A. Sharma et al., 2020; N. Singh et al., 2020). Therefore, it is crucial to identify its impact on job security in organisational contexts. This technology places various opportunities in the spheres, including entertainment and education. For example, it can be used in multilingual advertisement promotions, develop technologies for people who are speaking impaired for a certain period or permanently, and bring deceased artists alive for a better experience as visitors go through museums. Although it has these positive impacts, deepfake technology creates many problems for aural and visual integrity and can be abused to produce fake news. Developing strategies to counter the deceitfulness of deepfakes from an educational and cultural perspective may be effective, particularly for individuals with lower susceptibility to willfully misleading claims (Adow et al., 2022; Kamal, Shende, et al., 2022; Kamal, Shobha, et al., 2022; Painuli et al., 2022). There is a high likelihood for people to fall victim to the content because of the unknown realities of deepfakes, but with this level of knowledge, people can learn how to scrutinise the content for the real deal from the fake ones. Awareness also enhances societal immunity against the wrong use of deepfake technology. A similar observation was made for deepfake videos whereby after watching the exposure material, the participants' scores significantly improved, supporting the exposure strategy for deepfake detection skills. Moreover, they reported that people's awareness of deepfakes is somewhat sensitive to their social media activity. This is because those more engaged on social media will likely be more aware of the presence and possible consequences of deepfake technology (Giri et al., 2022; Juyal & Sharma, 2021; Rakhra et al., 2022). In this way, employee knowledge about this technology defines the organisation's further actions in the fight against deepfakes. Previous research has emphasised the importance of employee awareness in mitigating cybersecurity risks, but little is understood about how such awareness training, in this case for deepfakes, plays out within an organisation (Adhikari et al., 2021; Godbole et al., 2021; Gupta et al., 2021; Mitra et al., 2022).

Knowledge of deepfake identification is one significant organisational measure to combat threats from deepfakes. Training prepares the organisation's employees to recognise and report deepfake content and bolsters their confidence in its defence strategy for protecting human capital. (Bisht et al., 2024; Pramanik et al., 2023; A. Sharma, Mohan, et al., 2024; Tamta et al., 2024)In some organisations, methods based on semantic artefacts became ineffective with improved, newer, and better-generation techniques of deepfakes. In response, data-driven solutions have been initiated to train human resources in organisations to identify deepfakes. These solutions use localisation information, multi-task learning, attention mechanisms, and ensembles of convolutional neural networks (CNNs).

Trust in management is another factor of consideration in this regard. Organisational trust is a critical organisational antecedent as it defines employees' functioning, motivation, commitment level, and satisfaction. Other studies have explored the trust-uncertainty relation where trust is assumed to mitigate social uncertainty; something that makes an individual uncertain is always assumed to be relevant for trust (Dhayal et al., 2024; A. Joshi et al., 2024; Tina et al., 2024). It becomes even more important for management to encourage trust in light technology such as deepfakes. This study aims to establish whether there is a possibility of a decrease in the levels of trust that the employees have for their management and, consequently, the perceived job security as a result of awareness of deepfake technology. Further, deepfakes are a considerable threat to employment since visual and audible content can be generated and twisted to lay the blame on an innocent target. Addressing this risk necessitates organisational strategies focused on improving detection capabilities and minimising the impact of misleading media on employee trust and stability (Barthwal et al., 2024; Mahajan et al., 2024; Naik et al., 2024; Walia et al., 2024).

Based on this, this study posits that heightened familiarity with deepfake technology can spur improvement in training programs aimed at helping employees detect deepfakes or, in other words, strengthen the employees' capacity to differentiate accurate content from fake content. (Kaushik et al., 2024; Ray et al., 2024; Sunori et al., 2024). Therefore, this study's research question is as follows: What is the nature of the relationship between awareness of deepfake technology, trust in management, training on deepfake recognition, and perceived job security? Through these interconnections, the study will offer insights that might be useful to the organisation in containing the issues typically linked with deepfakes while, at the same time, improving the security and trust of the employees. (Duong et al., 2024; Jain et al., 2023; Tomar et al., 2024).

In essence, deepfake technology is a double-edged sword, offering a broad spectrum of opportunities and innovations for the various industries but also potential threats and problems. Therefore, these risks must be managed, and the benefits of this developing technology must be well exploited through awareness, good organisational preparedness, adequate training, and trust. (Rani et al., 2024; Samantaray et al., 2024; Sneha et al., 2024). This research is significant because it builds on the existing knowledge of the organisational consequences of new technologies by pinpointing the consequences of deepfakes. Therefore, this paper underlines the need for awareness, trust, and training to address the issues around employees' perceptions and behaviours and achieve a safer and more secure organisational system as emerging digital advancements challenge it. (S. Joshi et al., 2024; Ramesh et al., 2024; Solanki et al., 2024; Srivastava et al., 2024).

4.2 Review of Literature

With the help of AI, it has become easy to produce large quantities of "deepfakes" – synthetic videos that look real. That is why, for a person, it seems essential to know the potential consequences of deepfakes in affecting online disinformation. Deepfakes enhance the degree of uncertainty, hence diminishing the trust in social media news. Moreover, the uncertainty and scepticism caused by deepfakes compound distrust in public questioning. These challenges are important for persons as citizens and promoting awareness of such outcomes is crucial to avoid the worst impact. Involvement of deepfake technology presents huge threats to democracy and the credibility and reliability of elected officials, corporate leaders and social bonds. There should be proper legislation, corporate governance measures, educational campaigns and improvement on such technologies (S. P. Singh et al., 2024). Deepfakes pose certain risks, but they also generate possibilities for cybersecurity and the development of AI, and they need to involve various actors to develop trusted content within digital environments. Nevertheless, deepfakes have certain disadvantages, such as misrepresentation, ethical problems, data privacy problems, and technical drawbacks. It is therefore important in today's digital world that the masses understand these complexities. Deepfake technology does both benefits and harm, hence, it is important to outweigh the former with considerations of the latter. Criminals are using this malicious technology in a variety of ways, causing harm to society. However, keeping in mind the further perspective and the opportunities opened for beneficial uses, the focus should be on protecting society from the distribution of damaging content instead of completely banning the distribution of deepfakes (A. Sharma, Kumar, et al., 2024). AI is an integration that signifies the change of business paradigm because it influences several facets of the business environment. AI holds the prospect of change and draws attention to the fact that employers must design spaces to accommodate change to optimise the use of AI. Deepfake also poses several threats, such as changing the opinions of the masses, altering the results of an election, conducting embezzlement and fraud, and tarnishing the image and reputation of a person or an organisation (Verma et al., 2024). Solving these threats has necessitated the use of digital authentication methods, detection algorithms AI, and video watermarking. It, therefore, requires a multi-faceted approach to technological methods, increased public awareness, and scepticism to fight deepfakes and refrain from causing severe social impacts. As a technology, deepfake influences and affects society and businesses, which implies new problems that cannot be solved with existing legislation, pointing out the necessity of regulation. The solution to the above involves how detection is done and awareness (Garg et al., 2024). Preventing deepfake abuse requires fresh legislation, technology controls and popular education. As a society, we currently have no adequate non-superficial strategy that would allow for addressing deepfakes sufficiently. This is mainly due to their development level, which is still somewhat less than perfect, so the degree of influence they exert does not seem significant. Solving this problem calls for the advancements of technology right now, improving education, training and governance (Thirumalaivasan et al., 2024). Deepfake technology has the potential to enhance collective critical thinking by reducing gullibility towards false news and promoting source verification. In the long run, it may transition from one kind of rationality, instrumental rationality, to another, which is social rationality based on trust. This change is oriented toward more efficient and reliable self-realisation within the chosen set of reliable connections compared to the information-based expectations (Fan et al., 2024).

Therefore, deepfake technology presents significant threats to the credibility and character of digital media content while simultaneously serving as an opportunity to enhance people's ability to think critically and become more sceptical when consuming content. Managing both aspects requires a combination of technology, policy, and education. This approach deals with ways of preventing and managing risks and allowing the beneficial operation of artificially intelligent technologies to develop a more trustworthy digital world.

4.3 Conceptual Model

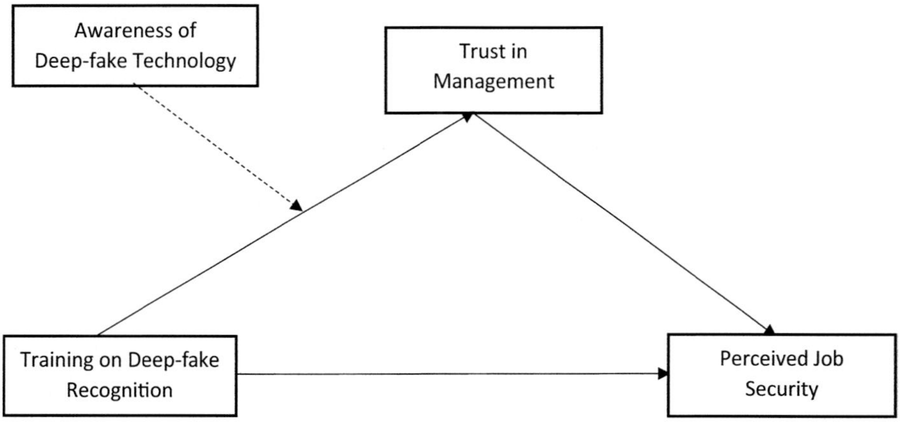

Figure 4.1 Conceptual model. Source: Authors compilations.

4.4 Research Methodology

4.4.1 Sampling and data collection

In the present examination, the cross-sectional research tool employed a multi-indicator model as presented in Figure 4.1. Using descriptive research design, several reflective components have been included to assess the impact of various latent factors. This study's data collection method is cross-sectional. The data for the study was collected using a survey questionnaire within two months from March 2023 to April 2024. The survey was conducted on corporate employees working in the IT sector in Delhi-NCR with the help of a purposive sampling technique. Several companies in the Delhi-NCR region were contacted physically by the researchers for data. The questionnaires were distributed only to those employees who had received training on identifying deepfake threats in the past year. (Badawy et al., 2024) A total of 350 questionnaires were distributed, out of which 297 employees returned with completed questionnaires. After data cleaning, the final data set of 286 respondents was acquired for data analysis. G*Power analysis has been employed to validate the suitability of the sample size. According to the G*Power study, a sample size of 172 is considered acceptable for obtaining a power of 90%. Therefore, in compliance with the aforementioned criteria, the sample size for the study was deemed acceptable.

4.4.2 Measures

The respondents were surveyed using a closed-ended, Likert-scaled, well-structured questionnaire to obtain direct feedback. The interviewees were asked to complete two questionnaire sections: Section I asked questions about their demographics, and Section II asked them to rate various items on a scale. All of the scales that were employed in this study were standardised, but they were all modified as per the study's objectives. A "five-point Likert scale" was used to measure the items for the various scales used in the study, which included Trust in Management adapted from the study Training on Deepfake Recognition taken and modified from the study of Dhar (2015), Perceived Job Security adapted from Yilmaz & Aydin (2023) Moreover, awareness of deepfake technology was adapted from a study.

4.4.3 Common method bias and multicollinearity

In this study, standard method bias was evaluated using "Harman's single-factor test", revealing that the total variance of the first factor accounted for only 32%, well below the threshold of 50%, indicating that "common method bias" is not a significant concern. Finally, to avoid the problem of multicollinearity. The obtained values of VIF varied from 1.04 to 1. All these values are less than the threshold of 5, implying that multi-collinearity is not an issue of concern in the current model. These assessments guarantee the validity of the analytical strategy used in the present research and the absence of methodological biases in the revealed relationships within the framework of the proposed model.

4.4.4 Statistical tools used

The data collected for this study was not standard. In case of non-normal distribution of data, PLS-SEM is considered suitable. Thus, based on the suitability of the data and conceptual model, the researchers used SmartPLS v.4.1.0.3 software to assess the construct reliability and validity and to test the above-stated hypotheses.

4.5 Results

4.5.1 Demographics of respondents

The demographic analysis of the sample population (N = 286) reveals a balanced gender distribution, with males constituting 54.19% and females 45.80%. Age-wise, a significant proportion of the respondents fall within the younger age brackets: 46.85% are between 18 and 25 years, followed by 37.06% in the 26–35 years range. The 36–45 years group represents 9.79%, while those aged 46–55 years and over 55 account for 5.24% and 1.05%, respectively. Regarding educational qualifications, the sample is predominantly well-educated, with 43.01% holding graduate degrees and 40.55% having post-graduate qualifications. High school graduates comprise 6.29%, and those with doctorates constitute 8.39%. A small proportion (1.75%) have completed diploma and certificate courses. The monthly income levels vary, with the highest concentration (29.72%) earning between Rs 25001 and Rs 50000. Those earning less than Rs. 25000 and between Rs 50001 and Rs 75000 represent 22.72% and 23.43%, respectively. Higher-income brackets, Rs 75001 to Rs 1 Lakh and above Rs 1 Lakh, account for 14.33% and 9.79%, respectively. Further, the job profiles indicate that most respondents are in middle (34.26%) or entry-level positions (29.02%), with fewer in senior (21.68%) and executive roles (15.03%). Experience levels show that nearly half (47.20%) have 1–3 years of experience, while 22.72% have 4–6 years, and a smaller segment has less than 1 year (11.18%) or over 10 years (3.14%) of experience.

4.5.2 Measurement model results

Table 4.2 illustrates the measurement model findings of the conceptual model. To establish the indicator reliability, the factor loading of each item to the construct is more than the threshold limit of 0.708. Moreover, it is pretty clear that each construct has fulfilled the threshold of AVE value more than 0.50, confirming the convergent validity of the model. Further, each construct has an alpha value of <0.80, which supports our constructs' internal consistency and trustworthiness. Additionally, the internal consistency of the constructs was further confirmed using Cronbach's alpha, whose values exceeded the required threshold of 0.7. Finally, the discriminant validity of the constructs is demonstrated using two more criteria, namely, the Fornell and Larcker Criterion (Table 4.4) and the HTMT ratio (Table 4.3).

Table 4.1 Demographics of the respondents.

	Characteristics	Frequency (N=286)	Percentage
Gender	Male	155	54.19
	Female	131	45.80
Age	18–25 years	134	46.85
	26–35 years	106	37.06
	36–45 years	28	9.79
	46–55 years	15	5.24
	More than 55 years	3	1.05
Educational Qualification	High School	18	6.29
	Graduate	123	43.01
	Post-graduate	116	40.55
	Doctorate	24	8.39
	Others (including Diploma and Certificate courses)	5	1.75
Monthly Income	"Less than Rs. 25,000"	65	22.72
	"Rs.25,001–Rs.50,000"	85	29.72
	"Rs.50,001–Rs.75,000"	67	23.43
	"Rs.75,001–Rs.1 Lakh"	41	14.33
	"Above Rs. 1 Lakh"	28	9.79
Job Profile	Entry level	83	29.02
	Middle level	98	34.26
	Senior Level	62	21.68
	Executive level	43	15.03
Experience (Years)	Less than 1	32	11.18
	1–3	135	47.20
	4–6	65	22.72
	7–9	45	15.73
	Ten and above	9	3.14

Source: Authors compilations.

Table 4.2 Construct reliability and validity.

Constructs	Indicators	Loadings	CR	AVE	α
Training in Deepfake Recognition	**TDR_1**	0.808	0.872	0.717	0.868
	TDR_2	0.853			
	TDR_3	0.812			
	TDR_4	0.911			
Trust in Management	**TIM_1**	0.792	0.861	0.714	0.81
	TIM_2	0.873			
	TIM_3	0.868			
Perceived Job Security	**PJS_1**	0.853	0.899	0.751	0.89
	PJS_2	0.895			
	PJS_3	0.832			
	PJS_4	0.884			
Awareness of Deepfake Technology	**ADT_1**	0.818	0.986	0.719	0.826
	ADT_2	0.81			
	ADT_3	0.913			

Author's Calculations.

Table 4.3 Discriminant validity-HTMT criteria.

Constructs	ADT	PJS	TDR	TiM	ADT X TDR
ADT					
PJS	0.722				
TDR	0.723	0.618			
TiM	0.138	0.089	0.228		
ADT X TDR	0.246	0.143	0.097	0.3	

Author's calculations.

Note: ADT-Awareness of Deepfake Technology; PJS-Perceived Job Security; TDR-Training on Deepfake Recognition; TiM-Trust in Management

Table 4.4 Discriminant Validity-Fornell and Larcker criteria.

Constructs	ADT	PJS	TDR	TiM
ADT	0.848			
PJS	0.586	0.867		
TDR	0.617	0.556	0.847	
TiM	–0.137	0.05	–0.206	0.845

Author's calculations.

Note: ADT-Awareness of Deepfake Technology; PJS-Perceived Job Security; TDR-Training on Deepfake Recognition; TiM-Trust in Management

4.5.3 Structural model results

In order to test the significance of proposed hypotheses, bootstrapping with 5,000 subsamples was performed. The results (Table 5, Figure 4.2) reveal that Training on Deepfake Recognition ($\beta = 0.592$, $p < 0.05$) significantly impacts Perceived Job Security. The relationship between Training on Deepfake Recognition and Trust in Management ($\beta = 0.206$, $p < 0.05$) has been found to be positive and significant. There is significant association between Trust in Management and Perceived Job Security ($\beta = 0.172$, $p < 0.05$). Thus, hypothesis (H1 to H3) are accepted in full. Next, the mediation effects were examined. The bootstrapped results show that Trust in Management significantly mediates the relationship between Training on Deepfake Recognition ($\beta = 0.135$, $p < 0.05$) and Perceived Job Security, supporting H4. The findings also show that awareness of Deepfake Technology ($\beta = -0.045$, $p < 0.05$) negatively moderates the relationship between Training on Deepfake Recognition and Perceived Job Security mediated through Trust in Management. Hence, hypothesis H5 is also supported.

Furthermore, the correlation between Awareness of Deepfake Technology and Training on Deepfake Recognition is illustrated in Figure 4.3 using three lines. As evidenced by the negative slope of the two lines, the relationship between Training on Deepfake Recognition and Trust in Management is negatively correlated which, in turn, affects perceived job security in the presence of the moderator. The presence of a negative moderating effect causes the influence of the moderator Awareness of Deepfake Technology to weaken the effect of Training on Deepfake Recognition on Perceived Job Security at high levels. Conversely, at lower levels of the moderator, the effect of Training on Deepfake Recognition on Perceived Job Security becomes stronger.

4.6 Discussion and Implications

The results of this research establish three primary objectives of the present study: Training on deepfake recognition and trust in management; the mediating role of trust in the management; and the moderating effect of perceived job security. Presenting the training on deepfake recognition was found to increase the level of perceived job security (H1) and perceived trust in the management (H2) suggesting that the provision of the requisite knowledge and skills to help prevent threats posed by deepfakes benefits the organisation's employees in the overall. This was in concordance to previous studies that have postulated that training and development procedures bring about change in the employees' perception with regard to Employment Security

Table 4.5 Hypothesis testing.

	Hypothesised Paths	**β**	**S.E.**	**t-value**	**R^2**	**R^2 adj.**	**Q^2**	**Lower Bound**	**Upper Bound**	**p value**	**Decision**
H1	**TDR->PJS**	0.592	0.054	10.947	0.338	0.330	0.296	0.493	0.699	0.000	Supported
H2	**TDR->TiM**	0.206	0.085	2.417	0.133	0.118	0.066	0.369	0.027	0.016	Supported
H3	**TiM->PJS**	0.172	0.062	2.766				0.057	0.291	0.006	Supported
H4	**TDR->TiM->PJS**	0.135	0.019	1.910				0.076	0.203	0.047	Supported
H5	**ADT->TDR->TiM->PJS**	−0.045	0.022	2.061				−0.087	−0.007	0.040	Supported

Author's Calculations

Note: ADT-Awareness of Deepfake Technology; PJS-Perceived Job Security; TDR-Training on Deepfake Recognition; TiM-Trust in Management

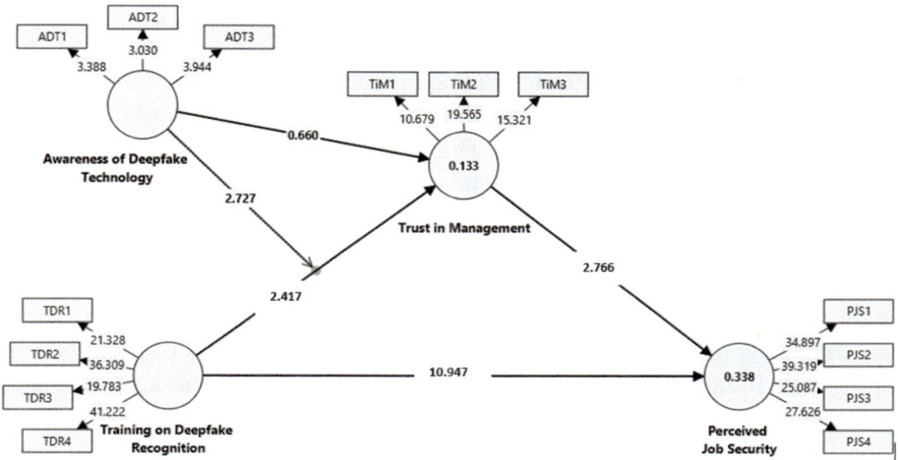

Figure 4.2 PLS algorithm (designed by authors).

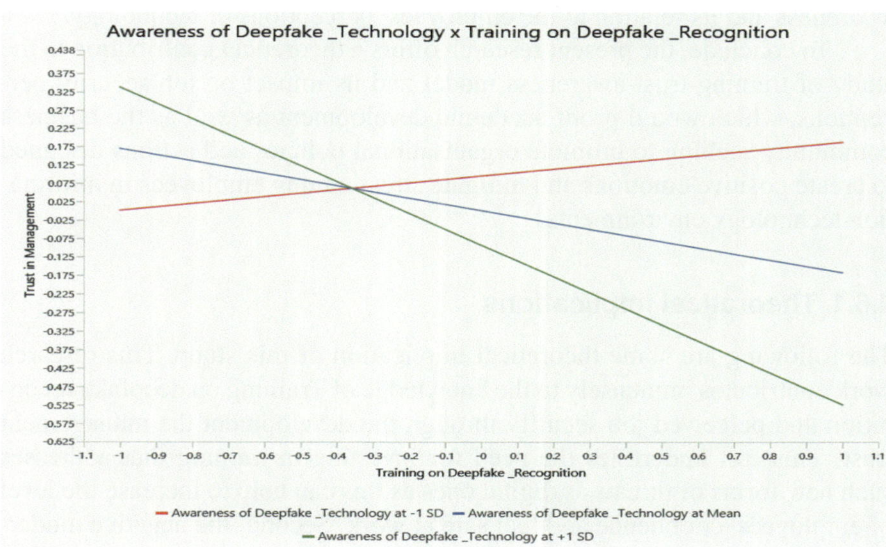

Figure 4.3 Two-way interaction effect Awareness of Deepfake Technology*Training on Deepfake Recognition on Trust in Management (Calculated by authors).

Note: The upper, middle, and lower lines show the correlation for higher, average and lower levels of the moderator variable, that is, Awareness of Deepfake Technology respectively.

and Organisational Trust. Additionally, the findings suggested that there is a positive correlation between trust in management and perceived job security, meaning that when employees trust their management, they are likely to have a perception of job security (H3). Thus, the studies underscore the significance of trust as the base of the organisational processes.

Further, the results reflected that trust in management acts as a mediator between training on deepfake recognition and perceived job security (H4). Such mediation has been evidenced in past studies where trust in management fully mediated the relationship between the organisational practices superordinate and subordinates and the outcome dimensions of the measure under test. Finally, the negative moderation effect of awareness of deepfake technology on the mediated relationship (H5) implied that though training has a positive effect on perceived job security through trust in management, high awareness of deepfake technology can reduce the effects. This could be as a result of awareness that might lead to enhanced rate of anxiety or perceived risk among the employees even if they are trained to deal with such threats. This extended perspective enriches the existing literature on apprehensive awareness and its relation to the employees' perceptions of technology.

To conclude, the present research offers a theoretical contribution to the study of training-trust-awareness model and its impact on job security perceptions, which would profit academic development as well as the business community seeking to promote organisational policies and actions designed to create positive emotions and mitigate stress among employees in information technology environments.

4.6.1 Theoretical implications

The following are some theoretical implication of this study. This research work contributes immensely to the knowledge of Training on deepfake recognition and perceived job security through the development the management trust. This fact underlines the need for investing in training that addresses such new forms of threats as digital ones as this can help to increase the level of employees' confidence and feel safe at work. Second, the negative moderation of the awareness of the deepfake technology to the relationship between training and job security paves way for the notion that mere awareness of deepfakes may result to high levels of anxiety among employees. This result has an implication that while awareness campaigns should be promoted to create awareness of potential negative effects, they should be effectively followed by training projects and educational exercises. Third, the research points to trust as a mediating variable whereby organisational management is significantly important. While job security reduces turnover intention, trust in management plays the intermediate role that can boost the impact of training program. Such theoretical implications of the study mean that further investigations should look at the overall effects of awareness and trust in threat management in a wider context in other industries and cultures. Furthermore, this research contributes to the theoretical and practical literature in terms of identifying key training and trust-building activities that might be generic enough to be adapted depending on the specific training and trust-building needs and contexts in which they are to be applied.

4.6.2 Practical Implications

In the present study, the relevance of implementing deepfake recognition training within IT sectors has been highlighted. Such measures can increase confidence in their employment among the personnel and can help to stabilise turnover levels and raise the retainment ratios. For optimum result, organisations should make sure that training initiatives are taken, which include awareness campaigns and skill-enhancement programmes. This approach also goes a long way to ease potential employee tensions elicited by an increase in the frequency of deepfake perils. The paper also confirms trust in management as a mediator that helps transform substantive competence into better organisational security perceptions. However, the study also highlights that although awareness of deepfake threats is crucial but excessive awareness can diminish the positive impacts of training on perceptions of job security. Therefore, organisational strategies need to strike a balance between awareness and training to optimise resilience against digital threats and maintain employee well-being in today's dynamic digital landscape.

4.7 Limitations and Future Directions

However, there are certain limitations of this study. First, due to the cross-sectional research design, it was impossible to identify causes and effects as the data were collected at one point in time. In future, the researchers can carry out more longitudinal studies in order to have better understanding of how perceptions concerning job security change. Second, there is limited generalisability of the findings due to the geographic-based sampling on the participants from the Delhi-NCR region. It will be necessary for future studies to expand the sample to include participants from other areas and having different cultural backgrounds to increase the generalisation of the findings. Third, the study is based on the questionnaires that have certain limitations self-reports may be influenced by social desirability. Employing objective measures or triangulating data sources could mitigate this issue. Fourth, the study examines only single factor – training on deepfake recognition – as predictor of perceived job security. Future research could explore additional factors such as risk perception, and perceived vulnerability. Fifth, while trust in management was identified as significant mediator, the study does not account for potential moderating variables like age, gender, and prior disappointing experience with technology. Incorporating these moderators in future studies could provide a more nuanced understanding of the relationships between these variables.

4.8 Declaration

The authors declare that the manuscript follows ethical standards and there are no potential conflicts of interest concerning this chapter's research, authorship, and/or publication.

4.9 Disclaimer

The authors express the contents and views of this chapter in personal capacities. The editor and the publisher don't need to agree with these viewpoints and are not responsible for any duty of care in this regard.

References

Adhikari, P., Jain, R., Sharma, A., & Pandey, A. (2021). Plant Growth Promotion at Low Temperature by Phosphate-Solubilizing Pseudomonas Spp. Isolated from High-Altitude Himalayan Soil. *Microbial Ecology*, *82*(3), 677–687. https://doi.org/10.1007/s00248-021-01702-1

Adow, A. H., Shrivas, M. K., Mahdi, H. F., Zahra, M. M. A., Verma, D., Doohan, N. V., & Jalali, A. (2022). Analysis of Agriculture and Food Supply Chain through Blockchain and IoT with Light Weight Cluster Head. *Computational Intelligence and Neuroscience*, *2022*. https://doi.org/10.1155/2022/1296993

Badawy, A. A., Husen, A., & Salem, S. S. (2024). Use of nanobiotechnology in augmenting soil–plant system interaction for higher plant growth and production. In *Essential Minerals in Plant-Soil Systems: Coordination, Signaling, and Interaction under Adverse Situations.* Elsevier. https://doi.org/10.1016/B978-0-443-16082-0.00006-0

Barthwal, R., Kathuria, D., Joshi, S., Kaler, R. S. S., & Singh, N. (2024). New trends in the development and application of artificial intelligence in food processing. *Innovative Food Science and Emerging Technologies, 92*. https://doi.org/10.1016/j.ifset.2024.103600

Bisht, B., Begum, J. P. S., Dmitriev, A. A., Kurbatova, A., Singh, N., Nishinari, K., Nanda, M., Kumar, S., Vlaskin, M. S., & Kumar, V. (2024). Unlocking the potential of future version 3D food products with next generation microalgae blue protein integration: A review. *Trends in Food Science and Technology, 147*. https://doi.org/10.1016/j.tifs.2024.104471

Debasis, M., Ganeshamurthy, A. N., Komal, S., Radha, T. K., & Rupa, T. R. (2020). Plant growth promotion and biocontrol activity of some typical harsh environment rhizo-microbes and their effects on Amaranthus cruentus plants. *Research Journal of Biotechnology, 15*(1), 35–45.

Dhayal, K. S., Agrawal, S., Agrawal, R., Kumar, A., & Giri, A. K. (2024). Green energy innovation initiatives for environmental sustainability: current state and future research directions. *Environmental Science and Pollution Research, 31*(22), 31752–31770. https://doi.org/10.1007/s11356-024-33286-x

Duong, L., Kumar, V., & Van Binh, T. (2024). Supply chain collaboration in the food industry: a literature review. In *Future Food Systems: Exploring Global Production, Processing, Distribution and Consumption*. Elsevier. https://doi.org/10.1016/B978-0-443-15690-8.00007-2

Fan, L., Aspy, N. N., Smrity, D. Y., Dewan, M. F., Kibria, M. G., Haseeb, M., Kamal, M., & Rahman, M. S. (2024). Moving towards food security in South Asian region: Assessing the role of agricultural trade openness, production and employment. *Heliyon, 10*(13). https://doi.org/10.1016/j.heliyon.2024.e33522

Garg, S., Nain, P., Kumar, A., Joshi, S., Punetha, H., Sharma, P. K., Siddiqui, S., Alshaharni, M. O., Algopishi, U. B., & Mittal, A. (2024). Next generation plant biostimulants & genome sequencing strategies for sustainable agriculture development. *Frontiers in Microbiology, 15*. https://doi.org/10.3389/fmicb.2024.1439561

Giri, N. C., Mohanty, R. C., Shaw, R. N., Poonia, S., Bajaj, M., & Belkhier, Y. (2022). Agriphotovoltaic System to Improve Land Productivity and Revenue of Farmer. *2022 IEEE Global Conference on Computing, Power and Communication Technologies, GlobConPT 2022*. https://doi.org/10.1109/GlobConPT57482.2022.9938338

Godbole, V., Pal, M. K., & Gautam, P. (2021). A critical perspective on the scope of interdisciplinary approaches used in fourth-generation biofuel production. *Algal Research*, *58*. https://doi.org/10.1016/j.algal.2021.102436

Gupta, S., Verma, D., Tufchi, N., Kamboj, A., Bachheti, A., Bachheti, R. K., & Husen, A. (2021). Food, fodder and fuelwoods from forest. In *Non-Timber Forest Products: Food, Healthcare and Industrial Applications*. Springer International Publishing. https://doi.org/10.1007/978-3-030-73077-2_17

Jain, M., Soni, G., Verma, D., Baraiya, R., & Ramtiyal, B. (2023). Selection of Technology Acceptance Model for Adoption of Industry 4.0 Technologies in Agri-Fresh Supply Chain. *Sustainability (Switzerland)*, *15*(6). https://doi.org/10.3390/su15064821

Joshi, A., Gupta, A. K., Mansi, Semwal, S., Deoli, N., Rather, M. A., Naik, B., Kumar, V., Jha, A. K., Rustagi, S., & Preet, M. S. (2024). Sustainable solutions for food security: Evaluating pre-treatment technologies in the growing fruits and vegetables industry of India. *Sustainable Chemistry and Pharmacy*, *39*. https://doi.org/10.1016/j.scp.2024.101580

Joshi, S., Sharma, M., Luthra, S., Agarwal, R., & Rathi, R. (2024). Role of industry 4.0 in augmenting endurability of agri-food supply chains amidst pandemic: organisation flexibility as a moderator. *Operations Management Research*. https://doi.org/10.1007/s12063-023-00436-2

Juyal, P., & Sharma, S. (2021). Strawberry Plant's Health Detection for Organic Farming Using Unmanned Aerial Vehicle. *Proceedings of the 2021 IEEE International Conference on Innovative Computing, Intelligent Communication and Smart Electrical Systems, ICSES 2021*. https://doi.org/10.1109/ICSES52305.2021.9633825

Kamal, S., Shende, V. G., Swaroopa, K., Bindhu Madhavi, P., Akram, P. S., Pant, K., Patil, S. D., & Sahile, K. (2022). FCN Network-Based Weed and Crop Segmentation for IoT-Aided Agriculture Applications. *Wireless Communications and Mobile Computing*, *2022*. https://doi.org/10.1155/2022/2770706

Kamal, S., Shobha, K. R., Francis, F., Khilar, R., Tripathi, V., Lakshminarayana, M., Kannadasan, B., & Sahile, K. (2022). IOT Automation with Segmentation Techniques for Detection of Plant Seedlings in Agriculture. *Wireless Communications and Mobile Computing*, *2022*. https://doi.org/10.1155/2022/6466555

Kaushik, P., Jain, E., Gill, K. S., Upadhyay, D., & Devliyal, S. (2024). Comparative Analysis of Cassava Leaf Disease Prediction Using the Deep Learning Approach. *2nd International Conference on Sustainable Computing and Smart Systems, ICSCSS 2024 - Proceedings*, 1369–1373. https://doi.org/10.1109/ICSCSS60660.2024.10625585

Khoshru, B., Mitra, D., Khoshmanzar, E., Myo, E. M., Uniyal, N., Mahakur, B., Mohapatra, P. K. Das, Panneerselvam, P., Boutaj, H., Alizadeh, M., Cely, M. V. T., Senapati, A., & Rani, A. (2020). Current scenario and future prospects of plant growth-promoting rhizobacteria: an economic valuable resource for the agriculture revival under stressful conditions. *Journal of Plant Nutrition*, *43*(20), 3062–3092. https://doi.org/10.1080/01904167.2020.1799004

Kumar, P., Thakur, S., Dhingra, G. K., Singh, A., Pal, M. K., Harshvardhan, K., Dubey, R. C., & Maheshwari, D. K. (2018). Inoculation of siderophore producing rhizobacteria and their consortium for growth enhancement of wheat plant. *Biocatalysis and Agricultural Biotechnology*, *15*, 264–269. https://doi.org/10.1016/j.bcab.2018.06.019

Kunwar, S., Bhatt, S., Pandey, D., & Pandey, N. (2021). Field Application of the Microbial Technology and Its Importance in Sustainable Development. In *Microbial Technology for Sustainable Environment*. Springer Nature. https://doi.org/10.1007/978-981-16-3840-4_20

Mahajan, M., Upadhyay, D., Aeri, M., Kukreja, V., & Sharma, R. (2024). Advancing Agricultural Health: Hybrid CNN-SVM Framework for Classifying Tomato Diseases. *2024 IEEE 9th International Conference for Convergence in Technology, I2CT 2024*. https://doi.org/10.1109/I2CT61223.2024.10544232

Mangla, S. K., Sharma, Y. K., Patil, P. P., Yadav, G., & Xu, J. (2019). Logistics and distribution challenges to managing operations for corporate sustainability: Study on leading Indian diary organizations. *Journal of Cleaner Production*, *238*. https://doi.org/10.1016/j.jclepro.2019.117620

Mitra, D., Saritha, B., Janeeshma, E., Gusain, P., Khoshru, B., Abo Nouh, F. A., Rani, A., Olatunbosun, A. N., Ruparelia, J., Rabari, A., Mosquera-Sánchez, L. P., Mondal, R., Verma, D., Panneerselvam, P., Das Mohapatra, P. K., & Guerra Sierra, B. E. (2022). Arbuscular mycorrhizal fungal association boosted the arsenic resistance in crops with special responsiveness to rice plant. *Environmental and Experimental Botany*, *193*. https://doi.org/10.1016/j.envexpbot.2021.104681

Naik, B., Kumar, V., Rizwanuddin, S., Mishra, S., Kumar, V., Saris, P. E. J., Khanduri, N., Kumar, A., Pandey, P., Gupta, A. K., Khan, J. M., & Rustagi, S. (2024). Biofortification as a solution for addressing nutrient deficiencies and malnutrition. *Heliyon*, *10*(9). https://doi.org/10.1016/j.heliyon.2024.e30595

Painuli, S., Quispe, C., Herrera-Bravo, J., Semwal, P., Martorell, M., Almarhoon, Z. M., Seilkhan, A., Ydyrys, A., Rad, J. S., Alshehri, M. M.,

Daştan, S. D., Taheri, Y., Calina, D., & Cho, W. C. (2022). Nutraceutical Profiling, Bioactive Composition, and Biological Applications of Lepidium sativum L. *Oxidative Medicine and Cellular Longevity*, *2022*. https://doi.org/10.1155/2022/2910411

Pant, J., Pant, R. P., Kumar Singh, M., Pratap Singh, D., & Pant, H. (2021). Analysis of agricultural crop yield prediction using statistical techniques of machine learning. In S. Y. (Ed.), *Materials Today: Proceedings* (Vol. 46, pp. 10922–10926). Elsevier Ltd. https://doi.org/10.1016/j.matpr.2021.01.948

Pant, M., & Thakur, P. (2021). Forest-based plants in beautification and their medicinal significance. In *Non-Timber Forest Products: Food, Healthcare and Industrial Applications*. Springer International Publishing. https://doi.org/10.1007/978-3-030-73077-2_16

Pramanik, A., Sinha, A., Chaubey, K. K., Hariharan, S., Dayal, D., Bachheti, R. K., Bachheti, A., & Chandel, A. K. (2023). Second-Generation Bio-Fuels: Strategies for Employing Degraded Land for Climate Change Mitigation Meeting United Nation-Sustainable Development Goals. *Sustainability (Switzerland)*, *15*(9). https://doi.org/10.3390/su15097578

Rajput, V., Saini, I., Parmar, S., Pundir, V., Kumar, V., Kumar, V., Naik, B., & Rustagi, S. (2024). Biochar production methods and their transformative potential for environmental remediation. *Discover Applied Sciences*, *6*(8). https://doi.org/10.1007/s42452-024-06125-4

Rakhra, M., Bhargava, A., Bhargava, D., Singh, R., Bhanot, A., & Rahmani, A. W. (2022). Implementing Machine Learning for Supply-Demand Shifts and Price Impacts in Farmer Market for Tool and Equipment Sharing. *Journal of Food Quality*, *2022*. https://doi.org/10.1155/2022/4496449

Ramesh, J. V. N., Khandekar, S. D., Baburao, D., Singh, M., Biban, L., Muniyandy, E., & Desingurajan, N. (2024). Harnessing Remote Sensing and Geographic Information Systems to Address Soil Degradation and Water Scarcity in Climate Change Era. *Remote Sensing in Earth Systems Sciences*, *7*(2), 139–147. https://doi.org/10.1007/s41976-024-00108-0

Rani, A., Pundir, A., Verma, M., Joshi, S., Verma, G., Andjelković, S., Babić, S., Milenković, J., & Mitra, D. (2024). Methanotrophy: A Biological Method to Mitigate Global Methane Emission. *Microbiology Research*, *15*(2), 634–654. https://doi.org/10.3390/microbiolres15020042

Rawat, K. S., Singh, S. K., Ray, R. L., & Szabo, S. (2020). Parameterization of the modified water cloud model (MWCM) using normalized difference vegetation index (NDVI) for winter wheat crop: a case study from Punjab, India. *Geocarto International*, 1–14. https://doi.org/10.1080/10106049.2020.1783579

Rawat, K. S., Singh, S. K., Ray, R. L., Szabó, S., & Kumar, S. (2020). Parameterizing the modified water cloud model to improve soil moisture data retrieval using vegetation models. *Hungarian Geographical Bulletin*, *69*(1), 17–26. https://doi.org/10.15201/hungeobull.69.1.2

Ray, A., Kundu, S., Mohapatra, S. S., Sinha, S., Khoshru, B., Keswani, C., & Mitra, D. (2024). An Insight into the Role of Phenolics in Abiotic Stress Tolerance in Plants: Current Perspective for Sustainable Environment. *Journal of Pure and Applied Microbiology*, *18*(1), 64–79. https://doi.org/10.22207/JPAM.18.1.09

Samantaray, A., Chattaraj, S., Mitra, D., Ganguly, A., Kumar, R., Gaur, A., Mohapatra, P. K. D., Santos-Villalobos, S. de los, Rani, A., & Thatoi, H. (2024). Advances in microbial based bioinoculum for amelioration of soil health and sustainable crop production. *Current Research in Microbial Sciences*, *7*. https://doi.org/10.1016/j.crmicr.2024.100251

Semwal, P., Painuli, S., Jugran, A., Palni, L. M. S., Verma, S., Thapliyal, A., & Tewari, D. (2020). Genetic Diversity of Scanty Available Himalayan Saussurea obvallata (DC.) Edgew. *Iranian Journal of Science and Technology, Transaction A: Science*, *44*(3), 587–594. https://doi.org/10.1007/s40995-020-00862-y

Shakya, A. K., Ramola, A., Sawant, K., Tiwari, S., Aarfin, S., & Mittal, P. (2018). Visual Representation of Change in Vegetation Area of Dehradun, Uttarakhand, India using Normalized Difference Vegetation Index (NDVI). *2018 2nd IEEE International Conference on Power Electronics, Intelligent Control and Energy Systems, ICPEICES 2018*, 1087–1092. https://doi.org/10.1109/ICPEICES.2018.8897376

Sharma, A., Bachheti, A., Sharma, P., Bachheti, R. K., & Husen, A. (2020). Phytochemistry, pharmacological activities, nanoparticle fabrication, commercial products and waste utilization of Carica papaya L.: A comprehensive review. *Current Research in Biotechnology*, *2*, 145–160. https://doi.org/10.1016/j.crbiot.2020.11.001

Sharma, A., Kumar, V., & Musunur, L. P. (2024). The Good, The Bad and The Ugly: An Open Image Dataset for Automated Sorting of Good, Bad, and Imperfect Produce Using AI and Robotics. *Sustainability (Switzerland)*, *16*(15). https://doi.org/10.3390/su16156411

Sharma, A., Mohan, A., Johri, A., & Asif, M. (2024). Determinants of fintech adoption in agrarian economy: Study of UTAUT extension model in reference to developing economies. *Journal of Open Innovation: Technology, Market, and Complexity*, *10*(2). https://doi.org/10.1016/j.joitmc.2024.100273

Sharma, Y. K., Patil, P. P., & Mangla, S. K. (2018). Analyzing risks in safety and security of food using grey relational analysis. *International Journal of Mechanical Engineering and Technology*, *9*(12), 9–19.

Singh, N., Negi, A. S., & Pant, M. (2020). Tissue culture interventions in soybean production: Significance, challenges and future prospects. *Ecology, Environment and Conservation*, *26*, S96–S102.

Singh, S. P., Singh, P., Diwakar, M., & Kumar, P. (2024). Improving quality of service for Internet of Things(IoT) in real life application: A novel adaptation based Hybrid Evolutionary Algorithm. *Internet of Things (Netherlands)*, *27*. https://doi.org/10.1016/j.iot.2024.101323

Sneha, Singh, P. D., & Tripathi, V. (2024). Cloud-based scheduling optimization for smart agriculture. In S. S., K. S., & J. P.K. (Eds.), *AIP Conference Proceedings* (Vol. 3121, Issue 1). American Institute of Physics. https://doi.org/10.1063/5.0221549

Solanki, M. K., Wang, Z., Kaushik, A., Singh, V. K., Roychowdhury, R., Kumar, M., Kumar, D., Singh, J., Singh, S. K., Dixit, B., & Kumar, A. (2024). From orchard to table: Significance of fruit microbiota in postharvest diseases management of citrus fruits. *Food Control*, *165*. https://doi.org/10.1016/j.foodcont.2024.110698

Srivastava, A., Rawat, B. S., Bajpai, P., & Dhondiyal, S. A. (2024). Potato Leaf Disease Detection Method Based on the YOLO Model. *IEEE International Conference on Data Engineering and Communication Systems, ICDECS 2024*. https://doi.org/10.1109/ICDECS59733.2023.10502511

Sunori, S. K., Negi, P. B., Joshi, N. C., Mittal, A., & Juneja, P. (2024). Soil Fertility Assessment Using Ensemble Methods in Machine Learning. *Proceedings - 2024 5th International Conference on Intelligent Communication Technologies and Virtual Mobile Networks, ICICV 2024*, 17–21. https://doi.org/10.1109/ICICV62344.2024.00010

Suravajhala, P., Kumar, A., Pandeya, A., Malik, G., Sharma, M., P., H. K., S., A. K., Gahlaut, V., Gajula, M. N. V. P., Singh, K. P., Balyan, H. S., & Gupta, P. K. (2018). A web resource for nutrient use efficiency-related genes, quantitative trait loci and microRNAs in important cereals and model plants. *F1000Research*, *7*. https://doi.org/10.12688/f1000research.14561.1

Tamta, S., Vimal, V., Verma, S., Gupta, D., Verma, D., & Nangan, S. (2024). Recent development of nanobiomaterials in sustainable agriculture and agrowaste management. *Biocatalysis and Agricultural Biotechnology*, *56*. https://doi.org/10.1016/j.bcab.2024.103050

Thirumalaivasan, N., Nangan, S., Kanagaraj, K., & Rajendran, S. (2024). Assessment of sustainability and environmental impacts of renewable energies: Focusing on biogas and biohydrogen (Biofuels) production. *Process Safety and Environmental Protection, 189*, 467–485. https://doi.org/10.1016/j.psep.2024.06.063

Tina, Pant, M., Pant, K., Chauhan, A., Negi, A. S., Nainwal, P., Srivastava, A., & Kumar, V. (2024). Molecular marker-assisted genetic diversity analysis in soybean cultivars from Himalayan region of Uttarakhand, India. *Ecological Genetics and Genomics, 31*. https://doi.org/10.1016/j.egg.2024.100237

Tomar, S., Sharma, N., & Kumar, R. (2024). Effect of organic food production and consumption on the affective and cognitive well-being of farmers: analysis using prism of NVivo, etic and emic approach. *Environment, Development and Sustainability, 26*(5), 11027–11048. https://doi.org/10.1007/s10668-023-03195-z

Verma, A., Zaheer, A., Ahsan, A., Anand, A., Abu Serhan, H., Nazli Khatib, M., Syed Zahiruddin, Q., Gaidhane, A. M., Kukreti, N., Rustagi, S., Satapathy, P., Sharma, D., Arora, M., & Kumar Sharma, R. (2024). Noma in the WHO's list of neglected tropical diseases: A review of its impact on undeveloped and developing tropical regions. *Preventive Medicine Reports, 43*. https://doi.org/10.1016/j.pmedr.2024.102764

Walia, N., Sharma, R., Kumar, M., Choudhary, A., & Jain, V. (2024). Optimized VGG16 Model for Advanced Classification of Cotton Leaf Diseases. *2024 4th International Conference on Intelligent Technologies, CONIT 2024*. https://doi.org/10.1109/CONIT61985.2024.10627057

5

Data-driven Decision-making in Insurance Industry

S. Ullah[1], M. Kukreti[2] and M. R. Shaukat[3]

[1]University of Central Punjab, Pakistan
[2, 3]University of Technology and Applied Sciences, Ibri, Oman

Email: dr.samiullah@ucp.edu.pk; mohit.kukreti@utas.edu.om; muhammad.shaukat@utas.edu.om

Abstract

This chapter explains the transformational impacts of data-driven decision-making in the insurance industry. It identifies the evolutionary development from practices hitherto based on manual underwriting and risk assessment to more modern data-centric processes. Historically, the industry was very much based on actuarial data and manual practice, which resulted in inflexibility and delayed response to emerging trends. The integration of data analytics has entirely revolutionised this landscape. Data analytics personalised insurance opened dynamic risk assessment models, allowing for efficient claims processing. The chapter underlines the shift from 17th-century London coffee houses' data aggregation to sophisticated big data technologies today through this historical perspective. These innovations allow predictive modelling, real-time analytics, and the application of artificial intelligence and machine learning to update risk assessments and customer engagement and improve benefits related to these areas. Another fact discussed in the paper is how different data types and technological tools, such as IoT, blockchain, and AI, can change the approach to decision-making, enabling significant improvements in the fight against industry-specific challenges and problems, including fraud detection, regulatory compliance, and cybersecurity. This storyline is about how these technologies not only revamp insurance practices but also coincide with broader standards on sustainability and ethics that send the industry toward becoming more agile and consumer-focused.

5.1 Introduction

Traditional insurance industry decision processes were based on age-old practices, with a history bent toward data, actuarial science, and manual underwriting (Gangwar & Srivastva, 2020; Ritika et al., 2024; A. Sharma et al., 2024). This, of course, is laborious, but unfortunately, it cannot account for individual variations and emerging trends (M. Gupta et al., 2024; P. Kumar et al., 2024). The second significant factor is claims processing, which, through manual inspections and paperwork, was often a delay-introducing, error-prone operation. The customer relations were standardised as much as possible (Rawat, Sharma, et al., 2023; Yadav et al., 2024). There was little customisation of the products or services. The risks were not perfectly managed; most were reactive, mitigating known risks from previous data while unable to take advantage of opportunistic risks (Agarwal et al., 2024; Jena et al., 2024).

Data analytics have significantly revolutionised these old practices worldwide. More customised policies, risk appraisal in the United States, Germany, and Japan, and microinsurance innovation in Kenya and India. The overall world of insurance is becoming data-driven (C. Gupta et al., 2022; Srivastava et al., 2024). This factor reveals that data is used to manage risks better, carry out operations efficiently, and engage customers more effectively in insurance organisations globally. This, in turn, has led to a new wave in the insurance industry with more dynamic, efficient, and customer-centric decision-making processes (Gopal et al., 2023; Rawat, Goyal, et al., 2023). Thus, with this paradigm shift, there is improved risk assessment and management capability to create innovative insurance solutions well-suited to the needs of the new age (Bhatt & Dani, 2024; Mukul et al., 2024).

5.2 The Evolution of Big Data in Insurance

The insurance industry is arguably one of the oldest sectors of the global economy but has constantly evolved, especially in its application of data analytics. Its historical evolution in data analytics is a journey from manual processing to complex uses of digital data (Deng et al., 2024; Mishra et al., 2024). These changes transform how insurers determine risks, compute premiums, process claims, and deal with customers (Caiado et al., 2023; Govindarajan et al., 2023).

5.2.1 Late 17th century: The dawn of insurance data

In the 17th century, the London coffee houses became some of the busiest social and commercial institutions that attracted people from all walks of life, mainly merchants, owners of ships, and mariners. Establishments, such as Edward Lloyd's shop, started at the end of 1680 and gained remarkable popularity because of their location on Tower Street, by the River Thames, the city's shipping business centre (Pramanik et al., 2023; A. B. Singh et al., 2023). Lloyd's Coffee House began collecting and disseminating shipping news and information on maritime affairs. Such a systematic collection of shipping information served as the foundation upon which marine insurance could be based. In Lloyd's Coffee House, merchants and ship owners started to congregate with potential underwriters. These underwriters would agree to reimburse the owner of a ship or cargo in case of loss for a fee or premium (Garai et al., 2023; Rajput et al., 2023). Such practices developed underwriting that established and set the precedence for modern insurance. In this case, the underlying principle is a division of risks amongst several underwriters, and the role that accurate information plays in a risk assessment is central to the ideas in insurance fostered in this environment (Bharadwaj et al., 2023; V. Kumar et al., 2023).

5.2.2 Early beginnings: Manual processing and actuarial tables

Nineteenth century up to the mid-20th century: The fundamental framework of insurance decision-making was established during the 19th century and early 20th century. At this time, the industry relied heavily on manual processing and actuarial science (Jaiswal et al., 2023; Kashyap et al., 2023). Actuaries determine mathematical and statistical techniques to create actuarial tables, which form the heart of risk computation and premium charging. Such methods relied upon historical statistics, mortality trends, and demographic information. The process was cumbersome and time-consuming based on paper records (Gwak et al., 2023; H. Kaur et al., 2023).

5.2.3 The advent of computers and basic data processing

Late 20th century: The computers took over during the late 20th century. This was when the big companies started using essential data processing tools to take care of and store a large chunk of data efficiently (Liao et al., 2023; Naveen et al., 2023). The days passed from paper-based record-keeping to digital methods, but the analytical methods were very crude compared to what is happening today. The computers enhanced the speed at which policy and claims data is processed but had limited capacity to analyse complex datasets (Bisht et al., 2024; Jaiswal et al., 2023).

5.2.4 Early stages of data analytics and predictive modelling

1990s to early 2000s: This was the early age of data analytics in insurance. Over time, insurers learned to begin using more complex statistical models and testing predictive modelling (A. Gupta & Kumar, 2022; S. Gupta et al., 2024). Computer technology and many packages of software contributed to this. Insurers could analyse a lot more than they previously were, therefore, greater accuracy in assessing risk. Underwriting has also witnessed the emergence of credit scoring, particularly in auto and home insurance, marking a significant shift towards data-centric decision-making for this era (Garg & Shrivastava, 2024; B. Kaur et al., 2023; S. K. Singh et al., 2024).

5.2.5 The big data revolution and advanced analytics

Late 2000s to 2020: The big data revolution in the late 2000s drastically changed the insurance landscape. Big data is characterised by its volume, velocity, variety, and veracity and has redefined how insurance companies operate. The computing power, data storage, and analytics tools have propelled the transition from the traditional data processing methods to the significant data age (Arora et al., 2023; Datta et al., 2023; Swain et al., 2024). In the wake of AI, machine learning, the Internet of Things, and cloud computing, insurers can tap into vast, diversified datasets, from behavioural data for customers to natural environmental data. It has built significantly advanced predictive models that enable personalised products at the insurance level, real-time risk assessment, and proactive fraud detection. Data analytics is used to gain insights into customer needs and preferences. This allows insurers to offer more personalised products and services. Based on individual customer data, customised insurance packages are created. Insurers are now using big data for more accurate risk assessment, hence more customised models for pricing. Companies such as Lemonade and Progressive have developed advanced data analytics in dynamic pricing and customer engagement (Chandel et al., 2024; P. Sharma et al., 2023; Taneja et al., 2023).

5.2.6 The age of AI and advanced analytics

2020s and beyond: The industry stands at the threshold of a new era dominated by AI-driven analytics. The near future will, therefore, witness IoT, blockchain, and much more complex AI models converge into an even more personalised and efficient service insurance. These technologies are expected to automate the more complex underwriting and claim processing aspects and even assist with the predictive personalisation of policies. Data privacy and responsible usage of AI will be the need of the hour. The use of AI is poised to transform the customer experience. Bots and assistants using natural language processing will lead to many customer interactions with immediate 24/7 hours of availability. For instance, Lemonade Insurance allows handling claims and underwriting processes with the help of AI bots, thereby increasing efficiency by leaps and bounds and customer satisfaction.

This historical perspective shows how the insurance industry has moved from dependence on manual-based processes and basic statistical methods to embracing the full potential of digital data and advanced analytics. By introducing big data into the insurance sector, risk assessment has been improved while enabling innovative product development to detect fraud properly. Improved operational efficiencies, risk assessments, and risk profiling have enhanced the customer experience in this insurance revolution.

5.3 Various Forms of Data Used in Insurance

Data will form the basis of the insurance industry's decision-making. Various types of data are used to attain specific purposes, and each has several elements in the operation of the insurance business. Data-based activities ensure accurate risk evaluation, customised policies, expeditious claims processing, and enhanced service to policyholders. With technological advancement, using data will be more holistic, bringing more innovations and strategies into the insurance business.

5.3.1 Personal data

Personal information may include age, gender, marital status, occupation, medical history, and lifestyle. Such details are crucial when establishing the risk profiles of those who take the policies. For example, the health insurance policy mainly relies on personal information, such as age, smoking habits, and medical history, to assess an individual's risk profile and premium rates. A non-smoking young person with no history of chronic illness will pay much less for an insurance premium than an older person who might have a long history of some chronic disease.

5.3.2 Actuarial data

Actuarial data forms the insurance industry's core due to its integration of statistical foundations for risk assessment and pricing policies and sustaining a financial course. It includes statistical data in calculating risk and premiums associated with insurance. Some examples of actuarial data include mortality rates, morbidity rates, and life expectancy. For example, a life insurance company will use mortality tables among the actuarial data to approximate the years a client could survive. Such information will assist in the determination of the premiums; for instance, a higher life expectancy often attracts lower premiums. Essentially, actuarial data is used by underwriters to determine the risk associated with the insurance of a specific individual or entity. With this assessment, they tailor insurance policies according to specific risk profiles. They examine the previous claims data to determine possible future pay outs of claims. This ensures that the insurance has sufficient reserve for potential liabilities.

5.3.3 Claims data

Claims data provides information on past claims filed, such as the type of claim, the amount in dollars, and what circumstances led to the claim. It is convenient in predicting future claims and determining risk. For instance, automobile insurers trace previous claims data to find trends and factors of risk. For example, insurers may use such information to revise premiums if there is a surge in accidents in specific regions or age groups.

5.3.4 Financial data

Financial data refers to the history of one's or his group of individuals' credit, income, and financial standing. This data determines the risk over one's finances associated with the policyholder. In assessing life insurance applications, for example, an insurer may examine a customer's credit score as part of their financial discipline and, indirectly, risk level. Such a person with a good credit score and constant income would be less likely to default premium payments; hence, they qualify for better insurance rates.

5.3.5 Property data

Property data includes information concerning properties insured. It may consist of location, construction materials, age of the property, type of use-whether it is a residential home, commercial establishment, or used for industrial purposes, and the number of occupants and proximity to hazards. For example, for home insurance, the kind of location (flood zones, crime rates) and structural details (age of the building, the type of construction would be important information for risk assessment and premium determinations. Furthermore, property data that helps an insurance firm understand the market value of properties is vital in a policy that will have coverage for the replacement value of the property.

5.4 Tools and Technologies for Data Analytics

An integrated managed data source has sufficient depth to generate informed decision-making. An insurance company involves, therefore, various data types and subtypes, such as structured data, policyholder information, and unstructured data, such as claims notes or telematics data. Integrating different data streams into a coherent, unified system is complex. This variety requires sophisticated processing tools and algorithms to interpret and merge data effectively, often leading to higher costs and technical complexity. It may result in poor decision-making due to inaccurate, incomplete, or outdated data. Therefore, the modern insurance company employs several data analytics tools and technologies essential in processing, analysing, and interpreting large datasets. These tools and technologies improve the accuracy of the risk assessment and decision-making processes; all operations are refined, and customers' experiences are promising.

5.4.1 Big data platforms

The big data platform encompasses storing and processing significant amounts of data, as Apache Hadoop and Spark facilitated. Hadoop and Spark have strengths that can be used efficiently for the required data analytics tasks in the insurance sector. While Hadoop can hold large amounts of data at lower storage costs, Spark is apt for real-time processing and high analytics jobs. In practical terms, most insurance organisations often use the two platforms together; one is the base that holds data and puts it through batch processing using Hadoop, while the other employs Spark for real-time analytics. For example, Allstate Insurance tracks innovation and employs Hadoop-based systems for extensive data analysis. They analyse voluminous amounts of information from divergent sources to support the refinement of best practices in decision-making related to customer segmentation and risk assessment.

5.4.2 Data warehousing

Data warehousing technologies, such as Amazon Redshift, Google BigQuery, and Microsoft Azure SQL Data Warehouse, facilitate companies to store and manage structured data in vast quantities. Insurers use warehouses to aggregate data relating to claims, customer interactions, and policy information for efficient reporting and analysis. State Farm uses data warehousing technologies; among them are solutions like Teradata that aggregate and analyse data from many of its policyholders. This analysis of the provided data gives way to more accurate risk assessment and pricing strategies.

5.4.3 Business Intelligence (BI) and visualisation tools

BI tools can collate data from various claims databases, CRM systems, and external market data. This centralisation is critical for insurance companies to understand their operations and customers better. BI tools, such as Tableau, Microsoft Power BI, and QlikView, provide the flexibility to produce complex visualisations and uncover some hidden insights. They create dashboards with KPIs on renewals policy, claims processing, and other satisfaction metrics for the customer. Zurich Insurance Group uses BI and visualisation tools such as Tableau to analyse massive datasets, which enables them to make data-driven decisions, optimise business processes, and improve the customer experience.

5.4.4 Customer Relationship Management (CRM) systems

CRMs have become the central location for a customer's information, combining details obtained from all touchpoints, including policy applications, claims processing, customer service calls, and more. This centralisation provides a holistic view of the customer, which is very important for analytics. Most modern CRMs, such as Salesforce and Microsoft Dynamics, have also transcended their traditional general role of serving as simple customer management tools. They are highly used as robust bases for analytics, offering numerous capabilities in enhancing decision-making processes, interactions with customers, and work system efficiency. Through these systems, insurance companies can track every client's interaction, tailor communications with the clients, and offer customised products according to the customers' needs on their part. MetLife uses Salesforce as its CRM. It can allow them to better monitor their contact with customers, simplifying processes and efficiency in sales and marketing activities.

5.4.5 Internet of Things (IoT) platforms

IoT platforms combine several devices, collate and transfer data, and will thus result in real-time insights into various aspects that matter to insurance.

Examples include the IBM Watson IoT and Cisco IoT Cloud Connect. Health insurers employ data from fitness trackers to track policyholders' activity and health levels; for instance, discounts or rewards are available for healthy habits. With the Vitality program, John Hancock's Manulife company monitors clients' health and lifestyle information through IoT platforms and devices, including wearables. Reward-based incentives can be accrued for healthful behaviours tracked by such smart devices. IoT devices like sensors and smart home systems can also measure various aspects of risk factors and fire hazards, leakages, or break-ins, which could be reported to insurers in real time. It allows home insurance companies to estimate risks and tailor rates with enhanced accuracy.

5.4.6 Regulatory compliance and data governance tools

Insurance regulatory compliance is following various laws, policies, and standards that establish the nature of the industry. The regulations guard consumers but also help promote fair practices and support financial stability. However, these regulations are getting so complex and voluminous that many insurance companies find it hard to follow them. Data governance, in the case of insurance, relates to the availability, usability, integrity, and security of data in place. Effective data governance is essential in an industry entirely reliant on data, whether underwriting, claims processing, or customer service. The confluence of regulatory compliance with data governance also works both ways. As emphasised above, data governance facilitates compliance because it ensures integrity and accuracy in data, which are the two most necessary provisions for compliance. On the other hand, stringent compliance triggers a call for robust data governance frameworks. Tools such as Collibra and Talend help govern the data and compliance with the rules, such as GDPR. These tools help insurance firms maintain data integrity and security, track data lineage, and adhere appropriately to privacy laws and industry regulations. Liberty Mutual Insurance uses Collibra to support its data management, privacy, and regulatory compliance efforts. More innovative ways of data analytics in the insurance industry are yet to emerge in regulatory compliance and data governance. These will help with compliance and governance and boost the industry's efficiency and competitiveness.

5.5 Applications of Data Analytics in Insurance

Indeed, the insurance business is rapidly changing, shifting paradigms by integrating data analytics into its core processes. Thus, today, insurers can analyse vast and diverse datasets, such as personal information, social media activity, sensor data from connected devices, and much more. It can gather more precise risk and a tailor-made pricing model where the finer data can be utilised, way beyond the one-size-fits-all model of yesteryears.

5.5.1 Personalised risk profiling

Unlike old-school, one-size-fits-all traditional insurance models, data analytics personalises risk assessment. For example, insurers can build a better risk profile for each customer based on various data points, including lifestyle habits, health records, driving behaviour, and online activities. Enhanced risk assessment may focus more on the individual's behaviour than demographic factors. For instance, two individuals of the same age and health profile still had diverse risk profiles because of their lifestyle behaviours, for example, exercise frequency, diet type, and smoking status. For example, health insurers can leverage fitness trackers' data to break down lifestyle-related risk factors. John Hancock was one of the pioneers of this space. It has created interactive forms of life insurance where the premiums are linked to healthy behaviour tracked through wearable devices. It inspires healthier lifestyles and allows insurers to mitigate the risks posed by lifestyle diseases.

5.5.2 Understanding customer behaviour and preferences

Data analytics provides advanced machine learning algorithms and models that enable companies to predict future risks. This gives insurance companies a profound understanding of their customers' behaviours, preferences, and needs. Insurers can determine what a customer values by collecting data from social media, customer feedback, and interaction history. Predictive models analyse historical data, and then such an analysis is used to identify patterns that may point to a higher or lower risk, thus allowing insurers to predict the claims that will be filed more accurately in advance. For instance, Progressive Insurance uses data analytics to understand what customers want and adjusts communication and offerings appropriately, enhancing customer satisfaction while encouraging loyalty.

5.5.3 Dynamic pricing models

Data analytics helps create dynamic pricing models where the premiums are not fixed but vary according to real-time data. Premiums will be pretty adjusted according to the actual risk; that is, people with low-risk behaviour may earn lower premiums and be encouraged to change positive behaviour for policyholders. A prime example is usage-based car insurance: Companies like Progressive use telematics data from devices installed in vehicles to monitor drivers' behaviour and then update premiums accordingly. Safe driving leads to lower premiums and thus brings the insurance cost closer to the actual risk posed by the person driving.

5.5.4 Fraud detection and prevention

Insurance fraud is a significant issue, costing billions annually. Data analytics tools are adept at identifying patterns in claims data indicative of fraudulent activities. These could be unusual patterns in billing, discrepancies in claim details, or abnormal claim frequency from a particular source. Anomaly detection involves flagging claims that deviate significantly from the norm. It could include unusually high costs for certain types of claims or multiple claims from the same policyholder in a short period. Machine learning algorithms, a subset of data analytics, can continually improve and adapt predictive models as they are exposed to more data, enhancing their accuracy over time. By identifying fraudulent claims more efficiently, insurance companies can significantly reduce the costs associated with fraud, which ultimately benefits customers through lower premiums. For instance, Allstate Insurance uses a combination of predictive modelling, text mining, and other analytics techniques to identify potentially fraudulent claims. Their system flags claims that show signs of fraud for further investigation by an exceptional team. AXA employs advanced analytics to detect patterns and anomalies in claims data. They use machine learning algorithms that continuously learn from new data, improving their ability to detect fraud over time.

5.5.5 Geographical risk assessment

Applying geospatial data and analytics has transformed the risk assessment process in property insurance. Now, advanced analytics for mapping areas of risk, such as natural disaster risks (like floods, earthquakes, hurricanes) and human-induced risks (such as rates of urban crime or industrial hazards). It aids in understanding how climate change changes those landscapes of risk. For instance, regions that had never seen flooding or wildfires may experience these today due to climate change. Zurich Insurance uses satellite data, drones, and other sources to evaluate environmental risks such as floods, earthquakes, and wildfires. All these data will be critical in correctly pricing property insurance over areas prone to natural disasters. A global reinsurance leader, Munich Re, uses its NatCatSERVICE database for natural catastrophe risk assessment. This database contains geospatial data on natural disasters, which helps assess and price insurance for such risks more accurately.

5.5.6 Underwriting processes

Data analytics enables automation in many aspects of the underwriting process. Algorithms can process large volumes of data quickly, reducing the time it will take to assess the risk to offer policy terms. Automation often ensures policies become available sooner and allows for a maximum level of customer satisfaction. The underwriters use predictive models to forecast future trends and potential risks. Such models will supply the likelihood of claims upon some risky events and then process better prices and risk correction. For example, MetLife ensures the underwriting process is efficient by applying advanced analytics to its underwriting process, which saves it much time and cost to scrutinise policy applications. Lemonade, an insurance firm primarily run by technology, uses AI and machine learning in its underwriting process. Their AI algorithms cross-reference data from multiple sources to assess risk and price policies quickly.

5.6 The Future of Data-Driven Decision-Making in Insurance

Historically cautious and conservative, the insurance industry has transformed in directions that are more agile, innovative, and data-driven. This transformation is highly driven by emerging trends and technologies transforming the landscape of data-driven decision-making in insurance. Amidst the globally acclaimed revelation that data has been termed the new oil, the insurance industry is leading in using data to drive decisions to transform a business. Insurers increasingly tap large datasets, combining old data sources with new ones, such as IoT device data, social media activity, and telematics. For example, Progressive Insurance has been at the forefront of using telematics data through its Snapshot program to calculate auto insurance rates strictly based on driving behaviour. This trend will deepen with more granular data, leading to better risk assessments and personalised pricing.

5.6.1 Opportunities

5.6.1.1 Artificial intelligence and machine learning

In the rapidly evolving world of insurance, AI and machine learning have marked a paradigm shift. These technologies are not just futuristic concepts but are currently at the forefront of revolutionising the insurance industry's operations. AI and machine learning are critical players in driving data-driven decision-making, from automating underwriting processes to enhancing customer service. At its heart, the insurance industry is about risk assessment and management. These technologies offer cutting-edge tools to analyse large datasets, predict outcomes, and automate complicated processes. They enable data to power insurance companies' operations in ways previously unimaginable and lead to more accurate risk assessments and personalised policy pricing, as well as fraud detection and all-around operational efficiency. Risk assessment and policy pricing are significant contributions in the context of AI and ML for insurance. Traditional methods usually depend on historical data through manual processes, which can be time-consuming and inaccurate. Contrastingly, AI algorithms can process vast volumes of data, including no traditional sources such as social media profiles, IoT device outputs, and telematics. They can detect subtle patterns and correlations that human analysts might miss, leading to a more nuanced understanding of risk. Lemonade Insurance, a tech-driven startup, utilises AI for everything from policy issuance to claims processing, significantly reducing overhead costs and improving customer experience. AI algorithms continuously learn from data, which means they can adapt to new patterns in risk or customer behaviour, making the insurance process more responsive and dynamic.

5.6.1.2 Blockchain technology

Blockchain is a distributed ledger technology. It allows data to be stored across a network of computers and requires that once the information is recorded, it is virtually impossible to change or delete. Initially developed for the digital currency, Bitcoin, blockchain has potential applications that extend far beyond the realm of cryptocurrencies. In the insurance sector, data integrity and security are paramount. Immutability and decentralisation are inherent characteristics of blockchain that ensure data is secure and non-manipulative. With blockchain, insurance companies can hold tamper-proof policies, claims, and customer information records. This creates trust among stakeholders and reduces potential data breaches and fraud risks. Smart contracts in blockchain can, therefore, automate claim processes and administration of policies, with reduced fraud and increased efficiency. A notable example is AXA's Fizzy – an innovative contract-based insurance product that automatically pays customers for delayed flights, avoiding the classic claim processing procedure.

5.6.1.3 Predictive analytics

The core of insurance lies in the concept of risk. Predictive analytics has transformed the art of risk assessment, giving insurers a window to analyse multiple factors that were impossible to quantify before this innovation. For example, predictive models could assess risk factors in health insurance based on individual lifestyle choices, genetic information, and even social media behaviour. In auto insurance, telematics data provides real-time insights into driving habits, enabling insurers to tailor premiums to individual risk levels. This granularity ensures fairer pricing and encourages policyholders to adopt safer habits. For example, MetLife uses predictive analytics to identify customers likely to churn, enabling proactive engagement to improve retention rates. Therefore, the insurance industry's future is inextricably linked to the advancement of predictive analytics. On the horizon, that perfected accuracy and scope of prediction models will mean much more innovation in product offerings, risk assessment, and customer engagement. To insurers, embracing this data-driven approach will mean leading in a market that values precision, efficiency, and personalisation.

5.6.2 Challenges

5.6.2.1 Bridging the talent gap

Adopting data-driven strategies in insurance is highly dependent on talent but lags significantly in the skill gap, particularly in data analytics, machine learning, and digital innovation. Liberty Mutual and MetLife are among the insurers that invest in recruiting and training programs to attract data scientists and analytics experts. All these programs help create a data-driven workforce. Collaboration with academia and institutions of learning can help create targeted courses and research to benefit the insurance sector. This can be strategically used to create an orderly well of skilled personnel. Instead of hiring experts, a requirement is being built to develop a data-driven culture in the organisation. It means training the existing workforce in the value and application of data analytics in their work and embedding data-driven decision-making at every level of an organisation. Only talented companies will be able to seize opportunities to enter new markets, especially those previously underserved, which lack the traditional data that businesses have used. This is evident in the context of expansions in developing countries, supported by mobile data and alternative data sources.

5.6.2.2 Cybersecurity

Insurers gather, store, and process sensitive information in this data-driven decision-making generation, including personal, financial, and health-related data. Even though such information is fundamental for business insights, it remains a cyber-attacker's target. Therefore, cybersecurity measures are no longer an option but necessary. It supports data integrity, confidentiality, and availability. For example, Anthem Inc., a prominent health insurer, experienced a significant data breach in 2015 that exposed the sensitive personal information of more than 78 million individuals. The occurrence highlighted the requirement for robust cybersecurity measures when handling sensitive information. Cyber threats and attacks evolve with attackers becoming more sophisticated. Insurers should stay on their toes by regularly updating their cybersecurity. It includes technological solutions, employee training, and company-wide culture awareness. For example, AIG, the cyber insurance leader, modifies its present cybersecurity practices according to new and emerging threats.

5.6.2.3 Regulatory compliance

One of the challenges is that the regulatory landscape is constantly evolving. Insurers will need to ensure that the use of their data aligns with all relevant legal requirements, which differ by jurisdiction. Different regions have different regulations, such as GDPR in Europe and CCPA in California. Insurers such as AIG and Prudential need to ensure that their practices around data align with the rules, which entails significant investment in data governance and legal expertise. Regulatory bodies increasingly pay attention to the transparency and fairness of insurance practices, especially concerning using personal data in decision-making on pricing and coverage levels. Insurers need robust data governance frameworks to ensure that their use of data is compliant but, above all, fair and transparent. Thus, compliance is a legal necessity and a foundation for maintaining customer trust and corporate reputation.

5.6.2.4 Enhancing sustainability practices

The insurer can leverage data analytics to help with aligning with sustainable goals. Insurance companies are regarded as significant institutional investors; data analytics can inform their investment decisions, thus favouring companies and projects following sustainable practices–the way global efforts are being made to align with the UN Sustainable Development Goals. Data analytics helps create insurance products that encourage sustainable behaviour. Auto insurers can use a lower premium for electric or hybrid vehicles to promote environmentally friendly transportation. Green insurance products can be developed using environmental impact data to guide policyholders in environmentally friendly practices. For instance, Munich Re and Swiss Re use big data analytics in climate change risk assessment. They base their assessments on the probable impacts of climate-related events on their policyholders and use the information to devise products that encourage sustainable practices.

5.6.2.5 Ethical use of data and privacy concerns

Data ethics and privacy concerns will be important in the future. The insurer would have to draw a fine line where, on the one hand, there is better decision-making, and on the other hand, there is no breach of the customer's right to privacy. The industry may also witness more stringent regulations on this front, just like what is known as the General Data Protection Regulation in the European Union. For instance, firms such as Zurich Insurance Group have remained active in their initiatives to implement data governance frameworks, retaining customer confidentiality yet remaining strong proponents of analytics solution uses.

5.7 Conclusion

In the chapter itself, it can be seen how analytics has transformed the insurance industry. From their traditional method of simply processing the data manually based on history, the industrial sector has evolved into adopting digital data and more sophisticated analytics today. It has heralded better risk assessment, claims processing, and, most importantly, customer interaction toward dynamic, efficient, and personalised forms of insurance services. Furthermore, of course, this has much to do with big data, AI, and machine learning–the trilogy, so to say, has animated all elements of this change. They have enabled insurers to be more nuanced in terms of the offering they bring to market, increase efficiency on the operational side, and better understand and manage risks. In short, the industry's future will become even more data-centric, with new entrants like IoT and blockchain making them more potent for innovation and efficiency. However, cybersecurity concerns, regulatory compliance, and guaranteeing that information is used ethically remain significant concerns. In this context, the chapter underlines the great strides the insurance industry made toward more data-driven and customer-centric approaches, signalling a new era of opportunities and challenges.

5.8 Declaration

The authors declare that the manuscript follows ethical standards and that there are no potential conflicts of interest concerning this chapter's research, authorship, and/or publication.

5.9 Disclaimer

The authors express the contents and views of this chapter in personal capacities. The editor and the publisher do not need to agree with these viewpoints and are not responsible for any duty of care.

References

Agarwal, M., Gill, K. S., Upadhyay, D., Dangi, S., & Chythanya, K. R. (2024). The Evolution of Cryptocurrencies: Analysis of Bitcoin, Ethereum, Bit connect and Dogecoin in Comparison. *2024 IEEE 9th International Conference for Convergence in Technology, I2CT 2024*. https://doi.org/10.1109/I2CT61223.2024.10543872

Arora, M., Mishra, K. K., & Ghai, S. (2023). Green HRM practices and their impact on environmental sustainability. In *Green Management - A New Paradigm in the World of Business*. Nova Science Publishers, Inc.

Bharadwaj, G., Chopde, S., Taluja, R., Lalitha, G., Chandrashekar, R., & Dhahi, H. A. (2023). Closing the Loop: Advances in Materials, Energy, and Waste Management. In S. K.K. (Ed.), *E3S Web of Conferences* (Vol. 453). EDP Sciences. https://doi.org/10.1051/e3sconf/202345301024

Bhatt, S., & Dani, R. (2024). Social media and community engagement: Empowering local voices in regenerative tourism. In *Examining Tourist Behaviors and Community Involvement in Destination Rejuvenation*. IGI Global. https://doi.org/10.4018/979-8-3693-6819-0.ch009

Bisht, B., Lohani, U. C., Nanda, M., Kumar, S., Vlaskin, M., Dsouza, A., Joshi, S., & Kumar, V. (2024). Synergistic interaction between hydrocolloids and kinnow peel biowaste for the development of edible fillers using response surface methodology. *Environmental Science and Pollution Research International*, *31*(2), 2595–2613. https://doi.org/10.1007/s11356-023-31247-4

Caiado, R. G. G., Scavarda, L. F., Vidal, G., de Mattos Nascimento, D. L., & Garza-Reyes, J. A. (2023). A taxonomy of critical factors towards sustainable operations and supply chain management 4.0 in developing countries. *Operations Management Research*. https://doi.org/10.1007/s12063-023-00430-8

Chandel, N. S., Tripathi, V., Singh, H. B., & Vaishnav, A. (2024). Breaking seed dormancy for sustainable food production: Revisiting seed priming techniques and prospects. *Biocatalysis and Agricultural Biotechnology*, *55*. https://doi.org/10.1016/j.bcab.2023.102976

Datta, S., Hamim, I., Jaiswal, D. K., & Sungthong, R. (2023). Sustainable agriculture. *BMC Plant Biology*, *23*(1). https://doi.org/10.1186/s12870-023-04626-9

Deng, Q., Usman, M., Irfan, M., & Haseeb, M. (2024). The role of financial inclusion and tourism in tackling environmental challenges of industrialization and energy consumption: Redesigning Sustainable Development Goals policies. *Natural Resources Forum*. https://doi.org/10.1111/1477-8947.12522

Gangwar, V. P., & Srivastva, S. P. (2020). Impact of micro finance in poverty eradication via SHGs: A study of selected districts in U.P. *International Journal of Advanced Science and Technology*, *29*(2), 3818–3829.

Garai, T., Garg, H., & Biswas, G. (2023). A fraction ranking-based multi-criteria decision-making method for water resource management under bipolar neutrosophic fuzzy environment. *Artificial Intelligence Review*, *56*(12), 14865–14906. https://doi.org/10.1007/s10462-023-10514-3

Garg, N., & Shrivastava, S. (2024). Valorisation of ceramic insulator waste in rendering mortar for enhanced mechanical, durability and sustainability performance. *Innovative Infrastructure Solutions*, *9*(1). https://doi.org/10.1007/s41062-023-01326-z

Gopal, S., Gupta, P., & Minocha, A. (2023). Advancements in Fin-Tech and Security Challenges of Banking Industry. *4th International Conference on Intelligent Engineering and Management, ICIEM 2023*. https://doi.org/10.1109/ICIEM59379.2023.10165876

Govindarajan, H. K., Ganesh, L. S., Sharma, N., & Agarwal, R. (2023). Indian Energy Scenario: A Critical Review. *Indian Journal of Environmental Protection*, *43*(2), 99–107.

Gupta, A., & Kumar, H. (2022). Multi-dimensional perspectives on electric vehicles design: A mind map approach. *Cleaner Engineering and Technology*, *8*. https://doi.org/10.1016/j.clet.2022.100483

Gupta, C., Jindal, P., & Malhotra, R. K. (2022). A Study of Increasing Adoption Trends of Digital Technologies - An Evidence from Indian Banking. In D. N. & C. A. (Eds.), *AIP Conference Proceedings* (Vol. 2481). American Institute of Physics Inc. https://doi.org/10.1063/5.0104572

Gupta, M., Kumari, I., & Singh, A. K. (2024). Impact of human capital on SDG1 in selected G20 countries. In *Interlinking SDGs and the Bottom-of-the-Pyramid Through Tourism*. IGI Global. https://doi.org/10.4018/979-8-3693-3166-8.ch002

Gupta, S., Gilotra, S., Rathi, S., Choudhury, T., & Kotecha, K. (2024). Plant Disease Recognition Using Different CNN Models. In T. S.,

G. R., S. A., K. S., K. S., A. R., & S. K. R. (Eds.), *Proceedings of the 14th International Conference on Cloud Computing, Data Science and Engineering, Confluence 2024* (pp. 787–792). Institute of Electrical and Electronics Engineers Inc. https://doi.org/10.1109/Confluence60223.2024.10463383

Gwak, J., Garg, H., & Jan, N. (2023). Investigation of Robotics Technology Based on Bipolar Complex Intuitionistic Fuzzy Soft Relation. *International Journal of Fuzzy Systems*, *25*(5), 1834–1852. https://doi.org/10.1007/s40815-023-01487-0

Jaiswal, K. K., Dutta, S., Banerjee, I., Pohrmen, C. B., & Kumar, V. (2023). Photosynthetic microalgae–based carbon sequestration and generation of biomass in biorefinery approach for renewable biofuels for a cleaner environment. *Biomass Conversion and Biorefinery*, *13*(9), 7403–7421. https://doi.org/10.1007/s13399-021-01504-y

Jena, S., Cao, S., & Gairola, A. (2024). Cyclonic wind loads and structural mitigation measures – vulnerability assessment of traditional housings in Odisha. *Journal of Earth System Science*, *133*(2). https://doi.org/10.1007/s12040-024-02255-w

Kashyap, A., Shukla, O. J., Jha, B. K., Ramtiyal, B., & Soni, G. (2023). Enhancing Sustainable Dairy Industry Growth through Cold-Supply-Chain-Integrated Production Forecasting. *Sustainability (Switzerland)*, *15*(22). https://doi.org/10.3390/su152216102

Kaur, B., Mansi, Dimri, S., Singh, J., Mishra, S., Chauhan, N., Kukreti, T., Sharma, B., Singh, S. P., Arora, S., Uniyal, D., Agrawal, Y., Akhtar, S., Rather, M. A., Naik, B., Kumar, V., Gupta, A. K., Rustagi, S., & Preet, M. S. (2023). Insights into the harvesting tools and equipment's for horticultural crops: From then to now. *Journal of Agriculture and Food Research*, *14*. https://doi.org/10.1016/j.jafr.2023.100814

Kaur, H., Hussain, S. J., Mir, R. A., Chandra Verma, V., Naik, B., Kumar, P., & Dubey, R. C. (2023). Nanofertilizers – Emerging smart fertilizers for modern and sustainable agriculture. *Biocatalysis and Agricultural Biotechnology*, *54*. https://doi.org/10.1016/j.bcab.2023.102921

Kumar, P., Taneja, S., Bhatnagar, M., & Kaur, A. K. (2024). Navigating the digital paradigm shift: Designing CBDCs for a transformative financial landscape. In *Exploring Central Bank Digital Currencies: Concepts, Frameworks, Models, and Challenges*. IGI Global. https://doi.org/10.4018/979-8-3693-1882-9.ch006

Kumar, V., Gururani, P., Parveen, A., Verma, M., Kim, H., Vlaskin, M., Grigorenko, A. V, & Rindin, K. G. (2023). Dairy Industry wastewater and stormwater energy valorization: effect of wastewater nutrients on microalgae-yeast biomass. *Biomass Conversion and Biorefinery*, *13*(15), 13563–13572. https://doi.org/10.1007/s13399-022-02947-7

Liao, N., Cai, Q., Garg, H., Wei, G., & Xu, X. (2023). Novel Gained and Lost Dominance Score Method Based on Cumulative Prospect Theory for Group Decision-Making Problems in Probabilistic Hesitant Fuzzy Environment. *International Journal of Fuzzy Systems*, *25*(4), 1414–1428. https://doi.org/10.1007/s40815-022-01440-7

Mishra, D., Kandpal, V., Agarwal, N., & Srivastava, B. (2024). Financial Inclusion and Its Ripple Effects on Socio-Economic Development: A Comprehensive Review. *Journal of Risk and Financial Management*, *17*(3). https://doi.org/10.3390/jrfm17030105

Mukul, Taneja, S., Özen, E., & Bansal, N. (2024). Challenges and Opportunities for Skill Development in Developing Economies. *Contemporary Studies in Economic and Financial Analysis*, *112B*, 1–22. https://doi.org/10.1108/S1569-375920240000112B001

Naveen, Y., Lokanadham, D., Naidu, D. R., Sharma, R. C., Palli, S., & Lila, M. K. (2023). An Experimental Study on the Influence of Blended Karanja Biodiesel on Diesel Engine Characteristics. *International Journal of Vehicle Structures and Systems*, *15*(2), 154–160. https://doi.org/10.4273/ijvss.15.2.02

Pramanik, B., Sar, P., Bharti, R., Gupta, R. K., Purkayastha, S., Sinha, S., Chattaraj, S., & Mitra, D. (2023). Multifactorial role of nanoparticles in alleviating environmental stresses for sustainable crop production and protection. *Plant Physiology and Biochemistry*, *201*. https://doi.org/10.1016/j.plaphy.2023.107831

Rajput, S., Parida, S., Sharma, A., & Sonika. (2023). Dielectric Materials for Energy Storage and Energy Harvesting Devices. In *Dielectric Materials for Energy Storage and Energy Harvesting Devices*. River Publishers.

Rawat, R., Goyal, H. R., & Sharma, S. (2023). Artificial Narrow Intelligence Techniques in Intelligent Digital Financial Inclusion System for Digital Society. *2023 6th International Conference on Information Systems and Computer Networks, ISCON 2023*. https://doi.org/10.1109/ISCON57294.2023.10112133

Rawat, R., Sharma, S., & Goyal, H. R. (2023). Intelligent Digital Financial Inclusion System Architectures for Industry 5.0 Enabled Digital Society. *Winter Summit on Smart Computing and Networks, WiSSCoN 2023*. https://doi.org/10.1109/WiSSCoN56857.2023.10133858

Ritika, Bora, B., Ismail, B. B., Garba, U., Mishra, S., Jha, A. K., Naik, B., Kumar, V., Rather, M. A., Rizwana, Preet, M. S., Rustagi, S., Kumar, H., & Gupta, A. K. (2024). Himalayan fruit and circular economy:

nutraceutical potential, traditional uses, challenges and opportunities. *Food Production, Processing and Nutrition*, *6*(1). https://doi.org/10.1186/s43014-023-00220-6

Sharma, A., Mohan, A., & Johri, A. (2024). Impact of Financial Technology (Fin-Tech) on the Restructuring of the Agrarian Economy: A Comprehensive Systematic Review. In M. H. (Ed.), *Proceedings - 2024 6th International Conference on Computational Intelligence and Communication Technologies, CCICT 2024* (pp. 249–252). Institute of Electrical and Electronics Engineers Inc. https://doi.org/10.1109/CCICT62777.2024.00049

Sharma, P., Hussain, S. S., Taneja, S., & Sheikh, R. (2023). Gig economy, workplace culture and talent crunch: A conceptual model for future work. In *Green Management - A New Paradigm in the World of Business*. Nova Science Publishers, Inc.

Singh, A. B., Khandelwal, C., Sarkar, P., Dangayach, G. S., & Meena, M. L. (2023). Achieving Sustainable Development in the Hospitality Industry: An Evidence-Based Empirical Study. *Evergreen*, *10*(3), 1186–1198. https://doi.org/10.5109/7148439

Singh, S. K., Chauhan, A., & Sarkar, B. (2024). Strategy planning for sustainable biodiesel supply chain produced from waste animal fat. *Sustainable Production and Consumption*, *44*, 263–281. https://doi.org/10.1016/j.spc.2023.10.012

Srivastava, B., Kandpal, V., & Jain, A. K. (2024). Financial well-being of women self-help group members: a qualitative study. *Environment, Development and Sustainability*. https://doi.org/10.1007/s10668-024-04879-w

Swain, K. P., Ranjan Nayak, S., Ravi, V., Mishra, S., Alahmadi, T. J., Singh, P., & Diwakar, M. (2024). Empowering Crop Selection with Ensemble Learning and K-means Clustering: A Modern Agricultural Perspective. *Open Agriculture Journal*, *18*. https://doi.org/10.2174/0118743315291367240207093403

Taneja, S., Bansal, N., & Kumar, P. (2023). Tech-driven sustainability: Fintech innovations revolutionizing green banking. In *Green Management - A New Paradigm in the World of Business*. Nova Science Publishers, Inc.

Yadav, S., Samadhiya, A., Kumar, A., Luthra, S., & Pandey, K. K. (2024). Nexus between fintech, green finance and natural resources management: Transition of BRICS nation industries from resource curse to resource blessed sustainable economies. *Resources Policy*, *91*. https://doi.org/10.1016/j.resourpol.2024.104903

6

Role of Fintech in Revamping the Banking World

Vivek Sharma[1], Sanjay Taneja[2], J.P. Davim[3] and Bupiinderpal Singh[4]

[1]Chandigarh University, India
[2]Graphic Era Deemed to be University, India
[3]Universidade de Aveiro, Portugal
[4]Yorkville University, Canada

Email: vivek9781987681@gmail.com; drsanjaytaneja1@gmail.com; pdavim@ua.pt; bchahal@yorkvilleu.ca

Abstract

This dynamic technology-driven era has seriously impacted the way we save, spend, and invest in an almost irreversible manner. This has opened the avenues for a new kind of tech-driven business model in the form of fintech (financial technology). Amidst the increased craze of Blockchain technology, the rapid pace of globalisation, and the global financial crisis of 2008 (US sub-prime lending crisis) and 2021 (China Evergrande), the role of technology in revamping the BFSI (banking financial and services sector) has become even more critical by offering various innovations in terms of Bitcoins, Regtech (regulatory technology), Insurtech (insurance technology), Robo-advisory services. Fintech as an emerging technology includes all software, mobile applications, and technologies that aim to improve and automate the traditional process of delivering financial services. At its core, it uses specialised software and algorithms that are run on mobile devices and computers to cater to the needs of businesses and retail consumers in managing their financial affairs. Such companies include Coinbase Global, Inc., Revolt, PayPal, Google Pay, etc. The present chapter aims to explain the role of fintech technology in reshaping the banking world by resolving the issues related to regulatory compliances, data security, lack of mobile and tech expertise, credit score assessments such as CIBIL, window dressing, and risk management. A brief discussion has also been made regarding the difference between fintech companies and techfin (technology finance) Companies and the future of fintechin the metaverse.

6.1 Introduction

The twenty-first century has witnessed the most significant technological revolution in finance, known as fintech technology. Fintech has brought significant improvements in the areas of lending, payment systems, insurance, and financial advising. One of its key roles is to promote financial inclusion by ensuring the availability of financing for the unbanked areas. Fintech will play a pivotal role in cost reduction, i.e., the aim of improving and automating the traditional process of delivering financial services. At its core, it makes use of specialised software and algorithms that are run on mobile devices and computers to cater to the needs of businesses and retail consumers in managing their financial affairs. Examples of such companies are Coinbase Global, Inc., Revolt, PayPal, Google Pay, etc. Initially, it was more of a back-end technology directed toward well-established financial institutions. However, later on, it became an increasingly consumer-centric service. At present, it covers major fields and industries such as cryptocurrencies, wealth management, retail banking, regtech, and fundraising, to name a few. As per EY's 2017 Fintech Adoption Index, one-third of customers use two or more fintech services, and these consumers are becoming more conscious of fintech as a part of their daily lives (B. Pramanik et al., 2023).

6.1.1 History and evolution of fintech

It must be well-managed evolution, not a revolution that has witnessed some critical global economic events from the Great Depression of the 1930s to the 2008 US subprime lending crisis. The first phase was more focused on establishing the basic telecommunication infrastructure (A. Kaur, Kukreja, Malhotra, et al., 2024; Shao et al., 2023; Širić et al., 2023). The second phase involved the application of technology to the global banking sector in terms of opening the first ATM (Automated Teller Machine) by Barclays Bank in London and developing Internet banking. In the advent of severe global financial crises and major geopolitical shifts, the third phase witnessed the

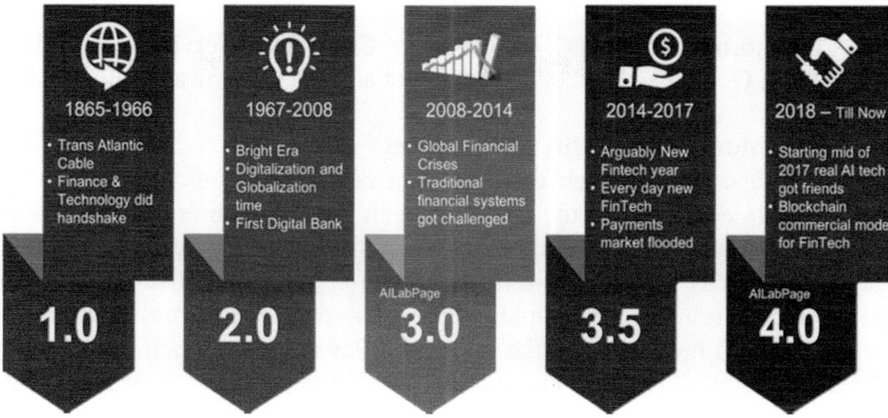

Figure 6.1 Evolution of fintech. Designed by authors.

emergence of fintech companies that capitalised on the available opportunities to serve the needs of the information–and technology-driven economy. The fourth phase will offer the tremendous capabilities of artificial intelligence (AI) and metaverse (a melding of the physical and virtual worlds) to leverage the investment avenues available with real-time information with almost zero system downtime. (A. Arya et al., 2024; P. Arya et al., 2023; A. Kaur, Kukreja, Kumar, et al., 2024b).

6.1.2 Revenue generation models of fintech companies

In this technology-driven environment, various unique business models have been developed using blockchain, digital platforms, transaction processing systems, and decision support systems. Key revenue streams mainly include pay-per-use, subscription, revenue sharing, kickback, and charging of interest or fees on loans (Dutta et al., 2023; Gupta et al., 2024; Sharma et al., 2023; Swain et al., 2024). This allows the fintech companies to open up new markets and client contacts, offer various innovative revenue-generating products, and practice cutting-edge techniques for creating customer-centric goods and services. With the latter, fintechs can collaborate with their clients to create value, allowing both the supply and demand sides to contribute to the production of resources and activity-based competitive advantages. Product offerings mainly cover data collection, brokerage, foreign exchange conversion, imparting education regarding financial inclusion, investment management, payment services, personal assistantship, lending/credit, credit score monitoring, and KYC (Know Your Customers) services (Bhandari et al., 2023; G. Garg et al., 2023; H. Kaur et al., 2023; Semwal et al., 2023).

6.1.2.1 Fintech vs techfin companies

After the success of fintech companies, a new class of technology-based players also emerged in the form of tech fin companies. Techfins are technology-driven companies that provide software and application solutions that are primarily not finance-related but are supplementary to their original product offering. For example, the popular social media messaging platform Whatsapp has launched the Whatsapp Pay feature in their application (Adelodun et al., 2024; Al-Huqail et al., 2023; Deepti et al., 2023; A. Kaur, Kukreja, Kumar, et al., 2024a). Similarly, e-commerce giant Amazon has also launched Amazon Pay for its existing set of users in order to provide a one-stop solution instead of a third-party payment application. One big difference between fintech companies and techfin companies is that the former have their primary business purely financial. However, the latter are such companies that provide finance-related solutions merely as a part of their original product. Techfin companies exist to improve the existing capabilities in the financial services industry, which are less disruptive and incremental. (R. Kaur, Gupta, Tripathi, et al., 2024; Khosravi et al., 2024; Kukreti et al., 2024).

6.1.2.2 Fintech users

There are four main groups of fintech users: i) B2B for banks, ii) their corporate clients, iii) B2C for small businesses, and iv) consumers. Due to trends toward mobile banking, increased information and data, more accurate analytics, and decentralised access, all four groups will have the chance to connect in previously unheard-of ways. In terms of clients, the younger you are, the more probable it is that you are familiar with fintech and can define it precisely, as with most forms of technology (S. Garg et al., 2024). Millennials are the main target of consumer-focused fintech due to their vast size and growing earning (and inheritance) potential. Some fintech industry watchers believe that the focus on millennials is more a result of the size of that market than of Gen Xers' and baby boomers' interest in or competency with fintech. Fintech typically has little to offer older consumers because it does not solve their needs. Before the creation and application of fintech, a business owner or startup would have gone to a bank to obtain financing or bridge finance. If they wanted to accept credit card payments, they would need to partner with a credit provider and install equipment, such as a landline-connected card reader. These barriers are no longer an issue because of mobile technologies (Pal et al., 2024).

6.1.2.3 Scope of fintech in the banking field

Some of the most prominent areas of fintech innovation include or revolve around the following areas:

a. Cryptocurrency: The terms cryptocurrency and fintech always go together. There is intense competition among traditional players in the banking and financial sectors. The cryptocurrency market has grown at an unpredictable pace, offering more than 550 competing cryptocurrencies. Among all these, the most popular is Bitcoin, which has contributed significantly to the fluidity of the industry despite the stringent government regulations. The idea of Bitcoin was pioneered by Satoshi Nakamoto, who published it in his book in 2008 (a peer-to-peer electronic cash system). Although the idea of digital money has been around since the late 1980s, the first decentralised cryptocurrency to be a success is Bitcoin, which was introduced in 2009 by the mysterious (and as of yet unidentified) creator Satoshi Nakamoto. Considering the bright prospects, almost all the central banks in the countries have introduced their digital currency (Jain et al., 2024a). Reserve Bank of India, on 1 December 2022, launched a retail version of the CBDC (E-₹-). Cryptocurrencies make use of cryptographic techniques in order to ensure a safe end-to-end transaction. Cryptocurrencies are the most popular application of blockchain technology. By disseminating the currency and releasing it from hierarchical power structures, Bitcoin revolutionised the digital coin market. Through the use of end-to-end secured networks, people and corporations can conduct an exchange of coins. After Bitcoin, several other cryptocurrencies were introduced, such as Ethereum, Tether, BNB, USD Coin, Binance USD, and Cardano (ADA). In 2011, its demand sharply rose, and altcoins– the collective term for all cryptocurrencies became popular. Beginning in 2011, it attracted a lot of interest, and several altcoins – a collective term for all currencies released after Bitcoin – soon emerged (Jain et al., 2024b).

b. Regulatory technology (Regtech): It refers to a sub-part of fintech that involves using such technology, which ensures compliance with the applicable regulatory environment more effectively and efficiently. This term was first adopted by the UK's Financial Conduct Authority in 2015. The overall foundation of regtech is based on the four key pillars, which are (1) data protection regulations, (2) increased competition due to the increase in the number of open banking platforms, (3) the emergence of global financial crises such as US Sub-Prime lending crisis of

2008 and recent China's Evergrande liquidity crisis (2021) (4) Rapidly changing Legislative Framework for user identity authentication.

6.1.2.3.1 Critical drivers for the use of Regtech in the BFSI sector

- Increased cost of regulatory compliance: According to The Trade, banks reportedly spent over $100 billion on regulatory compliance in 2016 alone.
- Complex business models: These refer to the intricacies of organisational structures, products and services offered, processes involved, and markets served. Effective monitoring of special watch accounts and compliance with global prudential norms such as BASEL norms have also been the biggest challenges in controlling non-performing assets (NPAs). (BASEL norms are the major prudential regulations applicable to all the banks of member countries).
- Interdependence among global financial institutions: Several issues are involved in terms of process-related controls and selected target markets. Monitoring, interpreting, and complying with the current and planned regulations is a challenge, even for the largest banks. Much of the budget is dedicated to hiring consultants and professionals to offer specialised information technology services.
- Information and data-related drivers: According to past studies done in the UK and USA related to the regulatory and financial environment, key issues are a lack of comprehension skills and a holistic approach, ineffective risk management strategies, and poor market studies done to understand client needs.

c. Insurtech: Insurance and banking have long been related but are also distinct. Insurtech is a combination of two words: "Insurance plus Technology". It involves the innovative use of technology and traditional insurance products to bring savings and efficiency to the traditional insurance business model. For a good period, banks have become popular insurance service providers. To capture the major market share, all the banks and financial institutions are focusing on creating differentiating value for their clients compared to their rivals. This strong urge to create value differentiation has resulted in the emergence of Insurtech companies. Banks and financial institutions already have valuable customer data, such as purchasing a car, house, jewellery, or foreign trip. So, banks can directly offer insurance concerning these purchases at the time of purchase, which will not only be time- and cost-effective but also minimise the time gap in the realisation of revenue. Some famous examples are Zipari, Corvus Insurance, Lemonade, Acko, and Policybazaar. It offers smooth workflows for handling the claims process at scale through AI (Artificial Intelligence) technology. Due to the emergence of the COVID-19 pandemic, the revenue of these insurance companies has increased significantly as people have realised the actual value of medical insurance and allied life coverage schemes. These companies also provide a financial shield to tackle the medical ailment. Banks and FI's can also offer embedded insurance schemes for providing comprehensive insurance coverage against all possible risks related to principal purchases, such as the time of buying a laptop package will include risk coverage from theft or any other act of sabotage (Banerjee et al., 2024).

d. Cybersecurity: Cybersecurity risks have put the assets and information of businesses, institutions, governments, and individuals at constant risk in the new and developing digitalised world. Not an exception are banks. Offering low interest rates is becoming a crucial part of banks' survival strategies. The availability of sophisticated communication and advanced transaction mechanisms caused the formation of a new class of competitors known as financial technology services in response to the rising demand for a personalised portfolio of financial goods (Jain et al., 2024b). In order to better serve customers and meet the demands of expanding markets, these fintech companies and banks have recently intensified their cooperation. However, this partnership between banks and fintech companies has raised severe cybersecurity concerns. Businesses using fintech run the risk of cybersecurity because of integration problems, including compatibility and outdated technology. Data privacy issues may arise due to fintech integration with conventional banking systems. Large volumes of client data, susceptible personal data, are gathered by fintech companies, making them attractive targets for hackers (Banerjee et al., 2024).

Thanks to fintech, people who previously had difficulty accessing these services now have simple access to fundamental banking functions. However, these new bank customers may be more vulnerable to hackers since they have little to no prior knowledge of cybersecurity risks (Tamta et al., 2024).

API banking refers to the practice of using application programming interfaces (APIs) created specifically for banks to access fintech platforms and provide easily available services. By using open APIs, third-party developers can create applications and services tailored to users' demands.

Key cybersecurity issues involved are

- Blockchain risks, such as hacking and malware attacks, may cause unwanted downtime and a massive loss of money and reputation for the user.
- Risk of money laundering due to the use of cryptography technology that is not fully regulated. The use of any unregulated technology may increase the risk of terror funding. Due to the pseudonymous nature of fintech, it is impossible to identify the beneficiary in any fintech-enabled transactions, which can significantly aid money laundering operations.
- Issues related to outdated and sub-standard CBS (Core et al.) systems can also cause incompatibility issues.
- Security risks related to cloud environment: One of the critical enablers of a finance ecosystem is cloud computing. Payment gateways are one of the specialised cloud computing services offered in a fintech ecosystem. Other services include digital wallets and safe online transactions. For instance, cloud computing makes it simple and quick to make payments. Maintaining the privacy and security of financial information is essential for banks and financial services. This sensitive information may be compromised and corrupted without cloud security safeguards. This risk can be eliminated with a robust encryption method for the cloud platform.

e. Robo-advisors: Fintech Robo advisers are commonly utilised in the mutual fund sector, where investor behaviour is assessed through an online survey, and mutual funds are assigned to the investor in order to generate a well-maintained portfolio based on the investor's expectations for risk and return. Robo advisors employ online tools to assist investors in selecting the best investment options while considering their expectations. It is a process where automated algorithms are used to generate guidance. Robotic advisors require little assistance from humans. By taking an online poll, they learn about an investor's requirements and then offer suggestions for where to put the money. The least expensive method of obtaining financial advice on investments is through Robo-advisors. Since Robo advising services do not require human labour and can be accessed 24/7 with internet connectivity, online platforms can offer them a reasonable price. The Robo advisors are thought to be the most appropriate for beginning investors. Entry-level investors typically have less wealth and experience. In these circumstances, Robo-advisors are the ideal choice for investments. Only a smaller beginning balance is needed for Robo advisers compared to other platforms that offer the same services. Since Robo advising services require less human connection, one of their primary criticisms is that automated portfolio management lacks intelligence and empathy. Robo advising services are considered particularly well suited for traditional investment instead of complex investing. For this reason, they use the term "Robo". Advisors are appropriate for beginning investors or novices. Earlier, only a small group had access to the Robo advising services. However, they are accessible to everyone, and the services can be delivered straight to the client. Since 2000, automated algorithms have been used by human wealth managers to build portfolios. Most Robo advisors today employ passive indexing, concentrating on higher returns with little stock buying and selling. These strategies are optimised by utilising some of the characteristics of Modern Portfolio Theory (MPT).

6.1.2.3.2 Popular robo-advisors: Which investors can select

- Wealthfront: This is the oldest and most popular Robo-advisor for financial goal setting. Tax planning and portfolio management services are also provided according to the applicable tax slab and the nature of the profession/business at a very modest fee of 0.25 percent. Thus, it is at the top due to its cost-effectiveness and easy-to-use interface.
- Interactive advisors: They are the best choice for developing strong portfolios as they use rigorous data investigation and screening to select funds.
- Betterment: This is the best choice for newcomers due to its on-demand services and complete transparency in the administration and distribution of funds. It offers its users educational resources, and its user accounts are not subject to any minimum fees.
- Personal capital: Personal capital is considered the most excellent choice for investors when managing a portfolio. It is regarded as the

best due to its diversification and tax optimisation. It offers account aggregation and a variety of investment management solutions to investors. Additionally, it puts much effort into offering advanced support to investors who require specialised advice from professionals.

- M1 finance: For veterans, it is the best choice. The supporting reasons for this are portfolio customisation and sound, comprehensive portfolio controls. They concentrate on offering pre-built portfolios for customers and provide 80 distinct combinations.
- Merrill: Merrill is well known for providing a learning-based environment through valuable articles, videos, and other value-added tools for maximising wealth.
- E*trade: It makes the best possible efforts to provide standardised services ranging from smartphones to computers. Its main features are an easy-to-use interface and affordable fees.

6.1.2.4 How the fintech industry can adopt the metaverse

In Lyman's terms, the Metaverse can be defined as a melding of the physical and the virtual world. Being receptive to the opportunities offered by metaverse world fintech companies will enjoy more autonomy, including direct participation and flexibility for improving overall customer engagement beyond the physical offices and smartphone-based applications. The story has a substantial financial component, even though augmented reality (AR) and virtual reality (VR) currently dominate metaverse developments. Consumers are increasingly lured to immersive digital experiences, which call for new digital financial models, but are also drawn to virtual assets. This involves crypto, non-fungible tokens (NFTs), and other elements that play a significant role in the metaverse's layers. Authentication and digital identity services, financial infrastructure, and data management firms will greatly facilitate value exchanges in this virtual world.

6.2 Conclusion

Fintech technologies will play a game-changer role in reshaping the banking world by addressing key issues, such as regulatory compliance, window dressing, and risk management. They require a positive attitude from the regulatory authorities in catering to the infrastructural challenges and disseminating financial and technology literacy across the country, especially in the rural sector. Traditional banks can also enter into strategic partnerships with fintech companies to leverage the benefits offered by fintech (Elsaid, 2023). From the theoretical point of view, promoting competition in the financial markets should result in less stringent regulations than in the case of traditional financial services. However, the challenges involved during execution are also unavoidable regarding financial stability (Pozzolo, 2017). However, a trade-off must be maintained with sustainability by ensuring proper alignment with the Sustainable Development Goals (SDGs), demanding harmony among global policymakers.

References

Adelodun, B., Agbelusi, O. O., Soma, T., Odey, G., Adeyi, Q., Kumar, P., Ajibade, F. O., Goala, M., Silva, L. F. O., Mostafa, Y. S., Singh, R., Choi, K. S., & Eid, E. M. (2024). Rethinking food loss and waste to promote sustainable resource use and climate change mitigation in agri-food systems: A review. *Waste Management and Research*. https://doi.org/10.1177/0734242X241257655

AL-Huqail, A. A., Singh, R., Širić, I., Kumar, P., Abou Fayssal, S., Kumar, V., Bachheti, R. K., Andabaka, Ž., Goala, M., & Eid, E. M. (2023). Occurrence and Health Risk Assessment of Heavy Metals in Lychee (Litchi chinensis Sonn., Sapindaceae) Fruit Samples. *Horticulturae*, *9*(9). https://doi.org/10.3390/horticulturae9090989

Arya, A., Bachheti, A., Bachheti, R. K., Singh, M., & Chandel, A. K. (2024). Role of Artificial Intelligence in Minimizing Carbon Footprint: A Systematic Review of Recent Insights. *Green Energy and Technology*, *Part F2511*, 365–386. https://doi.org/10.1007/978-3-031-51601-6_14

Arya, P., Shreya, S., & Gupta, A. (2023). Amazing potential and the future of fungi: Applications and economic importance. In *Microbial Bioactive Compounds: Industrial and Agricultural Applications*. Springer Nature. https://doi.org/10.1007/978-3-031-40082-7_2

Banerjee, D., Sharma, N., Chauhan, R., Singh, M., & Kumar, B. V. (2024). A Deep Dive into Precision Horticulture: Unravelling Olive Peacock Spot Intensity with Hybrid Deep Learning. *2024 5th International Conference for Emerging Technology, INCET 2024*. https://doi.org/10.1109/INCET61516.2024.10593619

Bhandari, G., Dhasmana, A., Chaudhary, P., Gupta, S., Gangola, S., Gupta, A., Rustagi, S., Shende, S. S., Rajput, V. D., Minkina, T., Malik, S., & Slama, P. (2023). A Perspective Review on Green Nanotechnology in Agro-Ecosystems: Opportunities for Sustainable Agricultural Practices

& Environmental Remediation. *Agriculture (Switzerland)*, *13*(3). https://doi.org/10.3390/agriculture13030668

Chandel, N. S., Tripathi, V., Singh, H. B., & Vaishnav, A. (2024). Breaking seed dormancy for sustainable food production: Revisiting seed priming techniques and prospects. *Biocatalysis and Agricultural Biotechnology*, *55*. https://doi.org/10.1016/j.bcab.2023.102976

Datta, S., Hamim, I., Jaiswal, D. K., & Sungthong, R. (2023). Sustainable agriculture. *BMC Plant Biology*, *23*(1). https://doi.org/10.1186/s12870-023-04626-9

Deepti, Bachheti, A., Arya, A. K., Verma, D. K., & Bachheti, R. K. (2023). Allelopathic activity of genus Euphorbia. In G. D., P. B., M. U., M. R., & G. R. (Eds.), *AIP Conference Proceedings* (Vol. 2782). American Institute of Physics Inc. https://doi.org/10.1063/5.0154514

Dutta, A., Singh, P., Dobhal, A., Mannan, D., Singh, J., & Goswami, P. (2023). Entrepreneurial Aptitude of Women of an Aspirational District of Uttarakhand. *Indian Journal of Extension Education*, *59*(2), 103–107. https://doi.org/10.48165/IJEE.2023.59222

Garg, G., Gupta, S., Mishra, P., Vidyarthi, A., Singh, A., & Ali, A. (2023). CROPCARE: An Intelligent Real-Time Sustainable IoT System for Crop Disease Detection Using Mobile Vision. *IEEE Internet of Things Journal*, *10*(4), 2840–2851. https://doi.org/10.1109/JIOT.2021.3109019

Garg, S., Nain, P., Kumar, A., Joshi, S., Punetha, H., Sharma, P. K., Siddiqui, S., Alshaharni, M. O., Algopishi, U. B., & Mittal, A. (2024). Next generation plant biostimulants & genome sequencing strategies for sustainable agriculture development. *Frontiers in Microbiology*, *15*. https://doi.org/10.3389/fmicb.2024.1439561

Gupta, S., Gilotra, S., Rathi, S., Choudhury, T., & Kotecha, K. (2024). Plant Disease Recognition Using Different CNN Models. In T. S., G. R., S. A., K. S., K. S., A. R., & S. K. R. (Eds.), *Proceedings of the 14th International Conference on Cloud Computing, Data Science and Engineering, Confluence 2024* (pp. 787–792). Institute of Electrical and Electronics Engineers Inc. https://doi.org/10.1109/Confluence60223.2024.10463383

Jain, R., Kukreja, V., Chattopadhyay, S., Verma, A., & Sharma, R. (2024a). Hierarchy in Disease Severity Classification in Banana Leaves through the Integration of Convolutional Neural Network and Decision Tree Models. *2024 5th International Conference for Emerging Technology, INCET 2024*. https://doi.org/10.1109/INCET61516.2024.10593446

Jain, R., Kukreja, V., Chattopadhyay, S., Verma, A., & Sharma, R. (2024b). Hybrid CNN-RNN Modelling for Precisely Classifying the Seriousness of Mustard White Rust Disease at Five Levels. *2024 5th International Conference for Emerging Technology, INCET 2024*. https://doi.org/10.1109/INCET61516.2024.10593033

Kaur, A., Kukreja, V., Kumar, M., Choudhary, A., & Sharma, R. (2024a). A Fine-tuned Deep Learning-based VGG16 Model for Cotton Leaf Disease Classification. *2024 5th International Conference for Emerging Technology, INCET 2024*. https://doi.org/10.1109/INCET61516.2024.10593164

Kaur, A., Kukreja, V., Kumar, M., Choudhary, A., & Sharma, R. (2024b). A Fine-Tuned DenseNet Model for an Efficient Maize Leaf Disease Classification. *2024 IEEE International Conference on Interdisciplinary Approaches in Technology and Management for Social Innovation, IATMSI 2024*. https://doi.org/10.1109/IATMSI60426.2024.10503026

Kaur, A., Kukreja, V., Malhotra, S., Joshi, K., & Sharma, R. (2024). Rice Sheath Rot Disease Detection and Severity Classification: A Novel Framework Leveraging CNN-LSTM Models for Multi-Classification. *2024 IEEE International Conference on Interdisciplinary Approaches in Technology and Management for Social Innovation, IATMSI 2024*. https://doi.org/10.1109/IATMSI60426.2024.10502629

Kaur, B., Mansi, Dimri, S., Singh, J., Mishra, S., Chauhan, N., Kukreti, T., Sharma, B., Singh, S. P., Arora, S., Uniyal, D., Agrawal, Y., Akhtar, S., Rather, M. A., Naik, B., Kumar, V., Gupta, A. K., Rustagi, S., & Preet, M. S. (2023). Insights into the harvesting tools and equipment's for horticultural crops: From then to now. *Journal of Agriculture and Food Research*, *14*. https://doi.org/10.1016/j.jafr.2023.100814

Kaur, H., Hussain, S. J., Mir, R. A., Chandra Verma, V., Naik, B., Kumar, P., & Dubey, R. C. (2023). Nanofertilizers – Emerging smart fertilizers for modern and sustainable agriculture. *Biocatalysis and Agricultural Biotechnology*, *54*. https://doi.org/10.1016/j.bcab.2023.102921

Kaur, R., Gupta, S., Tripathi, V., & Bharadwaj, A. (2024). Unravelling the secrets of soil microbiome and climate change for sustainable agroecosystems. *Folia Microbiologica*. https://doi.org/10.1007/s12223-024-01194-9

Khosravi, H., Khoshru, B., Nosratabad, A. F., & Mitra, D. (2024). Exploring the landscape of biofertilizers containing plant growth-promoting rhizobacteria in Iran: Progress and research prospects. *Current Research in Microbial Sciences*, *7*. https://doi.org/10.1016/j.crmicr.2024.100268

Kukreti, B., Chaudhary, P., & Sharma, A. (2024). Visualization of synergistic interaction between inorganic nanoparticle and bioinoculants. *Vegetos*. https://doi.org/10.1007/s42535-024-01022-y

Pal, A. K., Patro, B. D. K., Chaudhary, P., Richa, Kumar, A., & Garg, N. (2024). An Improved Analysis of Weed Prediction in Precision Agriculture using Deep Learning. *Proceedings of International Conference on Communication, Computer Sciences and Engineering, IC3SE 2024*, 936–941. https://doi.org/10.1109/IC3SE62002.2024.10593570

Pramanik, A., Sinha, A., Chaubey, K. K., Hariharan, S., Dayal, D., Bachheti, R. K., Bachheti, A., & Chandel, A. K. (2023). Second-Generation Bio-Fuels: Strategies for Employing Degraded Land for Climate Change Mitigation Meeting United Nation-Sustainable Development Goals. *Sustainability (Switzerland)*, *15*(9). https://doi.org/10.3390/su15097578

Pramanik, B., Sar, P., Bharti, R., Gupta, R. K., Purkayastha, S., Sinha, S., Chattaraj, S., & Mitra, D. (2023). Multifactorial role of nanoparticles in alleviating environmental stresses for sustainable crop production and protection. *Plant Physiology and Biochemistry*, *201*. https://doi.org/10.1016/j.plaphy.2023.107831

Semwal, P., Painuli, S., Begum J.P, S., Jamloki, A., Rauf, A., Olatunde, A., Mominur Rahman, M., Mukerjee, N., Ahmed Khalil, A., Aljohani, A. S. M., Al Abdulmonem, W., & Simal-Gandara, J. (2023). Exploring the nutritional and health benefits of pulses from the Indian Himalayan region: A glimpse into the region's rich agricultural heritage. *Food Chemistry*, *422*. https://doi.org/10.1016/j.foodchem.2023.136259

Shao, D., Kombe, C., & Saxena, S. (2023). An ensemble design of a cash crops-warehouse receipt system (WRS) based on blockchain smart contracts. *Journal of Agribusiness in Developing and Emerging Economies*, *13*(5), 762–774. https://doi.org/10.1108/JADEE-02-2022-0032

Sharma, M., Joshi, S., & Govindan, K. (2023). Overcoming barriers to implement digital technologies to achieve sustainable production and consumption in the food sector: A circular economy perspective. *Sustainable Production and Consumption*, *39*, 203–215. https://doi.org/10.1016/j.spc.2023.04.002

Širić, I., Alhag, S. K., Al-Shuraym, L. A., Mioč, B., Držaić, V., Abou Fayssal, S., Kumar, V., Singh, J., Kumar, P., Singh, R., Bachheti, R. K., Goala, M., Kumar, P., & Eid, E. M. (2023). Combined Use of TiO2 Nanoparticles and Biochar Produced from Moss (Leucobryum glaucum (Hedw.) Ångstr.) Biomass for Chinese Spinach (Amaranthus dubius L.) Cultivation under Saline Stress. *Horticulturae*, *9*(9). https://doi.org/10.3390/horticulturae9091056

Swain, K. P., Ranjan Nayak, S., Ravi, V., Mishra, S., Alahmadi, T. J., Singh, P., & Diwakar, M. (2024). Empowering Crop Selection with Ensemble

Learning and K-means Clustering: A Modern Agricultural Perspective. *Open Agriculture Journal*, *18*. https://doi.org/10.2174/0118743315291367240207093403

Tamta, S., Vimal, V., Verma, S., Gupta, D., Verma, D., & Nangan, S. (2024). Recent development of nanobiomaterials in sustainable agriculture and agrowaste management. *Biocatalysis and Agricultural Biotechnology*, *56*. https://doi.org/10.1016/j.bcab.2024.103050-

7

A Multidisciplinary Approach to Building Resilience Against Deepfakes in the Financial Sector

Manpreet Kaur[1] and Babli Dhiman[1]

[1]Lovely Professional University, India

Email: manpreet1277@yahoo.com; babli.dhiman@lpu.co.in

Abstract

The swift progress of deepfake technology presents substantial risks to multiple industries, especially the financial industry. Deepfake, synthetic media utilising internet visual datasets and machine learning, provides new information damages and image-based misuse risks. These can be employed by unscrupulous individuals to commit fraud and deception, leading to significant financial damages and undermining trust in monetary establishments. Fraudsters and deceivers employ deep, which uses AI to generate audio and video that looks genuine but fake- to steal money or damage people's faith in banks, insurance, etc. One effective way to lessen the impact of deepfake attacks is to increase people's knowledge of personal finance. This study proposes a framework for an AI and data literacy paradigm to address deepfake harms in the financial sector, exploring an integrated approach to mitigate the spread of deepfake and emphasising the crucial role of media literacy towards social media, apps, and fake calls/messages. The qualitative approach was used for framework and investigating advanced AI detection tools and encryption methods to prevent the creation and dissemination of deepfakes in this area. This study develops a multifaceted framework combining technological solutions, regulatory measures, and educational initiatives to safeguard information integrity. To enhance media literacy and promote public awareness against cybercriminals' advanced technology and public trust, the financial industry can cultivate a culture of understanding and ongoing learning to navigate the digital environment safely.

7.1 Introduction

The financial sector is undergoing a transition towards the fourth industrial revolution, also known as an automated process, characterised by the growing integration of digital technology into society, which is blurring the distinction between the physical and digital realms and consequently redefining the concept of humanity (Aloo et al., 2023; Jindal, Kukreja, Mehta, Yadav, et al., 2023; Mehta et al., 2023; Vishalli et al., 2023). Disruptive technologies and developments like mobile internet, robots, autonomous payment machines (UPI, Cards, ATM, etc), and, most importantly, artificial intelligence (AI) have defined this era. The worldwide artificial intelligence (AI) market, a relatively new technical development, is proliferating. From 2022 to 2030, the market for artificial intelligence (AI) applications is expected to rise from its 2021 valuation of $93.5 billion, with a compound annual growth rate (CAGR) of 38.1%.

When it comes to achieving sustainable development, the banking institutions' role is crucial, as they are the backbone of the financial system and the economy (Kaur et al., 2023; Rather et al., 2023; Wongchai et al., 2022). As a result, banking services and products have evolved in recent years to meet customer demands and adapt to the digital transition period. In 2023, Indonesia's digital bank transactions amounted to 58.478 trillion rupiahs. It is projected to experience a growth rate of 9.11% in 2024. Presently, a majority of 72% of Indonesians opt for digital means to carry out their day-to-day financial operations. In 2021, the number of bank account transactions will increase as technology development which requires more security, protection, and customised services to save personal data (Jindal, Kukreja, Mehta, Chamoli, et al., 2023; Jindal, Kukreja, Mehta, Gupta, & Joshi, 2023; G. Kumar et al., 2023; Sunori et al., 2023).

Deepfakes are created using advanced artificial intelligence (AI) techniques to build highly realistic depictions. These representations are becoming difficult to differentiate from actual reality It involves a neural network that allows the AI to generate scenarios. The growing accessibility of high-performing computing resources and the Internet are crucial for deepfakes. According to research conducted in 2019, the frequency of deepfakes has increased by over 550%.

For instance 2019, UAE employees were fired for allegedly using this technology and deceiving money. In Singapore in 2021, an individual incurred a financial loss of $14,000 because of falling victim to a deceptive video call utilising deepfake technology. The perpetrator assumed the identity of the victim's acquaintance and requested a monetary transfer. Thankfully, this catastrophe was averted. In 2022, a bank employee in Hong Kong fell victim to a deception where an individual utilised deepfake technology to imitate the voice of the employee's client, resulting in the loss of millions of dollars. An identical occurrence occurred in a bank in India in 2023. A private bank employee was contacted by a deepfake scammer who falsely claimed to be their superior and requested a funds transfer. Fortunately, both endeavours were identified.

These highly accurate fabrications, driven by artificial intelligence, are becoming powerful tools for criminals, taking advantage of the weaknesses inherent in the digital financial environment. Since it is difficult for the average person to tell the difference between authentic and deep, fake – manipulated content, this problem has only worsened. Although the technology has great creative potential, it has already been used in harmful ways, leading to actual losses in the real world.

Using deepfake films in video KYC (Know Your Customer), fraudsters can present significant risks to banks and other financial services. The result states that recognising fraud cases requires quick and regulated restrictions on using deepfakes to ensure a smooth flow of transactions through digital tools. To mitigate the potential for deepfake fraud, the Reserve Bank of India (RBI) has implemented a mandate for live video verification during the Know Your Customer (KYC) process. Security enhancements, such as customised dynamic randomised surveys for each user, aim to fortify security protocols and diminish the probability of fraudulent activities, particularly in credit applications. Thus, this study proposes a framework for an AI and data literacy paradigm to address profound fake harms in the financial sector, exploring an integrated approach to mitigate the spread of deepfake and emphasising the crucial role of media literacy and education towards social media, apps, and fake calls/messages. A graphical representation addresses the spread of deepfake information and highlights the importance of media literacy and education.

Zerodha, a leading stock market platform, reported a noteworthy event involving a close call when a customer narrowly avoided a potential loss of Rs 1.80 lakh owing to a scam tied to deepfake technology. Nithin Kamath, the CEO, emphasised the growing occurrence of AI-driven apps producing deepfakes, leading to increased fraudulent attacks.

According to the above description, this study talks explicitly about how deepfakes could threaten the digitalisation of financial institutions, which is where other possible technology risks need to be addressed. Criminals could target the safety of people's personal information, like financial data and customer savings if rules and safeguards in this sector are not put in place right now. Thus, this study will examine the potential hazards of deepfakes and investigate a comprehensive strategy to address this issue. This study aims to enhance consciousness through literacy to devise effective prevention strategies.

7.2 Mitigation Strategies

To mitigate the risks posed by deepfakes, it is imperative to implement a thorough and multifaceted approach. The following Figure 2.1 provides the framework to ensure the preservation of information integrity within the financial industry.

7.2.1 Technological solutions

There is a need for AI detection techniques and encryption technology to effectively prevent the production and dissemination of deepfakes. It must include digital content and cryptographic measures to learn these algorithms to improve their accuracy over time (Jaswal et al., 2023; Pargaien et al., 2023; Sneha et al., 2023). Encryption techniques may enhance security and save internet users' data. There are Elliptic Curve Cryptography (ECC) signatures to authenticate media material, in addition to a blockchain-based system to guarantee the traceability and authenticity of the information (Jindal, Kukreja, Mehta, Gupta, & Sharma, 2023; N. C. Joshi & Gururani, 2023; Pant et al., 2023).

7.2.2 Regulatory measures

The role of government in tackling the legal and ethical ramifications of deepfake plays a crucial role in the economy. Thus, if the proper rules of regulation in the form of a code of conduct and norms are established, the individual's behaviour may change their intention regarding deceiving, which creates public trust in technology development. The strict guidelines, auditing, and penalties ensure the safety of society. Furthermore, creating agreements with other developed economies and global cooperations makes a comprehensive and standardised regulatory framework to combat the global threat (Dwivedi et al., 2013; Gonfa et al., 2023; A. Joshi et al., 2016; V. Kumar et al., 2021).

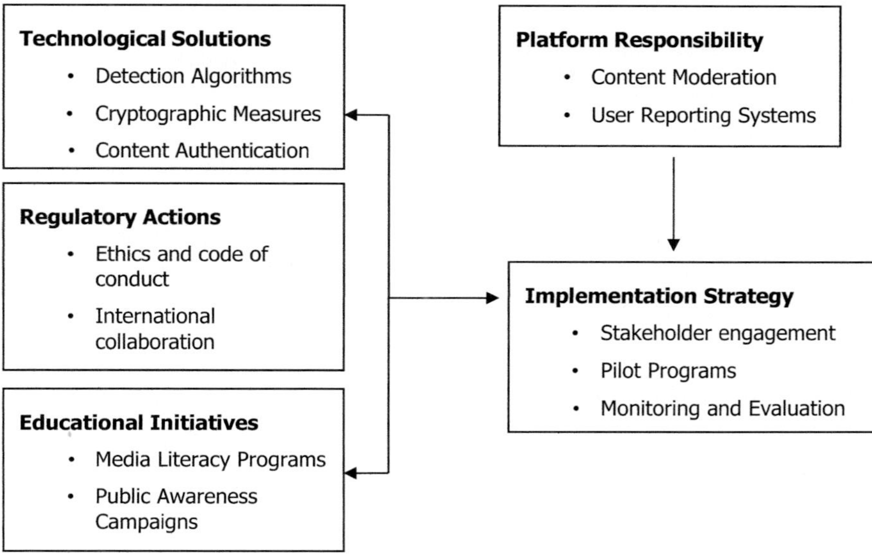

Figure 7.1 Framework to mitigate the deepfake information. Source: The author

7.2.3 Educational initiatives

Increasing awareness about deepfake technology and media literacy is pivotal in educating the public and detecting fraud. Furthermore, implementing marketing campaigns to educate the public about deepfakes, including their associated risks and strategies for detection, might be beneficial in spreading educational content. AI and data literacy educational programs can improve user's capacity to recognise and tackle deepfake content. These actions should give priority to the importance of verifying the authenticity of information collected through digital platforms, such as social media, applications, and telephone calls. By fostering a culture that encourages scepticism and critical thinking, the financial industry can enhance its ability to withstand and protect against fraudulent activities and deceptive practices involving deepfakes (A. Kumar et al., 2024; Nijhawan & Jain, 2018; Sharma et al., 2024; Zahra et al., 2024).

7.2.4 Platform responsibilities

Content moderation requires social media platforms to implement robust policies, including automatic detection and removal of deepfake content. The user report system may enhance user reporting mechanisms to allow swift action against suspected deepfake content.

7.2.5 Implementation strategy

It establishes connections and collaborates with technological companies, educational institutions, government agencies, and civil society organisations to guarantee the thorough execution of the project. It conducts pilot projects to evaluate the efficacy of detection tools, instructional modules, and regulatory measures before widespread use. Thus, a system should be implemented to assess the effects of the framework consistently and adapt it as needed in response to feedback and technological progress.

7.3 Components Used in the Proposed Framework

This study proposes a comprehensive framework for addressing deepfake harms in the financial sector, focusing on AI and data literacy. The framework included the following components.

7.3.1 AI detection tools

Protecting information from loss, misuse, manipulation, or disclosure requires data security measures. The extent of data security guaranteed by the project's chief investigator or lead researcher varies with the specific data. Cloud-Data Security System (C-DSS) protects data stored in the cloud from breaches, exfiltration, fraudulent access, misuse, and unauthorised access, disclosure, and alteration. For devices with limited power, there is a type of encryption called data security, also known as lightweight encryption. Protecting limited network resources using lightweight encryption technology necessitates employing less resource-intensive procedures. Creating and implementing sophisticated AI techniques that can accurately identify deepfakes. These tools ought to be incorporated into the security systems of financial institutions to oversee and authenticate digital communications and transactions in real time.

7.3.2 Encryption methods

Utilising robust encryption techniques to ensure the security of data and communication connections. This measure will effectively thwart any attempts of unwanted access and tampering with sensitive information using deepfake technologies. A sizable dataset of images is compiled using NSFW JS data to facilitate NSFW image classification. Subsequently, two pre-trained neural network models, ResNet and Squeeze Net, are assessed and refined for the NSFW classification task leveraging the dataset. Evaluation of these models initially yielded accuracy scores of 93% and 72%, respectively. The developed solution is seamlessly integrated into the Arquivo.pt Image Search System, accessible at https://nsfwjs.com/. This integration ensures that users can efficiently identify and filter out NSFW content while exploring the extensive image repository maintained by NSFW JS, enhancing the platform's overall user experience and usability.

7.3.3 Regulatory compliance

Ensuring that financial institutions adhere to current regulations and actively support the creation of new legislation to tackle the difficulties presented by deepfakes. This article examines the potential impact of the risk of fraud and comprehensively describes their unlawful and unethical use within an organisational context. Using speech-generating software in combination with other fraudulent techniques, such as business email compromise, enhances the persuasiveness of the offenders towards their victims, who are more likely to be deceived due to their familiarity with the voice and email. Based on the findings, every firm is susceptible to the risks posed by technology. Adhering to regulatory requirements requires conducting regular audits and executing security system improvements to keep up with developing hazards.

7.3.4 Media literacy education

Educational programs for financial institutions, workers, and clients can support responsible data science (RDS), including data quality, algorithmic fairness and diversity, privacy, security, transparency of data and algorithms, legal compliance, and ethics in AI. The study suggests integrating RDS with current research in learning analytics and learning science while establishing effective teaching strategies for technical data science and artificial intelligence sources. These initiatives should educate customers on differentiating deepfake content and implement appropriate methods to verify information before making any decisions.

7.3.5 Public awareness campaign

This component comprises human rights. The best solution to raise awareness is to add a subject in schools or colleges. The result could create knowledge and use human rights to jeopardise our well-being.

7.4 Conclusion

Due to the substantial risks involved in transactions and the reliance on trust in financial relationships, the financial sector is particularly susceptible to the malicious exploitation of deepfakes. This study presents a framework for AI and data literacy paradigms to tackle the negative impacts of deepfakes in the financial sector. It explores a comprehensive approach to reducing the dissemination of deepfakes and highlights the importance of media literacy and education about social media, apps, and fraudulent calls/messages. A visual depiction is employed to tackle disseminating deepfake information and emphasise the significance of media literacy and education. This framework includes technology solutions, regulatory measures, and educational initiatives to safeguard information integrity in the financial industry.

7.5 Declaration

The authors declare that the manuscript follows ethical standards and that there are no potential conflicts of interest regarding this chapter's research, authorship, and publication.

References

Aloo, B. N., Dessureault-Rompré, J., Tripathi, V., Nyongesa, B. O., & Were, B. A. (2023). Signalling and crosstalk of rhizobacterial and plant hormones that mediate abiotic stress tolerance in plants. *Frontiers in Microbiology*, *14*. https://doi.org/10.3389/fmicb.2023.1171104

Dwivedi, S., Parshav, V., Sharma, N., Kumar, P., Chhabra, S., & Goudar, R. H. (2013). Using technology to make farming easier and better: Simplified E-Farming Support (SEFS). *2013 International Conference on Human Computer Interactions, ICHCI 2013*. https://doi.org/10.1109/ICHCI-IEEE.2013.6887806

Gonfa, Y. H., Gelagle, A. A., Hailegnaw, B., Kabeto, S. A., Workeneh, G. A., Tessema, F. B., Tadesse, M. G., Wabaidur, S. M., Dahlous, K. A., Abou Fayssal, S., Kumar, P., Adelodun, B., Bachheti, A., & Bachheti, R. K. (2023). Optimization, Characterization, and Biological Applications of Silver Nanoparticles Synthesized Using Essential Oil of Aerial Part of Laggera tomentosa. *Sustainability (Switzerland)*, *15*(1). https://doi.org/10.3390/su15010797

Jaswal, N., Kukreja, V., Sharma, R., Chaudhary, P., & Garg, A. (2023). Citrus Leaf Scab Multi-Class Classification: A Hybrid Deep Learning

Model for Precision Agriculture. *2023 4th IEEE Global Conference for Advancement in Technology, GCAT 2023*. https://doi.org/10.1109/GCAT59970.2023.10353507

Jindal, V., Kukreja, V., Mehta, S., Chamoli, S., & Sharma, M. (2023). The Role of Federated Learning and CNNs in the Detection and Classification of Zucchini Leaf Diseases: A Severity-Based Analysis. *2023 4th IEEE Global Conference for Advancement in Technology, GCAT 2023*. https://doi.org/10.1109/GCAT59970.2023.10353311

Jindal, V., Kukreja, V., Mehta, S., Gupta, A., & Joshi, K. (2023). Addressing Zucchini Leaf Diseases: An Innovative Approach Using Federated Learning and CNN. *2023 4th IEEE Global Conference for Advancement in Technology, GCAT 2023*. https://doi.org/10.1109/GCAT59970.2023.10353452

Jindal, V., Kukreja, V., Mehta, S., Gupta, A., & Sharma, M. (2023). Tackling Agricultural Challenges of Red Globe Grapes Leaf Diseases: A Federated Learning CNN Approach. *2023 3rd Asian Conference on Innovation in Technology, ASIANCON 2023*. https://doi.org/10.1109/ASIANCON58793.2023.10270032

Jindal, V., Kukreja, V., Mehta, S., Yadav, R., & Mohd, N. (2023). Evolving Agritech: Implementing Federated Learning & CNN for Parsley Leaf Disease Detection. *2023 3rd Asian Conference on Innovation in Technology, ASIANCON 2023*. https://doi.org/10.1109/ASIANCON58793.2023.10270228

Joshi, A., Bachheti, R. K., Sharma, A., & Mamgain, R. (2016). Parthenium hysterophorus. L. (Asteraceae): A boon or curse? (A review). *Oriental Journal of Chemistry*, *32*(3), 1283–1294. https://doi.org/10.13005/ojc/320302

Joshi, N. C., & Gururani, P. (2023). A mini review on heavy metal contamination in vegetable crops. *International Journal of Environmental Analytical Chemistry*. https://doi.org/10.1080/03067319.2023.2210058

Kaur, A., Kukreja, V., Yadav, R., Tanwar, S., & Sharma, M. (2023). Harmonizing Nature and Technology: CNN-SVM for Cercospora Leaf Spot Disease Recognition in Chilli Plants. *2023 4th IEEE Global Conference for Advancement in Technology, GCAT 2023*. https://doi.org/10.1109/GCAT59970.2023.10353509

Kumar, A., Singh, N., & Joshi, R. (2024). Comprehensive characterization of bioactive peptides in rice bran protein hydrolysates: A multi-platform approach for metabolomic profiling, identification, and molecular docking analysis. *Cereal Chemistry*, *101*(5), 1000–1019. https://doi.org/10.1002/cche.10802

Kumar, G., Kumar, A., Singhal, M., Singh, K. U., Kumar, L., & Singh, T. (2023). Revolutionizing Plant Disease Management Through Image Processing Technology. *Proceedings of International Conference on Computational Intelligence and Sustainable Engineering Solution, CISES 2023*, 521–528. https://doi.org/10.1109/CISES58720.2023.10183408

Kumar, V., Mitra, D., Rani, A., Suyal, D. C., Singh Gautam, B. P., Jain, L., Gondwal, M., Raj, K. K., Singh, A. K., & Soni, R. (2021). Bio-inoculants for Biodegradation and Bioconversion of Agrowaste: Status and Prospects. In *Bioremediation of Environmental Pollutants: Emerging Trends and Strategies*. Springer International Publishing. https://doi.org/10.1007/978-3-030-86169-8_16

Mehta, S., Kukreja, V., Vats, S., & Verma, A. (2023). A Paradigm Shift in Pomegranate Leaf Disease Detection with Federated Learning and CNN. *2023 14th International Conference on Computing Communication and Networking Technologies, ICCCNT 2023*. https://doi.org/10.1109/ICCCNT56998.2023.10308132

Nijhawan, R., & Jain, K. (2018). Glacier terminus position monitoring and modelling using remote sensing data. *Communications in Computer and Information Science*, *906*, 11–23. https://doi.org/10.1007/978-981-13-1813-9_2

Pant, B., Obaidat, M. S., Singh, S., Pant, M., Wazid, M., Das, A. K., & Hsiao, K.-F. (2023). SLA-SCA: Secure and Lightweight Authentication and Key Agreement Mechanism for Smart City Applications. In O. M.S., N. Z., H. K.-F., N. P., & G. Y. (Eds.), *Proceedings of the 2023 IEEE International Conference on Communications, Computing, Cybersecurity and Informatics, CCCI 2023*. Institute of Electrical and Electronics Engineers Inc. https://doi.org/10.1109/CCCI58712.2023.10290729

Pargaien, S., Prakash, R., Dubey, V. P., & Singh, D. (2023). Machine Learning Techniques in Wheat Crop Yield Prediction Using NDVI Indices and Meteorological Parameters. *International Conference on Sustainable Communication Networks and Application, ICSCNA 2023 - Proceedings*, 1165–1169. https://doi.org/10.1109/ICSCNA58489.2023.10370097

Rather, M. A., Thakur, R., Hoque, M., Das, R. S., Lima Miki, K. S., Teixeira-Costa, B. E., Mishra, P., & Gupta, A. K. (2023). Sorghum (Sorghum bicolor): Phytochemical Composition, Bio-Functional, and Technological Characteristics. In *Nutri-Cereals: Nutraceutical and Techno-Functional Potential*. CRC Press. https://doi.org/10.1201/9781003251279-3

Sharma, A., Dheer, P., Rautela, I., Thapliyal, P., Thapliyal, P., Bajpai, A. B., & Sharma, M. D. (2024). A review on strategies for crop improvement against drought stress through molecular insights. *3 Biotech*, *14*(7). https://doi.org/10.1007/s13205-024-04020-8

Sneha, Singh, P., & Tripathi, V. (2023). Optimizing Cloud-Based Smart Agriculture. *2023 International Conference on Computer Science and Emerging Technologies, CSET 2023*. https://doi.org/10.1109/CSET58993.2023.10346687

Sunori, S. K., Kant, S., Agarwal, P., & Juneja, P. (2023). Development of Rainfall Prediction Models using Linear and Non-linear Regression Techniques. *2023 4th IEEE Global Conference for Advancement in Technology, GCAT 2023*. https://doi.org/10.1109/GCAT59970.2023.10353508

Vishalli, Kukreja, V., Mehta, S., Das, P., & Singh, V. (2023). Dissecting Parsley Leaf Disease Severity: A Federated Learning and CNN Perspective. *2023 3rd Asian Conference on Innovation in Technology, ASIANCON 2023*. https://doi.org/10.1109/ASIANCON58793.2023.10270195

Wongchai, A., Shukla, S. K., Ahmed, M. A., Sakthi, U., Jagdish, M., & kumar, R. (2022). Artificial intelligence - enabled soft sensor and internet of things for sustainable agriculture using ensemble deep learning architecture. *Computers and Electrical Engineering*, *102*. https://doi.org/10.1016/j.compeleceng.2022.108128

Zahra, N., Kausar, A., Abdelghani, H. T. M., Singh, S., Vashishth, D. S., Bachheti, A., Bachheti, R. K., & Husen, A. (2024). Serotonin improves plant growth, foliar functions and antioxidant defence system in Ethiopian mustard (Brassica carinata A. Br.). *South African Journal of Botany*, *170*, 1–9. https://doi.org/10.1016/j.sajb.2024.05.002

8

Unmasking Influence: A Bibliometric Analysis of Deepfake Technology in Social Media Marketing

Ankita Bansal[1], Soni Mitali[2], Raj Kumar Singh[3], Vikas Agrawal[4] and Pirtibha Sharma[5]

[1]Vivekananda Institute of Professional Studies, India
[2]Faculty of Management Studies, University of Delhi, India
[3]SOM, Graphic Era Hill University, India
[4]Amrapali University Haldwani, India
[5]TMIMT, Teerthanker Mahaveer University, India

Email: ankitabansal358@gmail.com; sonimitali77@gmail.com; rajkumarsingh001@gmail.com; vikashaldwani4@gmail.com; ica.pratibha.pdp@gmail.com

Abstract

This research explores the intricate relationship between deepfake technology and social media marketing, exposing its potential as a cutting-edge tool for promotion and a major risk. Deepfakes are artificial intelligence-generated, incredibly realistic synthetic media that raise severe issues about misinformation, privacy violations, and risks to democratic processes. This research highlights the increased interest in deepfake studies since 2019 by identifying significant patterns and themes using a bibliometric analysis of the available literature. The study delves into multiple domains, such as computer science, social sciences, and marketing. It reveals noteworthy subjects like the development of deepfake detection technology, the use of deepfakes in disseminating false information, and the moral dilemmas they present for marketing strategies. The findings underline the need for interdisciplinary collaboration in solving the problems faced by deepfake technology. Deepfakes have particular chances for captivating marketing tactics but can jeopardise customer confidence and brand integrity if handled unethically. Therefore, this study calls for a holistic approach that combines the creative potential of deepfakes with the need to defend individual rights and societal norms.

8.1 Introduction

A deepfake is a technique that has come up as the fastest-evolving area of research in artificial intelligence, and it showcases the possibility of blurring reality with fake information (Kunwar et al., 2023). This advanced AI technology manipulates the elements of sight and sound, creating hyper-realistic but entirely false multimedia content (A. Sharma et al., 2024). The consequences of deepfake technology are far-reaching, leading to questions about the nature of truth and trust in our hyper-connected society (M. Chauhan et al., 2023). The production calibre of deepfakes, which replicate facial expressions, voice, and gestures accurately, makes it almost impossible for the layman to discern them against authentic content (Gaur et al., 2024; Sardana et al., 2024). It is now an area of concern to have deepfakes that can produce a wide range of adverse side effects in different arenas, such as politics and social and personal privacy (Santoyo et al., 2024; K. D. Singh et al., 2023).

Despite deepfake technology showing promise as a creative tool in film and digital art, it also carries plenty of inherent dangers (Yıldız et al., 2024). These risks include, but are certainly not limited to, the spread of disinformation, violations of privacy, and threats to democracy. Counterfeit speeches, movies, and interviews often involving prominent individuals to spread intentional lies have utilised deepfakes (Srinivasan, 2024). The speedy dissemination of incorrect info via social media platforms undermines public belief in institutions, distorts public thought, and can harm people and agencies substantially (A. K. Singh et al., 2024). Therefore, diverse detection techniques and the corresponding legal framework and regulatory body should be implemented to cater to increasing deepfakes (G. Kumar et al., 2023).

One of the most frightful sides is how fast it can spread these revolutionary deepfakes through social networks (R. Kumar et al., 2023). Social media channels are designed for fast broadcasting, and the material's viral characteristics enable deepfakes to be rapidly shared with a broad audience – potentially ones in millions or even billions within a limited time duration. Amplification makes deepfakes even more potent as a weapon against malicious actors seeking to use them to influence public opinion and damage reputational harm and societal unrest (A. Chauhan & Joshi, 2024)This large amount of information traded on social media makes it harder for platforms to trace harmful deepfakes and eliminate them as quickly as possible (Mitra et al., 2020; Sudarsan et al., 2024). Advanced detection algorithms and hardened platform rules are needed to restrict these risks associated with deep fake content (Behera & Singh Rawat, 2023).

While deepfakes offer attractive possibilities and challenges for marketers (Bisht et al., 2024), the ability to produce highly realistic content presents new avenues for creative advertising and personalised marketing (Gupta et al., 2022; Khanna et al., 2023; R. Kumar & Khanna, 2023; V. Kumar et al., 2021; Rana et al., 2022; Upreti & Malhotra, 2024). Brands that use deepfake technology can provide people with an emotional and fulfilling experience, meaning more engaged viewers and higher revenues. However, using deepfakes in marketing also brings ethical concerns (viz., transparency and consumer trust) to count (Meena et al., 2024). Customers cannot distinguish between genuine and counterfeits, or if they suspect manipulation from companies using deepfakes, it can lead to a decrease in trust and discredit for the brand (Hossain et al., 2024). Thus, organisations must be cautious in using deepfakes while encouraging inventiveness, making a trade-off with ethical matters, and ensuring the views of all stakeholders are taken into account. A holistic approach is needed to face the challenges inherent to deepfake technology (Sadiq et al., 2023; Saravani et al., 2021). Thus, an all-around strategy includes developing detection technology, formulating and structuring legal/lawful foundations, and public awareness activities to confront deepfakes (Gonfa et al., 2023). As AI-generated content becomes increasingly sophisticated, the corresponding detection algorithms must evolve to keep pace (A. Kumar et al., 2023). Studies have focused on identifying deepfakes by examining minor irregularities in the manipulated media – like lighting, shadows, or facial expressions (Tomar et al., 2023). Despite this, detection techniques must evolve further due to the continual progress of deepfake technology. Along with technological solutions, the deepfake challenge can also be addressed through legal and legislative measures. The legal frameworks around deepfakes are fragmented and slow to evolve to keep pace with rapidly advancing technology (Kukreti et al., 2024). Consequently, deepfakes present further complications; many countries still have not amended legislation, such as libel offences, to account for the specifics of the fake video technology, restricting potential victims' access to justice (Preeti et al., 2022; P. Sharma et al., 2024). Non-consensual deep fake pornography – the use of deepfake technology to create sexually explicit material without the subject's consent – may present potential legal ambiguities (Joshi et al., 2024). To remedy these gaps, legislators should aim to enact comprehensive laws that protect individuals from the adverse effects of deepfake technology and provide explicit principles for the ethical usage of such technology (Malik et al., 2023).

In addition, social media platforms have a crucial role in mitigating the risks associated with deepfakes. Facebook, Twitter, and YouTube have now started to enforce measures dealing with problematic content that may cause harm. However, given the volume of material these systems pass back and forth daily, it isn't feasible to rely on human moderation alone to ensure deepfakes are quickly detected and destroyed (Papageorgiou et al., 2023). Moreover, platforms must be transparent in their rules and processes – providing users with the information they need to recognise (and report) deepfakes. Successfully combating deepfakes in the digital landscape will require a collective effort from technology companies, governments, and academics to develop best practices and protocols (Shajar et al., 2024).

As dangerous as they are, deepfakes also open the gates for several opportunities – particularly in digital marketing. AI-powered content generation helps companies explore new strategies to engage with their target audiences and create personalised customer experiences. Nevertheless, as with every emerging technology, deepfakes should be used responsibly (Mekala et al., 2023). Businesses must tread carefully with the ethical implications of using deepfake technology and ensure that marketing strategies are transparent and respect consumer rights (S. Sharma et al., 2023). Companies can benefit from the possibilities allowed by deepfakes without losing customer trust if they use ethical marketing strategies (Mitra et al., 2021; Salini & Harikiran, 2023; Yanagi et al., 2024). While previous research has explored techniques to produce deepfakes, the mechanisms of their propagation, and methods for detection, a comprehensive analysis of the spectrum of deepfake types and underlying behaviour is notably lacking (Al-Khazraji et al., 2023; Mitra et al., 2022; Narayan et al., 2022; Qureshi et al., 2024). Similarly, although the marketing and age of deepfakes have been explored or exist (Ramarajan et al., 2024), less research is available to analyse the risks and possible benefits of using deep fake algorithms for advertising impacts. Furthermore, the fragmented nature within different disciplines of what is known about deepfakes in terms of theory and research provides a lack of holistic understanding, creating gaps between the influence of technology (Rao et al., 2023). Scholars have also explained the new characteristics and impacts of deepfakes and social media marketing via bibliometric analysis, also popularly known as depth analyses, conducted in their respective research (Tamta et al., 2024). Deepfake research covers several areas and points to some emerging topics and future trends. However, the specific characteristics of deepfake content on different social media platforms remain unanswered. The findings of this study highlight the importance of studying deepfake technology and its interactive relationship with social networking marketing. This study highlights

Table 8.1 Selection criteria.

Selection criteria	Eliminated	Accepted
Database: "Scopus" Date of Search: "26 August 2024" Initial search result (on the search term): "Deepfakes" OR "Deepfake Technology" AND "Social media" OR "Social Media Marketing" OR "Digital Marketing"		**218**
Period of Publications: 2004 to 2024	1	**217**
Subject area: "Business, management and accounting, Economics, Econometrics and Finance, decision science, Social sciences, Arts and Humanities"	128	**89**
Publication type: "Articles, Conference Paper, Books, Book Chapter, and Review"	5	**84**
Language screening: "Include documents published in English only" Screening (based on content)	1	**83**

Source: Scopus database.

the need for a more robust detection technique and addressing ethical issues. This study begins with an overview of the relevance of deepfake technology in social media and digital marketing. The research is organised from a bibliometric perspective through co-authorship, co-citation, co-occurrence analyses, and thematic trend analysis.

8.2 Bibliometric Research Method

8.2.1 Determining the appropriate search keywords

8.2.2 Data collection

Scopus has been utilised as the primary source for data collection in this study, as outlined in Table 1, which details the selection criteria. The research employed a variety of keywords, including "deepfakes," "Deepfake Technology," "social media," "Social Media Marketing," and "Digital Marketing," resulting in an initial retrieval of 218 papers. Publications from the period from 2004 to 2024 were then considered for inclusion. Further, the author has selected works published solely in English across several disciplines like "Business, management and accounting, Economics, Econometrics and Finance, Decision Science, Social Sciences, Arts, and Humanities". Additionally, Screening based on the content was the final step to align the study with the intended scope.

8.2.3 Selecting the techniques for analysis

A bibliometric analysis assessed the research state and development trends of deepfake technology in the marketing era. It uses statistical techniques to highlight the trends and patterns of the study done in this area over a particular period. This research provides an overview of the prominent journals, authors, countries, and institutions. Additionally, bibliometric applies scientific collaboration by visualising a network of co-authorship institutional partnerships highlighting the key partners and collaborative network. A keyword trend has been analysed to assess the results of the present research era.

8.3 Findings

8.3.1 Performance analysis

Figure 8.1 depicts the performance analysis for the period 2004 to 2024. The chart shows that the research on Deepfake started in 2019. Before that, no research had been observed, and a steady increase in research interest had been observed since 2019, starting with two publications and peaking at 21 publications in 2023. It concludes a growing phase of the research on deepfake; this consistent upward trend suggests scholarly interest, signifying its emerging importance in social media and digital marketing studies.

8.3.2 Most influential authors for research on deep fake and social media marketing

Table 8.2 depicts the most influential authors who have made their contributions, the most influential author S. Ahmed has published four articles, closely followed by Bee, A.W.T., Gelfand, J., Hameleers, M., and Nour, N. having published two articles each. Other authors Acosta, J., Adkins, J., Aggarwal, N. et al, followed by other authors have published a single document each indicating either more exploratory efforts or initial participation in this research area. Deepfake has reached a stage of development and recognition, and its future progress will largely depend on advancements in technology and cooperation across other fields of study.

8.3.2.1 Most prominent discipline for Research on deepfake and social media marketing

Figure 8.2 examines the most prominent research areas on deep fake and social media marketing through a pie chart. The pie chart represents the distribution of research in deepfake technology and social media marketing. The

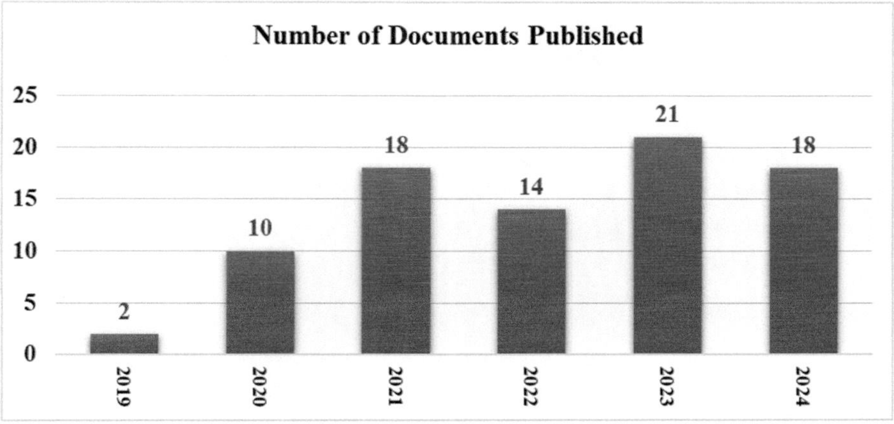

Figure 8.1 Performance analysis. Source: Scopus database.

Table 8.2 Top 20 authors.

Author	Number of Documents	Author	Number of Documents
Ahmed, S.	4	Aldoseri, D.T.	1
Bee, A.W.T.	2	Alharabi, Y.O.	1
Gelfand, J.	2	Ali, S.	1
Hameleers, M.	2	Alkholidi, A.	1
Nour, N.	2	Alsharabi, N.A.	1
Acosta, J.	1	Ascott, T.	1
Adkins, J.	1	Ayerdi, K.M.	1
Aggarwal, N.	1	Bakir, V.	1
Agarwal, P.	1	Bazarkina, D.	1
Akbar, M.H.	1	Ben Jabra, M.	1

Source: Authors' Preparation Based on Vos Viewer Output.

most influential field is Social Sciences, having 31.5% of the contribution. The dominance of Computer Science at 24.9% reflects the technology and algorithmic developments necessary for deepfake detection and analysis. This is further backed by engineering (11.6%), which showcases the development and counter of deepfake technology. Additional necessary fields include decision science (9.4%), which indicates strategic implications for businesses and policymakers, and psychology (5.0%), which shows curiosity about the cognitive and behavioural effects of deepfakes. Minor contributions from business management and arts and humanities (each 4.4%) indicate an interest in marketing and ethical tales, highlighting the extensive influence of deepfakes in both societal and technical domains.

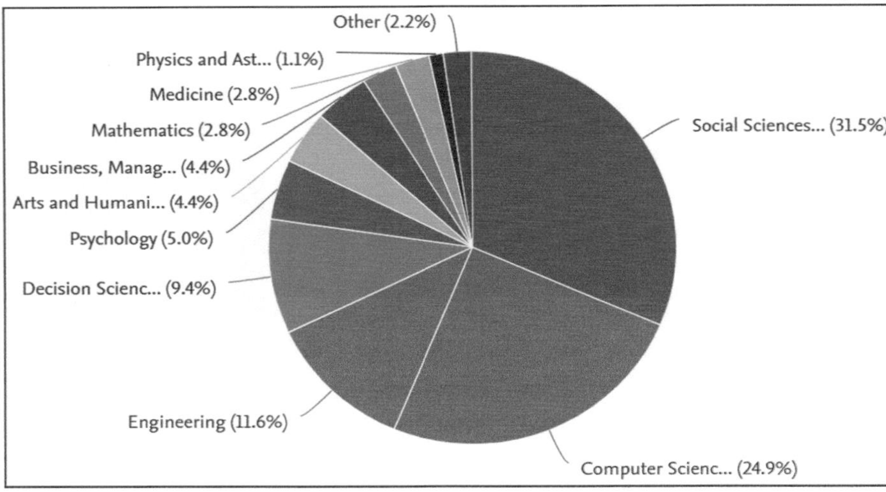

Figure 8.2 Prominent disciplines. Source: Scopus database

8.3.3 Prominent authors, organisations, and countries for research on deepfake and social media marketing

Table 8.3 shows the record of notable authors, institutions, and countries in deepfake technology and social media marketing based on the total citations and publications. The analysis shows that Mika Westerlund is the most referenced author, having 432 total citations with a single publication, demonstrating substantial influence. The most productive author is Saifuddin Ahmed, with the highest publication count (4); however, a comparatively lower total citation tally (53) indicates steady contributions with modest influence. Other extensively referenced authors, including Andrew Chadwick and Cristian Vaccari, have each garnered 296 citations for a single article, underscoring the significant impact of their study. Similarly, the list of prominent Institutions, "Carleton University, Canada," nailed the list with 432 total citations having one publication, closely followed by "Loughborough University, UK", having 296 citations, indicating robust research productivity. The top 20 list of institutions includes 3 institutes from India, namely "IIT Mandi, Manas Lab, India", "Mandi, RFSL, India", and "Department of Management, Symbiosis Institute of Business Management, Symbiosis International (Deemed University), Maharashtra, Pune, India" which shows that Institutes from India having their contribution in the research era of deep fake. Further, the list of countries shows that Canada and the United Kingdom are the two most prominent countries, with 490 and 484 total citations. The

Table 8.3 Prominent list of authors, institutes, and countries.

TC	Author	TP	TC	Institution	TP	TC	Country	TP
432	Westerlund, Mika	1	432	Carleton University In Ottawa, Canada	1	490	Canada	4
296	Chadwick, Andrew	1	296	Loughborough University, United Kingdom	1	484	United Kingdom	13
296	Vaccari, Cristian	1	91	University Of Oxford, Oxford, United Kingdom	1	238	United States	25
91	Brennen, J. Scott	1	60	Iit Mandi, Manas Lab, India	1	110	India	11
91	Nielsen, Rasmus Klei	1	60	Mandi, Rfsl, India	1	53	Singapore	6
91	Simon, Felix M.	1	36	Hadassah Academic College, Israel	1	50	Spain	3
60	Bhavsar, Arnav	1	36	The University Of Haifa, Israel	1	38	Ireland	2
60	Kumar, Akash	1	34	School Of Applied Psychology, University College Cork, Cork, Ireland	1	36	Israel	1
60	Verma, Rajesh	1	33	Faculty Of Communication Sciences, University Of Santiago De Compostela, Santiago De Compostela, 15782, Spain	1	32	Finland	1
53	Ahmed, Saifuddin	4	33	Gustavson School Of Business, University Of Victoria, Victoria, Bc, Canada	1	32	France	1
36	Oppenheim, Yael	1	33	King's College London, Bush House, London, United Kingdom	1	26	China	3
36	Yadlin-Segal, Aya	1	33	Loyola University New Orleans, New Orleans, La, United States	1	20	Italy	1
34	Flynn, Emma	1	32	Department Of Management, Symbiosis Institute Of Business Management, Symbiosis International (Deemed University), Maharashtra, Pune, India	1	20	Portugal	1

(Continued)

Table 8.3 *Continued*

TC	Author	TP	TC	Institution	TP	TC	Country	TP
34	Murphy, Gillian	1	32	Department Of Marketing & International Business, Turku School Of Economics, University Of Turku, Finland	1	13	Netherlands	3
33	Kietzmann, Jan	1	32	Department Of Marketing And Sales Management, Ieseg School Of Management, Univ. Lille, Cnrs, Umr 9221 - Lem - Lille Economie Management, France	1	8	Germany	1
33	López-García, Xosé	1	32	Hanken School Of Economics, Finland	1	4	Pakistan	1
33	Mills, Adam J.	1	32	Massachusetts Institute Of Technology, United States	1	2	New Zealand	1
33	Plangger, Kirk	1	32	School Of Management, Swansea University, Bay Campus, Fabian Bay, Swansea, United Kingdom	1	1	Saudi Arabia	1
33	Vaz-Álvarez, Martín	1	32	Turku School Of Economics, Finland	1	1	Tunisia	1
33	Vizoso, Ángel	1	32	University Of Vaasa, Finland	1	1	Turkey	1

Note(s): TC = total citations, TP = total number of article(s) publications
Source: Authors' Preparation Based on Vos Viewer Output

Table 8.4 Prominent journals.

Journal	TC	TP	2004–2014	2014–2024
Technology Innovation Management Review	432			1
Social Media and Society	309	2		2
International Journal of Press/Politics	91	1		1
Cyberpsychology, Behaviour, and Social Networking	89	6		6
Convergence	57	2		2
Media and Communication	45	2		2
Memory	34	1		1
Porn Studies	34	2		2
International Journal of Advertising	33	1		1
Computers and Eduction: Artifical Intelligence	32	1		1
Journal of Business Research	32	1		1
Journal of Intellectual Property Law and Practice	30	2		2
Journal of Strategic Studies	28	1		1
Journal of Broadcasting and Electronic Media	27	1		1
New Media and Society	25	1		1
Journalism Practice	24	1		1
Information and Communications Technology Law	20	1		1
Vanderbilt Law Review	19	1		1
2020 Ieee International Workshop on Information Forensics and Security, Wifs 2020	17	1		1
Journal of Human Rights Practice	15	1		1

Note(s): TC = total citations, TP = total number of article(s) publications
Source: Authors' Preparation Based on Vos Viewer Output

United States is the most productive country and nailed the list with the most publications (25).

8.3.4 Most influential journals for research on deep fake & social media marketing

Table 8.4 lists top journals with publications for deepfakes and social media marketing research across distinct fields. The most influential journal is "Technology Innovation Management Review", with 432 total citations for a single publication, followed by "Social Media and Society", with 309 citations with two articles, demonstrating its consistency. The most productive journal is "Cyberpsychology, Behavior, and Social Networking", with the most publications (6), making it a leading deepfake research journal.

8.3.5 Most influential articles for research on deep fake and social media marketing

Table 8.5 shows the list of most influential articles based on their total citations, and the most influential article is "The Emergence of Deepfake Technology: A Review," authored by (Westerlund, 2019), with 432 citations. "Deepfakes and Disinformation," with 296 citations [13], is another influential paper. COVID-19 misleading research (91 citations) shows deepfakes' relevance today [5]. Deepfake detection via metric learning (60 citations) [8] emphasises technological advances, whereas (Yadlin-Segal & Oppenheim 2021) article – Social Media Regulation Study (36 citations) emphasises regulatory and ethical issues. This comprehensive collection of articles addresses deepfake technology's issues, tactics, and potential ramifications.

Knowledge Foundations for Research on deep fake and Social Media Marketing

Figure 8.3 illustrates the co-authorship network, emphasising the collaboration patterns among researchers in deepfake and social media marketing. The visualisation illustrates that Cynthia Breazeal is a pivotal person, sustaining robust links with other writers, including Safinah Ali, Grace Kim, Ryan Blumofe, Victor Sindato, and Daniella Dipaola, signifying her substantial contribution to promoting interdisciplinary research. This network structure indicates that research in this field is collaborative and interrelated, with several authors often co-authoring publications. Other significant nodes are Safinah Ali and Irene Lee, who also function as network connections. The intricate connections among these writers signify a unified research community dedicated to tackling the intricacies of deepfake technology and its ramifications in digital and social media domains.

Figure 8.4 The co-citation analysis diagram for pivotal studies in deepfake technology and social media marketing, top clusters represent distinct research themes tied together by shared citations, highlighting their reciprocal relationships. The largest cluster (left) includes authors like Vosoughi S., Roy D., and Aral S., who focus on deepfakes and misinformation. This prominence indicates this cluster's central role in capturing social effects and spreading deepfake disinformation technology. Further, Denham H., Korshunov P., Marcel S. et al.: the smaller cluster to the right indicates increased importance of deep fake detection and forgery localisation. The lines linking the separate areas imply that many studies include social and ethical implications in discussing detection technologies. It illustrates how technical and social studies fit together to understand deepfake impacts better.

Table 8.5 Influential articles.

Author(S)	Title	Tc
(Westerlund, 2019)	The Emergence of Deepfake Technology: A Review	432
(Vaccari & Chadwick, 2020)	Deepfakes and Disinformation: Exploring The Impact of Synthetic Political Video on Deceptio, Uncertainty, and Trust in News	296
(Brennen et al., 2021)	Beyond (Mis) Representation: Visuals in Covid-19 Misinformation	91
(Kumar et al., 2020)	Detecting Deepfakes with Metric Learning	60
(Yadin-Segal & Oppenhelm, 2021)	Whose Dystopia is it Anyway? Deepfakes and Social Media Regulation	36
(Murphy & Flynn, 2022)	Deepfake False Memories	34
(Kietzmann et al., 2021)	Deepfakes: Perspectives on the Future "Reality" of Advertising and Branding	33
(Vizoso et al., 2021)	Fighting Deepfakes: Media and Internet Giants' Converging and Diverging Strategies Against Hi-Tech Misinformation	33
(Mustak et al., 2023)	Deepfakes: Deceptions, Mitigations, and Opportunities	32
(Ali et al., 2021)	Children as Creators, Thinkers and Citizens in an Ai-Driven Future	32
(Johnson, 2022)	Delegating Strategic Decision-Making to Machines: Dr. Strangelove Redux?	28
(Ahmed, 2023)	Disinformation Sharing Thrives with Fear of Missing Out Among Low Cognitive News Users: A Cross-National Examination of Intentional Sharing of Deep Fakes	27
(Ahmed, 2023)	Navigating The Maze: Deepfakes, Cognitive Ability, and Social Media News Skepticism	25
(Karasavva & Noorbhai, 2021)	The Real Threat of Deepfake Pornography: A Review of Canadian Policy	24
(Wahl-Jorgensen & Carlson 2021)	Conjecturing Fearful Futures: Journalistic Discourses on Deepfakes	24
(van der Nagel, 2020)	Verifying Images: Deepfakes, Control and Consent	23
(Bode, 2021)	Deepfaking Keanu: Youtube Deepfakes, Platform Visual Effects, and The Complexity of Reception	21
(Iacobucci et al., 2021)	Deepfakes Unmasked: The Effects of Information Priming and Bullshit Receptivity on Deepfake Recognition and Sharing Intention	20
(Kirchengast, 2020)	Deepfakes and Image Manipulation: Criminalisation and Control	20
(Gieseke, 2020)	"The New Weapon of Choice": Law's Current Inability to Properly Address Deepfake Pornography	19

Note(s): TC = total citations, TP = total number of article(s) publications
Source: Authors' Preparation Based on Vos Viewer Output

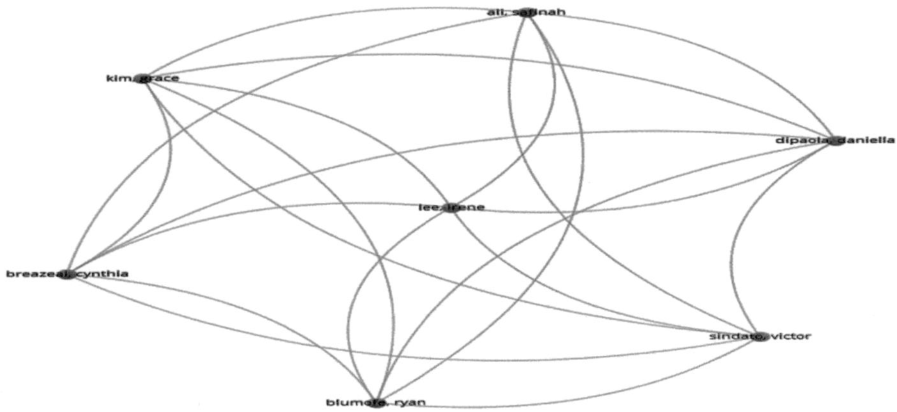

Figure 8.3 Co-authorship analysis (designed by authors).

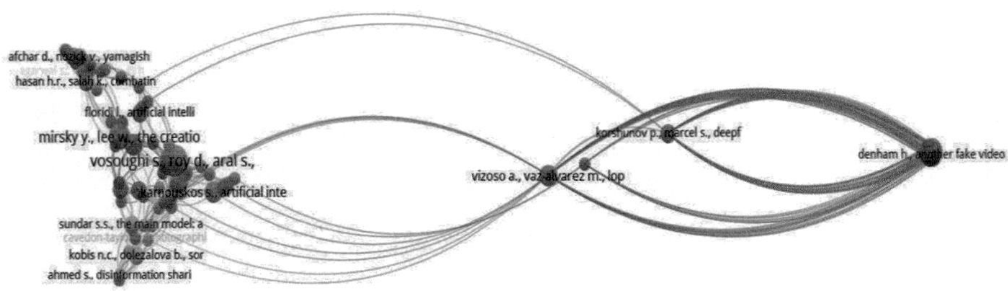

Figure 8.4 Co-citation analysis (designed by authors).

8.3.6 Thematic and influence structure analysis through bibliographic coupling

Table 8.6 presents various themes using bibliographic coupling, including research studies in relation to deepfake and social media marketing. Four themes are considered to be the prominent themes in the present. First theme: Deepfake Technology and Detection: This theme shows articles related to technological advancements and detection approaches; [14] is a well-referenced review emphasising the need for practical tools to combat deepfakes. The second theme related to Disinformation and Misinformation highlights deepfakes impact on falsehoods spreading specifically within political (along with COVID-19) frameworks, supported by the various study from [1]; [2]; [5]; [13]; [14]. Theme 3: Deepfake Impacts on Society and Media identifies sociological implications, including altering media strategy and advertising. Theme 4: Ethical, Legal and Future Concerns deals with tricky ethical dilemmas and legal constraints, especially regarding deepfake

Table 8.6 Cluster analysis.

Theme	Author(s)	Title	TC
Theme 1: Deepfake Technology and Detection	(Westerlund, 2019)	The emergence of deepfake technology: A review	432
	(Kumar et al., 2020)	Detecting Deepfakes with Metric Learning	60
	(Yadlin-Segal & Oppenheim, 2021)	Whose Dystopia is it Anyway? Deepfakes and Social Media Regulation	36
	(Mustak et al., 2023)	Deepfakes: Deceptions, Mitiagations and Opportunities	32
	(Kirchengast, 2020)	Deepfakes and Image Manipulation: Criminalisation and Control	20
Theme 2: Disinformation and Misinformation	(Vaccari & Chadwick, 2020)	Deepfakes and Disinformation: Exploring the Impact of Synthetic Political Video on Deception, Uncertainity, and Trust in News	296
	(Brennen et al., 2021)	Beyond (Mis)Representaion: Visuals in COVID-19 Misinformation	91
	(Ahmed, 2022)	Disinformation Sharing Thrives with Fear of Missing Out among Low Cognitive News Users: A Cross-national Examination of Deep Fakes	27
	(Ahmed, 2022)	Navigating the Maze: Deepfakes, Cognitive Ability and Social Media News Skepticism	25
	(Wahl-Jorgensen & Carlson, 2021)	Conjecturing Fearful Futures: Journalistic Discourses on Deepfakes	24
Theme 3: Deepfake Impacts on Society and Media	(Kietzmann et al., 2021	Deepfakes: Perspective on the Future "Reality" of Advertising and Branding	33
	(Vizoso et al., 2021)	Fighting Deepfakes: Media and Internet Giants' Converging and Diverging Strategies against Hi-Tech Misinformation	33
	(Bode, 2021)	Deepfaking Keanu: YouTube Deepfakes, Platform Visual Effects, and the Complexity of Reception	21
	(Iacobucci et al., 2021)	Deepfakes Unmasked: The Effects of Information Priming and Bullshit Receptvigty on Deepfake Recognition and Sharing Intention	20
	(van der Nagel, 2020)	Verifying Images: Deepfakes, Control, and Consent	23
Theme 4: Ethical Legal, and Future Concerns	(Karasavva & Noorbhai, 2021)	The Real Threat of Deepfake Pornography: A Review of Canadian Policy	24
	(Gieseke, 2020)	"The New Weapon of Choice": Law's Current Inability to Properly Address Deepfake Pornography	19
	(Ali et al., 2021)	Children as Creators, Thinkers and Citizens in an Ai-Driven Future	32
	(Murphy & Flynn, 2022)	Deepfake False Memories	34
	(Johnson, 2022)	Delegating Strategic Decision-making to Machines: Dr. Strangelove Redux?	28

Note(s): TC = total citations
Source: Authors' Preparation Based on Vos Viewer Output

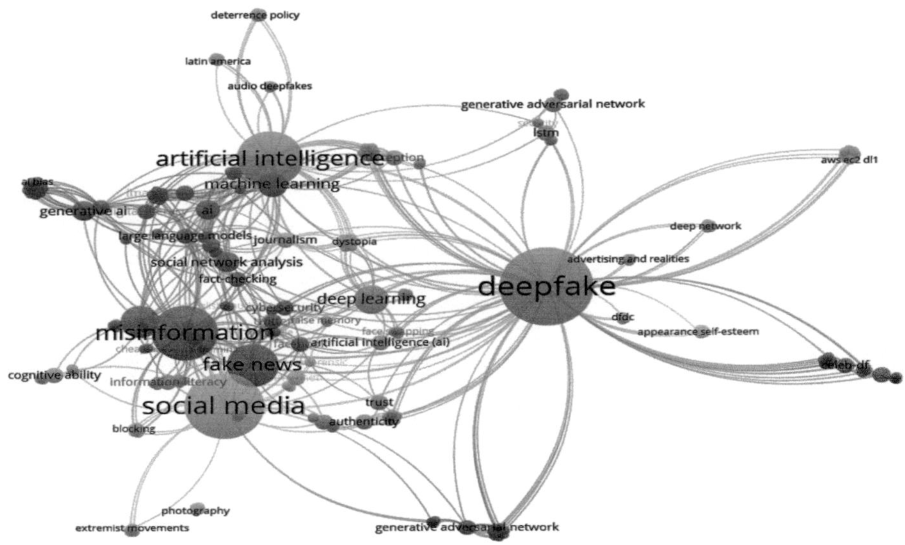

Figure 8.5 Co-occurrence analysis (designed by authors).

pornography and AI governance, emphasising the urgent necessity of coherent regulation. These topics demonstrate the multi-disciplinary and multifaceted nature of deepfake research.

8.3.7 Prominent keywords used for research on neuromarketing

Figure 8.5 illustrates the co-occurrence analysis, highlighting significant terms in deepfake research and elucidating essential topic domains and trends within the discipline. The predominant node is "deepfake", functioning as the core axis around which other themes are interrelated. Terms such as "artificial intelligence," "machine learning", and "generative adversarial network (GAN)" are intricately connected, representing the technological foundation of deepfake creation and identification methodologies. The grouping of "social media," "fake news", and "misinformation" indicates a significant focus on examining the sociological and ethical ramifications of deepfakes, especially with digital misinformation and public trust. A significant cluster comprises "trust," "authenticity," and "deception", underscoring apprehensions over information dependability and media manipulation. The inclusion of words such as "celebrity", "appearance", and "self-esteem" in a smaller cluster signifies an examination of deepfake effects on personal identity and social dynamics. The figure illustrates a multidisciplinary approach, including technological and sociological aspects, highlighting the complexity and extensive range of deepfake research.

8.4 Conclusion

This bibliometric study thoroughly analyses the emerging area of deepfake technology. The study has mapped the trends and patterns to identify the significant contributions and highlight the influential studies done in social marketing and deepfake. The highly recognised data source has been chosen to get an accurate and exhaustive analysis of the goal set. The co-occurrence, co-citation, and co-authorship made the study more comprehensive by identifying the critical collaborations for advancing the field. The study focused on fundamental and theoretical analysis and new research areas to help future researchers thoroughly understand multidisciplinary viewpoints. Future scholars may use this study to find out the gap in the studies and also use this in the real world. Even when the exhaustive discussion has been done, there remains a limitation to this study. The limitation is that a single database, i.e., Scopus, has been chosen, which restricted the author in the study. Thus, subsequent studies may be done considering more databases that may investigate new questions. Hence, scholars must make networks and collaborate to continue developing in the area.

8.5 Implications

Deepfake technology and social media marketing are the most discussed among all the stakeholders. This is not restricted to the area of marketing. Instead, it is multidisciplinary, as all the departments of the business and all the stakeholders are affected by the advent of artificial intelligence. Although it is a two-sided coin with opportunities and challenges, it must be used carefully. Although regulations need to be framed to counteract the malicious use of deepfakes. Thus, educational institutions and researchers must explore strategies to maintain integrity and ethics in technological advancements and their use.

8.6 Acknowledgements

During the preparation of this work, the author(s) used the Grammarly professional version in order to correct grammatical errors and improve readability. After using this tool/service, the author(s) reviewed and edited the content as needed and take(s) full responsibility for the publication's content.

8.7 Declaration

The authors declare that the manuscript follows ethical standards and there are no potential conflicts of interest concerning this chapter's research, authorship, and publication.

References

Al-Khazraji, S. H., Saleh, H. H., Khalıd, A. I., & Mıshkhal, I. A. (2023). Impact of Deepfake Technology on Social Media: Detection, Misinformation and Societal Implications. In O. M. (Ed.), *Eurasia Proceedings of Science, Technology, Engineering and Mathematics* (Vol. 23, pp. 429–441). ISRES Publishing. https://doi.org/10.55549/epstem.1371792

Behera, A., & Singh Rawat, K. (2023). A brief review paper on mining subsidence and its geo-environmental impact. *Materials Today: Proceedings*. https://doi.org/10.1016/j.matpr.2023.04.183

Bisht, B., Begum, J. P. S., Dmitriev, A. A., Kurbatova, A., Singh, N., Nishinari, K., Nanda, M., Kumar, S., Vlaskin, M. S., & Kumar, V. (2024). Unlocking the potential of future version 3D food products with next generation microalgae blue protein integration: A review. *Trends in Food Science and Technology*, *147*. https://doi.org/10.1016/j.tifs.2024.104471

Chauhan, A., & Joshi, H. C. (2024). Recent Developments and Applications in Bioconversion and Biorefineries. *Trends in Mathematics*, *Part F3197*, 247–307. https://doi.org/10.1007/978-981-99-7250-0_6

Chauhan, M., Rani, A., Joshi, S., & Sharma, P. K. (2023). Role of psychrophilic and psychrotolerant microorganisms toward the development of hill agriculture. In *Advanced Microbial Technology for Sustainable Agriculture and Environment*. Elsevier. https://doi.org/10.1016/B978-0-323-95090-9.00002-9

Gaur, A., Singh, S. K., & Saxena, P. (2024). Performance Analysis of Deepfake Text Detection Techniques on Social-media. *International Conference on Distributed Computing and Optimization Techniques, ICDCOT 2024*. https://doi.org/10.1109/ICDCOT61034.2024.10515626

Gonfa, Y. H., Gelagle, A. A., Hailegnaw, B., Kabeto, S. A., Workeneh, G. A., Tessema, F. B., Tadesse, M. G., Wabaidur, S. M., Dahlous, K. A., Abou Fayssal, S., Kumar, P., Adelodun, B., Bachheti, A., & Bachheti, R. K. (2023). Optimization, Characterization, and Biological Applications of Silver Nanoparticles Synthesized Using Essential Oil of Aerial Part of Laggera tomentosa. *Sustainability (Switzerland)*, *15*(1). https://doi.org/10.3390/su15010797

Gupta, C., Jindal, P., & Malhotra, R. K. (2022). A Study of Increasing Adoption Trends of Digital Technologies - An Evidence from Indian Banking. In D. N. & C. A. (Eds.), *AIP Conference Proceedings* (Vol. 2481). American Institute of Physics Inc. https://doi.org/10.1063/5.0104572

Hossain, M. R., Dash, D. P., Das, N., Hossain, M. E., Haseeb, M., & Cifuentes-Faura, J. (2024). Do Trade-Adjusted Emissions Perform Better in Capturing Environmental Mishandling among the Most Complex Economies of the World? *Environmental Modeling and Assessment*. https://doi.org/10.1007/s10666-024-09994-6

Joshi, H. C., Bagauli, R., Ahmad, W., Bisht, B., & Sharma, N. (2024). A review on carbonaceous materials for fuel cell technologies: An advanced approach. *Vietnam Journal of Chemistry*. https://doi.org/10.1002/vjch.202300407

Khanna, R., Jindal, P., & Noja, G. G. (2023). Blockchain technologies, a catalyst for insurance sector. In *The Application of Emerging Technology and Blockchain in the Insurance Industry*.

Kukreti, B., Chaudhary, P., & Sharma, A. (2024). Visualization of synergistic interaction between inorganic nanoparticle and bioinoculants. *Vegetos*. https://doi.org/10.1007/s42535-024-01022-y

Kumar, A., Goyal, H. R., & Sharma, S. (2023). Sustainable Intelligent Information System for Tourism Industry. *2023 IEEE 8th International Conference for Convergence in Technology, I2CT 2023*. https://doi.org/10.1109/I2CT57861.2023.10126400

Kumar, G., Kumar, A., Singhal, M., Singh, K. U., Kumar, L., & Singh, T. (2023). Revolutionizing Plant Disease Management Through Image Processing Technology. *Proceedings of International Conference on Computational Intelligence and Sustainable Engineering Solution, CISES 2023*, 521–528. https://doi.org/10.1109/CISES58720.2023.10183408

Kumar, R., & Khanna, R. (2023). Role of Artificial Intelligence in Digital Currency and Future Applications. *Proceedings of the 2023 2nd International Conference on Augmented Intelligence and Sustainable Systems, ICAISS 2023*, 42–46. https://doi.org/10.1109/ICAISS58487.2023.10250480

Kumar, R., Lamba, A. K., Mohammed, S., Asokan, A., Aswal, U. S., & Kolavennu, S. (2023). Fake Currency Note Recognition using Extreme Learning Machine. *Proceedings of the 2nd International Conference on Applied Artificial Intelligence and Computing, ICAAIC 2023*, 333–339. https://doi.org/10.1109/ICAAIC56838.2023.10140824

Kumar, V., Gupta, S., & Khanna, R. (2021). Dengue fever-a worldwide study. *Journal of Medical Pharmaceutical and Allied Sciences*, *10*, 102–108. https://doi.org/10.22270/jmpas.vic2i1.2014

Kunwar, S., Joshi, A., Gururani, P., Pandey, D., & Pandey, N. (2023). Physiological and Al-based study of endophytes on medicina A mini review. *Plant Science Today*, *10*, 53–60. https://doi.org/10.14719/pst.2555

Malik, D., Kukreja, V., Mehta, S., Gupta, A., & Singh, V. (2023). Mitigating the Impact of Guava Leaf Diseases Using CNNs and Federated Learning. *2023 3rd Asian Conference on Innovation in Technology, ASIANCON 2023*. https://doi.org/10.1109/ASIANCON58793.2023.10270236

Meena, C. S., Kumar, A., Singh, V. P., & Ghosh, A. (2024). Sustainable Technologies for Energy Efficient Buildings. In *Sustainable Technologies for Energy Efficient Buildings*. CRC Press. https://doi.org/10.1201/9781003496656

Mekala, K., Laxmi, V., Jagruthi, H., Dhondiyal, S. A., Sridevi, R., & Dabral, A. P. (2023). Coffee Price Prediction: An Application of CNN-BLSTM Neural Networks. *Proceedings of the 2nd IEEE International Conference on Advances in Computing, Communication and Applied Informatics, ACCAI 2023*. https://doi.org/10.1109/ACCAI58221.2023.10199369

Mitra, A., Mohanty, S. P., Corcoran, P., & Kougianos, E. (2020). A Novel Machine Learning based Method for Deepfake Video Detection in Social Media. *Proceedings - 2020 6th IEEE International Symposium on Smart Electronic Systems, ISES 2020*, 91–96. https://doi.org/10.1109/iSES50453.2020.00031

Mitra, A., Mohanty, S. P., Corcoran, P., & Kougianos, E. (2021). A Machine Learning Based Approach for Deepfake Detection in Social Media Through Key Video Frame Extraction. *SN Computer Science*, *2*(2). https://doi.org/10.1007/s42979-021-00495-x

Mitra, A., Mohanty, S. P., Corcoran, P., & Kougianos, E. (2022). EasyDeep: An IoT Friendly Robust Detection Method for GAN Generated Deepfake Images in Social Media. *IFIP Advances in Information and Communication Technology*, *641 IFIP*, 217–236. https://doi.org/10.1007/978-3-030-96466-5_14

Narayan, K., Agarwal, H., Mittal, S., Thakral, K., Kundu, S., Vatsa, M., & Singh, R. (2022). DeSI: Deepfake Source Identifier for Social Media. *IEEE Computer Society Conference on Computer Vision and Pattern Recognition Workshops*, *2022-June*, 2857–2866. https://doi.org/10.1109/CVPRW56347.2022.00323

Papageorgiou, G., Loukis, E., Pappas, G., Rizun, N., Saxena, S., Charalabidis, Y., & Alexopoulos, C. (2023). Open Government Data in Educational

Programs Curriculum: Current State and Prospects. *Lecture Notes in Business Information Processing*, *493 LNBIP*, 311–326. https://doi.org/10.1007/978-3-031-43126-5_22

Preeti, Kumar, M., & Sharma, H. K. (2022). A GAN-Based Model of Deepfake Detection in Social Media. In S. V. (Ed.), *Procedia Computer Science* (Vol. 218, pp. 2153–2162). Elsevier B.V. https://doi.org/10.1016/j.procs.2023.01.191

Qureshi, S. M., Saeed, A., Almotiri, S. H., Ahmad, F., & Ghamdi, M. A. Al. (2024). Deepfake forensics: a survey of digital forensic methods for multimodal deepfake identification on social media. *PeerJ Computer Science*, *10*, 1–40. https://doi.org/10.7717/PEERJ-CS.2037

Ramarajan, M., Dinesh, A., Muthuraman, C., Rajini, J., Anand, T., & Segar, B. (2024). AI-driven job displacement and economic impacts: Ethics and strategies for implementation. In *Cases on AI Ethics in Business*. IGI Global. https://doi.org/10.4018/9798369326435.ch013

Rana, M. S., Cavaliere, L. P. L., Mishra, A. B., Padhye, P., Singh, R. R., & Khanna, R. (2022). Internet of Things (IOT) Based Assessment for Effective Monitoring Data Against Malicious Attacks on Financial Collectors. *2022 2nd International Conference on Advance Computing and Innovative Technologies in Engineering, ICACITE 2022*, 177–181. https://doi.org/10.1109/ICACITE53722.2022.9823612

Rao, K. V. G., Kumar, M. K., Goud, B. S., Krishna, D., Bajaj, M., Saini, P., & Choudhury, S. (2023). IOT-Powered Crop Shield System for Surveillance and Auto Transversum. *2023 IEEE 3rd International Conference on Sustainable Energy and Future Electric Transportation, SeFet 2023*. https://doi.org/10.1109/SeFeT57834.2023.10245773

Sadiq, S., Aljrees, T., & Ullah, S. (2023). Deepfake Detection on Social Media: Leveraging Deep Learning and FastText Embeddings for Identifying Machine-Generated Tweets. *IEEE Access*, *11*, 95008–95021. https://doi.org/10.1109/ACCESS.2023.3308515

Salini, Y., & Harikiran, J. (2023). Multiplicative Vector Fusion Model for Detecting Deepfake News in Social Media. *Applied Sciences (Switzerland)*, *13*(7). https://doi.org/10.3390/app13074207

Santoyo, G., Orozco-Mosqueda, M. del C., Afridi, M. S., Mitra, D., Valencia-Cantero, E., & Macías-Rodríguez, L. (2024). Trichoderma and Bacillus multifunctional allies for plant growth and health in saline soils: recent advances and future challenges. *Frontiers in Microbiology*, *15*. https://doi.org/10.3389/fmicb.2024.1423980

Saravani, S. M., Ray, I., & Ray, I. (2021). Automated Identification of Social Media Bots Using Deepfake Text Detection. *Lecture Notes in Computer*

Science (Including Subseries Lecture Notes in Artificial Intelligence and Lecture Notes in Bioinformatics), 13146 LNCS, 111–123. https://doi.org/10.1007/978-3-030-92571-0_7

Sardana, F., Mishra, K. K., Singh, A., & Saini, N. (2024). Transforming social media marketing through deepfake technology. In *Navigating the World of Deepfake Technology*. IGI Global. https://doi.org/10.4018/979-8-3693-5298-4.ch022

Shajar, S. N., Kashif, M., George, J., & Nasir, S. (2024). The future of green finance: Artificial intelligence-enabled solutions for a more sustainable world. In *Harnessing Blockchain-Digital Twin Fusion for Sustainable Investments*. IGI Global. https://doi.org/10.4018/9798369318782.ch013

Sharma, A., Mohan, A., Johri, A., & Asif, M. (2024). Determinants of fintech adoption in agrarian economy: Study of UTAUT extension model in reference to developing economies. *Journal of Open Innovation: Technology, Market, and Complexity*, *10*(2). https://doi.org/10.1016/j.joitmc.2024.100273

Sharma, P., Kumar, M., & Sharma, H. K. (2024). GAN-CNN Ensemble: A Robust Deepfake Detection Model of Social Media Images Using Minimized Catastrophic Forgetting and Generative Replay Technique. In S. V., A. V.K., L. K.-C., & C. R.G. (Eds.), *Procedia Computer Science* (Vol. 235, pp. 948–960). Elsevier B.V. https://doi.org/10.1016/j.procs.2024.04.090

Sharma, S., Kadayat, Y., & Tyagi, R. (2023). Artificial Intelligence Enabled Sustainable Life Cycle System Using Vedic Scripture and Quantum Computing. *2023 3rd International Conference on Intelligent Technologies, CONIT 2023*. https://doi.org/10.1109/CONIT59222.2023.10205771

Singh, A. K., Singh, R., & Singh, S. (2024). Ecological footprint and its enhancing factors in SAARC Countries. In *Biodiversity Loss Assessment for Ecosystem Protection*. IGI Global. https://doi.org/10.4018/979-8-3693-3330-3.ch014

Singh, K. D., Deep Singh, P., Bansal, A., Kaur, G., Khullar, V., & Tripathi, V. (2023). Exploratory Data Analysis and Customer Churn Prediction for the Telecommunication Industry. *ACCESS 2023–2023 3rd International Conference on Advances in Computing, Communication, Embedded and Secure Systems*, 197–201. https://doi.org/10.1109/ACCESS57397.2023.10199700

Srinivasan, S. (2024). Empowerment and leadership quality improve unorganized women migrant workers in Karur District, Tamil Nadu, India.

In *Empowering and Advancing Women Leaders and Entrepreneurs*. IGI Global. https://doi.org/10.4018/979-8-3693-7107-7.ch004

Sudarsan, A., Chua, H. N., Jasser, M. B., & Wong, R. T. K. (2024). Deepfake Characterization, Propagation, and Detection in Social Media - A Synthesis Review. *2024 20th IEEE International Colloquium on Signal Processing and Its Applications, CSPA 2024 - Conference Proceedings*, 219–224. https://doi.org/10.1109/CSPA60979.2024.10525373

Tamta, S., Vimal, V., Verma, S., Gupta, D., Verma, D., & Nangan, S. (2024). Recent development of nanobiomaterials in sustainable agriculture and agrowaste management. *Biocatalysis and Agricultural Biotechnology*, *56*. https://doi.org/10.1016/j.bcab.2024.103050

Tomar, S., Sharma, N., & Nehra, N. S. (2023). A sustainable rural entrepreneurship model developed by the organic farmers of India. *Emerald Emerging Markets Case Studies*, *13*(2), 1–17. https://doi.org/10.1108/EEMCS-09-2022-0329

Upreti, H., & Malhotra, R. K. (2024). Bridging The Urban-Rural Education Gap In India Through CSR (Corporate Social Responsibility) Initiatives: A Conceptual Study With Special Reference To Sustainable Development Goal 4 (Quality Education). In P. P.K. (Ed.), *E3S Web of Conferences* (Vol. 556). EDP Sciences. https://doi.org/10.1051/e3sconf/202455601032

Yanagi, Y., Orihara, R., Tahara, Y., Sei, Y., Alumäe, T., & Ohsuga, A. (2024). The Proposal of Countermeasures for DeepFake Voices on Social Media Considering Waveform and Text Embedding. *Annals of Emerging Technologies in Computing*, *8*(2), 15–31. https://doi.org/10.33166/AETiC.2024.02.002

Yıldız, H. G., Ayvaz, B., Kuşakcı, A. O., Deveci, M., & Garg, H. (2024). Sustainability assessment of biomass-based energy supply chain using multi-objective optimization model. *Environment, Development and Sustainability*, *26*(6), 15451–15493. https://doi.org/10.1007/s10668-023-03258-1

9

The Influence of Deepfake Technology on Political Affairs

Swati Gupta[1], Umang Sharma[2] and Luan Vardari[3]

[1]Chitkara Business School, Chitkara University, India
[2]Chandigarh Group of Colleges, India
[3]University "Ukshin Hoti" Rruga e shkronjave Nr., prizren, Kosova

Email: Swati.gupta@chitkara.edu.in; Umang.hr@cgc.ac.in; luan.vardari@uni-prizren.com

Abstract

The increased creativity of AI hastened the creation of deepfake technology capable of altering audio, video, and images brought about by humans into high-quality fakes. Initially designed for entertainment, deepfakes have evolved into a tool for malicious uses, particularly in political contexts. The following paper, therefore, aims to discuss the effects of deepfake in the political realm, particularly in politics, elections, policy-making, and trust. This plunges into how deepfakes are created using GAN, giving a glimpse into the possibility of having fake media that is as real as the original media. Deepfakes act as a menace to democracies as they accomplish the job of confusing and sowing uncertainties into governments. Furthermore, it paints a picture and changes people's perceptions, especially during elections and political turmoil.

Even as technology for fighting deepfakes is developing, the creation of these synthetic media is becoming increasingly advanced, which calls for more robust legal and regulatory measures against using the noted technology. It is possible only through a coordinated approach involving governments, technological companies, and civil society organisations to tackle the menace of deepfakes in the political realm, enhance political stability and restore public confidence in the democratic systems.

9.1 Introduction

The availability of artificial intelligence means the creation of technologies that affect people in many ways (Arya et al., 2023). One of them is the "deepfake", an abbreviated form of deep learning fake, which is synthetic media with audio, video, or images that generative AI models have produced. Although deepfakes had been initially designed for entertainment and, more importantly, for creating fun content, their use for malicious purposes seems to be quite possible and quite relevant to current political events (Semwal et al., 2023; R. Yadav et al., 2023). Consequently, this paper examines the effects of deepfake technology on politics, elections, policy-making, and trust (Aloo et al., 2023; Behera & Singh Rawat, 2023).

As technology has developed in recent years, the deepfake generation is now as simple as making highly realistic videos and audios that are as good as the originals (Chand et al., 2023; Srivastava et al., 2023). This also encompasses synthetic text, synthetic audio, synthetic images, and synthetic video, making it even harder for people to sieve the truth from the falsehoods (Groh et.al., 2022; Rana et.al., 2022). Although deepfakes and other related synthetic media, including the simpler "cheapfakes", are in many fields, including entertainment, education, and fraud, a potentially dangerous application is politically influenced deepfakes. Recent examples are deepfakes directed at political personalities, including Donald Trump, Joe Biden, Emmanuel Macron, Nancy Pelosi, Vladimir Putin, and Volodymyr Zelensky. Deepfakes have been used to mobilise the votes (Christopher, 2020) and defame politicians for sexual misconduct (A. Kumar et al., 2023; G. Kumar et al., 2023) and for some socio-political factors, such as the Russian attack on Ukraine (B. Rawat et al., 2022; Širić et al., 2022).

Deepfakes are video-based disinformation generated using artificial intelligence (AI) (Gonfa et al., 2023; Vennila et al., 2022). Instead, cheapfakes refer to genuine images or videos in which the context is modified to intentionally give the content a different connotation (Paris & Donovan, 2020). Making cheapfakes can be done quickly; without specific skills, only basic editing and low-cost equipment, money and materials are needed. For instance, a cheapfake could crop a video of a missile strike, staged or authentic, and then edit it to suggest a Ukrainian bombardment of civilians in Russia. Despite a significant body of research dedicated to the technical aspects of deepfakes with enumeration of the detection methods (Pant et al., 2022; S. S. Rawat et al., 2022; Singla et al., 2023; Wongchai et al., 2022), deepfakes currently attract a minimal research focus in political communication. Researchers employed an existing deepfake to show how these fake videos destabilise people's understanding of the real and fabricated (Elbagory et al., 2022; Tyagi et al., 2022). With regards to the near and possible future trends, deepfakes shall be suggested to progress in two ways: the first is the increased sophistication of deepfakes in the future. Consequently, it is important to know how they are viewed at this current stage since there is increasing complexity (M. Sharma et al., 2022).

Several deepfake databases have been created, including Fake Catcher database, AI-Powered Video Archive, and Deepfake Detection Challenge Dataset, but these are primarily built for improving technical detection means and not systematised based on the range of politically and publicly important deepfakes and cheapfakes (Kholiya et al., 2023; Papageorgiou et al., 2023). This limitation makes systematic analysis rather challenging. Significantly, the increasing legislative concern, along with the rising capability of deepfakes, highlights the fact that much more detailed incident reporting is needed – which a robust and more comprehensive database would enable (V. Kumar & Korovin, 2023).

9.2 The Mechanism of Deepfake Technology

Deepfake is a term used to describe AI and machine learning fake content in which an individual's look, voice, or behaviour is modified or completely mimicked, usually through video or image. This is done by using other techniques like deep learning, which is a form of machine learning that mimics the functioning of the human brain to comprehend data and design intricate models for actions to be taken (K. Yadav et al., 2023).

GANs are at the centre of deepfake technology. GANs consist of two neural networks – generator and the discriminator (K. Yadav et al., 2023). The generator produces so-called "unreal" data, while the discriminator works on "real" data in differentiating the former from the latter. These two networks are in tension with one another – that's why the first one is called the "generator", while the second one is the "discriminator": the generator attempts to produce higher-quality counterfeit outputs than the discriminator can recognise. In the long run, such a process leads to extremely believable fake media involving even the slightest of facial expressions or voice alterations.

Here is a more detailed breakdown of how the mechanism works (Shao et al., 2023; Širić et al., 2023):

9.2.1 Data collection

Deepfake generation starts with scraping many images or videos of an intended target (Korkmaz et al., 2023). These datasets are used as the training data again so that the AI can train itself to recognise the subject's facial expressions, movements, and voice patterns. For instance, when it comes to videos, many frames of the involved person are needed to learn and model facial expressions.

9.2.2 Training of the generator and discriminator

In GANs, the initial generation begins with creating fake data, often including faces or videos. The discriminator takes the real and fake data as input and tries to distinguish between the two. Thus, a tight feedback loop between these two components is relevant. On the other hand, the generator loses with every fake that the discriminator points out but gets to adapt to facing such outcomes. It is like until the generator generates output, the discriminator is fooled into thinking it is accurate.

Generator: This authentic neural network creates artificial media by utilising actual patterns and features.

Discriminator: This neural network is the one giving feedback to the generated media to check the quality of fake data against real data.

9.2.3 Face and feature replacement

For the image and the video-based deepfakes, once the generator has been trained, the inserted face of a person in the given video is replaced with the face of another individual. This becomes the identification of facial features (eyes, nose, mouth, etc.) in relation to the target subject's face such that the facial muscle movements and lips match the speaker's words and movement. Such tools as face morphing algorithms are used to accomplish such a goal (Dutta et al., 2023).

9.2.4 Audio deepfakes

That is why audio deepfakes use the same method but replicate the fake speech. Voice cloning integrated with prognostic models reconstructs a person's voice by emulating phonetic patterns and paralinguistic features. Google's WaveNet is a convenient example of how AI systems play a major role in creating synthetic voices that sound very natural (Korkmaz et al., 2023).

9.2.5 Advanced processing and output finite elements and modelling advanced processing and output

Once the generator generates the fake content, post-processing methodologies like smoothing, frame interpolation, and colour correction are used to make the fake content look as real as possible. The reflections of this disagreement, the classic grey squares were known to combat fake media, are hidden through the fine-tuning of light, and shadows, among others by the AI to match the adjusted fake media with its natural environment or background (Bhandari et al., 2023).

9.2.6 Detection challenges

Despite the fact that these deepfakes are becoming all the more convincing, they are relatively difficult to identify. A number of detection methods have been invented, including pixel intensity variation, discrepancies in facial muscle coordination, and blinks. But with the current technological development it is becoming hard to trace whether the information one is getting is real or fake information; this calls for the creation of a better detection system (Pansare et al., 2023).

9.3 Deepfakes and Misinformation in Politics

In the last few years, the progress of artificial intelligence has raised a potent and discussing tool named "deepfakes". Deepfakes additionally apply machine learning techniques to create advanced fake media that can seem like the real life of the particular person by no means stated or done. Though the use of this technology has been relatively harmless for entertainment and more recently even art, the malicious end result it can produce is most worrisome in the spheres of politics (AL-Huqail et al., 2023).

These deepfakes have now grown to become a huge problem in political dialogues within the world, enhancing the spread of misinformation and disinformation. Since fake media tend to look quite realistic, mischievous individuals can achieve their aims – shift people's attitudes or opinions, cause confusion, and erode the population's confidence in politicians, organizations, and even the democratic processes (Deepti et al., 2023; Rajput et al., 2023). Therefore, deepfakes are beginning to be used for predatory purposes, to tell fake stories and twist elections, and to undermine governments. This growing phenomenon evokes crucial questions about the integration of technology in political manipulation and the prospective protection of societies from the malignant uses of deepfakes in political processes (Sapna et al., 2023; M. Sharma et al., 2023).

9.3.1 Deepfakes as a tool for disinformation

False information generally can be placed in one of three categories: disinformation, misinformation (fake news), or malinformation . Deepfakes fit best in the disinformation group, which includes "manipulated content", "imposter content", and "fabricated content" (Naveen et al., 2023). Disinformation can be seen as "intentional behaviour that purposively misleads" (Deepti et al., 2023). Quite frequently, disinformation is intended to serve some political purpose. Domestic actors can perform disinformation but can also be by foreign political actors. Thereby any domestic political actors with claims to legitimacy can employ tactics such as disinformation to achieve their goals. Deepfakes give the ability to spread fake news on a large scale. Depending on the skill set of these malign actors, easily fake videos or audio clips of politicians are used to distort political debate, mislead voters and manipulate public opinions. For example, a deepfake can portray a head of state as using obscene language or being involved in a certain scandal, while in fact, the latter is not true. A clear example of this risk was observed in the summer of 2020 when a user-generated deepfake video of a slowed-down Nancy Pelosi, the US House Speaker, to make her seem slurred in her speech (Garg et al., 2023). While this type of manipulated preview is not very realistic in regard to deepfake methods, it still shows how far the method can go in changing the perception regarding political personalities. Consequently, as technology progresses more realistic deepfakes will be developed presenting even more perils (Liao et al., 2023; Y. Singh et al., 2023).

9.3.2 Election manipulation

Among all the phenomena, elections are the most susceptible to deepfake-related manipulations of information. This means that even a deepfake that will be produced at a time when it can have a significant impact when released before an election can have significant impacts. According to research, deepfakes can be weaponised to defame political candidates or disrupt democratic processes. A fake video or audio with the candidate making racist or sexist comments, for example, would swing a close election and the timing of its release is all important especially just before the actual poll (Alexopoulos et al., 2023; Mishra et al., 2023). Also, there is a need to be aware of deepfakes since the campaigns may be a target of such fellowship. People in the 2024 US presidential primary elections have already produced advertisement videos using deepfakes (Suryavanshi et al., 2023). This is particularly pernicious as broadcast networks cannot opt not to air a campaign ad because The Communications Act of 1934 notes broadcasters possess "no power of censorship" over any legally qualified candidate for office (Tiwari et al., 2023). In response, the Federal Election Commission voted unanimously to investigate how to start assessing the rules surrounding the use of AI in campaigns (Rajput et al., 2023).

The most worrying aspect is that deepfakes may contribute to the future escalation of disinformation or "fake news" on social media, through which some adversaries may continue to fuel confusion and social tensions. (Banerjee et al., 2023; S. Sharma & Tyagi, 2023). For instance, during election periods, deepfakes can be applied to disown candidates or even manipulate the way people vote by using fake narratives. In addition, deepfakes challenge viewers' ability to discern the authenticity of content provided by trustworthy media outlets and thus erode the bases for political trust and openness (Kaur et al., 2023).

9.4 Impact on Public Trust and Political Stability

9.4.1 Erosion of public trust

Recognising deepfakes as a phenomenon that has affected or might impact politics in the future means it altered the public's trust in media and institutions. Apparently, the significant number of deepfake videos can lead to the appearance of a so-called "post-truth" scenario, in which the public loses faith in real news. When TV viewers and internet users cannot rely on their eyes and ears, it is sometimes difficult to distinguish between the truth and fake news, and faith in the popular vote weakens (Usmani et al., 2023).

9.4.2 Unpredictable political stability is another social risk

Osama A. Attia, the dissemination of deepfake videos also requires deliberate, intentional, and planned action and could cause political upheavals. Ethnic or religious hatred deepfake could be used to politic, instigate violence or increase ethnic and religious tensions, as was the case with the manipulation of media in Myanmar during the Rohingya genocide (Mozur, 2018). As the global society continues to get connected, deepfakes' negative effect could transcend and affect countries' relationships (Sapna et al., 2023).

9.5 Legal and Policy Responses

9.5.1 Regulatory frameworks

Several countries are gradually starting to speak about possible threats that may be connected with deepfake technology using legal and regulatory measures. For instance, The Deepfakes Accountability Act, which was passed in the United States in 2019, wants to require that synthetic media be disclosed.

In the same way, the EU has included provisions regarding deepfakes in the current DSA in order to come down on this threat of disinformation (Gupta et al., 2023).

9.5.2 Technological solutions

Besides, the state is not the only one trying to find ways to prevent the negative impact of deepfakes; technology companies are also seeking solutions. He noted that Facebook, Google, and Twitter have already started campaigns to create AI that can detect deepfakes. Though the present form of such technologies can be countered effectively, those are not perfect, and deepfake technology generation algorithms keep evolving.

9.6 Ethical Implications

The deepfake generation casts important ethical issues on practice concerning privacy, free speech or freedom of expression, and responsibility. A deeper philosophical issue arises from the potential of deepfakes to violate human dignity. (Kunwar et al., 2021)The ability to modify or perhaps create another person's character without knowledge may strip an individual of their true worth or inherent value. Such technology is ethically acceptable if human agency and freedom are not violated but, on the contrary, valued and recognised.

The large amounts of data needed to create convincing deepfakes pose significant privacy risks. Detailed facial and vocal recordings of individuals can be used to produce personalised deepfakes without their consent, increasing the threat of biometric data exposure (A. Singh et al., 2021). Transparency regarding the training data used by deepfake algorithms is essential, and obtaining third-party consent should be a priority where applicable. Implementing access controls and cybersecurity measures can help prevent the unauthorised use of biometric data. Watermarking synthetic media is another strategy to safeguard identities and reduce misuse. Ultimately, prioritising user privacy through proactive measures can help build trust. The media generated by AI could be used for positive intents, which may include the promotion of creativity of culture and making processes more accessible and cheaper. However, on the other hand, in politics, the government should make necessary rules regarding the usage of AI to balance the application of rules and technological advancements. The challenge lies in maintaining democratic processes and public trust in them while ensuring that freedom of speech is not compromised.

9.7 Conclusion

Deepfake technology, which in addition to forging realistic fake media content, can create fairly believable fake video content, is a profound threat to the political sphere and its honesty. As demonstrated in this research, deepfakes have, across the spectrum, extended their reach from election campaigns to influencing international relationships. The often-questioned opportunity to manipulate or create new video and audio material of political leaders can trigger misunderstandings, the distribution of fake news and affect democratic procedures. These technologies are most damaging in an age where new content is accessed, consumed, and passed across the Internet without proper evaluation. The deepfake technology has become one of the significant factors influencing the political process by adding new opportunities to mislead the audience. Regarding democracy and political stability, some measures must be taken before, during, and after preparing deepfake content to distribute to people. Deepfake-enabled disinformation is not easily solvable by technology and using technical solutions alone will lead to ethical concerns.

Deepfakes present many threats, and work to combat them is being done. Concerning risk reduction, improved technologies, regulation, and societal awareness of deepfakes will considerably contribute to battling fake videos. It is crucial for governments and technology companies, together with civil society, to create new policies and new technological instruments capable of managing deepfakes when they are used in political space. Such solutions will need advanced AI-based detection tools to act in conjunction with dos and don'ts and raise awareness among the general public about the threats of deepfakes. Maintaining political integrity and preventing corruption in the era of social media, along with the rapid growth of the internet and communication technologies, will require appropriate legal frameworks, the use of advanced information technologies, and raising public awareness of the deepfakes. It can be concluded that the current and future progression of deepfakes demands proactive and multi-stakeholder initiatives together with some existing legal and technological attempts to have an ethically sound political scenario.

References

AL-Huqail, A. A., Singh, R., Širić, I., Kumar, P., Abou Fayssal, S., Kumar, V., Bachheti, R. K., Andabaka, Ž., Goala, M., & Eid, E. M. (2023). Occurrence and Health Risk Assessment of Heavy Metals in Lychee

(Litchi chinensis Sonn., Sapindaceae) Fruit Samples. *Horticulturae*, *9*(9). https://doi.org/10.3390/horticulturae9090989

Alexopoulos, C., Saxena, S., Janssen, M., & Rizun, N. (2023). Whither the need and motivation for open government data (OGD) promotional strategies? *Digital Policy, Regulation and Governance*, *25*(2), 153–168. https://doi.org/10.1108/DPRG-07-2022-0078

Aloo, B. N., Dessureault-Rompré, J., Tripathi, V., Nyongesa, B. O., & Were, B. A. (2023). Signaling and crosstalk of rhizobacterial and plant hormones that mediate abiotic stress tolerance in plants. *Frontiers in Microbiology*, *14*. https://doi.org/10.3389/fmicb.2023.1171104

Arya, P., Shreya, S., & Gupta, A. (2023). Amazing potential and the future of fungi: Applications and economic importance. In *Microbial Bioactive Compounds: Industrial and Agricultural Applications*. Springer Nature. https://doi.org/10.1007/978-3-031-40082-7_2

Banerjee, D., Kukreja, V., Aeri, M., Hariharan, S., & Garg, N. (2023). Integrated CNN-SVM Approach for Accurate Radish Leaf Disease Classification: A Comparative Study and Performance Analysis. *2023 Annual International Conference on Emerging Research Areas: International Conference on Intelligent Systems, AICERA/ICIS 2023*. https://doi.org/10.1109/AICERA/ICIS59538.2023.10420119

Behera, A., & Singh Rawat, K. (2023). A brief review paper on mining subsidence and its geo-environmental impact. *Materials Today: Proceedings*. https://doi.org/10.1016/j.matpr.2023.04.183

Bhandari, G., Dhasmana, A., Chaudhary, P., Gupta, S., Gangola, S., Gupta, A., Rustagi, S., Shende, S. S., Rajput, V. D., Minkina, T., Malik, S., & Slama, P. (2023). A Perspective Review on Green Nanotechnology in Agro-Ecosystems: Opportunities for Sustainable Agricultural Practices & Environmental Remediation. *Agriculture (Switzerland)*, *13*(3). https://doi.org/10.3390/agriculture13030668

Chand, A., Agarwal, P., & Sharma, S. (2023). Real-Time Retrieving Vedic Sanskrit Text into Multi-Lingual Text and Audio for Cultural Tourism Motivation. *2023 International Conference for Advancement in Technology, ICONAT 2023*. https://doi.org/10.1109/ICONAT57137.2023.10080862

Deepti, Bachheti, A., Arya, A. K., Verma, D. K., & Bachheti, R. K. (2023). Allelopathic activity of genus Euphorbia. In G. D., P. B., M. U., M. R., & G. R. (Eds.), *AIP Conference Proceedings* (Vol. 2782). American Institute of Physics Inc. https://doi.org/10.1063/5.0154514

Dutta, A., Singh, P., Dobhal, A., Mannan, D., Singh, J., & Goswami, P. (2023). Entrepreneurial Aptitude of Women of an Aspirational

District of Uttarakhand. *Indian Journal of Extension Education*, *59*(2), 103–107. https://doi.org/10.48165/IJEE.2023.59222

Elbagory, M., El-Nahrawy, S., Omara, A. E.-D., Eid, E. M., Bachheti, A., Kumar, P., Abou Fayssal, S., Adelodun, B., Bachheti, R. K., Kumar, P., Mioč, B., Kumar, V., & Širić, I. (2022). Sustainable Bioconversion of Wetland Plant Biomass for Pleurotus ostreatus var. florida Cultivation: Studies on Proximate and Biochemical Characterization. *Agriculture (Switzerland)*, *12*(12). https://doi.org/10.3390/agriculture12122095

Garg, G., Gupta, S., Mishra, P., Vidyarthi, A., Singh, A., & Ali, A. (2023). CROPCARE: An Intelligent Real-Time Sustainable IoT System for Crop Disease Detection Using Mobile Vision. *IEEE Internet of Things Journal*, *10*(4), 2840–2851. https://doi.org/10.1109/JIOT.2021.3109019

Gonfa, Y. H., Gelagle, A. A., Hailegnaw, B., Kabeto, S. A., Workeneh, G. A., Tessema, F. B., Tadesse, M. G., Wabaidur, S. M., Dahlous, K. A., Abou Fayssal, S., Kumar, P., Adelodun, B., Bachheti, A., & Bachheti, R. K. (2023). Optimization, Characterization, and Biological Applications of Silver Nanoparticles Synthesized Using Essential Oil of Aerial Part of Laggera tomentosa. *Sustainability (Switzerland)*, *15*(1). https://doi.org/10.3390/su15010797

Gupta, S., Kushwaha, P., Chauhan, A. S., Yadav, A., & Badhotiya, G. K. (2023). A study on glazing to optimize daylight for improving lighting ergonomics and energy efficiency of a building. In S. Y., S. G., & B. G.K. (Eds.), *AIP Conference Proceedings* (Vol. 2521). American Institute of Physics Inc. https://doi.org/10.1063/5.0114766

Kaur, A., Kukreja, V., Chamoli, S., Thapliyal, S., & Sharma, R. (2023). Advanced Multi-Scale Classification of Onion Smut Disease Using a Hybrid CNN-RF Ensemble Model for Precision Agriculture. In G. R., H. K., P. R., G. S., T. A. J.V., V. R., M. R., & K. T. (Eds.), *Proceedings of the 2023 6th International Conference on Recent Trends in Advance Computing, ICRTAC 2023* (pp. 553–556). Institute of Electrical and Electronics Engineers Inc. https://doi.org/10.1109/ICRTAC59277.2023.10480840

Kholiya, D., Mishra, A. K., Pandey, N. K., & Tripathi, N. (2023). Plant Detection and Counting using Yolo based Technique. *2023 3rd Asian Conference on Innovation in Technology, ASIANCON 2023*. https://doi.org/10.1109/ASIANCON58793.2023.10270530

Korkmaz, M. E., Gupta, M. K., Ross, N. S., & Sivalingam, V. (2023). Implementation of green cooling/lubrication strategies in metal cutting industries: A state of the art towards sustainable future and challenges.

Sustainable Materials and Technologies, *36*. https://doi.org/10.1016/j.susmat.2023.e00641

Kumar, A., Goyal, H. R., & Sharma, S. (2023). Sustainable Intelligent Information System for Tourism Industry. *2023 IEEE 8th International Conference for Convergence in Technology, I2CT 2023*. https://doi.org/10.1109/I2CT57861.2023.10126400

Kumar, G., Kumar, A., Singhal, M., Singh, K. U., Kumar, L., & Singh, T. (2023). Revolutionizing Plant Disease Management Through Image Processing Technology. *Proceedings of International Conference on Computational Intelligence and Sustainable Engineering Solution, CISES 2023*, 521–528. https://doi.org/10.1109/CISES58720.2023.10183408

Kumar, V., & Korovin, G. (2023). A Comparision of Digital Transformation of Industry in the Russian Federation with the European Union. In K. V., K. G.L., A. V., & K. E. (Eds.), *Lecture Notes in Information Systems and Organisation: Vol. 61 LNISO* (pp. 45–57). Springer Science and Business Media Deutschland GmbH. https://doi.org/10.1007/978-3-031-30351-7_5

Kunwar, S., Bhatt, S., Pandey, D., & Pandey, N. (2021). Field Application of the Microbial Technology and Its Importance in Sustainable Development. In *Microbial Technology for Sustainable Environment*. Springer Nature. https://doi.org/10.1007/978-981-16-3840-4_20

Liao, N., Cai, Q., Garg, H., Wei, G., & Xu, X. (2023). Novel Gained and Lost Dominance Score Method Based on Cumulative Prospect Theory for Group Decision-Making Problems in Probabilistic Hesitant Fuzzy Environment. *International Journal of Fuzzy Systems*, *25*(4), 1414–1428. https://doi.org/10.1007/s40815-022-01440-7

Mishra, A., Shah, J. K., Sharma, R., Sharma, M., Joshi, S., & Kaushal, D. (2023). Enhancing Efficiency in Industrial Environments through IoT Connected Worker Solutions: Smart Wearable Technologies for the Workplace. *2023 International Conference on Advances in Computation, Communication and Information Technology, ICAICCIT 2023*, 1175–1179. https://doi.org/10.1109/ICAICCIT60255.2023.10466100

Naveen, Y., Lokanadham, D., Naidu, D. R., Sharma, R. C., Palli, S., & Lila, M. K. (2023). An Experimental Study on the Influence of Blended Karanja Biodiesel on Diesel Engine Characteristics. *International Journal of Vehicle Structures and Systems*, *15*(2), 154–160. https://doi.org/10.4273/ijvss.15.2.02

Pansare, R., Yadav, G., Garza-Reyes, J. A., & Raosaheb Nagare, M. (2023). Assessment of Sustainable Development Goals through Industry 4.0 and reconfigurable manufacturing system practices. *Journal of*

Manufacturing Technology Management, *34*(3), 383–413. https://doi.org/10.1108/JMTM-05-2022-0206

Pant, R., Gupta, A., Pant, G., Chaubey, K. K., Kumar, G., & Patrick, N. (2022). Second-generation biofuels: Facts and future. In *Relationship between Microbes and the Environment for Sustainable Ecosystem Services: Microbial Tools for Sustainable Ecosystem Services: Volume 3* (Vol. 3). Elsevier. https://doi.org/10.1016/B978-0-323-89936-9.00011-4

Papageorgiou, G., Loukis, E., Pappas, G., Rizun, N., Saxena, S., Charalabidis, Y., & Alexopoulos, C. (2023). Open Government Data in Educational Programs Curriculum: Current State and Prospects. *Lecture Notes in Business Information Processing*, *493 LNBIP*, 311–326. https://doi.org/10.1007/978-3-031-43126-5_22

Rajput, S., Sharma, A., Jately, V., & Ram, M. (2023). Recent advances in energy harvesting technologies. In *Recent Advances in Energy Harvesting Technologies*. River Publishers.

Rawat, B., Rawat, J. M., Purohit, S., Singh, G., Sharma, P. K., Chandra, A., Shabaaz Begum, J. P., Venugopal, D., Jaremko, M., & Qureshi, K. A. (2022). A comprehensive review of Quercus semecarpifolia Sm.: An ecologically and commercially important Himalayan tree. *Frontiers in Ecology and Evolution*, *10*. https://doi.org/10.3389/fevo.2022.961345

Rawat, S. S., Pant, S., Kumar, A., Ram, M., Sharma, H. K., & Kumar, A. (2022). A State-of-the-Art Survey on Analytical Hierarchy Process Applications in Sustainable Development. *International Journal of Mathematical, Engineering and Management Sciences*, *7*(6), 883–917. https://doi.org/10.33889/IJMEMS.2022.7.6.056

Sapna, Chand, K., Tiwari, R., & Bhardwaj, K. (2023). Impact of Welfare Measures on Job Satisfaction of Employees in the Industrial Sector of Northern India. *Finance India*, *37*(2), 613 – 626.

Semwal, P., Painuli, S., Begum J.P, S., Jamloki, A., Rauf, A., Olatunde, A., Mominur Rahman, M., Mukerjee, N., Ahmed Khalil, A., Aljohani, A. S. M., Al Abdulmonem, W., & Simal-Gandara, J. (2023). Exploring the nutritional and health benefits of pulses from the Indian Himalayan region: A glimpse into the region's rich agricultural heritage. *Food Chemistry*, *422*. https://doi.org/10.1016/j.foodchem.2023.136259

Shao, D., Kombe, C., & Saxena, S. (2023). An ensemble design of a cash crops-warehouse receipt system (WRS) based on blockchain smart contracts. *Journal of Agribusiness in Developing and Emerging Economies*, *13*(5), 762–774. https://doi.org/10.1108/JADEE-02-2022-0032

Sharma, M., Joshi, S., & Govindan, K. (2023). Overcoming barriers to implement digital technologies to achieve sustainable production and consumption in the food sector: A circular economy perspective. *Sustainable Production and Consumption*, *39*, 203–215. https://doi.org/10.1016/j.spc.2023.04.002

Sharma, M., Kumar, A., Luthra, S., Joshi, S., & Upadhyay, A. (2022). The impact of environmental dynamism on low-carbon practices and digital supply chain networks to enhance sustainable performance: An empirical analysis. *Business Strategy and the Environment*, *31*(4), 1776–1788. https://doi.org/10.1002/bse.2983

Sharma, S., & Tyagi, R. (2023). Digitalization of Farming Knowledge Using Artificial Intelligence and Vedic Scripture. *3rd IEEE International Conference on ICT in Business Industry and Government, ICTBIG 2023*. https://doi.org/10.1109/ICTBIG59752.2023.10456219

Singh, A., Sharma, S., Purohit, K. C., & Nithin Kumar, K. C. (2021). Artificial Intelligence based Framework for Effective Performance of Traffic Light Control System. *Proceedings of the 2021 IEEE International Conference on Innovative Computing, Intelligent Communication and Smart Electrical Systems, ICSES 2021*. https://doi.org/10.1109/ICSES52305.2021.9633913

Singh, Y., Singh, N. K., & Sharma, A. (2023). Biodiesel as an alternative fuel employed in CI engine to meet the sustainability criteria: A review. In S. Y., S. G., & B. G.K. (Eds.), *AIP Conference Proceedings* (Vol. 2521). American Institute of Physics Inc. https://doi.org/10.1063/5.0113825

Singla, A., Singh, Y., Singh, Y., Rahim, E. A., Singh, N. K., & Sharma, A. (2023). Challenges and Future Prospects of Biofuel Generations: An Overview. In *Biowaste and Biomass in Biofuel Applications*. CRC Press. https://doi.org/10.1201/9781003265597-4

Širić, I., Alhag, S. K., Al-Shuraym, L. A., Mioč, B., Držaić, V., Abou Fayssal, S., Kumar, V., Singh, J., Kumar, P., Singh, R., Bachheti, R. K., Goala, M., Kumar, P., & Eid, E. M. (2023). Combined Use of TiO2 Nanoparticles and Biochar Produced from Moss (Leucobryum glaucum (Hedw.) Ångstr.) Biomass for Chinese Spinach (Amaranthus dubius L.) Cultivation under Saline Stress. *Horticulturae*, *9*(9). https://doi.org/10.3390/horticulturae9091056

Širić, I., Eid, E. M., Taher, M. A., El-Morsy, M. H. E., Osman, H. E. M., Kumar, P., Adelodun, B., Abou Fayssal, S., Mioč, B., Andabaka, Ž., Goala, M., Kumari, S., Bachheti, A., Choi, K. S., & Kumar, V. (2022). Combined Use of Spent Mushroom Substrate Biochar and PGPR Improves Growth, Yield, and Biochemical Response of Cauliflower (Brassica oleracea var. botrytis): A Preliminary Study on Greenhouse Cultivation. *Horticulturae*, *8*(9). https://doi.org/10.3390/horticulturae8090830

Srivastava, A., Hassan, M., & Gangwar, R. (2023). Improving Railway Track System Using Soil Nails for Heavy Axle Load. *Lecture Notes in Civil Engineering, 338 LNCE*, 1–13. https://doi.org/10.1007/978-981-99-1886-7_1

Suryavanshi, A., Tanwar, S., Kukreja, V., Choudhary, A., & Chamoli, S. (2023). An Integrated Approach to Potato Leaf Disease Detection Using Convolutional Neural Networks and Random Forest. *Proceedings of the 2023 International Conference on Innovative Computing, Intelligent Communication and Smart Electrical Systems, ICSES 2023*. https://doi.org/10.1109/ICSES60034.2023.10465557

Tiwari, K., Bafila, P., Negi, P., & Singh, R. (2023). The applications of nanotechnology in nutraceuticals: A review. In S. Y., S. G., & B. G.K. (Eds.), *AIP Conference Proceedings* (Vol. 2521). American Institute of Physics Inc. https://doi.org/10.1063/5.0129695

Tyagi, S., Jindal, T., Krishna, S. H., Hassen, S. M., Shukla, S. K., & Kaur, C. (2022). Comparative Analysis of Artificial Intelligence and its Powered Technologies Applications in the Finance Sector. *Proceedings of 5th International Conference on Contemporary Computing and Informatics, IC3I 2022*, 260–264. https://doi.org/10.1109/IC3I56241.2022.10073077

Usmani, Z., Sharma, M., Tripathi, M., Nizami, A. S., Gong, L., Nguyen, Q. D., Reddy, M. S., Thakur, V. K., & Gupta, V. K. (2023). Converting biowaste streams into energy–leveraging microwave assisted valorization technologies for enhanced conversion. *Journal of the Energy Institute, 107*. https://doi.org/10.1016/j.joei.2022.101161

Vennila, H., Giri, N. C., Nallapaneni, M. K., Sinha, P., Bajaj, M., Abou Houran, M., & Kamel, S. (2022). Static and dynamic environmental economic dispatch using tournament selection based ant lion optimization algorithm. *Frontiers in Energy Research, 10*. https://doi.org/10.3389/fenrg.2022.972069

Wongchai, A., Shukla, S. K., Ahmed, M. A., Sakthi, U., Jagdish, M., & kumar, R. (2022). Artificial intelligence - enabled soft sensor and internet of things for sustainable agriculture using ensemble deep learning architecture. *Computers and Electrical Engineering, 102*. https://doi.org/10.1016/j.compeleceng.2022.108128

Yadav, K., Chirade, S., Banerjee, M., Sharma, M., Ramya, N. S., Aravinda, K., & Alwan, A. A. (2023). Digital Dimensions: Unveiling the Potential of E-Design and Virtual Prototyping. In S. K.K. (Ed.), *E3S Web of Conferences* (Vol. 453). EDP Sciences. https://doi.org/10.1051/e3sconf/202345301031

Yadav, R., Ingole, S., Verma, R. P., Khan, I., Ramana Devi, K. V., Revathi, V., & Abbas, H. A. (2023). Eco-Revolution: Exploration on Advancing Remanufacturing for a Greener Future. In S. K.K. (Ed.), *E3S Web of Conferences* (Vol. 453). EDP Sciences. https://doi.org/10.1051/e3sconf/202345301027

10

The Exposure of Deepfake Technology on Social Media and its Effects on Society

Naveen Negi[1,2], Deepak Kaushal[2], Sargam Bahl Walia[1] and Saurabh Fulara[1]

[1]Graphic Era Hill University, Dehradun, India
[2]Graphic Era (deemed to be) University, Dehradun, India

Email: dipak.kaushal@gmail.com; naveennegi7895@gmail.com; bahl.sargam@gmail.com; saurabhfulara@gmail.com; dipak.kaushal@gmail.com

Abstract

Deepfake technology has been trendy recently and could be used to edit & generate images, audio, and even video clips. Its rapid proliferation on social media makes Deepfakes an exciting domain to explore in terms of its impact and growth on social media. This research will highlight validation methods of multimedia integrity and then pragmatic steps detecting if the image or video is modified along with deepfake effects on society. The study presents an exhaustive narrative review to investigate the spread of deepfake and its undermining effect on trust in digital content. As such, this study aims to increase what is known and understood about the impact of deepfake in social media while at the same time informing detection and policy-making moving forward as it shines a light on these vital arenas.

10.1 Introduction

A deepfake is a type of artificial intelligence used to generate forgery video, image, and audio that intend to mislead viewers. It works on algorithms like generator-discriminator to create fake things, known as deepfake! Using a deep neural network to produce that video would enable a deepfake version that delivers the same utterance and motions. Deepfakes can be used for disinformation and character assassination (Singh & Bhatnagar, 2023). The media credibility puzzle. Many researchers are studying the nuances of deepfakes and pursuing research in this regard. They also investigate approaches such as deep neural networks and forensic analysis to distinguish between real and fake content. The agenda is to generate automated tools that can detect deepfakes accurately on social media. Deepfake technology is a noteworthy and unsettling development in media manipulation that calls for more study, technological safeguards, and moral reflection to address the risks. Another research path involves comprehension of the collision of deepfakes on society, politics, and social media (Bhatnagar et al., 2023). Researchers are exploring the psychological and sociological effects of deepfake on public trust. Such studies help take practical steps to control the harm caused by deepfakes. An author describes a method for identifying deepfake videos using the Haar wavelet transform based on the Haar wavelet form. Deepfake, also known as Photoshop for videos, is a breed of intelligence technologies that can create very hyper-realistic-looking fake videos, pictures, or even audio in today's world. This includes the usage of deep learning which is, in general, a subset of machine learning. Though this might sound stunning, it has been a problem for society and has a highly negative impact on the population; spreading misinformation and fake news articles heavily affects public opinions and various societal decisions that must be taken in charge. Political manipulation through fake visuals and audio recordings is widespread to defame multiple political leaders and parties. The best example of this is the deepfake video of the Ukrainian president Volodymyr Oleksandrovych Zelenskyy that was circulated just three weeks after the start of the Ukraine and Russia war in which he was portrayed giving a message to the Ukrainian soldiers where they were told to drop down the weapons and return home leaving the battlefield which was later on labelled as a fake video (Bhatnagar et al., 2024). Although deepfakes are often openly misused, they are still a prominent option for doing sensible work for the people. Education is where historical figures and scripts can be brought to visuals and audio. Entertainment and media are also places where deepfakes have grown their roots deep into the business, where actors who are no longer between us can still be brought to life in films and shows with their exact voice-overs, visual graphics, etc. After carefully analysing the above factors, we can conclude that deepfake is a gift to human society. However, we must use it, whether we use it for society or against it, totally depends on our mentality and morals. Deepfake is a powerful tool for spreading false information, which causes challenges to society (Ningthoujam et al., 2021). It has become a challenge to differentiate between reality and fake media. Spreading misinformation can quickly gain reliability when portrayed as an authentic video or image, making it more believable to individuals. Deepfake content can manipulate public opinion. Even many celebrities have faced deepfake threats, where their deepfake video saying or doing things which they never did (Hernandez-Sánchez et al., 2021). These false portrayals are designed to harm their public image and societal divisions. Deepfake videos and pictures can quickly go viral on social media due to their scandalous nature, which helps to captivate audiences' attention. In today's times, through social media, the speed at which deepfakes can spread makes it challenging to contain the circulation of misinformation (Chemerys, 2023). As deepfake is becoming more realistic, it is difficult to differentiate between real and fake content. This makes it possible for deepfakes to propagate misinformation over extended periods without being noticed (Agarwal et al., 2021).

10.2 The Rise of Deepfake Cybercrime

Deepfakes have evolved from mere unfamiliarity to becoming a notable threat in the digital world (D. K. Sharma et al., 2021). These enlighten influenced artificial intelligence algorithms to develop realistic recordings, videos and images that look real but are fake (Kushwah, Nathani, et al., 2021). Deepfakes are used for spreading misinformation and even defaming someone (Arora & Gupta, 2022). In recent years, we have seen tremendous growth where malevolent actors exploit this technology for financial benefits (R. R. Sharma & Chawla, 2021). Disclosed deepfake manipulation is a challenge. With better advancements in AI algorithms and access to enormous data online, creating deepfakes has become much easier than before (Saxena et al., 2021). Many researchers and tech companies are continuously working towards developing techniques to identify deep fake videos and images by analysing facial expressions and movements to fight against deepfake cybercrime (Boccignone et al., 2022). As people become more aware of deepfake, governments worldwide are taking legal action and reconnoitre legislation related to the illegal creation of deepfake content in collaboration with tech companies to detect deepfake technology. Unquestionably, as technology continues to expand into unexplored areas, so do its negative aspects (Siddiqui & Kushwah, 2021). Cybercrime, for example, is fostered by potent instruments such as deepfake technology. However, experts are investigating, and with the help of research and development, imitative and collaborative efforts between government and tech companies are being made to decrease deepfakes (Dincer et al., 2023).

Moreover, raising awareness about deepfakes is particularly important, and education plays a crucial role in authorising individuals to acknowledge and evaluate misleading content online (Bhatia & Jain, 2021). It can be done by promoting media literacy and a culture of cynicism towards fake information sources; we can strengthen our society's resistance to the damaging effects of deepfake manipulation (Kushwah, Singh, et al., 2021). We can effectively address the growing threat posed by deepfakes in our digital environment if we continue to progress research, boost public awareness through campaigns, and collaborate across industries (Y. Li et al., 2018).

10.3 Several Techniques for Detecting Deepfakes

Forensic analysis: Analysing the image's content and videography for lack of consistency proposes manipulation. For example, investigating the consistency of facial expressions and shadows of the person helps to identify the disparity. Digital forensics experts use specialised tools to analyse the digital footprints left while manipulating deepfake media.

Detection algorithms: Recently, AI has seen tremendous growth in many applications, such as predictive analysis and face recognition (Nafees et al., 2021). Currently, there are two types of object detection algorithms, which consist of two major classes: one-stage and two-stage detection algorithms (Ali et al., 2020). These algorithms help extract features from the media, such as facial expressions and visual representation of the spectrum of frequencies, and they are used as input to predict the genuineness of the content (Tiwari et al., 2021).

Blockchain and watermarking: Many platforms use blockchain and watermarking to check the originality of fake videos and images. They have also been used to authenticate multi-server environments.

Body language and facial expression: It is difficult to copy natural facial expressions and body language, so analysing eye movement and facial expression can help identify deep fake videos. Using a facial action coding system, we can detect deep fake videos.

Audio-visual mismatch: If there is an imprecise lip sync, you can easily detect the deep fake by analysing the mouth movement to match the spoken words. Analysing the voice quality and modulation, such as robotic or background noise, can also help detect deep fake videos and images.

10.4 Psychological Impact of Deepfake

What is deepfake? Let us understand it with an example in laypeople's terms. There is a video that appears to show cricket star Virat Kohli fluently speaking nine different languages when he says one or two. Deepfake can easily alter perceptions, fabricate reality, and eventually ruin trust in auditory and visual evidence, influencing people's opinions.

Some impacts are as follows:

1. **Depletion of trust:** Deepfake twists and fabricates the line between fiction and reality, leading towards boundless trust in institutions, personal relationships, and media.
2. **Anxiety and paranoia:** Constant disclosure to deepfake can intensify paranoia and anxiety as individuals become hesitant towards the authenticity of the content they come across. Hence, prolonged exposure can profoundly affect our state to trust the information at hand, leaving us in severe disbelief and constant paranoia.
3. **Emotional distress:** When or if you are the victim of a certain deepfake that was sought to create and spread false information or defame someone, it can lead to emotional distress, humiliation, and damage to self-esteem.
4. **Reputation damage:** Deepfake can stain reputations by portraying individuals engaging in criminal and inappropriate behaviour, leading to image spoiling and criticism.
5. **Loss of agency:** Victims of deepfakes may lose control over their image and chronology, leading to feelings of inadequacy and vulnerability.

The psychological impact of deep fakes can be profound and vary briefly, posing significant challenges to an individual's mental health, societal trust, and the integrity of information. Our report makes it quite evident that deep fakes can cause emotional distress, undermine personal reputations, and contribute to a pervasive sense of insecurity by blurring the line between reality and fabricated evidence.

10.5 Social Media Platforms Designed to Create Deepfakes

TikTok: has built-in filters that allow individuals to create deepfake videos and images often used for entertainment. Users can use face-swapping filters and creatively alter different effects (Gautam et al., 2020).

Snapchat: Snapchat provides an interactive experience like the real world with computer-generated information, which helps to create deepfake videos like face swapping and face morphing. The agenda is to make a short entertainment video to cater to customers (Manocha & Sharma, 2020).

Reface: Reface is an application designed for creating deepfake videos. Users can swap faces in videos and even put their faces onto famous celebrities and movie scenes, which makes them more realistic (Goparaj & Sharma, 2020).

Wombo: Wombo is an application that lets users build lip-sync deepfakes or images that sing along to well-known tunes. Whenever users upload or snap a selfie, the software animates the face to lip-synch to selected music, producing amusing and frequently hilarious outcomes (V. Sharma, 2020).

Jiggy: Jiggy is an application for transforming still images into dancing films. This technique can produce results like deepfake photography by convincingly making the subject of the shot move. Users can upload pictures of themselves or other people to create amusing dance movies (Ningthoujam et al., 2020).

10.5.1 Deepfake phishing

Deepfake is the imitative images, video and audio developed using deep learning. Anyone can identify deepfake technology from Photoshop that can change or alter the background, and with the help of filters, it can make people younger or older and also morph faces (M. Li & Wan, 2023). The principles that social engineering attacks follow, similarly to deepfake phishing, follow the same: to manipulate users and utilise their trust. There are several ways to deepfake phishing. These include:

Electronic mail or messages: Deepfake generates business email compromise, and shares personalised messages with the user, which makes it more credible. Businesses lose millions of dollars to business email compromise attacks every year. For example, attackers can develop fake professional profiles of CEOs and use them to tempt employees.

Video calls: An attacker can use deep fake video calls through Google Meet and Zoom calls to convince users to share important information and confidential data like credentials and manipulate them to make unauthorised financial transactions.

Voice messages: Cloning someone's voice is straightforward. All you need is a three-second video clip. The difference between reality and deception is further blurred by the ability to employ these deep fakes to hold live conversations or leave voicemail messages for recipients.

10.6 Businesses Affected by Deepfake

According to (Zandt, 2024) the rise of technology-assisted in identifying fraud and the share of experts with the following experience on advanced methods of identifying fraud. Today, deepfakes create false statements by business leaders and people associated with a company. This can lead to notable reputational damage if deepfake goes viral. When deepfake videos come to notice of customers where company leaders are making offensive statements, it can lead to a loss of business. The chart below shows the percentage of fraud committed by deepfakes. A survey by Regula conducted among more than 1,000 fraud detection and prevention professionals from the US, UK, France, and Germany reveals that one of three advanced identity fraud techniques was used to target a significant portion of their companies. 46% experienced synthetic identity fraud, 37% reported seeing voice deepfake used, and only 29% of respondents said they had already encountered such fraud attempts, as shown in Figures 10.1–10.3.

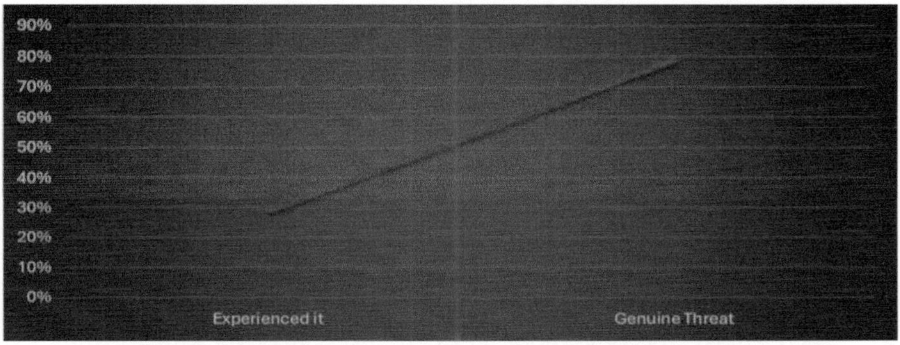

Figure 10.1 Synthetic identity fraud. Source: Complied by authors.

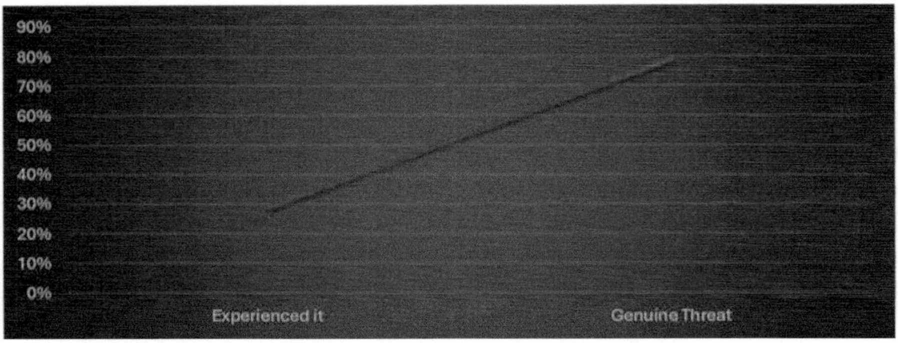

Figure 10.2 Voice deepfakes. Source: Complied by authors.

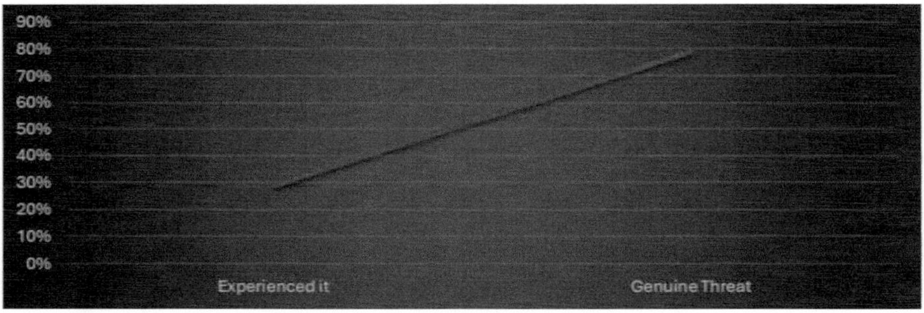

Figure 10.3 Video deepfakes. Source: Complied by authors.

10.7 Rise of Technology-Assisted In Identifying Fraud

- Deepfakes use artificial intelligence to create realistic fake videos, images, and recordings with important societal implications. The impact of deep fakes can be positive or negative on society, politics, and entertainment.
- Deepfakes can create fake news stories and headlines, which can mislead public opinion and influence elections. Even politicians and famous personalities can be targeted with deepfakes that show them doing and saying things that they never did, which harm their reputation.
- Deepfakes can be used to deceive people into disclosing sensitive information through sophisticated phishing attacks.
- As deepfakes become more prevalent, users may start mistrusting real media, leading to a broader cynicism towards all digital platforms.

- The film industry creates special effects or accurate animations to enhance storytelling and production capabilities.
- Deepfake is used artificial intelligence voices to assist in speech therapy

The deepfake threat is accurate, and it is the synthetic media in which a user in which someone replaces an individual video and image else. Deepfake is evolving fast and is an increasing threat to people and businesses.

- By reinforcing online platform guidelines, the issue of deep fakes can be reduced. This includes strict guidelines for individuals to verify content.
- By collaboration between tech companies, law enforcement and cybersecurity firms. By pooling resources and expertise, we can respond quickly to new dangers and encourage creative ways to counteract rapidly advancing technologies.
- Governments should allocate resources to research initiatives aimed at developing tools specifically designed for detecting and countering deep fakes effectively. This investment will help them stay ahead of cybercriminals who continually adapt their techniques.
- By allocating resources towards research initiatives to effectively develop tools for detecting deepfakes. This investment will help keep up with cybercriminals who are constantly changing their methods of deep faking.

10.8 Conclusion

Deepfake can create high-quality manipulative videos and images, making it difficult for viewers to distinguish between real and fake content. Nowadays, deepfake content is increasingly on social media platforms like Twitter, Facebook, and Instagram, which is spreading false information among people and creating false narratives. Deepfake can be used for financial fraud, which can hamper businesses and individuals. Today, it has become difficult for viewers to trust the actual content because of much misinformation circulating in society, which impacts the reputation of individuals and businesses, but with the help of various detection techniques like blockchain, watermarking and forensic analysis, it is easy to detect the threat. Deepfake technology is regularly evolving, and staying at the forefront of deepfake creation and detection is essential. Promoting deepfake education among people about the risks related to deepfake can reduce the threat of deepfake.

10.9 Acknowledgements

I would like to express my sincere gratitude to everyone who contributed to the successful completion of this project on "The Exposure of Deepfake Technology on Social Media and Society". Special thanks to my co-authors for their expert guidance and support throughout this research. I am also grateful to Graphic Era Deemed to be University Dehradun for providing the resources necessary to conduct this study. My heartfelt thanks go to the participants and colleagues whose insights and feedback helped shape this work. Lastly, I am deeply appreciative of my family and friends for their constant encouragement and support.

10.10 Declaration

The authors declare that the manuscript follows ethical standards and that there are no potential conflicts of interest regarding this chapter's research, authorship, and/or publication.

10.11 Disclaimer

The authors express the contents and views of this chapter in personal capacities. The editor and the publisher do not need to agree with these viewpoints and are not responsible for any duty of care.

References

Agarwal, S., Sharma, D. K., & Uniyal, A. S. (2021). Formulation & distribution of super primes. *Global and Stochastic Analysis*, *8*(2), 155–166.

Ali, S. S., Kaur, R., Ersöz, F., Altaf, B., Basu, A., & Weber, G.-W. (2020). Measuring carbon performance for sustainable green supply chain practices: a developing country scenario. *Central European Journal of Operations Research*, *28*(4), 1389–1416. https://doi.org/10.1007/s10100-020-00673-x

Arora, M., & Gupta, A. (2022). Impact of learning through live projects on sustainable employability generation: checking moderating role of education: an empirical study. *International Journal of Innovation and Sustainable Development*, *16*(2), 186–196. https://doi.org/10.1504/IJISD.2022.121783

Bhatia, P., & Jain, L. (2021). Lawful Sequence of Events and Cryptocurrency Anomalies: An Empirical Investigation. *FIIB Business Review*. https://doi.org/10.1177/23197145211042438

Bhatnagar, M., Rajaram, R., Taneja, S., & Kumar, P. (2024). Balancing acts: The Yin and Yang of debit and credit on the stage of financial well-being. In *Emerging Perspectives on Financial Well-Being*. IGI Global. https://doi.org/10.4018/979-8-3693-1750-1.ch002

Bhatnagar, M., Taneja, S., & Rupeika-Apoga, R. (2023). Demystifying the Effect of the News (Shocks) on Crypto Market Volatility. *Journal of Risk and Financial Management*, *16*(2), 136. https://doi.org/10.3390/jrfm16020136

Boccignone, G., Bursic, S., Cuculo, V., D'Amelio, A., Grossi, G., Lanzarotti, R., & Patania, S. (2022). DeepFakes Have No Heart: A Simple rPPG-Based Method to Reveal Fake Videos. In S. Sclaroff, C. Distante, M. Leo, G. M. Farinella, & F. Tombari (Eds.), *Image Analysis and Processing, ICIAP 2022, PT II* (Vol. 13232, pp. 186–195). Springer International Publishing AG. https://doi.org/10.1007/978-3-031-06430-2_16

Chemerys, H. Y. (2023). Truth & Trust in the Age of Deepfakes: Recognize & Overcome. Українські Студії в Європейському Контексті: Зб. Наук. Пр. Київ: ГО "Інноваційні Обрії України, *7*, 403–407.

Dincer, S., Ustubioglu, B., Tahaoglu, G., & Ulutas, G. (2023). Deep Fake Video Detection Based on Enhanced Capsule Network with Golden Ratio. *2023 31ST Signal Processing and Communications Applications Conference, SIU*. https://doi.org/10.1109/SIU59756.2023.10224003

Gautam, V., Basu, A., Basu, A., & Singh, T. (2020). Entrepreneurial attributes and intention among management students: A longitudinal approach to evolution and applicability of conceptual and empirical constructs. *Journal for International Business and Entrepreneurship Development*, *12*(2–3), 156–182. https://doi.org/10.1504/JIBED.2020.106189

Goparaj, H., & Sharma, R. R. (2020). A mare's nest: Broken promotion promise at combitech, india. *Journal of Organizational Behavior Education*, *13*, 61–62.

Hernandez-Sánchez, B. R., Sánchez-García, J. C., Sharma, R. R., & Moreira, A. C. (2021). Editorial: Women and Entrepreneurship. *Frontiers in Psychology*, *12*. https://doi.org/10.3389/fpsyg.2021.762028

Kushwah, S. V., Nathani, N., & Vigg, M. (2021). Impact of tax knowledge, tax penalties, and E-filing on tax compliance in India. *Indian Journal of Finance*, *15*(5–7), 61–74. https://doi.org/10.17010/ijf/2021/v15i5-7/164493

Kushwah, S. V., Singh, T., Vigg, M., & Singh, V. (2021). Role of entrepreneurship support in women empowerment: An empirical analysis. *Academy of Entrepreneurship Journal*, *27*(SpecialIssue 4), 1–5.

Li, M., & Wan, Y. (2023). Norms or fun? The influence of ethical concerns and perceived enjoyment on the regulation of deepfake information. *Internet Research*, *33*(5), 1750–1773. https://doi.org/10.1108/INTR-07-2022-0561

Li, Y., Chang, M. C., & Lyu, S. (2018). In Ictu Oculi: Exposing AI created fake videos by detecting eye blinking. *10th IEEE International Workshop on Information Forensics and Security, WIFS 2018*. https://doi.org/10.1109/WIFS.2018.8630787

Manocha, T., & Sharma, V. (2020). Study on the readiness among youth towards industry 4.0. *International Journal of Advanced Science and Technology*, *29*(3), 6324–6333.

Nafees, L., Mehdi, M., Gupta, R., Kalia, S., Banerjee, S., & Kapoor, S. (2021). Netflix in India: expanding to success. *Emerald Emerging Markets Case Studies*, *11*(2), 1–31. https://doi.org/10.1108/EEMCS-10-2019-0285

Ningthoujam, S., Bansal, V. M., Singh, T., Devi, O. H., Zafar, M., & Imran, M. (2021). Career Aspirations Among Youth in Manipur: Studying the Barriers to Aspiration in a Conflict Region. *Journal of Career Development*, *48*(5), 751–766. https://doi.org/10.1177/0894845319890923

Ningthoujam, S., Manna, R., Gautam, V., & Chauhan, S. (2020). Building customer engagement and brand loyalty through online social media: An exploratory study. *International Journal of Electronic Marketing and Retailing*, *11*(2), 143–160. https://doi.org/10.1504/IJEMR.2020.106846

Saxena, S., Agarwal, S., Kapoor, R., & Singh, B. K. (2021). Medical Consultation and Pandemic Investigation: Pertinence to Game Theory. *Global and Stochastic Analysis*, *8*(3 Special Issue), 167–185.

Sharma, D. K., Agarwal, S., & Uniyal, A. S. (2021). Distribution of Multi-Reverse Primes within the Given Interval & Their Application in Asymmetric Cryptographic Algorithm. *International Journal of Applied Engineering and Technology (London)*, *3*(1), 29–33.

Sharma, R. R., & Chawla, S. (2021). Gender equality & gender equity: Strategies for bridging the gender gap in the corporate world. In *Exploring Gender at Work: Multiple Perspectives*. Springer. https://doi.org/10.1007/978-3-030-64319-5_11

Sharma, V. (2020). IoT for crowd sensing and crowd sourcing. In *Internet of Things (IoT): Concepts and Applications*. Springer International Publishing. https://doi.org/10.1007/978-3-030-37468-6_15

Siddiqui, A. A., & Kushwah, S. V. (2021). Carbon emissions, economic growth and trade: Empirical evidence from trading nations. *International Journal of Technology Management and Sustainable Development*, *20*(1), 61–78. https://doi.org/10.1386/TMSD_00035_1

Singh, M., & Bhatnagar, M. (2023). Sustainability's Symphony: Orchestrating Talent Management for Creating Financial Impact. In *Sustainable Investments in Green Finance* (pp. 17–48). IGI Global. https://doi.org/10.4018/979-8-3693-1388-6.ch002

Tiwari, A., Sharma, R. R., & Sharma, T. (2021). A Case of Family Business Strategy of Expansion. *Global Business Review*. https://doi.org/10.1177/0972150921989667

11

The Impact of Deepfakes on Corporate Transparency: A Cross-disciplinary Study of Governance, Financial Reporting, and Marketing Communications

Nilesh P. Gokhale[1] and Vishwanathan Iyer[1]

[1]Sri Balaji University, India

Email: nilesh.gokhale@bitmpune.edu.in;
vishwanathan.iyer@biibpune.edu.in

Abstract

This study investigates the intricate relationships between corporate governance practices, deepfake technology usage, and corporate transparency through a cross-sectional quantitative analysis, revealing significant correlations and predictive power of governance and technology usage on transparency while highlighting the managerial implications of navigating the complexities of deepfake-induced misinformation, stakeholder trust, and regulatory compliance in contemporary corporate environments.

11.1 Introduction

As deepfake technologies exponentially evolve in sophistication, they engender a labyrinthine challenge for corporations (Parsola et al., 2019; Ram & Dohi, 2019; S. Sharma et al., 2019); they erode the foundational pillars of ethical governance, distort the accuracy of financial disclosures (Bansal et al., 2019; Joshi et al., 2019; Negi et al., 2019; Shalini & Naithani, 2019), and subverting the authenticity of marketing narratives, thereby precipitating a seismic recalibration of corporate accountability (Bhardwaj & Singh, 2019; Dev et al., 2018; Panchal et al., 2018; Y. K. Sharma, Mangla, & Patil, 2019), risk management strategies, and the very essence of stakeholder engagement (Luthra, Mangla, Venkatesh, et al., 2018; Malaviya et al., 2019; Ram & Davim, 2018b, 2018a; Ram & Goyal, 2018).

11.2 Important Definitions

- Corporate transparency, an intricate construct of organisational ethos, embodies the multifaceted obligation of corporations to meticulously disclose (Bhatti & Negi, 2018; Mangla et al., 2018; Singh et al., 2019), with unassailable clarity and veracity, their financial, operational, and governance-related information, thereby facilitating an unobstructed conduit of insight for stakeholders, regulators, and the broader public, while safeguarding against obfuscation, opacity, and malfeasance (Kumar et al., 2018; Y. K. Sharma et al., 2018; Y. K. Sharma, Mangla, Patil, et al., 2019; Sufi & Shojaie, 2018).
- Deepfake technology usage, a formidable and ethically contentious application of artificial intelligence, leverages advanced generative adversarial networks (GANs) to algorithmically synthesise hyper-realistic, yet fabricated audio-visual content that can seamlessly mimic authentic human expressions, voices, and appearances (Luthra, Venkatesh, Mangla, & Jakhar, 2017; Luthra, Garg, et al., 2018; Luthra, Mangla, Chan, et al., 2018; Mangla et al., 2017; Venkatesh et al., 2017), thereby posing profound implications for digital misinformation, corporate deception, and the erosion of trust across both public and private spheres (Ghosal et al., 2017; Luthra, Govindan, & Mangla, 2017; Luthra, Govindan, Kannan, et al., 2017; Luthra, Mangla, Kumar, Garg, et al., 2017; Pandey, Baliga, et al., 2017).
- Corporate governance practices, the quintessential framework of fiduciary protocols and strategic oversight, encompass a meticulously structured system of policies, controls, and ethical standards designed to ensure accountability, equitable decision-making, and transparency within corporate hierarchies while harmonising the interests of diverse stakeholders, mitigating agency conflicts, and safeguarding the long-term sustainability of the organisation against malfeasance and regulatory infractions (Nayak et al., 2016; Pandey, Negi, et al., 2017).

11.3 Literature Review

- The pervasive integration of deepfake technology within corporate communications fundamentally obfuscates the veracity of financial disclosures and public relations narratives, thereby engendering profound erosions in stakeholder trust and precipitating significant disruptions to organisational governance frameworks' perceived integrity and transparency.

- Robust corporate governance practices, encompassing stringent oversight mechanisms, ethical leadership, and comprehensive transparency protocols, serve as pivotal bulwarks against informational asymmetry, mitigating the opacity of corporate disclosures and fortifying the trustworthiness of financial reporting, thereby elevating the overall transparency and integrity of organisational operations within an increasingly scrutinised regulatory landscape (Gandhi et al., 2016; Luthra et al., 2016; Mangla et al., 2016).
- Corporate governance practices are instrumental in delineating the strategic contours of fiduciary responsibility, risk mitigation, and ethical stewardship. They safeguard the probity of organisational conduct and ensure adherence to regulatory mandates while preserving stakeholder confidence in corporate transparency and accountability (Ram & Goyal, 2016; C. Sharma & Jain, 2015; Verma et al., 2016).

11.4 Research Gap

The proposed research title fills a significant and unexplored research gap by addressing the confluence of rapidly advancing deepfake technology and its potential to obfuscate corporate disclosures, distort financial reporting, and erode stakeholder trust. These areas have largely been neglected in academic literature, particularly concerning the efficacy of corporate governance mechanisms in safeguarding organisational transparency and maintaining integrity across internal governance frameworks and external stakeholder communications within an increasingly digitised and vulnerable corporate ecosystem.

11.5 Research Methodology

The research methodology employed a quantitative cross-sectional design, leveraging descriptive statistics, Pearson correlations, multiple regression analysis, and collinearity diagnostics to examine the multifaceted relationships between corporate governance practices, deepfake technology usage, and corporate transparency, using a structured dataset of 213 respondents, thereby facilitating the rigorous identification of key predictors, variance explanations, and potential multicollinearity concerns through advanced statistical modelling and residual diagnostics.

Table 11.1 Descriptive statistics.

	Mean	Std. Deviation	N
Corporate_Transparency	3.7512	1.16111	213
Deepfake_Technology_Usage	3.6948	1.16790	213
Corporate_Governance_Practices	3.8357	1.14358	213

Source: Calculated by authors.

11.6 Data Analysis

- The descriptive statistics in Table 11.1 indicate that corporate governance practices (mean = 3.84) have the highest average score, followed by corporate transparency (mean = 3.75) and deepfake technology usage (mean = 3.69).
- All variables display similar levels of variability, as reflected by their standard deviations around 1.14 to 1.17 across a sample size of 213.

As per Table 11.2, the strong positive correlations between corporate transparency, deepfake technology usage, and corporate governance practices (ranging from 0.679 to 0.697, all significant at $p < 0.001$) suggest that in management contexts, effective governance and transparency are closely intertwined with how organisations navigate and respond to the challenges posed by deepfake technology.

The model explains 56.9% of the variance in Table 11.3 in corporate transparency ($R^2 = 0.569$), with both corporate governance practices and deepfake technology Usage being significant predictors ($p < 0.001$), indicating that these factors are crucial for enhancing transparency in organisational management.

The ANOVA results (Table 11.4) show that the model is statistically significant ($F (2, 210) = 138.568$, $p < 0.001$), indicating that corporate governance practices and deepfake technology usage together significantly explain variations in corporate transparency within the management context.

The negative correlation (Table 11.5) (–0.679) between corporate governance practices and deepfake technology usage indicates an inverse relationship. This suggests that as the emphasis on one increases, the reliance or use of the other decreases in the context of driving corporate transparency. This highlights a trade-off that management must balance effectively.

The collinearity diagnostics in Table 11.6 reveal a high condition index (10.350) for the third dimension, indicating potential multicollinearity between deepfake technology usage and corporate governance practices,

Table 11.2 Correlations.

		Corporate_ Transparency	Deepfake_ Technology_Usage	Corporate_ Governance_Practices
Pearson Correlation	Corporate_Transparency	1.000	0.685	0.697
	Deepfake_Technology_Usage	0.685	1.000	0.679
	Corporate_Governance_Practices	0.697	0.679	1.000
Sig. (1-tailed)	Corporate_Transparency	.	0.000	0.000
	Deepfake_Technology_Usage	0.000	.	0.000
	Corporate_Governance_Practices	0.000	0.000	.
N	Corporate_Transparency	213	213	213
	Deepfake_Technology_Usage	213	213	213
	Corporate_Governance_Practices	213	213	213

Source: Calculated by authors.

Table 11.3 Model summary.

					Change Statistics					
Model	R	R Square	Adjusted R Square	Std. Error of the Estimate	R Square Change	F Change	df1	df2	Sig. F Change	Durbin-Watson
1	0.754[a]	0.569	0.565	0.76598	0.569	138.568	2	210	0.000	1.726

a. Predictors: (Constant), Corporate_Governance_Practices, Deepfake_Technology_Usage
b. Dependent Variable: Corporate_Transparency
Source: Calculated by authors.

Table 11.4 ANOVA.

Model		Sum of Squares	df	Mean Square	F	Sig.
1	Regression	162.601	2	81.301	138.568	0.000[b]
	Residual	123.211	210	0.587		
	Total	285.812	212			

a. Dependent Variable: Corporate_Transparency
b. Predictors: (Constant), Corporate_Governance_Practices, Deepfake_Technology_Usage
Source: Calculated by authors.

Table 11.5 Coefficient correlations.

Model			Corporate_ Governance_ Practices	Deepfake_ Technology_ Usage
1	Correlations	Corporate_Governance_Practices	1.000	–0.679
		Deepfake_Technology_Usage	–0.679	1.000
	Covariances	Corporate_Governance_Practices	0.004	–0.003
		Deepfake_Technology_Usage	–0.003	0.004

a. Dependent Variable: Corporate_Transparency
Source: Calculated by authors.

Table 11.6 Collinearity diagnostics.

				Variance Proportions		
Model	Dimension	Eigenvalue	Condition Index	(Constant)	Deepfake_ Technology_ Usage	Corporate_ Governance_ Practices
1	1	2.923	1.000	0.01	0.01	0.01
	2	0.050	7.673	0.96	0.24	0.09
	3	0.027	10.350	0.03	0.76	0.91

a. Dependent Variable: Corporate_Transparency
Source: Calculated by authors.

which management should monitor to ensure that the model's predictors do not redundantly explain corporate transparency.

The case-wise diagnostics highlight significant outliers (Table 11.7), with large negative residuals (e.g., Case 205: –2.82). These suggest that certain observations substantially deviate from the model's predicted corporate transparency values, indicating areas where management practices may require closer examination or adjustments to align with expectations.

Table 11.7 Casewise diagnostics.

Case Number	Std. Residual	Corporate_ Transparency	Predicted Value	Residual
187	–3.107	2.00	4.3798	–2.37980
198	–3.206	1.00	3.4558	–2.45581
205	–3.678	2.00	4.8176	–2.81762

a. Dependent Variable: Corporate_Transparency
Source: Calculated by authors.

Table 11.8 Residuals statistics.

	Minimum	Maximum	Mean	Std. Deviation	N
Predicted Value	1.4601	6.0344	3.7512	0.87578	213
Residual	–2.81762	2.27906	0.00000	0.76235	213
Std. Predicted Value	–2.616	2.607	0.000	1.000	213
Std. Residual	–3.678	2.975	0.000	0.995	213

a. Dependent Variable: Corporate_Transparency
Source: Calculated by authors.

The residuals statistics show a well-centred model (Table 11.8) with a mean residual of 0. However, the wide range of residuals (–2.82 to 2.28) and standardised residuals (–3.68 to 2.98) indicate that some predictions for corporate transparency deviate considerably, signalling management should address potential inconsistencies or underlying factors not captured by the model.

11.7 Managerial Implications

The managerial implications of this study underscore the imperative for corporate leaders to meticulously integrate robust governance frameworks and adaptive strategies in response to the emergent risks posed by deepfake technology, fostering an ecosystem of heightened transparency, bolstered stakeholder trust, and resilient operational oversight, while concurrently mitigating the adverse impacts of misinformation and ensuring alignment with evolving regulatory and ethical standards.

11.8 Conclusion

In summation, the intricate interdependencies elucidated between corporate governance practices, deepfake technology usage, and corporate transparency highlight a complex paradigm wherein the meticulous orchestration of governance frameworks, strategic technological oversight, and enhanced transparency mechanisms is paramount for mitigating the pernicious effects of deepfake-induced misinformation, ensuring regulatory compliance, and sustaining stakeholder confidence in an increasingly digitised and ethically volatile corporate landscape.

References

Bansal, G., Singh, D. B., Virk, H. S., Devrani, A., & Bhandari, A. (2019). Microstructural characterisation, applications and process study of various additive manufacturing process: A review. In S. S.K., A. E.T., K. K., D. J.P., & S. K.K. (Eds.), *Materials Today: Proceedings* (Vol. 26, pp. 833–837). Elsevier Ltd. https://doi.org/10.1016/j.matpr.2020.01.048

Bhardwaj, A., & Singh, D. P. (2019). An efficient algorithm to minimise EVM over ZigBee. *Advances in Intelligent Systems and Computing*, *742*, 217–221. https://doi.org/10.1007/978-981-13-0589-4_20

Bhatti, K. K., & Negi, A. (2018). Green store attributes and infrastructure: A connecting link between retailers and consumers to bring sustainability. *International Journal of Civil Engineering and Technology*, *9*(11), 190–198.

Dev, A., Jha, P. K., & Parkash, V. (2018). Effect of Automation on GRR in Tactile Measurement. *Mapan - Journal of Metrology Society of India*, *33*(4), 449–458. https://doi.org/10.1007/s12647-018-0269-1

Gandhi, S., Mangla, S. K., Kumar, P., & Kumar, D. (2016). A combined approach using AHP and DEMATEL for evaluating success factors in the implementation of green supply chain management in Indian manufacturing industries. *International Journal of Logistics Research and Applications*, *19*(6), 537–561. https://doi.org/10.1080/13675567.2016.1164126

Ghosal, A., Manna, A., & Patil, P. (2017). Optimization process during laser machining of 2 mm thick Al/Al2O3 MMC. *Materials Science Forum, 900 MSF*, 121–126. https://doi.org/10.4028/www.scientific.net/MSF.900.121

Joshi, A., Sharma, A., Bachheti, R. K., Husen, A., & Mishra, V. K. (2019). Plant-Mediated Synthesis of Copper Oxide Nanoparticles and Their Biological Applications. In *Nanomaterials and Plant Potential*. Springer International Publishing. https://doi.org/10.1007/978-3-030-05569-1_8

Kumar, S., Luthra, S., Haleem, A., Garg, D., Singh, S., & Mangla, S. (2018). An integrated approach to analyse requisites of product innovation management. *International Journal of Business Innovation and Research*, *16*(1), 36–62. https://doi.org/10.1504/IJBIR.2018.091081

Luthra, S., Garg, D., Mangla, S. K., & Singh Berwal, Y. P. (2018). Analyzing challenges to Internet of Things (IoT) adoption and diffusion: An Indian context. In S. A.K. & J. J. (Eds.), *Procedia Computer Science* (Vol. 125, pp. 733–739). Elsevier B.V. https://doi.org/10.1016/j.procs.2017.12.094

Luthra, S., Govindan, K., Kannan, D., Mangla, S. K., & Garg, C. P. (2017). An integrated framework for sustainable supplier selection and evaluation in supply chains. *Journal of Cleaner Production*, *140*, 1686–1698. https://doi.org/10.1016/j.jclepro.2016.09.078

Luthra, S., Govindan, K., & Mangla, S. K. (2017). Structural model for sustainable consumption and production adoption—A grey-DEMATEL based approach. *Resources, Conservation and Recycling*, *125*, 198–207. https://doi.org/10.1016/j.resconrec.2017.02.018

Luthra, S., Mangla, S. K., Chan, F. T. S., & Venkatesh, V. G. (2018). Evaluating the Drivers to Information and Communication Technology for Effective Sustainability Initiatives in Supply Chains. *International Journal of Information Technology and Decision Making*, *17*(1), 311–338. https://doi.org/10.1142/S0219622017500419

Luthra, S., Mangla, S. K., Kumar, S., Garg, D., & Haleem, A. (2017). Identify and prioritise the critical factors in implementing the reverse logistics practices: A case of Indian auto component manufacturer. *International Journal of Business and Systems Research*, *11*(1–2), 42–61. https://doi.org/10.1504/IJBSR.2017.080834

Luthra, S., Mangla, S. K., Venkatesh, V. G., & Jakhar, S. K. (2018). Management of risks in sustainable supply chain using AHP and monte carlo simulation. In *Global Business Expansion: Concepts, Methodologies, Tools, and Appl.* IGI Global. https://doi.org/10.4018/978-1-5225-5481-3.ch075

Luthra, S., Mangla, S. K., Xu, L., & Diabat, A. (2016). Using AHP to evaluate barriers in adopting sustainable consumption and production initiatives in a supply chain. *International Journal of Production Economics*, *181*, 342–349. https://doi.org/10.1016/j.ijpe.2016.04.001

Luthra, S., Venkatesh, V. G., Mangla, S. K., & Jakhar, S. K. (2017). Management of risks in sustainable supply chain using AHP and Monte Carlo simulation. In *Managerial Strategies for Business Sustainability During Turbulent Times*. IGI Global. https://doi.org/10.4018/978-1-5225-2716-9.ch004

Malaviya, P., Sharma, R., & Sharma, P. K. (2019). Rain gardens as stormwater management tool. In *Sustainable Green Technologies for Environmental Management*. Springer Singapore. https://doi.org/10.1007/978-981-13-2772-8_7

Mangla, S. K., Govindan, K., & Luthra, S. (2016). Critical success factors for reverse logistics in Indian industries: A structural model. *Journal of Cleaner Production*, *129*, 608–621. https://doi.org/10.1016/j.jclepro.2016.03.124

Mangla, S. K., Govindan, K., & Luthra, S. (2017). Prioritizing the barriers to achieve sustainable consumption and production trends in supply chains using fuzzy Analytical Hierarchy Process. *Journal of Cleaner Production*, *151*, 509–525. https://doi.org/10.1016/j.jclepro.2017.02.099

Mangla, S. K., Luthra, S., Mishra, N., Singh, A., Rana, N. P., Dora, M., & Dwivedi, Y. (2018). Barriers to effective circular supply chain management in a developing country context. *Production Planning and Control*, *29*(6), 551–569. https://doi.org/10.1080/09537287.2018.1449265

Nayak, A., Bhushan, B., Gupta, V., & Rodriguez-Turienzo, L. (2016). Development of a green and sustainable clean up system from grape pomace for heavy metal remediation. *Journal of Environmental Chemical Engineering*, *4*(4), 4342–4353. https://doi.org/10.1016/j.jece.2016.10.001

Negi, P. K., Ram, M., & Yadav, O. P. (2019). Basics of CNC programming. In *Basics of CNC Programming*. River Publishers.

Panchal, D., Mangla, S. K., Tyagi, M., & Ram, M. (2018). Risk analysis for clean and sustainable production in a urea fertilizer industry. *International Journal of Quality and Reliability Management*, *35*(7), 1459–1476. https://doi.org/10.1108/IJQRM-03-2017-0038

Pandey, Y., Baliga, A. K., Srishti, Negi, S., & Kumar, B. (2017). Performance analysis of dual gate-OTFT with variation in OSC thickness and channel length. In S. A., S. M., A. P.N., & S. V. (Eds.), *Proceeding - IEEE International Conference on Computing, Communication and Automation, ICCCA 2016* (pp. 1521–1526). Institute of Electrical and Electronics Engineers Inc. https://doi.org/10.1109/CCAA.2016.7813964

Pandey, Y., Negi, S., Srishti, Baliga, A. K., & Kumar, B. (2017). Dual gate organic inverter circuit behavior analysis based on diode load logic configuration. *Advances in Intelligent Systems and Computing*, *479*, 1027–1033. https://doi.org/10.1007/978-981-10-1708-7_121

Parsola, J., Gangodkar, D., & Mittal, A. (2019). Mobile Application for Storage and Retrieval of e-learning videos Using Hadoop. *Proceedings of the 4th International Conference on Communication and*

Electronics Systems, ICCES 2019, 757–762. https://doi.org/10.1109/ICCES45898.2019.9002272

Ram, M., & Davim, J. P. (2018a). Advanced applications in manufacturing enginering. In *Advanced Applications in Manufacturing Engineering*. Elsevier. https://doi.org/10.1016/C2017-0-00582-7

Ram, M., & Davim, J. P. (2018b). Advanced mathematical techniques in science and engineering. In *Advanced Mathematical Techniques in Science and Engineering*. River Publishers.

Ram, M., & Dohi, T. (2019). Advances in applied mathematical analysis and applications. In *Advances in Applied Mathematical Analysis and Applications*. River Publishers.

Ram, M., & Goyal, N. (2016). Automated teller machine network inspection under stochastic modelling. *Journal of Engineering Science and Technology Review*, *9*(5), 1–8. https://doi.org/10.25103/jestr.095.01

Ram, M., & Goyal, N. (2018). Stochastic Design Exploration with Rework of Flexible Manufacturing System under Copula-Coverage Approach. *International Journal of Reliability, Quality and Safety Engineering*, *25*(2). https://doi.org/10.1142/S0218539318500079

Shalini, & Naithani, P. (2019). Adsorption of heavy metals using mixture of waste products. *Asian Journal of Chemistry*, *31*(5), 1009–1012. https://doi.org/10.14233/ajchem.2019.21783

Sharma, C., & Jain, A. (2015). PV Based Green Computing System for ICT Sustainable Development. *Proceedings - 2015 2nd IEEE International Conference on Advances in Computing and Communication Engineering, ICACCE 2015*, 240–244. https://doi.org/10.1109/ICACCE.2015.40

Sharma, S., Ghanshala, K. K., & Mohan, S. (2019). Blockchain-based internet of vehicles (IoV): An efficient secure ad hoc vehicular networking architecture. *IEEE 5G World Forum, 5GWF 2019 - Conference Proceedings*, 452–457. https://doi.org/10.1109/5GWF.2019.8911664

Sharma, Y. K., Mangla, S. K., & Patil, P. P. (2019). Analyzing Challenges to Transportation for Successful Sustainable Food Supply Chain Management Implementation in Indian Dairy Industry. *Lecture Notes in Networks and Systems*, *40*, 409–418. https://doi.org/10.1007/978-981-13-0586-3_41

Sharma, Y. K., Mangla, S. K., Patil, P. P., & Liu, S. (2019). When challenges impede the process: For circular economy-driven sustainability practices in food supply chain. *Management Decision*, *57*(4), 995–1017. https://doi.org/10.1108/MD-09-2018-1056

Sharma, Y. K., Yadav, A. K., Mangla, S. K., & Patil, P. P. (2018). Ranking the Success Factors to Improve Safety and Security in Sustainable Food Supply Chain Management Using Fuzzy AHP. In X. M.A., Y. P.K.D.V., J. P., & J. J. (Eds.), *Materials Today: Proceedings* (Vol. 5, Issue 5, pp. 12187–12196). Elsevier Ltd. https://doi.org/10.1016/j.matpr.2018.02.196

Singh, R. K., Luthra, S., Mangla, S. K., & Uniyal, S. (2019). Applications of information and communication technology for sustainable growth of SMEs in India food industry. *Resources, Conservation and Recycling*, *147*, 10–18. https://doi.org/10.1016/j.resconrec.2019.04.014

Sufi, T., & Shojaie, N. (2018). A hotel classification framework for quality service. *Bridging Tourism Theory and Practice*, *9*, 229–244. https://doi.org/10.1108/S2042-144320180000009016

Venkatesh, V. G., Zhang, A., Luthra, S., Dubey, R., Subramanian, N., & Mangla, S. (2017). Barriers to coastal shipping development: An Indian perspective. *Transportation Research Part D: Transport and Environment*, *52*, 362–378. https://doi.org/10.1016/j.trd.2017.03.016

Verma, P., Patel, N., Nair, N.-K. C., & Sikander, A. (2016). Design of PID controller using cuckoo search algorithm for buck-boost converter of LED driver circuit. *2016 IEEE 2nd Annual Southern Power Electronics Conference, SPEC 2016*. https://doi.org/10.1109/SPEC.2016.7846102

12

The Impact of Deepfake Technology on Public Trust in Economic Policies

Pragti Dixit[1], Manjeet Kaur[2] and Larisa Mistrean[3]

[1]University School of Business, Chandigarh University, India
[2]School of Management Studies and Commerce, RIMT University, Mandi Gobindgarh, India
[3]Academy of Economic Studies of Moldova, Moldova

Email: pragatidixit.pd@gmail.com; India.manjeet16oct@gmail.com; mistrean_larisa@ase.md

Abstract

Deepfake technology has emerged as one of the most controversial tools of the present generation. Deepfakes use artificial intelligence to produce convincingly manipulated audio and visual material. They may be used as a weapon to fabricate images of decision-makers, spreading false information and undermining public trust in government economic policies. Against this backdrop, the present study has tried to investigate the impact of deepfake technology on public trust in economic policies. The study uses primary data collected from people residing in the New Delhi region of India. The study's findings reveal that public trust in economic policies decreases due to exposure to deepfake technology and increases due to media literacy and trust in credible sources. The study suggests that the government must take appropriate steps and concerned agencies to curb the derogatory effects of deepfake technology. Alongside this, there must be increased media literacy and the number of credible sources of information in the country.

12.1 Introduction

In recent years, deepfake technology has arisen as one of the most captivating yet controversial advancements in artificial intelligence and machine learning (Gupta et al., 2015, 2015; D. Kumar et al., 2015; Mamgain et al., 2014). The expression "deepfake" is a combination of "deep learning" and "fake", mirroring its establishment in a sophisticated AI algorithm that can make exceptionally realistic yet completely made-up sound, video, and picture content. By utilising deep learning techniques and incredibly generative adversarial networks (GANs), deepfake technology can superimpose one individual's similarity onto another's body, control speech to make forged audio, and even produce hyper-realistic synthetic images from scratch. Deepfake technology, powered by advanced artificial intelligence, has swiftly evolved to create hyper-realistic virtual audio, video, and photos forgeries. While often seen through a cynical lens because of its potential for misuse, deepfake technology offers numerous advantages (Goyal et al., 2014; M. Pant et al., 2014).

Creative content in films, TV and advertising can be created through deepfake technology. The technology allows for bringing historical figures back to life, placing actors' faces onto stunt duplicates and creating new scenes without reshooting (Dwivedi, Gairola, et al., 2013; Goswami et al., 2013; Tyagi et al., 2013). In animated films, computer games, and other media where character continuity is indispensable, technology can replicate voices and generate computerised adaptations of characters. Technology can also generate important people to give interviews and talks, providing enriching educational experiences (Agrawal et al., 2011; Govind et al., 2012; M. Sharma & Joshi, 2012).

Deepfake can be used as a tool for patients to communicate with the computerised representations of their lost ones or rehearse specific social situations for therapeutic reasons. The technology simulates real patient encounters and clinical cases, allowing students and physicians to gain first-hand experience in controlled settings. Deepfake technology can restore and preserve old films (Anzaar, Shahnawaz, Mukesh, Gupta, & Gowri, 2010; Anzaar, Shahnawaz, Mukesh, Gupta, Gowri, et al., 2010; Khanna & Arora, 2009), photographs, and audio recordings so that future generations can enjoy cultural and unique treasures in their original quality. Computer-generated aliases of artists, items, and historical characters can enhance museum displays and make them more appealing and accessible to the global community (Dutta et al., 2023; Grover et al., 2024; Kumari et al., 2024).

The pros, however, do not work independently of the cons. Since deepfakes can create believable but fake videos and audio of politicians, fake news and misinformation can be spread using deepfake technology (Mishra et al., 2024; P. Singh & Singh, 2023; Srivastava et al., 2024). This can defame, change perception, and even tilt the balance in the political race. Based on the recent advances in deepfakes, the public may lose faith in online content. Individuals are likely to doubt the authenticity of legit content, thereby reversing the credibility of news agencies and influencers (Belwal & Belwal, 2017; Gangwar & Srivastva, 2020; Indu et al., 2023).

Deepfake technology can be used for the creation of unofficial videos and audio recordings of a person, causing theft of identity and violation of privacy rights (Ajay et al., 2023; Padhi et al., 2024; Shrivastava et al., 2023). The technology can also be leveraged in life to replicate a person's presence in video calls, voice calls, and other forms of electronic communication, which is causing significant cybersecurity threats to organisations and individuals. Addressing the misuse of deepfakes requires considering viable legal frameworks, which are pretty complex (Aiyappa et al., 2024; Arora et al., 2024; Khandelwal et al., 2023). Balancing the protection of individuals and society against the preservation of free speech and freedom of expression in creative work offers several problems for governing bodies (A. K. Singh et al., 2024; K. U. Singh et al., 2024; Zhang et al., 2023).

Deepfakes lead to the erosion of public trust in economic policies. Deepfakes have the capability of generating videos of economic figures like the governors of the central banks or the ministers of finance, where they are seen and heard saying things they never said, which can lead to panic among the public (Pandey et al., 2023; Tripathi & Mohan, 2016) Due to fake policy announcements, financial markets can experience unnecessary fluctuations. Deepfake videos or audio clips may present economic leaders in a bad light or compromising situations, discrediting the leaders, even if the information is fake. Deepfakes are improving continuously, making it challenging for the public to differentiate between real and fake news. This has resulted in the public's negative attitude towards the media, even if it is a vital source of information on the government's economic policies.

The consequences of deepfake technology are vast and manifold. The technology that has breathed new life into entertainment and creative industries is also responsible for creating counterfeit recordings and audio clips, raising worries about misinformation, security infringement, and the potential for new types of cybercrime and political manipulations. Public trust in economic policies has deteriorated due to the spreading of false and misleading information. Keeping this in mind, the present chapter explores deepfake technology's impact on public trust in economic policies.

The rest of the chapter is organised as follows: Section 2 comprises a Literature Review encompassing the erosion of public trust in economic policies because of deepfake technology. Section 3 covers the research gaps. Section 4 includes the Research Methodology used in the present chapter. Section 5 covers Data Analysis, and Section 6 includes Managerial Implications. Section 7 incorporates a Conclusion followed by References.

12.2 Literature Review

Deepfake technology has raised a serious concern about the reliability of information within today's society. Deepfakes, derived from artificial intelligence (AI), create incredibly realistic albeit fake sound and video clips and have raised a serious concern for politics, media, and economics. Drawing from the literature, this section analyses the impact of deepfake technology. It discusses how it erodes trust in economic policies by exploring the prospects, shortcomings and solutions presented in the literature.

12.2.1 Creation and detection of deepfakes

Deepfake technology uses AI techniques, specifically deep learning and GANs, to produce realistic synthetic media. A detailed overview of threats in this area has been provided by researchers, pinpointing it as a rapidly evolving problem due to the availability of tools for creating high-quality fake content (Godbole et al., 2021; Painuli et al., 2022). This has led to using deepfakes in malicious matters, such as misinformation and swaying people's opinions. For instance, researchers explained how GANs can deliver fake images and videos through a framework that pits two neural networks against each other while making continuous improvements (Kamal et al., 2022). In recent times, deepfake creation processes have become so realistic that it has become challenging for a non-professional to distinguish deepfakes from original media sources and requires expert assistance in these matters (Rakhra et al., 2022).

Researchers studied the creation and recognition of deepfakes, detailing the technical complexity of such manipulations. They draw attention to the arms race between deepfake generation and detection methods, with new methods being developed to better the genuineness of fakes as the detectors attempt to refine themselves to detect the continually improving deepfakes (Pargaien et al., 2021). Previous studies introduced FaceForensics++, a significant advancement in detecting orchestrated face images essential for deepfakes detection. Their work emphasises the need for solid detection schemes that would help to mitigate the impact of deepfakes on public trust. Some of the modern techniques and challenges in deepfake detection are described by previous studies (Juyal & Sharma, 2021). They highlight that while necessary technical advancements have been made, the dynamic characteristics of deepfake algorithms make their detection more challenging (Adhikari et al., 2021).

12.2.2 Economic impacts and policy responses

Deepfakes have the potential to significantly undermine public trust, notably within economic policies and communications. As per previous studies, deepfakes can diminish trust in public figures and institutions by disseminating misinformation and creating confusion. When utilised in economic contexts, deepfakes could distort public perceptions of vital economic data, statements from financial authorities, or even international economic agreements (M. Pant & Thakur, 2021). Deepfakes can impact economic trust through various mechanisms. Deepfakes can generate fabricated speeches or interviews involving policymakers, wrongly attributing statements that could trigger market turbulence or excitement (Y. K. Sharma et al., 2020).

The mere existence of deepfake technology can cast doubt on authentic communications from economic leaders, potentially fostering scepticism. Previous studies highlight the emergence of a "liar's dividend" effect that can impede the public's ability to trust genuine messages. Deepfakes can be wielded as tools in political campaigns to smear opponents or fabricate endorsements, consequently impacting economic policies by swaying election results and shaping public sentiment towards economic agendas (Semwal et al., 2020).

Numerous incidents underscore the significant risks associated with deep fakes within the economic sector. For instance, a deepfake video featuring a CEO disseminating false financial data could trigger stock price manipulation, as examined by previous studies. Additionally, using deep fakes to propagate misinformation regarding economic crises has been scrutinised in terms of financial stability and investor trust (J. Pant et al., 2021). Previous studies analyse the possible effects of deepfake videos and recordings on financial markets, highlighting the dangers associated with market manipulation through misleading information. They stress the requirement for regulatory oversight to forestall deepfakes from impairing financial systems (A. Sharma et al., 2020).

Researchers scrutinise the risks deepfakes present to economic policy and recommend mitigation strategies. He highlights the significance of worldwide cooperation and the growth of technological shields to safeguard economic stability (Rawat, Singh, Ray, Szabó, et al., 2020). Previous studies discuss the ramifications of deepfake technology on public safety and economic stability. They contend deepfakes can subvert public trust in economic policies, prompting broader uncertainty. Previous studies outline the applications and regulatory responses of deepfake technology. They call for extensive legal frameworks to address the complex challenges presented by deepfakes (Debasis et al., 2020). Researches conducted earlier concentrate on the governance of deepfakes in worldwide security, proposing measures to deal with the risks related to deepfakes in international settings (N. Singh et al., 2020).

12.2.3 Psychological and societal impacts

The psychological and societal impacts of deepfakes are no less. Previous studies analysed the psychological effect of exposure to deepfakes, discovering that manipulated videos significantly influence public trust. The study demonstrates that deepfakes can change perceptions and lessen trust in media credibility, leading to broader societal distrust (Rawat, Singh, Ray, & Szabo, 2020). Researchers investigate public awareness of deepfake technology, discovering a general absence of awareness yet a high potential for doubt once individuals are educated about the capabilities of deepfakes (Shakya et al., 2018). This highlights the need for public education on the risks associated with deepfakes. Researchers discuss how deepfakes and misinformation impact public opinion and policy. They contend deepfakes can shape political talks and economic decisions, leading to critical societal consequences (P. Kumar et al., 2018).

12.2.4 Threat assessment and legal considerations

The fast-paced evolution of deepfake technology is presenting significant obstacles for both detection and counteraction. Previous studies discuss the difficulties in determining the genuineness of video evidence in the age of deepfakes. They stress the legal and forensic hardships presented by deepfakes, which entangle the verification process and possibly subvert the validity of authentic video evidence (Mangla et al., 2019). Research offers a grounded threat evaluation of deepfakes, specifying their capability to disrupt various sectors, including politics and finance. He outlines the significance of understanding deepfakes' socio-political ramifications to foster successful countermeasures (Y. K. Sharma et al., 2018). Previous Studies investigate the legal and ethical considerations of deepfake technology. They advocate for advancing regulatory frameworks to address the abuse of deepfakes and safeguard individuals and establishments from their harmful effects (Joshi et al., 2016).

Like previous studies, current detection strategies hinge on detecting disparities in visual and audio data. However, these techniques must continuously progress to keep up with the increasing realism of deepfakes. Furthermore, there is a surging demand for public awareness campaigns and educational initiatives to empower individuals to identify and critically assess potential deepfakes (Dwivedi, Parshav, et al., 2013; Nijhawan & Jain, 2018; Suravajhala et al., 2018). Governments and international organisations have begun to respond to the severe threat of fraud through legal and regulatory measures. The EU General Data Protection Regulation (GDPR) and similar laws in other jurisdictions have been amended to include provisions prohibiting the use of artificial intelligence. The policy's recommendations also highlight the need for international cooperation in monitoring and combating fraud, as well as the development of ethical codes regarding the nature of intelligence and media (Mehta et al., 2023).

Deepfake technology presents a massive threat to public trust and economic policies. The rapid advancement of deepfake creation techniques challenges existing detection and alleviation efforts, requiring constant innovation and regulatory transformation.

12.3 Research Gaps

Amidst an expanding body of literature exploring the intricate dynamics of public trust in economic policies, a conspicuous research void endures in rigorously examining the compounded effects of exposure to deepfake technology, source credibility, and media literacy as interdependent variables, where the intricate interplay between digital manipulation, perceived reliability of information sources, and the moderating role of media literacy in shaping public trust remains insufficiently theorised and empirically substantiated.

12.4 Research Methodology

The present study uses primary data to examine the impact of deepfake technology on public trust in economic policies. The goal is to investigate how exposure to deepfake technology affects people's trust in economic policies while taking media literacy and trust in credible sources into account.

To achieve this purpose, a Google Form was designed to collect data. The form was pre-tested with a small group of individuals to ensure the questions were pertinent and easy to understand. Feedback was incorporated into the questionnaire's revisions. The Google Form comprised five sections: Profile of the Respondent, Public Trust in Economic Policies, Exposure to Deepfake Technology, Media Literacy and Trust in Credible Sources. Section I comprised the Profile of the Respondents. Section II comprised seven statements about Public Trust in Economic Policies. Section III consisted of six statements related to Exposure to Deepfake Technology. Section IV included six statements on Media Literacy, and Section V encompassed 7 statements dealing with Trust in Credible Sources. The statements in all four sections were measured on a scale of 1 to 5 (Five-point et al.), where one indicated strong disagreement with the statement and five indicated strong agreement. The scores of various statements for each section were averaged out to obtain a unique score for each section, i.e., Public Trust in Economic Policies, Exposure to Deepfake Technology, Media Literacy and Trust on Credible Sources.

The survey's target population was people residing in the New Delhi region of India. The Google Form was disseminated to 500 individuals through various platforms like e-mail, social media, and messaging applications to reach potential respondents in the New Delhi region. Two weeks were allotted for data collection to provide enough time to the participants. Out of 500 individuals, 128 responded, yielding a response rate of 25.6 per cent.

Descriptive statistics (mean, standard deviation, skewness, and kurtosis) were obtained for a unique score for each section. Pearson correlation coefficients were calculated to identify the direction and degree of relationship among unique scores of each section. Multiple regression analysis was employed to compute the impact of exposure to deepfake technology, media literacy and trust in credible sources on public trust in economic policies by using the equation no. 1:

$$Y_i = \alpha + \beta_1 X_{1i} + \beta_2 X_{2i} + \dots\dots\dots\dots + \beta_k X_{ki} \quad (1)$$

Data analysis was performed using SPSS.

12.5 Data Analysis

Table 12.2 represents the gender of the respondents. There are a total of 128 respondents, 72 (56.25) of whom are male and 56 (43.75) of whom are female. This shows that the majority of participants in the survey were males.

Table 12.3 depicts that 19 respondents (14.84 per cent) belong to the age group of 18 to 25 years, 47 respondents (36.72 per cent) to the age group of

Table 12.1 Questionnaire.

Variable name	Question statement	Scale
Public Trust in Economic Policies	1. I believe the government's economic decisions are in the public's best interest. 2. I have confidence in the information provided by policymakers about the economy. 3. I trust the government's ability to manage economic crises. 4. I feel confident in the government's long-term economic plans. 5. I feel assured that the government's economic policies are fair. 6. I am aware of the existence of deepfake technology. 7. I believe that deepfake technology is commonly used in media.	1 (Strongly disagree) – 5 (Strongly agree)
Exposure to Deepfake Technology	1. I am aware of the existence of deepfake technology. 2. I often find videos or audio that I suspect might be deepfakes. 3. I have experienced deepfake content in social media. 4. I am concerned about the impact of deepfake technology on news reliability. 5. I have discussed deepfake technology with friends and family. 6. My exposure to deepfake technology has increased over the past year.	1 (Strongly disagree) – 5 (Strongly agree)
Media Literacy	1. I can usually tell when a video or audio is fake. 2. I know how to check the credibility of a news source. 3. I feel confident in identifying deepfake content. 4. I can differentiate between reliable and unreliable news sources. 5. I actively educate myself about media literacy. 6. I think being aware of media literacy skills is essential.	1 (Strongly disagree) – 5 (Strongly agree)
Public Trust on Credible Sources	1. I trust information from traditional media sources (e.g., newspapers, TV news). 2. I find digital media sources (e.g., blogs, social media) credible. 3. I believe that government websites provide reliable information. 4. I trust economic reports from recognised financial institutions. 5. I think social media is a reliable source of economic news. 6. I trust economic data provided by international organisations (e.g., IMF, World Bank). 7. I am sceptical of economic information from unverified sources.	1 (Strongly disagree) – 5 (Strongly agree)

Source: Designed by authors

Table 12.2 Gender of the respondents.

Gender	Number of Respondents
Male	72 (56.25)
Female	56 (43.75)
Others	0 (0)
Total	128 (100)

Source: Primary survey
Note: Figures in parentheses represent percentage values.

Table 12.3 Age of the respondents.

Age (in years)	Number of respondents
18–25	19 (14.84)
26–35	47 (36.72)
36–45	32 (25)
46–60	24 (18.75)
61 & above	6 (4.89)
Total	128 (100)

Source: Primary survey
Note: Figures in parentheses represent percentage values.

26–35 years, 32 respondents (25 per cent) to the age group of 36 to 45 years and 24 respondents (18.75 per cent) to the age group of 46 to 60 years. Only six respondents (4.89 per cent) belonged to the age group of 61 and above. The analysis reveals that most respondents belonged to the age group of 26 to 45 years.

Table 4 categorises respondents based on income. Three respondents (2.34 per cent) had income up to Rs. 100,000. 24 respondents (18.75 per cent) had income between Rs. 100,001 to 3,00,000. The income of 37 respondents (28.91 per cent) lay between Rs. 300,001 to 500,000, of 42 respondents (32.81 per cent) lay between Rs. 500,001 to 750,000 and 20 (15.62 per cent) lay between Rs. 750,001 to 10,00,000. Only two respondents had an income of more than Rs. 10,00,000.

Table 12.5 outlines the educational qualifications of the respondents. Most respondents (40.62 per cent) who participated in the survey had attained education up to graduation level. Seven respondents (5.47 per cent) had attained education up to the primary level, 18 (14.06 per cent) had it up to the secondary level, and 23 (17.97 per cent) had attained it up to the senior secondary level. In the survey, 22 respondents (17.19 per cent) were post-graduates, and 6 (4.69 per cent) were doctorates.

Table 12.4 Income of the respondents.

Income (in Rupees)	Number of respondents
0–100,000	3 (2.34)
100,001–300,000	24 (18.75)
300,001–500,000	37 (28.91)
500,001–750,000	42 (32.81)
750,001–10,00,000	20 (15.62)
10,00,001 & above	2 (1.56)
Total	128 (100)

Source: Primary survey
Note: Figures in parentheses represent percentage values.

Table 12.5 Educational qualification of the respondents.

Education	Number of respondents
Primary	7 (5.47)
Secondary	18 (14.06)
Senior Secondary	23 (17.97)
Graduation	52 (40.62)
Post Graduation	22 (17.19)
Doctorate	6 (4.69)
Total	128 (100)

Source: Primary survey.
Note: Figures in parentheses represent percentage values.

Table 12.6 depicts the descriptive statistics obtained by the unique score for each section. The number of valid responses for each variable is 128, indicating no missing data in the analysis. The average score of public trust in economic policies is 3.969, indicating people's high level of trust in economic policies. In the case of exposure to deepfake technology, the average score is 1.952, suggesting that respondents have low exposure to deepfake technology. The average score of respondents in the case of media literacy is 3.994, indicating a high level of media literacy among respondents. Trust in Credible Sources has an average score of 3.991, indicating that, on average, people have more trust in credible sources of information. Standard deviation and variance represent the spread of responses around the mean. The highest variability in responses exists in the case of Public Trust in Economic Policies, and the lowest variability exists for Trust in Credible Sources.

Table 12.7 displays the Pearson correlation coefficients between the four key variables in the study: Public Trust in Economic Policies, Exposure to Deepfake Technology, Media Literacy, and Trust in Credible Sources. The correlation coefficients indicate the strength and direction of the linear

Table 12.6 Descriptive statistics

	N	Mean	Std. deviation	Variance	Skewness		Kurtosis	
	Statistic	Statistic	Statistic	Statistic	Statistic	Std. error	Statistic	Std. error
Public Trust in Economic Policies	128	3.969	1.219	1.488	–1.125	0.214	0.024	0.425
Exposure to Deepfake Technology	128	1.952	1.153	1.329	1.226	0.214	0.226	0.425
Media Literacy	128	3.994	1.030	1.061	–1.173	0.214	0.414	0.425
Trust in Credible Sources	128	3.991	0.919	0.846	–1.190	0.214	0.663	0.425
Valid N (listwise)	128							

Source: Authors' calculations.

Table 12.7 Correlation matrix.

	Public Trust in Economic Policies	Exposure to Deepfake Technology	Media Literacy	Trust in Credible Sources
Public Trust in Economic Policies	1			
Exposure to Deepfake Technology	–0.653**	1		
Media Literacy	0.873**	–0.580**	1	
Trust in Credible Sources	0.816**	–0.482**	0.770**	1

Note: ** implies significant at 0.01 level (2-tailed).
Source: Authors' own calculations.

Table 12.8 Model summary.[b]

Model	R	R square	Adjusted R square	Std. error of the estimate
1	0.917[a]	0.840	0.837	0.49310

a. Predictors: (Constant), Trust on Credible Sources, Exposure to Deepfake Technology, Media Literacy
b. Dependent Variable: Public Trust in Economic Policies
Source: Authors' own calculations.

Table 12.9 ANOVA.[a]

Model		Sum of squares	df	Mean square	F	Sig.
1	**Regression**	158.821	3	52.940	217.730	0.000[b]
	Residual	30.150	124	0.243		
	Total	188.971	127			

a. Dependent Variable: Public Trust in Economic Policies
b. Predictors: (Constant), Trust on Credible Sources, Exposure to Deepfake Technology, Media Literacy
Source: Authors' own calculations.

relationships between these variables. Public Trust in Economic Policies is negatively significantly related to Exposure to Deepfake Technology ($r = -0.653$) which indicates that as Exposure to Deepfake Technology increases, Public Trust in Economic Policies tends to decrease. With a correlation coefficient of 0.873 and 0.816 respectively, Media Literacy and Trust on Credible Sources are positively significantly related to Public Trust in Economic Policies depicting that with an increase in Media Literacy and Trust on Credible Sources, Public Trust in Economic Policies tends to increase.

Table 12.8 provides the summary statistics for a multiple regression model where the dependent variable is Public Trust in Economic Policies, and the predictors are Exposure to Deepfake Technology, Media Literacy and Trust on Credible Sources. The Coefficient of Determination (R^2) has a value of 0.840 indicating that 84 per cent variance in the dependent variable is explained by the explanatory variables. The Adjusted R^2 (0.837) confirms the model's robustness, accounting for the number of predictors.

Table 12.9 depicts the ANOVA results for the regression. The F- statistic for the model is 217.730 and is significant at 1 per cent level of significance indicating that the dependent variables collectively (Trust on Credible Sources, Exposure to Deepfake Technology, Media Literacy) can explain a significant proportion of variance in the independent variable (Public Trust in Economic Policies).

Table 12.10 Coefficients.[a]

Model		Unstandardised Coefficients		Standardised Coefficients		
		B	Std. Error	Beta	t	Sig.
1	(Constant)	0.259	0.295		0.878	0.382
	Exposure to Deepfake Technology	–0.214	0.047	–0.203	–4.592	0.000
	Media Literacy	0.589	0.072	0.497	8.205	0.000
	Trust on Credible Sources	0.445	0.075	0.336	5.962	0.000

a. Dependent Variable: Public Trust in Economic Policies
Source: Authors' own calculations.

Table 12.10 indicates the relationship of Pubic Trust in Economic Policies with each of dependent variables. The β- coefficient of constant (0.259) is insignificant (p-value= 0.382) indicating that it does not significantly contributes to the model. Exposure to Deepfake Technology is negatively significantly ($p < 0.01$) related to Public Trust in Economic Policies. The results reveal that with a unit increase in Exposure to Deepfake Technology, Public Trust in Economic Policies decline by –0.214 units. Media Literacy and Trust on Credible Sources have a positive significant ($p < 0.01$) impact on Public Trust in Economic Policies. The results indicate that with a unit increase in Media Literacy, Public Trust in Economic Policies increase by 0.589 units and with a unit increase in Trust on Credible Sources, the same tends to increase by 0.445 units.

12.6 Managerial Implications

The managerial implications of this study underscore the imperative for policymakers, corporate communicators, and media strategists to rigorously integrate robust source verification mechanisms, enhance media literacy initiatives, and develop sophisticated countermeasures against deepfake incursions, as the confluence of these factors critically mediates public trust in economic policy frameworks, necessitating a recalibration of communicative strategies in a digitally manipulated information environment to sustain institutional credibility and avert the pernicious effects of misinformation, as corroborated by findings in studies on the erosion of trust through digital disinformation (Vaccari & Chadwick, 2020; Buchanan, 2021).

12.7 Conclusion

The present chapter seeks to explain the effect of Exposure to Deepfake Technology, Media Literacy and Trust on Credible Sources on Public Trust in Economic Policies. The findings of the study divulge that Public Trust in Economic Policies is significantly negatively affected by Exposure to Deepfake Technology and is positively significantly affected by Media Literacy and Trust on Credible Sources. This indicates that as Exposure to Deepfake Technology increases, Public Trust in Economic Policies decreases and with an increase in Media Literacy and Trust on Credible Sources, Public Trust in Economic Policies increases. The findings hence suggest that appropriate steps must be taken by concerned agencies to increase Media Literacy of people along with an increase in the number of Credible Sources of information. Appropriate steps must also be taken to contain the negative usage of deepfake technology.

There is a need to balance the opportunities presented by deepfake technology against its adverse effects through reasonable measures. This involves both technical solutions as well as ethical and legal structures to tackle the extensive social impacts. It is crucial to understand the capacities, opportunities, and challenges while operating deepfake technologies in an increasing digital environment. Deepfake technology results in the breakdown of Public Trust in Economic Policies, thus, emerging as a significant problem in the digital era. With the advancement of deepfakes, people will be more affected by wrong information and alternatively, its influence on public trust will increase. Solving this problem calls for a multi-pronged strategy which involves new technology, change of perception among public as well as an improvement in the system of governance.

References

Adhikari, P., Jain, R., Sharma, A., & Pandey, A. (2021). Plant Growth Promotion at Low Temperature by Phosphate-Solubilizing Pseudomonas Spp. Isolated from High-Altitude Himalayan Soil. *Microbial Ecology*, *82*(3), 677–687. https://doi.org/10.1007/s00248-021-01702-1

Agrawal, P. K., Gupta, B. B., Jain, S., & Pattanshetti, M. K. (2011). Estimating strength of a DDoS attack in real time using ANN based scheme. *Communications in Computer and Information Science*, *157 CCIS*, 301–310. https://doi.org/10.1007/978-3-642-22786-8_38

Aiyappa, S., Kodikal, R., & Rahiman, H. U. (2024). Accelerating Gender Equality for Sustainable Development: A Case Study of Dakshina Kannada District, India. *Technical and*

Vocational Education and Training, *38*, 335–349. https://doi.org/10.1007/978-981-99-6909-8_30

Ajay, D., Sharad, K., Singh, K. P., & Sharma, S. (2023). Impact of Prolonged Mental Torture on Housewives in Middle Class Families. *Journal for ReAttach Therapy and Developmental Diversities*, *6*(4), 1–7.

Anzaar, A., Shahnawaz, H., Mukesh, C., Gupta, S. C., & Gowri, R. (2010). ASSR Fair Load Distribution Using Efficiency Division Factor with Greedy Booster Approach for MANET. *Communications in Computer and Information Science*, *101*, 641–646. https://doi.org/10.1007/978-3-642-15766-0_112

Anzaar, A., Shahnawaz, H., Mukesh, C., Gupta, S. C., Gowri, R., & Mandoria, H. L. (2010). "Simulation study for performance comparison of routing protocols in mobile Adhoc network." *World Academy of Science, Engineering and Technology*, *46*, 683–685.

Arora, A., Singh, R., Malik, K., & Kestwal, U. (2024). Association of sexual performance and intimacy with satisfaction in life in head and neck cancer patients: A review. *Oral Oncology Reports*, *11*. https://doi.org/10.1016/j.oor.2024.100563

Belwal, R., & Belwal, S. (2017). Employers' perception of women workers in Oman and the challenges they face. *Employee Relations*, *39*(7), 1048–1065. https://doi.org/10.1108/ER-09-2016-0183

Debasis, M., Ganeshamurthy, A. N., Komal, S., Radha, T. K., & Rupa, T. R. (2020). Plant growth promotion and biocontrol activity of some typical harsh environment rhizo-microbes and their effects on Amaranthus cruentus plants. *Research Journal of Biotechnology*, *15*(1), 35–45.

Dutta, A., Singh, P., Dobhal, A., Mannan, D., Singh, J., & Goswami, P. (2023). Entrepreneurial Aptitude of Women of an Aspirational District of Uttarakhand. *Indian Journal of Extension Education*, *59*(2), 103–107. https://doi.org/10.48165/IJEE.2023.59222

Dwivedi, S., Gairola, R., Lavania, P., Mittal, L., & Goudar, R. H. (2013). Advanced advertising technique in Indian public transport system: A better way to disseminate information using electronic display. *2013 International Conference on Human Computer Interactions, ICHCI 2013*. https://doi.org/10.1109/ICHCI-IEEE.2013.6887805

Dwivedi, S., Parshav, V., Sharma, N., Kumar, P., Chhabra, S., & Goudar, R. H. (2013). Using technology to make farming easier and better: Simplified E-Farming Support (SEFS). *2013 International Conference on Human Computer Interactions, ICHCI 2013*. https://doi.org/10.1109/ICHCI-IEEE.2013.6887806

Gangwar, V. P., & Srivastva, S. P. (2020). Impact of micro finance in poverty eradication via SHGs: A study of selected districts in U.P.

International Journal of Advanced Science and Technology, *29*(2), 3818–3829.

Godbole, V., Pal, M. K., & Gautam, P. (2021). A critical perspective on the scope of interdisciplinary approaches used in fourth-generation biofuel production. *Algal Research*, *58*. https://doi.org/10.1016/j.algal.2021.102436

Goswami, P., Mahapatra, R., & Divyasukananda, S. (2013). Bridging the digital gap in rural India VIVEKDISHA: A novel experience. *2013 National Conference on Communications, NCC 2013*. https://doi.org/10.1109/NCC.2013.6488049

Govind, K., Pahwa, A., Aggarwal, N., & Balodhi, V. (2012). Ecosecurity energy harvesting using piezoelectric crystal. *2012 Students Conference on Engineering and Systems, SCES 2012*. https://doi.org/10.1109/SCES.2012.6199116

Goyal, P., Dwivedi, M., & Awais, M. (2014). Use of randomized algorithms for enhancing learning ability in algorithms course. *Proceedings of the 2014 IEEE International Conference on MOOCs, Innovation and Technology in Education, IEEE MITE 2014*, 352–357. https://doi.org/10.1109/MITE.2014.7020302

Grover, D., Sharma, S., Kaur, P., Mittal, A., & Sharma, P. K. (2024). Societal Elements that Impact the Performance of Women Entrepreneurs in Tier-II Cities: A Study of Rohilkhand Region of Uttar Pradesh. *2024 IEEE Zooming Innovation in Consumer Technologies Conference, ZINC 2024*, 114–117. https://doi.org/10.1109/ZINC61849.2024.10579316

Gupta, V. K., Nayak, A., & Agarwal, S. (2015). Bioadsorbents for remediation of heavy metals: Current status and their future prospects. *Environmental Engineering Research*, *20*(1), 1–18. https://doi.org/10.4491/eer.2015.018

Indu, R., Dimri, S. C., & Kumar, B. (2023). Identification of Location for Police Headquarters to Deal with Crime Against Women in India Using Clustering Based on K-Means Algorithm. *International Journal of Computing and Digital Systems*, *14*(1), 965–974. https://doi.org/10.12785/ijcds/140175

Joshi, A., Bachheti, R. K., Sharma, A., & Mamgain, R. (2016). Parthenium hysterophorus. L. (Asteraceae): A boon or curse? (A review). *Oriental Journal of Chemistry*, *32*(3), 1283 – 1294. https://doi.org/10.13005/ojc/320302

Juyal, P., & Sharma, S. (2021). Strawberry Plant's Health Detection for Organic Farming Using Unmanned Aerial Vehicle. *Proceedings of the 2021 IEEE International Conference on Innovative Computing, Intelligent Communication and Smart Electrical Systems, ICSES 2021*. https://doi.org/10.1109/ICSES52305.2021.9633825

Kamal, S., Shobha, K. R., Francis, F., Khilar, R., Tripathi, V., Lakshminarayana, M., Kannadasan, B., & Sahile, K. (2022). IOT Automation with Segmentation Techniques for Detection of Plant Seedlings in Agriculture. *Wireless Communications and Mobile Computing, 2022.* https://doi.org/10.1155/2022/6466555

Khandelwal, C., Kumar, S., Tripathi, V., & Madhavan, V. (2023). Joint impact of corporate governance and risk disclosures on firm value: Evidence from emerging markets. *Research in International Business and Finance*, *66*. https://doi.org/10.1016/j.ribaf.2023.102022

Khanna, A., & Arora, B. (2009). A study to investigate the reasons for bank frauds and the implementation of preventive security controls in indian banking industry. *International Journal of Business Science and Applied Management*, *4*(3), 1–21.

Kumar, D., Agrawal, A., & Goyal, P. (2015). Efficiently improving the security of OTP. *Conference Proceeding - 2015 International Conference on Advances in Computer Engineering and Applications, ICACEA 2015*, 912–915. https://doi.org/10.1109/ICACEA.2015.7164835

Kumar, P., Thakur, S., Dhingra, G. K., Singh, A., Pal, M. K., Harshvardhan, K., Dubey, R. C., & Maheshwari, D. K. (2018). Inoculation of siderophore producing rhizobacteria and their consortium for growth enhancement of wheat plant. *Biocatalysis and Agricultural Biotechnology*, *15*, 264–269. https://doi.org/10.1016/j.bcab.2018.06.019

Kumari, J., Singh, P., Mishra, A. K., Singh Meena, B. P., Singh, A., & Ojha, M. (2024). Challenges Hindering Women's Involvement in the Hospitality Industry as Entrepreneurs in the Era of Digital Economy. In *Revolutionizing the AI-Digital Landscape: A Guide to Sustainable Emerging Technologies for Marketing Professionals*. Taylor and Francis. https://doi.org/10.4324/9781032688305-9

Mamgain, N., Sharma, A., & Goyal, P. (2014). Learner's perspective on video-viewing features offered by MOOC providers: Coursera and edX. *Proceedings of the 2014 IEEE International Conference on MOOCs, Innovation and Technology in Education, IEEE MITE 2014*, 331–336. https://doi.org/10.1109/MITE.2014.7020298

Mangla, S. K., Sharma, Y. K., Patil, P. P., Yadav, G., & Xu, J. (2019). Logistics and distribution challenges to managing operations for corporate sustainability: Study on leading Indian diary organizations. *Journal of Cleaner Production*, *238*. https://doi.org/10.1016/j.jclepro.2019.117620

Mehta, S., Kukreja, V., Vats, S., & Verma, A. (2023). A Paradigm Shift in Pomegranate Leaf Disease Detection with Federated Learning and CNN. *2023 14th International Conference on Computing Communication and Networking Technologies, ICCCNT 2023*. https://doi.org/10.1109/ICCCNT56998.2023.10308132

Mishra, D., Kandpal, V., Agarwal, N., & Srivastava, B. (2024). Financial Inclusion and Its Ripple Effects on Socio-Economic Development: A Comprehensive Review. *Journal of Risk and Financial Management*, *17*(3). https://doi.org/10.3390/jrfm17030105

Nijhawan, R., & Jain, K. (2018). Glacier terminus position monitoring and modelling using remote sensing data. *Communications in Computer and Information Science*, *906*, 11–23. https://doi.org/10.1007/978-981-13-1813-9_2

Padhi, B. K., Singh, S., Gaidhane, A. M., Abu Serhan, H., Khatib, M. N., Zahiruddin, Q. S., Rustagi, S., Sharma, R. K., Sharma, D., Arora, M., & Satapathy, P. (2024). Inequalities in cardiovascular disease among elderly Indians: A gender perspective analysis using LASI wave-I (2017-18). *Current Problems in Cardiology*, *49*(7). https://doi.org/10.1016/j.cpcardiol.2024.102605

Painuli, S., Quispe, C., Herrera-Bravo, J., Semwal, P., Martorell, M., Almarhoon, Z. M., Seilkhan, A., Ydyrys, A., Rad, J. S., Alshehri, M. M., Daştan, S. D., Taheri, Y., Calina, D., & Cho, W. C. (2022). Nutraceutical Profiling, Bioactive Composition, and Biological Applications of Lepidium sativum L. *Oxidative Medicine and Cellular Longevity*, *2022*. https://doi.org/10.1155/2022/2910411

Pandey, R. P., Bansal, S., Awasthi, P., Dixit, V., Singh, R., & Yadava, V. (2023). Attitude and Myths Related to Stalking among Early and Middle Age Adults. *Psychology Hub*, *40*(3), 85–94. https://doi.org/10.13133/2724-2943/17960

Pant, J., Pant, R. P., Kumar Singh, M., Pratap Singh, D., & Pant, H. (2021). Analysis of agricultural crop yield prediction using statistical techniques of machine learning. In S. Y. (Ed.), *Materials Today: Proceedings* (Vol. 46, pp. 10922–10926). Elsevier Ltd. https://doi.org/10.1016/j.matpr.2021.01.948

Pant, M., Lal, A., & Rani, A. (2014). Hippophae salicifolia d don-a plant with multifarious benefits. *International Journal of Pharmacy and Pharmaceutical Sciences*, *6*(11), 37–40.

Pant, M., & Thakur, P. (2021). Forest-based plants in beautification and their medicinal significance. In *Non-Timber Forest Products: Food, Healthcare and Industrial Applications*. Springer International Publishing. https://doi.org/10.1007/978-3-030-73077-2_16

Pargaien, S., Prakash, R., & Dubey, V. P. (2021). Wheat Crop Classification based on NDVI using Sentinel Time Series: A Case Study Saharanpur

Region. *2021 International Conference on Computing, Communication and Green Engineering, CCGE 2021*. https://doi.org/10.1109/CCGE50943.2021.9776445

Rakhra, M., Bhargava, A., Bhargava, D., Singh, R., Bhanot, A., & Rahmani, A. W. (2022). Implementing Machine Learning for Supply-Demand Shifts and Price Impacts in Farmer Market for Tool and Equipment Sharing. *Journal of Food Quality, 2022*. https://doi.org/10.1155/2022/4496449

Rawat, K. S., Singh, S. K., Ray, R. L., & Szabo, S. (2020). Parameterization of the modified water cloud model (MWCM) using normalized difference vegetation index (NDVI) for winter wheat crop: a case study from Punjab, India. *Geocarto International*, 1–14. https://doi.org/10.1080/10106049.2020.1783579

Rawat, K. S., Singh, S. K., Ray, R. L., Szabó, S., & Kumar, S. (2020). Parameterizing the modified water cloud model to improve soil moisture data retrieval using vegetation models. *Hungarian Geographical Bulletin*, *69*(1), 17–26. https://doi.org/10.15201/hungeobull.69.1.2

Semwal, P., Painuli, S., Jugran, A., Palni, L. M. S., Verma, S., Thapliyal, A., & Tewari, D. (2020). Genetic Diversity of Scanty Available Himalayan Saussurea obvallata (DC.) Edgew. *Iranian Journal of Science and Technology, Transaction A: Science*, *44*(3), 587–594. https://doi.org/10.1007/s40995-020-00862-y

Shakya, A. K., Ramola, A., Sawant, K., Tiwari, S., Aarfin, S., & Mittal, P. (2018). Visual Representation of Change in Vegetation Area of Dehradun, Uttarakhand, India using Normalized Difference Vegetation Index (NDVI). *2018 2nd IEEE International Conference on Power Electronics, Intelligent Control and Energy Systems, ICPEICES 2018*, 1087–1092. https://doi.org/10.1109/ICPEICES.2018.8897376

Sharma, A., Bachheti, A., Sharma, P., Bachheti, R. K., & Husen, A. (2020). Phytochemistry, pharmacological activities, nanoparticle fabrication, commercial products and waste utilization of Carica papaya L.: A comprehensive review. *Current Research in Biotechnology*, *2*, 145–160. https://doi.org/10.1016/j.crbiot.2020.11.001

Sharma, M., & Joshi, S. (2012). Creating Silicon Valley in Europe: Public Policy Towards New Technology Industries. *International Journal of Social Economics*, *39*(9), 738–740. https://doi.org/10.1108/03068291211245745

Sharma, Y. K., Mangla, S. K., Patil, P. P., & Uniyal, S. (2020). Analyzing sustainable food supply chain management challenges in India. In *Research Anthology on Food Waste Reduction and Alternative Diets for*

Food and Nutrition Security. IGI Global. https://doi.org/10.4018/978-1-7998-5354-1.ch023

Sharma, Y. K., Patil, P. P., & Mangla, S. K. (2018). Analyzing risks in safety and security of food using grey relational analysis. *International Journal of Mechanical Engineering and Technology*, *9*(12), 9–19.

Shrivastava, A., Usha, R., Kukreti, R., Sharma, G., Srivastava, A. P., & Khan, A. K. (2023). Women Safety Precaution. *2023 1st International Conference on Circuits, Power, and Intelligent Systems, CCPIS 2023*. https://doi.org/10.1109/CCPIS59145.2023.10291594

Singh, A. K., Singh, R., & Singh, S. (2024). A review on factors affecting and performance of nutritional security of women and children in India. In *Impact of Women in Food and Agricultural Development*. IGI Global. https://doi.org/10.4018/979-8-3693-3037-1.ch019

Singh, K. U., Chaudhary, V., Sharma, P. K., Kumar, P., Varshney, N., & Singh, T. (2024). Integrating GPS and GSM Technologies for Enhanced Women's Safety: A Fingerprint-Activated Device Approach. *2024 International Conference on Automation and Computation, AUTOCOM 2024*, 657–662. https://doi.org/10.1109/AUTOCOM60220.2024.10486120

Singh, N., Negi, A. S., & Pant, M. (2020). Tissue culture interventions in soybean production: Significance, challenges and future prospects. *Ecology, Environment and Conservation*, *26*, S96–S102.

Singh, P., & Singh, K. D. (2023). Fog-Centric Intelligent Surveillance System: A Novel Approach for Effective and Efficient Surveillance. In K. R., K. R., G. M., G. M., S. R., & S. R. (Eds.), *2023 International Conference on Advancement in Computation and Computer Technologies, InCACCT 2023* (pp. 762–766). Institute of Electrical and Electronics Engineers Inc. https://doi.org/10.1109/InCACCT57535.2023.10141802

Srivastava, B., Kandpal, V., & Jain, A. K. (2024). Financial well-being of women self-help group members: a qualitative study. *Environment, Development and Sustainability*. https://doi.org/10.1007/s10668-024-04879-w

Suravajhala, P., Kumar, A., Pandeya, A., Malik, G., Sharma, M., P., H. K., S., A. K., Gahlaut, V., Gajula, M. N. V. P., Singh, K. P., Balyan, H. S., & Gupta, P. K. (2018). A web resource for nutrient use efficiency-related genes, quantitative trait loci and microRNAs in important cereals and model plants. *F1000Research*, *7*. https://doi.org/10.12688/f1000research.14561.1

Tripathi, V. M., & Mohan, A. (2016). Microfinance and empowering rural women in the Terai, Uttarakhand, India. *International Journal of Agricultural and Statistical Sciences*, *12*(2), 523–530.

Tyagi, P., Kapil, D., Joshi, R. C., & Pilli, E. S. (2013). Virtual machine portability - A novel approach. *Proceedings - 2013 International Conference on Cloud Computing and Big Data, CLOUDCOM-ASIA 2013*, 240–245. https://doi.org/10.1109/CLOUDCOM-ASIA.2013.108

Zhang, Y., Cao, C., Gu, J., & Garg, H. (2023). The Impact of Top Management Team Characteristics on the Risk Taking of Chinese Private Construction Enterprises. *Systems*, *11*(2). https://doi.org/10.3390/systems11020067

13

Unveiling Deepfake: Ethical Concerns in Social Media Discourse

Reepu Reepu[1] and Amar Johri[2]

[1]Chandigarh University, Punjab, India
[2]Saudi Electronic University, Saudi Arabia

Email: reepu.technowize@gmail.com; johriamar@gmail.com

Abstract

Deepfakes are images, pictures, or audio or video recordings altered to misrepresent someone doing things that have not occurred. Due to such practices, there have been high ethical concerns about social media recently. The advancements in AI have resulted in the manipulation of various pictures, audio, and video formats that look more like the original, thereby damaging the individual's reputation. Moreover, complex deepfakes make it challenging to differentiate between real and fake. This has raised various ethical issues. In recent years, there have been growing concerns about the newer roles and format of visual misrepresentations. Still, minimal discussion or analysis has been carried out to address them, and strategies must be taken to address the upcoming threat.

A recent investigation noted that deepfake is being applied to popular social media sites like YouTube, Reddit, and other related media sites. The study addresses the issues and ethical concerns related to deepfakes and states the problems that will impact society and public confidence in social media. It is noted that deepfakes possess the potential to use advanced technologies that will affect the privacy and reputation of individuals, corporations, society, etc.

13.1 Introduction

Deepfake is considered synthetic media, mainly created using AI and other related tools (Ahmad et al., 2024). This technology enables users to create more realistic audio, video or images that mimic the original events and real-world people. In the beginning, deepfakes were mainly applied to create content that needed high creativity and to provide a larger-than-life experience (A. Kaur et al., 2024). However, it gradually moved to manipulate content like audio, video, images, and other aspects. The individuals who apply deepfakes tend to tarnish the dignity and image of individuals by creating fake content and posting it on social media (Deepti et al., 2023).

The rapid growth of AI has enabled the application of deepfakes in different domains and social media aspects (Rajput et al., 2024). However, deepfakes are mainly stated as artificial tools that empower the alteration of digital data to make it resemble others (Suryavanshi, Kukreja, Dogra, et al., 2024). Recently, cybercrime accounts for more than 65% of the incidents in security breaches; this is becoming one of the most challenging issues from a national and worldwide perspective (A. Kaur, Kukreja, Upadhyay, et al., 2024a). Deepfakes, which are more realistic-looking, are generated based on deep learning algorithms and are used to swap the original with artificially created content (Husen et al., 2021). The AI-synthesised data tends to have adverse impacts, making it challenging to determine legitimacy. The application of deepfake has now been intended for a wide range of reasons, from targeting a specific person for revenge on personal or political aspects. Deepfakes are now published to provide incorrect or falsified images with non-existent landscapes for malicious reasons (Chattopadhyay et al., 2024).

13.2 Context

13.2.1 Overall creation and inception of deepfakes technology

Deepfake technology was incepted through a conceptual collaboration of deep learning-based tools and fake aspects (A. Kaur, Kukreja, Upadhyay, et al., 2024b). This technology possesses heavy contributions from different machine learning models and the application of AI tools like artificial neural networks and other elements to create fake but realistic images, audio, and other digital content (A. Kaur et al., 2024).

Initial foundation (2014–2017): In the mid-2010s, Ian Goodfellow developed a critical artificial neural network that laid the foundation steps for creating deepfake technology (A. P. S. Yadav et al., 2024). GAN provides the output that enables more realistic output based on continuous learning. Most initial applications were in the academic field and focused on providing better images for publishing in textbooks and enhancing the image resolution for better understanding for students and others (Saikumar et al., 2024).

Early adoption (2017–2019): The term "Deepfake" was first stated in 2017 when enthusiasts started to overlay some celebrity faces on unwanted films using the artificial network; this immediately caught the attention of many who began to abuse the potential of the purpose of applying technology. With the quick adoption of social media, the morphed pictures and videos tend to reach more followers. Hence, academics and educational content creators look for other acceptable applications (Banerjee, Sharma, et al., 2024; A. Kaur, Sharma, Rana, et al., 2024; Ojha et al., 2024; Yashu, Kukreja, Srivastava, & Garg, 2024).

Current scenario (2019–present): The application of deepfake technology has recently increased. With COVID-19 and lockdown, individuals use deepfake to falsify digital content that cannot be verified. The growing implementation of these digital fake technologies tends to impact legitimate data, and many privacy and copyright infringements exist.

13.3 Research Methodology

To meticulously unravel the nuances of "Unveiling Deepfake: Ethical Concerns in Social Media Discourse," this research chapter meticulously adheres to a qualitative paradigm interwoven with an ethnographic lens, facilitating an in-depth discourse analysis of social media dynamics surrounding deepfake controversies; by immersing within platforms such as Reddit and YouTube, it scrutinises approximately 320 user-generated conversations, dissecting the lexicon, sentiment, and ethical dichotomies articulated by digital communities, thereby meticulously encoding thematic patterns through an exhaustive coding schema, which encapsulates prevailing moral implications, amplifies societal reverberations, and provides a critically synthesised narrative that underpins the discourse's ethical breadth, illuminating the psychological, social, and legal ramifications that underpin the pervasiveness of deepfakes in contemporary digital ethos.

13.4 Ethical and Moral Issues

Due to these technologies' ill effects, various ethical and moral issues arise regarding adopting such technology (Gautam et al., 2024; M. Kumar, Aeri, Chandel, et al., 2024; V. Kumar, Banerjee, Chauhan, et al., 2024; S. Singh et al., 2024).

1. Providing misinformation to the users: Deepfake is mainly used to alter the original contents, primarily in digital format, to impact other

people's credibility. Hence, the data are false principally; for example, fake images or photos of the politicians, actors, or celebrities were shared to create divisive remarks as the post went viral. This will impact the individual's future and affect their personal and professional life (A. Kaur et al., 2024, 2024; Singla et al., 2024).

2. Consent: The second ethical issue associated with using Deepfake is that many sources create it more frequently and share it on social media platforms without the individuals' consent. When individuals' images, audio, or other digital content are used without permission, it raises moral issues, impacting their personal and professional lives (Kukrety et al., 2024; Suryavanshi, Kukreja, Rana, et al., 2024).
3. Trust: Applying deepfake technology decreases individuals' confidence in digital space. Since the application and sharing of deepfakes are increasing data by data, they become more complex, and people tend to doubt the overall genuineness of the image or audio (H. Kaur, Hussain, et al., 2023; Suryavanshi, Kukreja, Upadhyay, et al., 2024). This results in losing trust in individuals.
4. Abuse and harmful applications: Finally, deepfakes can be considered a weapon of mass destruction as they try to abuse and cause more significant damage to individuals. Deepfakes are now mainly used by cyberbullies and also to falsify individuals' data, which will impede various legal and other processes (Mir et al., 2024; Semwal et al., 2023).

13.5 AI Moral Guidelines

With the above-discussed points on ethical and moral concerns of deepfakes, it is essential to analyze the technology at the heart of accepted AI-related principles to address the ethical use of these technologies. Some of the fundamental guidelines are stated as follows:

13.5.1 Respect

Honouring and respecting individuals' liberty, freedom of speech, and other aspects is highly important (J. Joshi et al., 2024; A. Kaur et al., 2024; Nayak et al., 2024). Deepfakes tend to fabricate images and video or audio with the primary purpose of fabricating various unlawful aspects, changing appearances and possessing the potential to impact dignity and cause stress. Hence, it is vital to respect each individual, and deepfakes can be used only for lawful creative purposes and to avoid creating psychological stress for individuals (A. Kaur et al., 2024; Pramanik et al., 2023; Shao et al., 2023) .

13.5.2 Transparency

Deepfakes can be accessed by anyone who can use deep learning and other tools. Nowadays, with the growth of technology, natural senses are being manipulated using deepfakes (A. Kaur et al., 2024; Malhotra et al., 2024; Yashu, Kukreja, Srivastava, Garg, et al., 2024). Therefore, it is essential to enhance transparency by providing clear guidelines on communication and providing a general message that it is AI-generated content using deepfake, etc.

13.5.3 Confidentiality

The use of deepfake should improve society and provide clear pictures for education purposes and other uses. So, individuals' private or confidential information needs to be protected. Without their approval, creating deepfakes of individuals' voices, videos, or images is now possible (AL-Huqail et al., 2023; A. Kaur, Sharma, Thapliyal, et al., 2024; Širić et al., 2023). To ensure genuine approvals, cybersecurity needs to audit the IDs that use Deepfakes involving real-world people frequently, and appropriate actions must be taken (Agarwal et al., 2024; B. Kaur et al., 2023; G. Kaur et al., 2024; V. Kumar, Banerjee, Upadhyay, et al., 2024).

13.5.4 Techniques

The primary purpose of the study is to address the critical ethical concerns of using deepfakes in social media; for this purpose, the researcher intends to apply qualitative research design, which enables providing a clear and deep understanding of the technology, addresses the various ethical concerns in using the technology and suggest measures in using the technology for more ethical and moral aspects (R. R. Kumar, Jain, Sharma, et al., 2024; Shreshtha et al., 2024; Suryavanshi, Kukreja, Mehta, et al., 2024; Upadhyay et al., 2024). Researchers use this technology to involve themselves in social media sites, and many conversations are built around deepfakes. The researcher has used top social media sites like YouTube and Reddit to analyze the communications, contents and interactions which is around Deepfakes and to investigate the posts (Bhatt et al., 2023; Datta et al., 2023; Deepak et al., 2024; Savary et al., 2023).

In the current study, the researcher has considered nearly 320 posts on YouTube and Reddit, analyzed them more passively, and intended to gather needed data and information related to deepfakes. The researchers make critical analyses based on the conversations that users on social media sites discuss on deepfakes. The study intends to analyze the conversations and identify the main ethical issues surrounding deep fakes in the current context.

Deepfakes discussions in Reddit, considered one of the key social media sites where many community members interact on various issues, involve individuals providing their voice of concern related to multiple prevailing issues and also offering possible solutions to address the problems in a more sustainable manner (Avikal et al., 2023; V. Kumar, Banerjee, et al., 2023; A. Rana et al., 2023; Suryavanshi, Kukreja, et al., 2023). These conversations reflect more considerable social aspects and help use AI for better benefits like education and authenticating media usage for sustainable development (R. Joshi et al., 2024; A. Kaur et al., 2024; Prakash et al., 2023; Tanwar et al., 2023).

Moreover, YouTube is more of a video-sharing social media platform where users upload and share more visual content. Therefore, in extensive discussions on moral and ethical issues, digital creativity presents no limits that call for authentic information and fraudulent representation of digital content (A. Kaur, Kukreja, et al., 2023; G. Kaur, Sharma, et al., 2023; Rahat et al., 2024; Savita & Vimal, 2023). Liver discussion related to such aspects and the overall negative potential of the technology in media production are discussed in detail (Choudhary et al., 2023; A. Kaur et al., 2024; Saxena et al., 2024; Suryavanshi, Tanwar, et al., 2023).

The study is more focused on providing a comprehensive understanding of the technology by the users on Reddit and YouTube and discussing deep fakes through ethnography analysis. Based on the overall exploration of ethical issues, imaginative properties, and adverse impacts on society, the study also intends to provide critical perspectives on AI-driven technologies.

13.6 Data Gathering

The researcher intends to collect critical data and information from leading sources. Hence, Reddit and YouTube were chosen, as both are considered the most renowned and diverse users, so they can understand the technology and address various ethical issues. The researcher tends to choose Deepfake-related posts and analyze the comments, mainly examined using specific keywords and hashtags. The comments on each post are reviewed based on identification and pertinent posts. All the data were analyzed, combined, and then sent to a system for critical analysis to provide better insights into the knowledge and understanding of the technology.

13.7 Information Analysis

The coding technique helps readers understand the texts more comprehensively (Mathur et al., 2024; G. Rana et al., 2024; Tiwari et al., 2023). It focuses on particular themes or chosen topics that are current discussion topics. This part helps the researcher organise the information and streamlines exhaustive analysis.

The researcher then intends to group the coding segments to analyze the commonalities and organize the categories to differentiate the related thoughts and expressions shared by the users (Banerjee, Kukreja, et al., 2024; A. Kaur, Kukreja, Upadhyay, et al., 2024c; Mohapatra et al., 2023). This will help create a more comprehensive fact and organize the data (Garg et al., 2023).

The next step is to interpret the collected information; this involves making a critical analysis by classifying the data to arrive at a meaningful conclusion. Deep fake technology's ethical aspects and public opinions are analyzed and grouped separately. Moreover, the researcher uses a critical thought process and reflects the data more comprehensively to understand the insight, interpretations, and suggestions (Pithode et al., 2023). This also enables learning and understanding the impact of deep fake on public opinions and arriving at a meaningful conclusion about using these technologies (Kushwaha et al., 2023).

13.8 Information Analysis

The coding technique helps readers understand the texts more comprehensively. It focuses on particular themes or chosen topics that are current discussion topics (A. Kumar, Nirala, et al., 2023). This part helps the researcher organise the information and streamlines exhaustive analysis.

The researcher then intends to group the coding segments to analyze the commonalities and organise the categories to differentiate the related thoughts and expressions shared by the users. This will help create a more comprehensive fact, which helps manage the data (Chincholikar et al., 2023).

The next step is to interpret the collected information; this involves making a critical analysis by classifying the data to arrive at a meaningful conclusion. Deepfake technology's ethical aspects and public opinions are analyzed and grouped separately (Rawat et al., 2022). Moreover, the researcher makes a critical thought process and reflects the data more comprehensively to understand the insight interpretations and suggestions (Alam et al., 2023). This also enables learning and understanding the impact of deep fake on public opinions and arriving at meaningful conclusions using these technologies (Agrawal, Yugbodh, et al., 2023).

13.9 Analysis of Results

Based on the data collection and analysis of the data collected from the above step, the thematic analysis results reveal significant and critical issues in using the thematic analysis (Shrivastava et al., 2022). Deepfakes tend to create various societal, ethical, moral, and security concerns. This technology is now used mainly by users to manipulate and fake the original digital content to provide misleading information to the public. Furthermore, the risk of identity-related theft or fraud and the possibility of spreading various fake news, which can affect the public, creating social unrest and declining public confidence towards digital information, are on the rise (Dewangan et al., 2020). In general parlance, the deepfake phenomenon tends to impact the lives of individuals adversely. The sharing of fake digital content affects individuals' personal and professional lives. Hence, more proactive measures have to be taken to reduce technology's ill effects and use it for various educational and creative purposes (Mahor, Bijrothiya, Mishra, Rawat, et al., 2022).

13.9.1 Sharing of falsified information

The overall interactions and analysis of the conversation on social media sites show that deep fakes are mainly used to spread falsified data and information. The participants have provided the critical concern that deep fakes are circulated primarily to mislead users and possess detrimental effects in the long run (A. Kumar, Maithani, et al., 2023). Many individuals have expressed their concerns and stated that their images can be shared without prior approval or agreements (A. S. Yadav, Alam, et al., 2022).

13.9.2 Trust

A general understanding is that digital media was previously attributed as original and provides clear information and digital content to the users; however, with the use of deepfake, individuals around the world have now started to express their concerns related to the trust in the digital content, they are now mentioning that it is difficult to differentiate between the original and fake digital contents hence losing the trust on those aspects (Barwar et al., 2022). This lack of confidence in the validity of individual media and the overall validity of different digital data and information. Since deepfakes are becoming more common, they are considered a key concern, and appropriate measures must be taken to gain users' confidence (Kumari et al., 2022).

13.9.3 Editing and altering data

Though deepfakes were introduced to use AI-generated motion pictures, which support altering the material to appear more accurate, the technology was used only for malicious purposes in the real world (Khan et al., 2022). Recently, political parties have tended to use deepfakes as weapons to target opponents and look for character assassination, creating embarrassment and affecting their personal and professional lives (R. Kumar, Dwivedi, et al., 2023).

13.9.4 Principles of AI ethics and deepfakes

In this section, the researcher intends to collate the fundamental principles that can be applied to the overall creation, sharing, and dissemination of digital content through AI and deepfakes (Mahor, Pachlasiya, Garg, Chouhan, et al., 2022). These principles can be considered for future development of technologies, enabling their use for constructive purposes. This paper invokes critical discussion on ethical aspects, provides merits and addresses key risks mainly related to deepfake technology (Mahor, Bijrothiya, Mishra, & Rawat, 2022).

13.9.4.1 Respect

The first aspect that needs more focus in using deepfake is addressing the infringement of individuals' respect, privacy and dignity. It is noted that deepfake technology never gets authentic information or approval from the individuals who are being used in the digital content; this calls for privacy and copyright infringements (Mahor, Garg, Telang, Pachlasiya, et al., 2022). Deepfakes tend to use individuals' photos, audio, etc, without prior approval or consent; this has drawn criticism from various individuals (Bhatnagar et al., 2023). Hence, it is essential to address the ethical concerns, and appropriate permission and authorization must be received before using them in the deepfake technology (H. Sharma et al., 2023).

13.9.4.2 Openness

The next aspect is that deep fake production tends to produce more realistic counterfeit data and digital content, which is in contrast to traditional media, where the sources are valid. Many users and digital content consumers have stated that they cannot differentiate between the actual content and images produced using deepfake technology (Mahla et al., 2022). Hence, transparency and openness are required; if any photo, video, or audio content is modified using deepfake technology, a statutory message must be sent to the users. This will enable the entire disclosure of AI-generated material, and users can differentiate whether it is accurate content or modified information using deep fake technology (Barwar et al., 2021).

13.9.4.3 Respecting privacy

Another critical aspect is the privacy issues that are created by deepfake technology; the creators mainly misuse the private images and videos that are available on social media and apply deepfake to morph the pictures and provide inaccurate or falsified digital content, which results in producing misleading contents and impacting the privacy of the individuals (A. Kumar, Singh, et al., 2023). Hence, it is essential to enhance privacy regulations, and strict actions must be taken for creators who use images and pictures without the prior approval of the individuals (Dash et al., 2022).

13.9.4.4 Absence of malice

The last principle considered for the study is the need to stop the harm and reduce the critical risks related to the AI application. Hence, the principle of non-maleficence can be implemented to overcome these issues (A. S. Yadav, Mishra, et al., 2022). The analysis of social media data showed that more misleading data would affect individuals' reputations and dignity. Therefore, more proactive steps need to be taken to prevent such harm. Also, it is important to hold deepfake users accountable and support them in preserving their overall societal values (Prasad et al., 2023).

13.10 Ethical Frameworks and Their Significance for Policy

The above discussion presents critical insights into applications of AI and deepfakes by understanding the ethical frameworks. It also calls for significant policy changes, specifically ethical aspects so that these technologies can be used for a sustainable future (Agrawal, Bhagoria, et al., 2023). There is a growing demand and opportunities to use these technologies across industries. However, the primary focus should be on following ethical guidelines and principles for sustainability. Hence, it is stated that fairness of technology usage, making the creators more accountable, and providing transparency are the critical elements in achieving such technologies' sustainability and development, guaranteeing a responsible future (V. P. Singh et al., 2023).

It is further noted that there needs to be a higher level of understanding of these technologies and the damage that they can create to society at large. There needs to be strict policies that address deepfakes that target women and other vulnerable groups (Rathod et al., 2024). Creating better regulations enables the use of deepfake technology for the better good of society, sharing content and information for educational purposes, etc. Deepfakes can also support addressing inequalities effectively. Hence, the application of deepfake needs to be monitored through strict regulations. It can be further stated that lawmakers and governments must focus on creating critical policies enabling AI and deepfakes to improve society (A. Kaur, Kumar, et al., 2023).

The ethical and moral guidelines are that deepfakes need to be made with the focus on providing better services in the educational industry, like creating better pictures of the universe, galaxy, and Milky Way and images of the organs in the human body so that they can be helpful for students to read and memorise (Bhatnagar et al., 2024; P. Sharma et al., 2024). Moreover, deepfakes can be used to create motion pictures and other related videos for entertainment purposes without affecting individual privacy.

13.11 Conclusion

Based on the discussion above, deepfake technology is currently being applied to affect individual personalities and adversely impact ethical and moral aspects. The study results are more focused on creating better strategies to use the deepfake to enhance the community and world by applying them to education, entertainment, etc. Also, when any pictures, videos, or audio are created using deepfake, they need to be presented with the disclaimer that they are using deepfake or other related AI technology; this will enable the viewers to differentiate the difference between the original and deepfake digital content.

The study also stated that the current usage of deepfakes needs to focus on the ethical issues raised in the current context. The digital content, mainly videos, audio, and photos, needs to be applied with more focus and be included in the ethical aspects. It has been noted that the application of AI needs to lead to the modifications of different digital contents, which has resulted in creating the appearance of these aspects. Moreover, deepfakes are very effective and sophisticated, and it is not easy to differentiate between the original and the contents created by deepfakes. There must be impactful and ethical aspects related to the moral factors that must be considered for the growing concern in the current scenario.

In conclusion, AI and deepfake technology can be utilised for different industries using social media platforms; hence, more market potential and benefits are available and expected to grow in the future. However, the only focus must be on protecting privacy, addressing ethical aspects, and ensuring that the content is created using AI technology; this will benefit society.

References

Agarwal, M., Gill, K. S., Upadhyay, D., & Devliyal, S. (2024). From Pixels to Insights: Harnessing Deep Learning for Accurate Plant Pathology Diagnosis. In C. R., K. M., M. S., & G. Y. (Eds.), *2024 International Conference on Intelligent Systems for Cybersecurity, ISCS 2024*. Institute of Electrical and Electronics Engineers Inc. https://doi.org/10.1109/ISCS61804.2024.10581100

Agrawal, Y., Bhagoria, J. L., Gautam, A., Sharma, A., Yadav, A. S., Alam, T., Kumar, R., Goga, G., Chakroborty, S., & Kumar, R. (2023). Investigation of thermal performance of a ribbed solar air heater for sustainable built environment. *Sustainable Energy Technologies and Assessments*, *57*. https://doi.org/10.1016/j.seta.2023.103288

Agrawal, Y., Yugbodh, K., Ayachit, B., Tenguria, N., Kumar Nigam, P., Gautam, A., Singh yadav, A., Sharma, A., & Alam, T. (2023). Experimental investigation on thermal efficiency augmentation of solar air heater using copper wire for discrete roughened absorber plate. *Materials Today: Proceedings*. https://doi.org/10.1016/j.matpr.2022.12.244

Ahmad, A., Kandari, S., Sharma, C., & Saini, A. (2024). Cloud-Based Smart Cultivation System Using IoT Data Analytics. *Proceedings - International Conference on Computing, Power, and Communication Technologies, IC2PCT 2024*, 1509–1513. https://doi.org/10.1109/IC2PCT60090.2024.10486213

AL-Huqail, A. A., Singh, R., Širić, I., Kumar, P., Abou Fayssal, S., Kumar, V., Bachheti, R. K., Andabaka, Ž., Goala, M., & Eid, E. M. (2023). Occurrence and Health Risk Assessment of Heavy Metals in Lychee (Litchi chinensis Sonn., Sapindaceae) Fruit Samples. *Horticulturae*, *9*(9). https://doi.org/10.3390/horticulturae9090989

Alam, M. A., Kumar, R., Banoriya, D., Yadav, A. S., Goga, G., Saxena, K. K., Buddhi, D., & Mohan, R. (2023). Design and development of thermal comfort analysis for air-conditioned compartment. *International Journal on Interactive Design and Manufacturing*, *17*(5), 2777–2787. https://doi.org/10.1007/s12008-022-01015-8

Avikal, S., Pant, R., Barthwal, A., Ram, M., & Upadhyay, R. K. (2023). Factors implementing sustainable circular economy in agro-produce supply chain: DEMATEL-DANP-based approach. *Management of Environmental Quality: An International Journal*, *34*(4), 1158–1173. https://doi.org/10.1108/MEQ-03-2022-0088

Banerjee, D., Kukreja, V., Nisha Chandran, S., Khushboo, & Garg, N. (2024). Precision Diagnosis of Wheat Powdery Mildew Using CNN and Random Forest. *2024 International Conference on Emerging Smart Computing and Informatics, ESCI 2024*. https://doi.org/10.1109/ESCI59607.2024.10497264

Banerjee, D., Sharma, N., Upadhyay, D., Singh, M., & Chythanya, K. R. (2024). Decoding Sunflower Downy Mildew: Leveraging Hybrid Deep Learning for Scale Severity Analysis. *2024 5th International Conference for Emerging Technology, INCET 2024*. https://doi.org/10.1109/INCET61516.2024.10592879

Barwar, M. K., Sahu, L. K., Bhatnagar, P., Gupta, K. K., & Chander, A. H. (2021). A flicker-free decoupled ripple cancellation technique for LED driver circuits. *Optik*, *247*. https://doi.org/10.1016/j.ijleo.2021.168029

Barwar, M. K., Sahu, L. K., Bhatnagar, P., Gupta, K. K., & Chander, A. H. (2022). Performance analysis and reliability estimation of five-level rectifier. *International Journal of Circuit Theory and Applications*, *50*(3), 926–943. https://doi.org/10.1002/cta.3187

Bhatnagar, M., Kumar, P., Taneja, S., Sood, K., & Grima, S. (2024). From digital overload to trading Zen: The role of digital detox in enhancing intraday trading performance. In *Business Drivers in Promoting Digital Detoxification*. IGI Global. https://doi.org/10.4018/9798369311073.ch010

Bhatnagar, M., Taneja, S., & Kumar, P. (2023). The Effectiveness of Carbon Pricing Mechanism in Steering Financial Flows Toward Sustainable Projects. *International Journal of Environmental Impacts*, *6*(4), 183–196. https://doi.org/10.18280/ijei.060403

Bhatt, S. C., Kumar, V., Gupta, A. K., Mishra, S., Naik, B., Rustagi, S., & Preet, M. S. (2023). Insights on bio-functional properties of Myrica esculenta plant for nutritional and livelihood security. *Food Chemistry Advances*, *3*. https://doi.org/10.1016/j.focha.2023.100434

Chattopadhyay, S., Verma, A., Srivastava, A., Kukreja, V., Mehta, S., & Hariharan, S. (2024). Cauliflower Leaf Disease: Unraveling Severity Levels with Federated Learning CNN. *2024 3rd International Conference for Innovation in Technology, INOCON 2024*. https://doi.org/10.1109/INOCON60754.2024.10511798

Chincholikar, P., Singh, K. R. B., Natarajan, A., Kerry, R. G., Singh, J., Malviya, J., & Singh, R. P. (2023). Green nanobiopolymers for ecological applications: a step towards a sustainable environment. *RSC Advances*, *13*(18), 12411–12429. https://doi.org/10.1039/d2ra07707h

Choudhary, P., Pant, M., & Pant, K. (2023). Importance of antagonistic activities of microbes and their metabolites. In *Microbial Bioactive Compounds: Industrial and Agricultural Applications*. Springer Nature. https://doi.org/10.1007/978-3-031-40082-7_14

Dash, A. P., Alam, T., Siddiqui, M. I. H., Blecich, P., Kumar, M., Gupta, N. K., Ali, M. A., & Yadav, A. S. (2022). Impact on Heat Transfer Rate Due to an Extended Surface on the Passage of Microchannel Using Cylindrical Ribs with Varying Sector Angle. *Energies*, *15*(21). https://doi.org/10.3390/en15218191

Datta, S., Hamim, I., Jaiswal, D. K., & Sungthong, R. (2023). Sustainable agriculture. *BMC Plant Biology*, *23*(1). https://doi.org/10.1186/s12870-023-04626-9

Deepak, A., Sharma, K., Naik, G. R., Shah, D. U., Modi, G., Poonguzhali, S., & Singh, D. P. (2024). Image Processing based Robotic Car for Agricultural Ploughing using Machine Learning Approach. *International Journal of Intelligent Systems and Applications in Engineering*, *12*(2s), 718–724.

Deepti, Bachheti, A., Arya, A. K., Verma, D. K., & Bachheti, R. K. (2023). Allelopathic activity of genus Euphorbia. In G. D., P. B., M. U., M. R., & G. R. (Eds.), *AIP Conference Proceedings* (Vol. 2782). American Institute of Physics Inc. https://doi.org/10.1063/5.0154514

Dewangan, N. K., Gupta, K. K., & Bhatnagar, P. (2020). Modified reduced device multilevel inverter structures with open circuit fault-tolerance capabilities. *International Transactions on Electrical Energy Systems*, *30*(1). https://doi.org/10.1002/2050-7038.12142

Garg, G., Gupta, S., Mishra, P., Vidyarthi, A., Singh, A., & Ali, A. (2023). CROPCARE: An Intelligent Real-Time Sustainable IoT System for Crop Disease Detection Using Mobile Vision. *IEEE Internet of Things Journal*, *10*(4), 2840–2851. https://doi.org/10.1109/JIOT.2021.3109019

Gautam, A., Chauhan, A., Singh, A., Mundepi, S., Pant, M., & Husen, A. (2024). Use of seaweed extract-based biostimulants in plant growth, biochemical constituents, and productions. In *Biostimulants in Plant Protection and Performance*. Elsevier. https://doi.org/10.1016/B978-0-443-15884-1.00022-1

Husen, A., Bachheti, R. K., & Bachheti, A. (2021). Non-Timber Forest Products: Food, Healthcare and Industrial Applications. In *Non-Timber Forest Products: Food, Healthcare and Industrial Applications*. Springer International Publishing. https://doi.org/10.1007/978-3-030-73077-2

Joshi, J., Aeri, M., Kukreja, V., & Mehta, S. (2024). Revolutionizing in Agriculture: Federated CNN Models for Sunflower Leaf Diseases. In S. B., A. R., K. S.K., S. K.M., S. A.V., J. S., S. N., C. A., & G. R. (Eds.), *2024 11th International Conference on Reliability, Infocom Technologies and Optimization (Trends and Future Directions), ICRITO 2024*. Institute of Electrical and Electronics Engineers Inc. https://doi.org/10.1109/ICRITO61523.2024.10522441

Joshi, R., Sharma, G., Tripathi, V., & Nainwal, A. (2024). Classification of Weeds Using Neural Network Algorithms and Image Classifiers. *Lecture Notes in Computer Science (Including Subseries Lecture Notes in Artificial Intelligence and Lecture Notes in Bioinformatics), 14532 LNCS*, 26–36. https://doi.org/10.1007/978-3-031-53830-8_4

Kaur, A., Kukreja, V., Chamoli, S., Thapliyal, S., & Sharma, R. (2023). Advanced Disease Management: An Encoder-Decoder Approach for Tomato Black Mold Detection. *2023 IEEE Pune Section International Conference, PuneCon 2023*. https://doi.org/10.1109/PuneCon58714.2023.10450088

Kaur, A., Kukreja, V., Chamoli, S., Thapliyal, S., & Sharma, R. (2024). Bridging the Gap in Precision Agriculture: A CNN-Random Forest Fusion for Disease Classification. *2024 4th International Conference on Advances in Electrical, Computing, Communication and Sustainable Technologies, ICAECT 2024*. https://doi.org/10.1109/ICAECT60202.2024.10469081

Kaur, A., Kukreja, V., Gopal, L., Verma, G., & Sharma, R. (2024). A Hybrid Deep Learning Approach for Severity Classification of Pepper Leaf Mosaic Virus. *2024 4th International Conference on Advances in Electrical, Computing, Communication and Sustainable Technologies, ICAECT 2024*. https://doi.org/10.1109/ICAECT60202.2024.10469219

Kaur, A., Kukreja, V., Gopal, L., Verma, G., & Sharma, R. (2024). Next-Gen Hybrid Deep Learning for Accurate Pepper Leaf Mosaic Virus Classification. In M. J.R., R. P., S. Y.M., B. S., & V. K. (Eds.), *Proceedings of the 2nd International Conference on Intelligent and Innovative Technologies in Computing, Electrical and Electronics, ICIITCEE 2024*. Institute of Electrical and Electronics Engineers Inc. https://doi.org/10.1109/IITCEE59897.2024.10467359

Kaur, A., Kukreja, V., Kumar, M., Choudhary, A., & Sharma, R. (2024). Innovative Hybrid Deep Learning Strategy for Detecting and Classifying White Rot in Onions. *2024 IEEE 9th International Conference for*

Convergence in Technology, I2CT 2024. https://doi.org/10.1109/I2CT61223.2024.10543358

Kaur, A., Kukreja, V., Malhotra, S., Joshi, K., & Sharma, R. (2024). Rice Sheath Rot Disease Detection and Severity Classification: A Novel Framework Leveraging CNN-LSTM Models for Multi-Classification. *2024 IEEE International Conference on Interdisciplinary Approaches in Technology and Management for Social Innovation, IATMSI 2024*. https://doi.org/10.1109/IATMSI60426.2024.10502629

Kaur, A., Kukreja, V., Shukla, A. N., Garg, A., & Sharma, R. (2024). Mitigating Mustard Downy Mildew Disease: Early Detection and Prevention through a Hybrid CNN-SVM Model. *2024 IEEE International Conference on Interdisciplinary Approaches in Technology and Management for Social Innovation, IATMSI 2024*. https://doi.org/10.1109/IATMSI60426.2024.10503427

Kaur, A., Kukreja, V., Tiwari, P., Manwal, M., & Sharma, R. (2024). An Efficient Deep Learning-based VGG19 Approach for Rice Leaf Disease Classification. *2024 IEEE 9th International Conference for Convergence in Technology, I2CT 2024*. https://doi.org/10.1109/I2CT61223.2024.10544229

Kaur, A., Kukreja, V., Tiwari, P., Manwal, M., & Sharma, R. (2024). Fruitful Fusion: An Accuracy-Boosting Ensemble of VGG19 and Convolutional Neural Networks for Dragon Fruit Classification. *2024 IEEE International Conference on Interdisciplinary Approaches in Technology and Management for Social Innovation, IATMSI 2024*. https://doi.org/10.1109/IATMSI60426.2024.10502785

Kaur, A., Kukreja, V., Tiwari, P., Manwal, M., & Sharma, R. (2024). Optimized Tomato Rot Disease Severity Profiling: A Hybrid CNN-Random Forest Algorithm for Five-Tier Categorization. *2024 IEEE 9th International Conference for Convergence in Technology, I2CT 2024*. https://doi.org/10.1109/I2CT61223.2024.10544233

Kaur, A., Kukreja, V., Upadhyay, D., Aeri, M., & Sharma, R. (2024a). An Effective Pistachio Classification by Ensembling Fine-tuned ResNet20 and DenseNet Models. *2024 IEEE International Conference on Interdisciplinary Approaches in Technology and Management for Social Innovation, IATMSI 2024*. https://doi.org/10.1109/IATMSI60426.2024.10502708

Kaur, A., Kukreja, V., Upadhyay, D., Aeri, M., & Sharma, R. (2024b). An Integrated GoogleNet with Convolutional Neural Networks Model for Multiclass Bean Leaf Lesion Detection. *2024 IEEE International Conference on Interdisciplinary Approaches in Technology and*

Management for Social Innovation, IATMSI 2024. https://doi.org/10.1109/IATMSI60426.2024.10502575

Kaur, A., Kukreja, V., Upadhyay, D., Aeri, M., & Sharma, R. (2024c). ResPoultry: An Enhanced ResNet50 Model for Multiclass Classification of Poultry Diseases. *2024 IEEE International Conference on Interdisciplinary Approaches in Technology and Management for Social Innovation, IATMSI 2024*. https://doi.org/10.1109/IATMSI60426.2024.10502477

Kaur, A., Kumar, P., Taneja, S., & Ozen, E. (2023). Fintech emergence – an opportunity or threat to banking. *International Journal of Electronic Finance*, *13*(1), 1–19. https://doi.org/10.1504/IJEF.2024.135163

Kaur, A., Sharma, R., Rana, D. S., & Garg, A. (2024). Unveiling Kale Diversity in Indian Agriculture: CNN-Logistic Regression Classification. *2024 5th International Conference for Emerging Technology, INCET 2024*. https://doi.org/10.1109/INCET61516.2024.10593127

Kaur, A., Sharma, R., Thapliyal, N., & Manwal, M. (2024). Broccoli Classification: A Fusion of CNN and AdaBoost. *1st International Conference on Electronics, Computing, Communication and Control Technology, ICECCC 2024*. https://doi.org/10.1109/ICECCC61767.2024.10593946

Kaur, B., Mansi, Dimri, S., Singh, J., Mishra, S., Chauhan, N., Kukreti, T., Sharma, B., Singh, S. P., Arora, S., Uniyal, D., Agrawal, Y., Akhtar, S., Rather, M. A., Naik, B., Kumar, V., Gupta, A. K., Rustagi, S., & Preet, M. S. (2023). Insights into the harvesting tools and equipment's for horticultural crops: From then to now. *Journal of Agriculture and Food Research*, *14*. https://doi.org/10.1016/j.jafr.2023.100814

Kaur, G., Sharma, N., Chauhan, R., Singh, P., & Gupta, R. (2023). An Automated Approach for Detection and Classification of Plant Diseases. *2023 2nd International Conference on Futuristic Technologies, INCOFT 2023*. https://doi.org/10.1109/INCOFT60753.2023.10425170

Kaur, G., Sharma, N., Malhotra, S., Devliyal, S., & Kumar, B. V. (2024). Citrus Leaf Disease Classification Using VGG16 Convolutional Neural Network Architecture. *2024 IEEE 9th International Conference for Convergence in Technology, I2CT 2024*. https://doi.org/10.1109/I2CT61223.2024.10543761

Kaur, H., Hussain, S. J., Mir, R. A., Chandra Verma, V., Naik, B., Kumar, P., & Dubey, R. C. (2023). Nanofertilizers – Emerging smart fertilizers for modern and sustainable agriculture. *Biocatalysis and Agricultural Biotechnology*, *54*. https://doi.org/10.1016/j.bcab.2023.102921

Khan, S. A., Alam, T., Khan, M. S., Blecich, P., Kamal, M. A., Gupta, N. K., & Yadav, A. S. (2022). Life Cycle Assessment of Embodied Carbon in Buildings: Background, Approaches and Advancements. *Buildings*, *12*(11). https://doi.org/10.3390/buildings12111944

Kukrety, S., Godbole, V., Bisht, M., & Pal, M. K. (2024). Application of biosensors in agriculture and food industry. In *Biosensors for Foodborne Pathogen Detection: A Rapid Detection Approach*. Elsevier. https://doi.org/10.1016/B978-0-323-95586-7.00017-4

Kumar, A., Maithani, R., Ali, M. A., Gupta, N. K., Sharma, S., Alam, T., Majdi, H. S., Khan, T. M. Y., Yadav, A. S., & Eldin, S. M. (2023). Enhancement of heat transfer utilizing small height twisted tape flat plate solar heat collector: A numerical study. *Case Studies in Thermal Engineering*, *48*. https://doi.org/10.1016/j.csite.2023.103123

Kumar, A., Nirala, A., Singh, V. P., Sahoo, B. K., Singh, R. C., Chaudhary, R., Dewangan, A. K., Gaurav, G. K., Klemeš, J. J., & Liu, X. (2023). The utilisation of coconut shell ash in production of hybrid composite: Microstructural characterisation and performance analysis. *Journal of Cleaner Production*, *398*. https://doi.org/10.1016/j.jclepro.2023.136494

Kumar, A., Singh, V. P., Nirala, A., Singh, R. C., Chaudhary, R., Mourad, A.-H. I., Sahoo, B. K., & Kumar, D. (2023). Influence of tool rotational speed on mechanical and corrosion behaviour of friction stir processed AZ31/Al2O3 nanocomposite. *Journal of Magnesium and Alloys*, *11*(7), 2585–2599. https://doi.org/10.1016/j.jma.2023.06.012

Kumar, M., Aeri, M., Chandel, R., Kukreja, V., & Mehta, S. (2024). Federated Learning CNN for Smart Agriculture: A Modeling for Soybean Disease Detection. *2024 IEEE International Conference on Interdisciplinary Approaches in Technology and Management for Social Innovation, IATMSI 2024*. https://doi.org/10.1109/IATMSI60426.2024.10503189

Kumar, R., Dwivedi, R. K., Arya, R. K., Sonia, P., Yadav, A. S., Saxena, K. K., Khan, M. I., & Moussa, S. Ben. (2023). Current development of carbide free bainitic and retained austenite on wear resistance in high silicon steel. *Journal of Materials Research and Technology*, *24*, 9171–9202. https://doi.org/10.1016/j.jmrt.2023.05.067

Kumar, R. R., Jain, A. K., Sharma, V., Das, P., Midha, M., & Singh, M. (2024). Towards Precision Agriculture: A Unified CNN and Random Forest Framework for Jasmine Leaf Disease Recognition. *4th International Conference on Innovative Practices in Technology and Management 2024, ICIPTM 2024*. https://doi.org/10.1109/ICIPTM59628.2024.10563259

Kumar, V., Banerjee, D., Chauhan, R., Kukreti, S., & Singh Gill, K. (2024). Optimizing Citrus Disease Prediction: A Hybrid CNN-SVM Approach for Enhanced Accuracy. *2024 3rd International Conference for*

Innovation in Technology, INOCON 2024. https://doi.org/10.1109/INOCON60754.2024.10511309

Kumar, V., Banerjee, D., Chauhan, R., Rawat, R. S., & Gill, K. S. (2023). Revolutionizing Pear Tree Disease Detection: An In-Depth Investigation into CNN-Based Approaches. *2023 Global Conference on Information Technologies and Communications, GCITC 2023*. https://doi.org/10.1109/GCITC60406.2023.10426553

Kumar, V., Banerjee, D., Upadhyay, D., Singh, M., & Ravi Chythanya, K. (2024). CNN-Random Forest Hybrid Model for Improved Ginger Leaf Disease Classification. *International Conference on E-Mobility, Power Control and Smart Systems: Futuristic Technologies for Sustainable Solutions, ICEMPS 2024*. https://doi.org/10.1109/ICEMPS60684.2024.10559352

Kumari, N., Alam, T., Ali, M. A., Yadav, A. S., Gupta, N. K., Siddiqui, M. I. H., Dobrotă, D., Rotaru, I. M., & Sharma, A. (2022). A Numerical Investigation on Hydrothermal Performance of Micro Channel Heat Sink with Periodic Spatial Modification on Sidewalls. *Micromachines*, *13*(11). https://doi.org/10.3390/mi13111986

Kushwaha, A. D., Patel, B., Khan, I. A., & Agrawal, A. (2023). Fabrication and characterization of hexagonal boron nitride/polyester composites to study the effect of filler loading and surface modification for microelectronic applications. *Polymer Composites*, *44*(8), 4579–4593. https://doi.org/10.1002/pc.27421

Mahla, S. K., Goyal, T., Goyal, D., Sharma, H., Dhir, A., & Goga, G. (2022). Optimization of engine operating variables on performance and emissions characteristics of biogas fuelled CI engine by the design of experiments: Taguchi approach. *Environmental Progress and Sustainable Energy*, *41*(2). https://doi.org/10.1002/ep.13736

Mahor, V., Bijrothiya, S., Mishra, R., & Rawat, R. (2022). ML techniques for attack and anomaly detection in internet of things networks. In *Autonomous Vehicles* (Vol. 1). wiley. https://doi.org/10.1002/9781119871989.ch13

Mahor, V., Bijrothiya, S., Mishra, R., Rawat, R., & Soni, A. (2022). The smart city based on AI and infrastructure: A new mobility concepts and realities. In *Autonomous Vehicles* (Vol. 1). wiley. https://doi.org/10.1002/9781119871989.ch15

Mahor, V., Garg, B., Telang, S., Pachlasiya, K., Chouhan, M., & Rawat, R. (2022). Cyber Threat Phylogeny Assessment and Vulnerabilities Representation at Thermal Power Station. *Lecture Notes in Networks and Systems*, *481 LNNS*, 28–39. https://doi.org/10.1007/978-981-19-3182-6_3

Mahor, V., Pachlasiya, K., Garg, B., Chouhan, M., Telang, S., & Rawat, R. (2022). Mobile Operating System (Android) Vulnerability Analysis Using Machine Learning. *Lecture Notes in Networks and Systems, 481 LNNS*, 159–169. https://doi.org/10.1007/978-981-19-3182-6_13

Malhotra, S., Manwal, M., Kukreja, V., & Mehta, S. (2024). Technological Synergy in Agriculture: A Federated Learning CNNs Against Banana Leaf Diseases. In S. B., A. R., K. S.K., S. K.M., S. A.V., J. S., S. N., C. A., & G. R. (Eds.), *2024 11th International Conference on Reliability, Infocom Technologies and Optimization (Trends and Future Directions), ICRITO 2024*. Institute of Electrical and Electronics Engineers Inc. https://doi.org/10.1109/ICRITO61523.2024.10522379

Mathur, S., Kumar, S., & Choudhury, T. (2024). Prognostication of Weather Patterns using Meteorological Data and ML Techniques. *EAI Endorsed Transactions on Energy Web*, *11*, 1–10. https://doi.org/10.4108/ew.5648

Mir, T. A., Banerjee, D., Chauhan, R., & Singh, M. (2024). Diseases: CNN-SVM Integration. *2nd International Conference on Artificial Intelligence and Machine Learning Applications: Healthcare and Internet of Things, AIMLA 2024*. https://doi.org/10.1109/AIMLA59606.2024.10531355

Mohapatra, B., Chamoli, S., Salvi, P., & Saxena, S. C. (2023). Fostering nanoscience's strategies: A new frontier in sustainable crop improvement for abiotic stress tolerance. *Plant Nano Biology*, *3*. https://doi.org/10.1016/j.plana.2023.100026

Nayak, N., Kumar, D., Chattopadhay, S., Kukreja, V., & Verma, A. (2024). Improved Detection of Fusarium Head Blight in Wheat Ears through YOLACT Instance Segmentation. In S. B., A. R., K. S.K., S. K.M., S. A.V., J. S., S. N., C. A., & G. R. (Eds.), *2024 11th International Conference on Reliability, Infocom Technologies and Optimization (Trends and Future Directions), ICRITO 2024*. Institute of Electrical and Electronics Engineers Inc. https://doi.org/10.1109/ICRITO61523.2024.10522220

Ojha, N. K., Upadhyay, D., Manwal, M., Kukreja, V., & Sharma, R. (2024). Implementing CNN and RF Models for Multi-Level Classification: Deciphering Beetroot Aphid Disease Severity. *2024 5th International Conference for Emerging Technology, INCET 2024*. https://doi.org/10.1109/INCET61516.2024.10593519

Pithode, K., Singh, D., Chaturvedi, R., Goyal, B., Dogra, A., Hasoon, A., & Lepcha, D. C. (2023). Evaluation of the Solar Heat Pipe with Aluminium Tube Collector in different Environmental Conditions. *2023 3rd Asian Conference on Innovation in Technology, ASIANCON 2023*. https://doi.org/10.1109/ASIANCON58793.2023.10269867

Prakash, S., Kakumanu, U., Badhotiya, G. K., & Singh, R. (2023). Analysis of potato supply chain in Indian context using ISM. In S. Y., S. G., & B. G.K. (Eds.), *AIP Conference Proceedings* (Vol. 2521). American Institute of Physics Inc. https://doi.org/10.1063/5.0113701

Pramanik, B., Sar, P., Bharti, R., Gupta, R. K., Purkayastha, S., Sinha, S., Chattaraj, S., & Mitra, D. (2023). Multifactorial role of nanoparticles in alleviating environmental stresses for sustainable crop production and protection. *Plant Physiology and Biochemistry*, *201*. https://doi.org/10.1016/j.plaphy.2023.107831

Prasad, A. O., Mishra, P., Jain, U., Pandey, A., Sinha, A., Yadav, A. S., Kumar, R., Sharma, A., Kumar, G., Hazim Salem, K., Sharma, A., & Dixit, A. K. (2023). Design and development of software stack of an autonomous vehicle using robot operating system. *Robotics and Autonomous Systems*, *161*. https://doi.org/10.1016/j.robot.2022.104340

Rahat, I. S., Ghosh, H., Ramesh, J. V. N., Kiran, A., & Verma, P. (2024). Cassava Syndrome Scan a Pioneering Deep Learning System for Accurate Cassava Leaf Disease Classification. *Communications in Computer and Information Science*, *2047 CCIS*, 111–123. https://doi.org/10.1007/978-3-031-55486-5_9

Rajput, K., Manwal, M., Chauhan, R. K., Kukreja, V., & Mehta, S. (2024). Transforming Sugarcane Leaf Diseases Pathology with Convolutional Neural Networks and SVM. In S. B., A. R., K. S.K., S. K.M., S. A.V., J. S., S. N., C. A., & G. R. (Eds.), *2024 11th International Conference on Reliability, Infocom Technologies and Optimization (Trends and Future Directions), ICRITO 2024*. Institute of Electrical and Electronics Engineers Inc. https://doi.org/10.1109/ICRITO61523.2024.10522214

Rana, A., Tyagi, M., Rai, N., Arya, S. K., Husain, R., & Singh, A. (2023). Safety, nutritional quality, and health benefits of organic products. In *Transforming Organic Agri-Produce into Processed Food Products: Post-COVID-19 Challenges and Opportunities*. Apple Academic Press.

Rana, G., Singh, R., Chauhan, R., Singh Pokhariya, H., & Chhabra, A. (2024). Disease Recognition in ViticultureCNN-SVM Framework for Accurate Grapevine Disease Diagnosis. *2024 4th International Conference on Advances in Electrical, Computing, Communication and Sustainable Technologies, ICAECT 2024*. https://doi.org/10.1109/ICAECT60202.2024.10469456

Rathod, N. J., Chopra, M. K., Shelke, S. N., Chaurasiya, P. K., Kumar, R., Saxena, K. K., & Prakash, C. (2024). Investigations on hard turning using SS304 sheet metal component grey based Taguchi and regression methodology. *International Journal on Interactive Design and Manufacturing*, *18*(5), 2653–2664. https://doi.org/10.1007/s12008-023-01244-5

Rawat, R., Mahor, V., Chouhan, M., Pachlasiya, K., Telang, S., & Garg, B. (2022). Systematic Literature Review (SLR) on Social Media and the Digital Transformation of Drug Trafficking on Darkweb. *Lecture Notes in Networks and Systems*, *481 LNNS*, 181–205. https://doi.org/10.1007/978-981-19-3182-6_15

Saikumar, A., Singh, A., Dobhal, A., Arora, S., Junaid, P. M., Badwaik, L. S., & Kumar, S. (2024). A review on the impact of physical, chemical, and novel treatments on the quality and microbial safety of fruits and vegetables. *Systems Microbiology and Biomanufacturing*, *4*(2), 575–597. https://doi.org/10.1007/s43393-023-00217-9

Savary, S., Andrivon, D., Esker, P., Frey, P., Hüberli, D., Kumar, J., McDonald, B. A., McRoberts, N., Nelson, A., Pethybridge, S., Rossi, V., Schreinemachers,P.,Willocquet,L.,Bove,F.,Sah,S.,Singh,M.,Djurle,A., Xu, X., Ojiambo, P., … Yuen, J. (2023). A Global Assessment of the State of Plant Health. *Plant Disease*, *107*(12), 3649–3665. https://doi.org/10.1094/PDIS-01-23-0166-FE

Savita, & Vimal, V. (2023). Integrating IoT-Based Environmental Monitoring and Data Analytics for Crop-Specific Smart Agriculture Management: A Multivariate Analysis. In C. N. (Ed.), *Proceedings - International Conference on Technological Advancements in Computational Sciences, ICTACS 2023* (pp. 368–373). Institute of Electrical and Electronics Engineers Inc. https://doi.org/10.1109/ICTACS59847.2023.10390277

Saxena, V., Singh, M., Saxena, P., Singh, M., Srivastava, A. P., Kumar, N., Deepak, A., & Shrivastava, A. (2024). Utilizing Support Vector Machines for Early Detection of Crop Diseases in Precision Agriculture a Data Mining Perspective. *International Journal of Intelligent Systems and Applications in Engineering*, *12*(16s), 281–288.

Semwal, P., Painuli, S., Begum J.P, S., Jamloki, A., Rauf, A., Olatunde, A., Mominur Rahman, M., Mukerjee, N., Ahmed Khalil, A., Aljohani, A. S. M., Al Abdulmonem, W., & Simal-Gandara, J. (2023). Exploring the nutritional and health benefits of pulses from the Indian Himalayan region: A glimpse into the region's rich agricultural heritage. *Food Chemistry*, *422*. https://doi.org/10.1016/j.foodchem.2023.136259

Shao, D., Kombe, C., & Saxena, S. (2023). An ensemble design of a cash crops-warehouse receipt system (WRS) based on blockchain smart contracts. *Journal of Agribusiness in Developing and Emerging Economies*, *13*(5), 762–774. https://doi.org/10.1108/JADEE-02-2022-0032

Sharma, H., Rana, A., Singh, R. P., Goyal, B., Dogra, A., & Lepcha, D. C. (2023). Improving Efficiency of Panel Using Solar Tracker Controlled Through Fuzzy Logic. *2023 International Conference on Sustainable Emerging Innovations in Engineering and Technology, ICSEIET 2023*, 286–289. https://doi.org/10.1109/ICSEIET58677.2023.10303639

Sharma, P., Taneja, S., Kumar, P., Özen, E., & Singh, A. (2024). Application of the UTAUT model toward individual acceptance: emerging trends in artificial intelligence-based banking services. *International Journal of Electronic Finance*, *13*(3), 352–366. https://doi.org/10.1504/IJEF.2024.139584

Shreshtha, K., Raj, S., Pal, A. K., Tripathi, P., Choudhary, K. K., Mitra, D., Rani, A., Santos-Villalobos, S. de los, & Tripathi, V. (2024). Isolation and identification of Rhizospheric and Endophytic Bacteria from Cucumber plants irrigated with wastewater: Exploring their roles in plant growth promotion and disease suppression. *Current Research in Microbial Sciences*, *7*. https://doi.org/10.1016/j.crmicr.2024.100256

Shrivastava, V., Yadav, A. S., Sharma, A. K., Singh, P., Alam, T., & Sharma, A. (2022). Performance Comparison of Solar Air Heater with Extended Surfaces and Iron Filling. *International Journal of Vehicle Structures and Systems*, *14*(5), 607–610. https://doi.org/10.4273/ijvss.14.5.10

Singh, S., Banerjee, D., Chauhan, R., Joshi, K., & Singh Gill, K. (2024). Enhancing Sugarcane Crop Health: CNN and SVM-Based Predictive Analysis of Leaf Diseases. *2024 3rd International Conference for Innovation in Technology, INOCON 2024*. https://doi.org/10.1109/INOCON60754.2024.10511876

Singh, V. P., Kumar, R., Kumar, A., & Dewangan, A. K. (2023). Automotive light weight multi-materials sheets joining through friction stir welding technique: An overview. *Materials Today: Proceedings*. https://doi.org/10.1016/j.matpr.2023.02.171

Singla, M., Singh Gill, K., Upadhyay, D., Singh, V., & Kumar, G. R. (2024). Visualisation and Classification of Coffee Leaves via the Use of a Sequential CNN Model Based on Deep Learning. *4th International Conference on Innovative Practices in Technology and Management 2024, ICIPTM 2024*. https://doi.org/10.1109/ICIPTM59628.2024.10563812

Širić, I., Alhag, S. K., Al-Shuraym, L. A., Mioč, B., Držaić, V., Abou Fayssal, S., Kumar, V., Singh, J., Kumar, P., Singh, R., Bachheti, R. K., Goala, M., Kumar, P., & Eid, E. M. (2023). Combined Use of TiO2

Nanoparticles and Biochar Produced from Moss (Leucobryum glaucum (Hedw.) Ångstr.) Biomass for Chinese Spinach (Amaranthus dubius L.) Cultivation under Saline Stress. *Horticulturae*, *9*(9). https://doi.org/10.3390/horticulturae9091056

Suryavanshi, A., Kukreja, V., Bordoloi, D., Mehta, S., & Choudhary, A. (2023). Agricultural Insights Through Federated Learning CNN: A Case Study on Jackfruit Leaf Disease. In D. R.K., S. A.Kr., S. R., B. S., & K. V. (Eds.), *Proceedings of the 2023 12th International Conference on System Modeling and Advancement in Research Trends, SMART 2023* (pp. 36–42). Institute of Electrical and Electronics Engineers Inc. https://doi.org/10.1109/SMART59791.2023.10428321

Suryavanshi, A., Kukreja, V., Dogra, A., Bordoloi, D., & Joshi, K. (2024). A CNN and Random Forest Fusion with Optimized Convolutional Layers for Accurate Disease Identification in Rice Using Machine Learning. *2024 IEEE International Conference on Interdisciplinary Approaches in Technology and Management for Social Innovation, IATMSI 2024*. https://doi.org/10.1109/IATMSI60426.2024.10502936

Suryavanshi, A., Kukreja, V., Mehta, S., Chattopadhyay, S., & Verma, A. (2024). Disruptive Farming Intelligence: Federated Learning CNN for Broccoli Leaf Disease Classification. *2024 International Conference on Cognitive Robotics and Intelligent Systems, ICC - ROBINS 2024*, 697–702. https://doi.org/10.1109/ICC-ROBINS60238.2024.10534024

Suryavanshi, A., Kukreja, V., Rana, D. S., & Thapliyal, S. (2024). Harvesting Insights: An Innovative Framework for Maize Leaf Disease Detection through CNN and Random Forest Integrations. In M. S., T. H.K., M. J.R., M. S., G. T., & S. K.S. (Eds.), *Proceedings of 2nd International Conference on Advancements in Smart, Secure and Intelligent Computing, ASSIC 2024*. Institute of Electrical and Electronics Engineers Inc. https://doi.org/10.1109/ASSIC60049.2024.10507936

Suryavanshi, A., Kukreja, V., Upadhyay, D., Mehta, S., & Thapliyal, S. (2024). Federated Learning CNN for Broccoli Leaf Disease Control: A Path to Sustainable Farming. In S. B., A. R., K. S.K., S. K.M., S. A.V., J. S., S. N., C. A., & G. R. (Eds.), *2024 11th International Conference on Reliability, Infocom Technologies and Optimization (Trends and Future Directions), ICRITO 2024*. Institute of Electrical and Electronics Engineers Inc. https://doi.org/10.1109/ICRITO61523.2024.10522286

Suryavanshi, A., Tanwar, S., Kukreja, V., Choudhary, A., & Chamoli, S. (2023). An Integrated Approach to Potato Leaf Disease Detection Using

Convolutional Neural Networks and Random Forest. *Proceedings of the 2023 International Conference on Innovative Computing, Intelligent Communication and Smart Electrical Systems, ICSES 2023*. https://doi.org/10.1109/ICSES60034.2023.10465557

Tanwar, V., Anand, V., Chauhan, R., & Rawat, D. (2023). A Deep Learning for Early Tomato Leaf Disease Detection: A CNN Approach. *2023 2nd International Conference on Futuristic Technologies, INCOFT 2023*. https://doi.org/10.1109/INCOFT60753.2023.10425552

Tiwari, K., Bafila, P., Negi, P., & Singh, R. (2023). The applications of nanotechnology in nutraceuticals: A review. In S. Y., S. G., & B. G.K. (Eds.), *AIP Conference Proceedings* (Vol. 2521). American Institute of Physics Inc. https://doi.org/10.1063/5.0129695

Upadhyay, D., Manwal, M., Kukreja, V., & Sharma, R. (2024). Advancing Citrus Disease Diagnosis: Application of EfficientNetB3 for Precise Classification of Orange Tree Pathologies. *International Conference on Emerging Technologies in Computer Science for Interdisciplinary Applications, ICETCS 2024*. https://doi.org/10.1109/ICETCS61022.2024.10543447

Yadav, A. P. S., Thapliyal, N., Aeri, M., Kukreja, V., & Sharma, R. (2024). Advanced Deep Learning Approaches: Utilizing VGG16, VGG19, and ResNet Architectures for Enhanced Grapevine Disease Detection. In S. B., A. R., K. S.K., S. K.M., S. A.V., J. S., S. N., C. A., & G. R. (Eds.), *2024 11th International Conference on Reliability, Infocom Technologies and Optimization (Trends and Future Directions), ICRITO 2024*. Institute of Electrical and Electronics Engineers Inc. https://doi.org/10.1109/ICRITO61523.2024.10522276

Yadav, A. S., Alam, T., Gupta, G., Saxena, R., Gupta, N. K., Allamraju, K. V., Kumar, R., Sharma, N., Sharma, A., Pandey, U., & Agrawal, Y. (2022). A Numerical Investigation of an Artificially Roughened Solar Air Heater. *Energies*, *15*(21). https://doi.org/10.3390/en15218045

Yadav, A. S., Mishra, A., Dwivedi, K., Agrawal, A., Galphat, A., & Sharma, N. (2022). Investigation on performance enhancement due to rib roughened solar air heater. *Materials Today: Proceedings*, *63*, 726–730. https://doi.org/10.1016/j.matpr.2022.05.071

Yashu, Kukreja, V., Srivastava, P., & Garg, A. (2024). TuberVision: Unveiling Potato Diversity through Advanced Classification Techniques. *2024 IEEE International Conference on Interdisciplinary Approaches in Technology and Management for Social Innovation, IATMSI 2024*. https://doi.org/10.1109/IATMSI60426.2024.10502772

Yashu, Kukreja, V., Srivastava, P., Garg, A., & Hariharan, S. (2024). Fostering Sustainable Farming: A Novel Model for Automated Tomato Disease Detection. *2024 IEEE 9th International Conference for Convergence in Technology, I2CT 2024*. https://doi.org/10.1109/I2CT61223.2024.10543940

14

Risks to Individual Privacy and Security in the World of Deepfake Technology

Pawan Pant[1], K. K. Mishra[1] and Rajendra Rajaram[2]

[1]University School of Business, Chandigarh University, India
[2]Unisa School of Business and Leadership, University of South Africa, South Africa
Email: pawanpant04@gmail.com; kkmsitmbbk@gmail.com; rajaramr@unisa.ac.za

Abstract

The digital age accentuates threats to personal safety and privacy through deepfake technologies. This chapter critically discusses deepfakes and the individual risks involving security lapses and privacy breaches. The paper attempts to look at how deepfakes can result in a compromising of personal privacy through identity theft, impersonation, and even psychic hurt by reviewing the literature and using case studies. Other security implications of deepfake manipulation are estimated to include financial deception, reputational harm, and its use in cyber-attacks. This consists of several legal and regulatory challenges that deepfake technology must consider in the complications arising under present legal frameworks and possible future regulation to tamp down the dangers. The chapter addresses established and recently developed technologies to detect deepfake threats and their mitigation. The section concludes with some valuable tips that may help secure people against Deepfake-induced security threats and privacy violations. It emphasises the need for critical thinking and digital literacy, as these are crucial tools in the fight against deepfake technology. The chapter tries to underline that solving complex problems thrown up by deepfake technology essentially involves stakeholder collaboration to guarantee people's security and privacy in this digital era.

14.1 Introduction

The evolution of deepfake technology, thanks to the development of AI and machine learning algorithms, has led to a more severe and potentially threatening landscape. Its hyper-realistic synthetic media can manipulate images, video, and audio in an unprecedentedly precise way (Singh et al., 2024). What was once appreciated for its entertainment value has become a severe concern for personal security and privacy (Gupta et al., 2023; S. Sharma & Tyagi, 2023; Suryavanshi et al., 2024). Deepfakes make it possible to create believable, fake content, for instance, videos of people saying or doing things they never said or did. It is otherwise a tool of ill use in cases of disinformation campaigns, fraud, or blackmail. The more deepfakes appear, the greater the need for ethical, legal, and societal implications concerning this technology (A. Kaur et al., 2023, 2024; Nagabhooshanam et al., 2024; Ritika et al., 2024). Advanced manipulation tools are available online, with many tutorials and software. The chapter deliberates upon the threats of deepfake technology to personal security and privacy and proceeds to evaluate the threats and challenges that exist in the cyber world, along with mitigating measures (K. Kaur et al., 2024; Nautiyal et al., 2024; M. Sharma et al., 2023).

With the increasing usage of deepfake technologies in recent years, serious questions have been raised regarding how they can manipulate social norms and threaten people's security and privacy. One unique problem created within the digital domain in these times is the manufacture of artificial media dubbed "deep fakes", which depend on advanced algorithms in machine learning processes to build convincing images of people saying and acting in ways they never have (Bhandari et al., 2023; Upadhyay, Manwal, Deep, et al., 2024; Upadhyay, Manwal, Gupta, et al., 2024). It has also been noticed that doctored images, videos, and audio are increasingly used to conduct nefarious acts such as spreading disinformation, fraud, and reputational destruction. Deepfakes continue to rise with advancements and accessibility to their underlying technology, constituting grave dangers to people's security and privacy. Deepfake production tools and tutorials are being widely disseminated across internet platforms, empowering anyone with shallow technical expertise to create convincing synthetic media. In this light, the analysis of such complicated questions thrown up by deepfakes assumes the importance of finding some workable solutions to reduce the adverse impact of this technology on people and society.

14.2 Deepfake Technology: A Primer

The very term "deep fake" represents a postmodernism of the terms "deep learning" and "fake". It has massively picked up as a robust technique for creating synthetic media that looks and acts exactly like real people. [1]. Deepfake technology, in essence, makes highly realistic forgeries through deep learning algorithms that manipulate pre-existing audio, video, or image information with the seamless addition or removal of parts, with the help of generative adversarial networks, or GANs. Deepfake algorithms learn mappings of facial expressions, gestures, and speech patterns by training on large datasets of photos and videos. Realistic simulations are typically indistinguishable from actual recordings that they can make. Deepfakes – altered media – are now created with relative simplicity thanks to essential software tools at anyone's disposal. Those applications may range from benign amusement and digital art through harmful political manipulation, defamation, and propagation of misinformation. This technology instantly drives several deep, fake-related serious moral, legal, and societal challenges, for which a much greater understanding of the potential, limitations, and probable impact is needed (Dutta et al., 2023; Joshi et al., 2023).

Deepfakes represent a challenging fusion of AI with manipulated digital media, whereby technology is rendered easiest to produce inordinate counterfeit content, undermining the traditional concept of reality and truth. Deepfake algorithms synthesise and analyse vast volumes of audio-visual data with the help of deep learning techniques and, therefore, prepare synthetic media that can imitate and mimic with full swing the voices, gestures, and looks intended for the respective targets. Primarily, these algorithms utilise neural networks, including convolutional neural networks and auto-encoders, to encode and reconstruct face expressions or characteristics unbiasedly (Choudhary et al., 2023).

Deepfakes represent this challenging fusion of AI and manipulated digital media, whereby the technology becomes easiest to produce inordinate counterfeit content and undermine the traditional notion of reality and truth. Deepfake algorithms can synthesise and analyze large volumes of audiovisual data by utilising techniques in deep learning, thus setting up synthetic media that can precisely imitate and mimic voices, gestures, and looks intended for the respective targets. These mainly include neural networks, such as convolutional neural networks and auto-encoders, for the encoding and reconstruction of face expressions or characteristics in a truthful manner (Pai et al., 2023).

14.3 Risks Posed by Deepfakes to Individual Privacy

Advanced algorithms using deepfake technology to manipulate visual and audio information may jeopardise personal information and deplete public trust in digital media to the detriment of individual privacy. The primary concern is that deepfakes will simplify identity theft and impersonation, where people's likenesses are added to fake content without permission. This would make people do some things in deepfake videos or pictures, which, in real life, they would never do, thus spoiling their reputation and hurting their feelings. Serious privacy violations may be allowed. Furthermore, "deep nudes", or deep fake porn, may turn out to be highly hazardous regarding privacy and respect because the faces of people could be copied and added to some sexual material without knowing it. Deepfake information spreads rapidly in social networks and online forums; every moment increases the risk of privacy violations that may result in loss of reputation and social shaming. For this reason, it would be worth developing a multilayered approach: technological developments, legal mechanisms, and increasing public awareness to reduce the risks that can affect the privacy of individuals due to deep fakes (Niharika et al., 2023).

14.4 Case Studies on Deepfake Technology

14.4.1 Case study: Deepfake revenge pornography

14.4.1.1 Revenge pornography

There have been cases of deepfake content that has been created and shared as a means for revenge porn, also called non-consensual pornography. For example, in 2019, an explicit deepfake of a famous Indian actress whose face was pasted onto an adult actress went viral across the Internet. Deepfakes can trigger psycho-social unease and cyberbullying, as demonstrated by the sheer terror the actress was in when her video became the rage of the internet (Tomar et al., 2023).

14.4.1.2 Background

Deepfake revenge pornography was one of the very bothering instances that came up in 2019, pointing out the severe impact on privacy – one of the nastiest uses of deepfake technologies and the making and circulation of a movie that placed an Indian actress's image over an adult film actress's body. Subsequently, it plunged an actress into heavy emotional depression and public outrage due to the large-scale online circulation of the video (Banerjee et al., 2023).

14.4.1.3 Incident details

This pornographic deepfake video was, within no time, uploaded on the internet and began circulating, hence getting millions of viewers and sharers. Once the movie got online, it would never stop circulating, thus further traumatising the victim and infringing the right of the actress to privacy. Being falsely accused, the actress angrily disowned the movie and even questioned some sexually explicit activities she had been doing. This event called for more stringent measures to stop cyber exploitation (Khan et al., 2023). The incident sparked public debate on the moral and legal implications of deepfake revenge pornography.

14.4.1.4 Impact

The actress paid a heavy cost in a deepfake revenge pornography incident, subsumed in the sequelae of severe emotional trauma, hurt reputation, and possible professional and personal life damage. This further highlighted deeper worries that the use of deepfake can make humans easily fall victim to any exploitation and called for very secure systems that would not lead to cyber exploitation besides an immediate victim. The breadth of the incident further raised concerns over how effective the existing legal frameworks would be in prosecuting cases related to deepfakes and the obligations of online platforms to filter offensive information.

14.4.1.5 Lessons learned

The deepfake revenge pornography case serves as a pointed reminder of how destructive malevolent deepfake manipulation can be to people's privacy and dignity. More immediately, it shows the proactive measures required in technological solutions, legal reform, and raising public awareness for detecting and reducing deepfake technology-based violations. A need to support the victims of deepfake exploitation and their legal redress and defence against further harm has also been underlined.

14.4.2 Case study: Deepfake political manipulation

14.4.2.1 Political manipulation

Deepfakes have already been used to destroy the rights and privacy of people and even manipulate political discourses. For instance, there is an example of a deep fake video presented as a Belgian politician saying something that he never said, presented on social media. The example is highly relevant because its wide circulation by the political opponents and video advertisement stirred public outrage and defamed his reputation.

14.4.2.2 Background

Deepfake technology has recently infiltrated the manipulation of political debates and eroded faith in democratic processes. Another clear example was the creation and publishing online of a deepfake video depicting a Belgian politician uttering ghetto, divisive, and inaccurate rhetoric over climate change. Fully aware that this would divide public opinion and pressure citizens, the video was intentionally released via social networking sites.

14.4.2.3 Incident details

In 2020, a deepfake video went online with what looked like a speech by a Belgian politician where he was visibly unhappy with environmental campaigners and went on to say climate change was unreal. The politician's speech included all manner of real-life facial expressions and lip-syncing. Since then, fact-checkers have attempted to reveal the video as a deepfake. However, it has gone viral on social media, shared by many duped into believing it is accurate.

14.4.2.4 Impact

The deepfake political manipulation episode exacted a high price on the targeted politician and the greater political environment. To illustrate, even though the politician and his sympathisers quickly moved to label it an intentional fabrication of the highest order, the damage had already been caused in huge blocks – in the form of negative coverage – to his credibility and reputation. Other than perpetuating social difference and showcasing rotten political figures and institutions, the video did much to deepen the current cynicism and polarisation. The event, therefore, has shown just how easily manipulated online spaces are and how difficult it is to combat misinformation in the digital age.

14.4.2.5 Lessons learned

The deepfake case of political manipulation has brought out into the open the urgent need for solid safeguards that would forestall the ruthless exploitation of deepfake technology for political ends. It underlines the urgency to intensify detection and verification processes with a view to proper detection and the fight against deepfake content. Importantly, this episode has pointed out that media literacy and critical thinking are critical in distinguishing fact from fiction amidst a world of misinformation and manipulation.

14.4.3 Case study: Deepfake celebrity impersonation

14.4.3.1 Celebrity impersonation

The technology of deepfakes can create enough convincing evidence of celebrities that play into their public personas to the point of malice. In 2021, various churned-out deepfake videos on social media portrayed a famous musician misbehaving. The artist tried to discredit the videos, but they circulated online, greatly smearing his reputation and privacy.

14.4.3.2 Background

Deepfake technology has created credible impersonations of celebrities to lead to a range of illicit behaviours, from satire and entertainment to even deception. One such creation and sharing of a deep fake film depicted a world-famous singer misbehaving. Such films spread virally through social media, significantly harming this singer's reputation.

14.4.3.3 Incident details

In 2021, a set of deepfake videos went online that claimed to show a famous singer involved in intimate scenes. The videos were entirely fabricated. They used the most advanced deep fake technology to place the musician's likeness over the actors' bodies, and reconstructions of the musician misbehaving were quite convincing. The performer came out trying to debunk the videos and explain that they were deepfakes; however, they continued going viral on social media, receiving millions of views and shares.

14.4.3.4 Impact

The deepfake celebrity impersonation event caused the targeted musician tremendous emotional suffering and reputation loss. The videos meant a reputation taint for the musicians and exposed them to unfair media, public scrutiny, and criticism. Due to the wide circulation of deepfake content, the musician's situation worsened, entrenching negative stereotypes and misconceptions. That incident was a real danger lurking in the manipulation using deepfakes and how tough it is to fight disinformation and libel in a digital age.

14.4.3.5 Lessons learned

Deepfake is a case of celebrity impersonation that stirred demands for more excellent protection against deepfake's mischievous manipulations, which cause harm to the reputation and privacy of people. It, therefore, calls for protective measures in developing technological solutions, changing the law, and raising public awareness to reduce threats that come with deep fake technology. Above all, this incident once again pushes to the fore the role that media literacy and critical thinking play in enabling citizens to sift fact news from fiction and not to spread disinformation.

14.4.4 Case study: Deepfake identity theft

14.4.4.1 Deepfake identity theft

The deepfake identity theft case with a well-known political figure unravels the severe possibility that manipulated media could amount to irreparable damage in the lives and reputations of individuals. Deepfake videos surfaced of the victim, highly sophisticated in their algorithms of artificial intelligence. These went viral, further fueling rumours regarding the victim and thus compromising his reputation. The sufferings of the victims were increased by the posting of this misinterpreted material continuously on social media and news networks. It completely erased the public's confidence despite trying to refute such baseless allegations. A vital safeguard against deepfake identity theft by tight authentication mechanisms is required as such cases point to dire needs and legislation that can endanger the safety and privacy of people in the present digital world. This also points to the crucial element of media literacy education and awareness campaigns within this quest for empowering people to recognise and prevent further distribution of false information on the Internet. It will require cooperation among governments, technology companies, and civil society organisations to develop solutions for protecting digital media integrity from deepfakes and to maintain fundamental values related to honesty and transparency.

14.4.4.2 Background

A famous case of profound fake identity theft from 2021 raised red flags about the risks of manipulating the media to fraud and impersonate crimes. Without his consent, a man's voice and likeness had been used to make deep, fake audio recordings and movies.

14.4.4.3 Incident details

She was a public figure and came to know that profound fake audio records and films featuring her misbehaving and spurious claims had been uploaded on the internet. Since these media items are of advanced deepfake technology, one may be unable to distinguish them from real happenings. The deepfake identity thieves tried to create a double victim in the media to access private data and financial accounts.

14.4.4.4 Impact

It resulted in severe consequences for the victim in terms of financial loss, privacy violation, and harm to his reputation. The manipulation of the media was used to spread a falsely portrayed image of the victim for the mockery of the public and the media. This shows the level of fraud and how easily people can fall prey to certain identity thefts using deep fake technology.

14.4.4.5 Lessons learned

This case revealed that much-improved security is required against impersonation and deepfake identity theft. More importantly, this indicates the need for a strong authentication mechanism with robust identity verification to avoid undesirable access to financial information and personal data. The incident further calls for raising awareness through proper education of people regarding deepfake risks and their identification and response.

14.4.5 Case study: Deepfake social engineering attack

14.4.5.1 Deepfake social engineering attack

Such a social engineering attack, using manipulated media with deepfakes against a multinational company, can be one of the latest but most critical threats to cybersecurity. In that scenario, attackers have used the most advanced technologies in the face of deepfakes to masquerade themselves as close colleagues and high-ranking executives. With the robust state of cybersecurity in a corporation such as this, the criminals managed to wiretap the media for social influence and social engineering to perpetrate unauthorised access to important personal data and finances from such an organisation. This incident should teach agile enterprises to deploy layered cyber defences, best complemented by advanced technologies in threat detection, employee awareness training, and policies on incident response, deep fakes, and social engineering attacks. Otherwise, this case verifies the role that vigilance and working together through staff, cybersecurity professionals, and law enforcement agencies play in identifying and mitigating deepfake-facilitated attacks. Proactive, all-inclusive cybersecurity approaches can help an organisation safeguard its digital assets and reduce the deepfake-based social engineering attack vectors.

14.4.5.2 Background

A 2020 deepfake social engineering case showed how much-manipulated media can be leveraged for ill purposes by capitalising on human weaknesses. In another case, a deepfake tool deceived targets into spilling sensitive information by pretending to be a trusted person in a social engineering scheme.

14.4.5.3 Incident details

In the deepfake social engineering attack, attackers used deepfake technology to imitate the voices of specimens, corporate executive officers, and other employees in convincing audio and video clips. Using these synthesised media assets, they targeted privileged information, passwords, and financial operations by contacting employees and vendors through telephone calls, emails, or video calls. In most cases, targets generally could not make out that they were engaging with AI-generated media assets because of the believability of this deepfake forgery.

14.4.5.4 Impact

Some serious consequences that affected the targeted persons and organisations were data breaches, monetary losses, and reputational damage. By using and abusing people's trust and media, these attackers could ride over security processes that would guide and clear them toward attaining the required information. This incident highlighted the need for advanced cybersecurity knowledge and defences against deepfake and social engineering attacks.

14.4.5.5 Lessons learned

Social engineering attacks using deepfakes are advancing, and this case proves that the state of the cybersecurity threat environment is never the same. Vigilance against deepfake social engineering attacks may be created, and their impact on the staff may be decreased through training, the implementation of multi-factor authentication, and suitable communication protocols.

14.5 Threats to Individual Security

Deepfake technology can seriously endanger individual security because it consists of many destructive operations that leverage manipulated media to achieve illicit ends. Among the most worrying risks in financial fraud schemes, deepfakes change individuals' voices or images to trick others into approving fraudulent transactions or disclosing sensitive information. In addition, spreading such deepfake details will result in reputational damage from social engineering – one of the mainstays hackers use to take over people's accounts or influence public opinion to their own needs, ideological or political. These risks fail the affected people's financial stability, personal security, and well-being, and our belief in digital media erodes. Multimodal approach Improvement in technology, government legislation, and awareness creation campaigns need to be initiated; these would work in detecting and reducing adverse effects of manipulated media and address concerns about personal security due to deepfake technology.

That being said, there are many more risks to individual security from distorted media that deepfake technology has adapted as a tool to crush confidence and commit various cybercrimes beyond financial fraud and extortion. All these are risks to an individual beyond financial fraud and extortion. Phishing attempts can be made to trick victims into giving out important information or downloading risky software. These impersonation threats work by making simple audio or editing alterations to mimic a friend, employer, or influential colleague. Besides, deepfakes could apply to social engineering activities and, as such, they can adversely impact the interpersonal relations of an individual through media manipulation in a bid to raise emotions, simulate controversy, or get some private information with ill intentions. Deepfakes could lead to broader social chaos after their more pervasive use in direct attacks and disseminating fake news, instigating violence, and meddling with democratic processes. Proactive measures are needed to recognise and reduce the risks associated with deepfake technology, as such risks inherently affect individuals' safety, digital security, and overall well-being. Thus, there is a need to invest in detection technology, conduct public awareness campaigns on cybersecurity, and have solid legislative frameworks to prevent the myriad risks from manipulated media.

14.6 Legal and Regulatory Considerations

A rising number of people in the audience are becoming aware that manipulated media calls for robust legal and regulatory frameworks concerning the moral, legal, and societal consequences of deepfake technology. Deepfake technology is vast and fast developing; lawmakers and policymakers must combat several challenges. Current legal regimes regarding matters such as libel, confidentiality, copyright, and fraud over the Internet may not provide appropriate coverage for the special problems deepfakes pose. This requires new legislation and regulations explicitly targeted toward the misuse of deepfake technology in a manner that protects fundamental freedoms and rights. In this regard, a few things to be kept in mind include defining deepfakes precisely and enumerating the repercussions of their creation, sharing, and manipulation for other purposes. Secondly, any effort at regulating deepfakes will have to balance harming people versus protecting the right to free speech and artistic expression. Therefore, it becomes imperative that complete legal and regulatory frameworks on deepfake technology be developed, accounting for all kinds of challenges. They need to come out of collaborative efforts between governments, tech corporations, and organisations working in civil society, together with legal professionals.

Deepfake technology has considerably improved and become more available; in this regard, it is a significant challenge for policymakers to find some legal and regulatory measures to alleviate this issue. Among them are increasing demands for accountability and transparency while creating and sharing deepfakes. Citron and Chesney have proposed policies for undeniably labelling altered material and establishing systems for tracing source and legitimacy. Moreover, the need for global coordination and cooperation in response to the international dimensions of the deepfake threat is increasing.

In that respect, initiating efforts toward creating standardised legal frameworks and standards across countries will help cross-border enforcement and collaboration in combatting deepfake-related crimes. Deepfake manipulation demands active protection through education and awareness campaigns related to detecting and responding to manipulated media. This would thus go a long way in toning down the hazards of deepfake technology and defending the rights and interests of the citizens in the digital era, in which policymakers can go a long way in encouraging an all-encompassing and proactive approach toward the relevant legal and regulatory issues.

14.7 Detection and Mitigation Strategies

Deepfake technology represents those challenges that enforce the development and usage of effective detection and mitigation methods. This is partly done by leveraging the advantages of technology advancements in areas such as computer vision and machine learning algorithms, where the appearance of an abnormality or inconsistency with information from media could show manipulation. Researchers devise automated means of detection through speech patterns, facial expressions, and other ocular telltales to identify the signs of artificial manipulation. Blockchain technology and digital watermarking offer even more ways to find traceability and authentication in media content that testifies to the integrity of content and its origin.

Further development of the standard process and detection tools related to authenticity verification also relies on multidisciplinary cooperation among engineers, researchers, policy actors, and business actors. Finally, besides the technical countermeasures, digital literacy campaigns raise public awareness about deep fakes' prevalence and risks, which helps people evaluate media material and, thus, resist manipulation critically. Deepfake technology risks can be mitigated by integrating technological innovation with collaborative partnerships and educational programs, identifying potential harms and developing a more comprehensive strategy for all stakeholders.

An integrated approach toward deepfake risks would encompass technological development, legislative initiatives, and human capability. This can be further enhanced using context-aware automated detection algorithms and human intuition in a human-in-the-loop approach. More concretely, the challenge here is interdisciplinarity research collaboration to advance the current state of the art in deepfake detection and develop effective defences. The need for industry standards and regulatory measures is admittedly in order through policy interventions that will punish maligned uses of deepfake technology while incentivising content providers and platforms to act responsibly. Second, enhanced accountability and transparency in developing and deploying deepfake detection technologies would lead to greater public trust in those technologies themselves. Technical know-how can identify and reduce risks only if they are integrated with broad policy initiatives and participation from stakeholders.

14.8 Best Practices for Individual Protection

The technology of deepfakes is becoming ever so complex and pervasive; thus, people must keep themselves alert through continuous steps that ensure their protection against potential harm. Developing digital literacy and applying critical thinking skills in identifying and judging the authenticity of media material is vital. Every information on the web should be taken with a grain of salt. One should try to verify the authenticity of the sources and data one share. Protecting digital assets and personal data requires further scrutiny: turning on multi-factor authentication, making trickier passwords, and keeping security software current. Besides, the threat of manipulations due to deepfakes could be reduced by users with more direct limitations in how private photos and videos are shared on public platforms and through being vigilant about interacting with unknown material or questionable material. Users are further advised to follow well-known fact-checking organisations and keep themselves updated with the most advanced technology regarding the development of deepfake detection so that users can know how to navigate such an ever-changing environment of manipulated media. These recommended procedures can help people minimise the dangers of deepfake technology while ensuring digital safety, security, and privacy.

People might increase their defence against deepfake threats by harbouring scepticism and verification, developing digital literacy, and establishing strong cybersecurity. The credibility of media content, especially if it sounds sensational or out of the person's style, has to be doubted. Besides, one has to be careful when interacting with people one has never met or has not established credibility with, especially on social networking sites where most deepfake videos are posted. Open, honest discussions with friends, family, or co-workers on the likelihood of deepfake manipulation can further enhance understanding and urge peer social groups to act as watchdogs against deception by using misinformation. Individuals could also help their course against deepfake by actively reporting suspicious material to network stakeholders and endorsing programmes that foster responsible media engagement. Individuals can help mitigate risks by becoming aware of these best practices and actively working to counter deepfake perils, thereby reducing their risks and those of their communities to some of the threatening consequences of doctored media.

14.9 Conclusion

Deepfake technology's problems range from complex ones, such as security and privacy, to even trust in digital media. The moral, ethical, legal, and technological discourse has underscored how deepfakes can manipulate, deceive, and injure people and society. The risks can only be kept at bay, and the negative consequences of manipulated media can be decreased, provided that the stakeholders of the respective industries collaborate as the deepfake technology develops. Indeed, a varied approach is required, including technical, legislative, and public awareness campaigns that will also entail proactive action by people. By collaborating on the challenge presented by deepfake technology, we can retain principles such as truth, integrity, and human dignity in the digital environment while ensuring everybody can access a safer, more trustworthy online environment.

14.10 Acknowledgements

We express our heartfelt gratitude to all those who have helped in this research by providing their input directly or indirectly through their research works as references or direct input as respondents. We express our heartfelt indebtedness to the almighty God, who has given us the strength to complete the research.

References

Banerjee, D., Kukreja, V., Sharma, V., Manwal, M., & Jindal, V. (2023). An Ensemble Approach of CNN and SVM for Precise Classification of Sweet Corn Leaf Diseases. *2023 14th International Conference on Computing Communication and Networking Technologies, ICCCNT 2023*. https://doi.org/10.1109/ICCCNT56998.2023.10306754

Bhandari, G., Dhasmana, A., Chaudhary, P., Gupta, S., Gangola, S., Gupta, A., Rustagi, S., Shende, S. S., Rajput, V. D., Minkina, T., Malik, S., & Slama, P. (2023). A Perspective Review on Green Nanotechnology in Agro-Ecosystems: Opportunities for Sustainable Agricultural Practices & Environmental Remediation. *Agriculture (Switzerland)*, *13*(3). https://doi.org/10.3390/agriculture13030668

Choudhary, N., Kukreja, V., Sharma, R., Gopal, L., & Rawat, D. (2023). Cutting-Edge AI for Helianthus Disease Detection: A CNN-KNN Hybrid Model. *2023 4th IEEE Global Conference for Advancement in Technology, GCAT 2023*. https://doi.org/10.1109/GCAT59970.2023.10353358

Dutta, A., Singh, P., Dobhal, A., Mannan, D., Singh, J., & Goswami, P. (2023). Entrepreneurial Aptitude of Women of an Aspirational District of Uttarakhand. *Indian Journal of Extension Education*, *59*(2), 103–107. https://doi.org/10.48165/IJEE.2023.59222

Gupta, A. K., Pratiksha, Das, T., Kumar, H., Rastogi, S., Espinosa, E., Rincón, E., Morcillo-Martín, R., Rather, M. A., Kumar, V., Naik, B., Makroo, H. A., Xiao, H.-W., Ranjan, R., & Mishra, S. (2023). Novel food materials: Fundamentals and applications in sustainable food systems for food processing and safety. *Food Bioscience*, *55*. https://doi.org/10.1016/j.fbio.2023.103013

Joshi, S., Sharma, M., Kaushal, D., Misra, A., Gupta, P., & Gopal, S. (2023). Optimizing Productivity and Efficiency in Agriculture through the Integration of Digital Technologies: A Smart Agriculture Perspective. *9th International Conference on Smart Computing and Communications: Intelligent Technologies and Applications, ICSCC 2023*, 119–125. https://doi.org/10.1109/ICSCC59169.2023.10335086

Kaur, A., Kukreja, V., Aggarwal, P., Thapliyal, S., & Sharma, R. (2024). Amplifying Apple Mosaic Illness Detection: Combining CNN and Random Forest Models. *2024 IEEE International Conference on Interdisciplinary Approaches in Technology and Management for Social Innovation, IATMSI 2024*. https://doi.org/10.1109/IATMSI60426.2024.10503272

Kaur, A., Kukreja, V., Nisha Chandran, S., Garg, N., & Sharma, R. (2023). Automated Mango Rust Severity Classification: A CNN-SVM Ensemble Approach for Accurate and Granular Disease Assessment in Mango Cultivation. In G. R., H. K., P. R., G. S., T. A. J.V., V. R., M. R., & K. T. (Eds.), *Proceedings of the 2023 6th International Conference on Recent*

Trends in Advance Computing, ICRTAC 2023 (pp. 486–490). Institute of Electrical and Electronics Engineers Inc. https://doi.org/10.1109/ICRTAC59277.2023.10480836

Kaur, K., Chattopadhyay, S., Verma, A., Kukreja, V., & Mehta, S. (2024). A Synergistic Approach to Cucurbit Leaf Disease Classification with Federated Learning CNNs. *2024 IEEE International Conference on Interdisciplinary Approaches in Technology and Management for Social Innovation, IATMSI 2024*. https://doi.org/10.1109/IATMSI60426.2024.10503438

Khan, S., Ambika, Rani, K., Sharma, S., Kumar, A., Singh, S., Thapliyal, M., Rawat, P., Thakur, A., Pandey, S., Thapliyal, A., Pal, M., & Singh, Y. (2023). Rhizobacterial mediated interactions in Curcuma longa for plant growth and enhanced crop productivity: a systematic review. *Frontiers in Plant Science*, *14*. https://doi.org/10.3389/fpls.2023.1231676

Nagabhooshanam, N., Verma, R., Kaliappan, S., Patil, P. P., Kumar, D. S., Vijay, K. M., & Kishore, K. L. (2024). Role of carbon quantum dots from lychee fruit husk waste and discarded caster bean stem fiber on load bearing, fatigue, and water uptake properties of epoxy composite. *Biomass Conversion and Biorefinery*. https://doi.org/10.1007/s13399-024-05625-y

Nautiyal, D., Sharma, V., Dangi, S., & Sharma, S. (2024). Applications of Technology Assisted Ultrasonic Repellers in Current Era of Indian Agriculture. *2024 2nd International Conference on Computer, Communication and Control, IC4 2024*. https://doi.org/10.1109/IC457434.2024.10486691

Niharika, Kukreja, V., Sharma, R., Das, P., & Mohd, N. (2023). Empowering Rice Farmers: Automated Multi-Classification of Rice Diseases using YOLOv5. *2023 4th IEEE Global Conference for Advancement in Technology, GCAT 2023*. https://doi.org/10.1109/GCAT59970.2023.10353514

Pai, H. A., Agarwal, J., Kumar, A. S., Mahesh, T. R., Mokashi, S. S., & Guruprasad, M. S. (2023). Enhancing Urban Farming Through Smart Systems and Water Conservation: An IoT Based Approach. In C. N. (Ed.), *Proceedings - International Conference on Technological Advancements in Computational Sciences, ICTACS 2023* (pp. 82–86). Institute of Electrical and Electronics Engineers Inc. https://doi.org/10.1109/ICTACS59847.2023.10390048

Ritika, Mansi, Rizwana, Kumar, H., Bora, B., Rather, M. A., Naik, B., Kumar, V., Ranjan, R., & Gupta, A. K. (2024). Traditional and Underutilized Fruits and Vegetables for Attaining Zero Hunger. *Advances in*

Science, Technology and Innovation, Part F2519, 89–111. https://doi.org/10.1007/978-3-031-51647-4_8

Sharma, M., Joshi, S., & Govindan, K. (2023). Overcoming barriers to implement digital technologies to achieve sustainable production and consumption in the food sector: A circular economy perspective. *Sustainable Production and Consumption*, *39*, 203–215. https://doi.org/10.1016/j.spc.2023.04.002

Sharma, S., & Tyagi, R. (2023). Digitalization of Farming Knowledge Using Artificial Intelligence and Vedic Scripture. *3rd IEEE International Conference on ICT in Business Industry and Government, ICTBIG 2023*. https://doi.org/10.1109/ICTBIG59752.2023.10456219

Singh, P., Singh, K. D., Kaur, R., Singh, D., & Tripathi, V. (2024). FATEH: A Novel Framework for Internet-of-Things-Based Smart Agriculture Monitoring System. In *Precision Agriculture for Sustainability: Use of Smart Sensors, Actuators, and Decision Support Systems*. Apple Academic Press. https://doi.org/10.1201/9781003435228-27

Suryavanshi, A., Kukreja, V., Bordoloi, D., Mehta, S., & Choudhary, A. (2024). Redefining Tea Cultivation: A Federated Approach to Detecting Leaf Diseases with CNN. *2024 4th International Conference on Advances in Electrical, Computing, Communication and Sustainable Technologies, ICAECT 2024*. https://doi.org/10.1109/ICAECT60202.2024.10469335

Tomar, S., Sharma, N., & Nehra, N. S. (2023). A sustainable rural entrepreneurship model developed by the organic farmers of India. *Emerald Emerging Markets Case Studies*, *13*(2), 1–17. https://doi.org/10.1108/EEMCS-09-2022-0329

Upadhyay, D., Manwal, M., Deep, P., Kukreja, V., & Sharma, R. (2024). Enhancing Agricultural Precision: A Hybrid CNN-SVM Approach for Multidimensional Weed Disease Classification. *Proceedings - International Conference on Computing, Power, and Communication Technologies, IC2PCT 2024*, 1525–1528. https://doi.org/10.1109/IC2PCT60090.2024.10486389

Upadhyay, D., Manwal, M., Gupta, A. K., Kukreja, V., & Sharma, R. (2024). Progressive Expression of Bean Leaf Lesions: A Comprehensive Analysis Using Spatio-Temporal Disease Classification Solutions Based on CNN and LSTM Networks. *Proceedings - International Conference on Computing, Power, and Communication Technologies, IC2PCT 2024*, 1519–1524. https://doi.org/10.1109/IC2PCT60090.2024.10486224

15

Deepfake Disruption: Leveraging AI for Marketing Innovation and Financial Resilience

Tushar K. Savale[1], Sandeep M. Kamble[1], Dilpreet Kaur[1] and Mohammad Ahsan[2]

[1]Sri Balaji University, India
[2]Imam Abdulrahman Bin Faisal University Dammam, Saudi Arabia

Email: tushar.savale@bimmpune.edu.in; sandeep.kamble@bimmpune.edu.in; Dilpreet.kaur2818@gmail.com; dr.mohammad.ahsan@gmail.com

Abstract

Deepfake technology is about to bring a tremendous revolution for leveraging AI for market innovation and financial resilience. For a particular business, marketing and finance are considered to be significant parameters for its future upliftment and growth. In today's world, where the acceptance of artificial intelligence in the field of business is rapidly increasing, it is necessary to take a grip on the recent advancements in the field of new sophisticated technology. Present research tries to bring insight into the utility of profound fake disruption through AI in order to foster marketing innovation and financial resilience.

15.1 Introduction

The significance of this research lies in its pioneering exploration of the profound and multidimensional impact that the prevalence of deepfake incidents in marketing and investment in AI-based detection tools have on the intricate relationship between brand trust and financial resilience, as it delves into an uncharted domain at the intersection of artificial intelligence, digital ethics, and financial sustainability, addressing a critical gap in existing literature by empirically assessing how the proliferation of deepfakes – a growing threat in today's digital ecosystem – erodes consumer confidence and undermines brand integrity, while concurrently evaluating the efficacy of AI-driven safeguards in restoring trust and fortifying organisations against the fiscal vulnerabilities posed by synthetic media, thus offering invaluable insights for both academics and practitioners in navigating the ethical, technological, and financial complexities of modern marketing strategies.

15.2 Important Definitions

- *Financial resilience* can be defined as an organisation's intrinsic capacity to absorb, adapt to, and recover from external economic shocks and market disruptions, while maintaining operational continuity, liquidity (Bhatnagar, Kumar, et al., 2024; Bhatnagar, Rajaram, et al., 2024; P. Kumar, Taneja, Bhatnagar, et al., 2024), and revenue streams, achieved through the strategic allocation of resources, robust risk management frameworks, and the cultivation of flexible financial structures that enable sustained growth and long-term fiscal stability in an increasingly volatile and unpredictable business environment (Bhatnagar, Sharma, et al., 2024; Kangotra & Bhatnagar, 2024; Miglani et al., 2024; R. Sharma, Sharma, et al., 2024).
- *Brand trust* is the deeply entrenched psychological construct characterised by a consumer's unwavering confidence in the reliability, authenticity, and ethical integrity of a brand's communications, products, and promises, which fosters a profound sense of loyalty and emotional security (Abhishek et al., 2024), thereby serving as a pivotal determinant of sustained customer engagement, market differentiation, and long-term relational equity in a competitive landscape fraught with increasing skepticism and digital manipulation (A. Arya et al., 2024).
- The *prevalence of deepfake incidents* guides to the increasing frequency of manipulated media, often videos or audio (Bijalwan et al., 2024), being used for misinformation, fraud, or malicious purposes in various sectors like politics, entertainment, and cybersecurity (Chandel et al., 2024).
- *Investment in AI detection tools* refers to the allocation of resources towards developing technologies that can identify and mitigate the misuse of artificial intelligence (P. Sharma et al., 2023), particularly in detecting deepfakes, cyber threats, and other AI-driven malicious activities (P. Arya et al., 2023).

15.3 Literature Review

- The consequence of the prevalence of deepfake incidents in marketing on brand trust is profoundly destructive, as the escalating use of manufactured, misleading scope deteriorates customer conviction (Kashif et al., 2024; Kaur et al., 2024), heightening incredulity toward the verisimilitude of trademark transmissions, thereby vandalising the foundational faith that operates as a significant portion of brand equity, while simultaneously exhilarating institutions to embrace cultivated AI-based detection tools to reduce reputational risks and correct customer confidence in an increasingly contrived digital terrain (Arora et al., 2024).
- The investment in AI detection tools exercises a profoundly optimistic and transformative consequence on brand trust, as associations that proactively deploy developed artificial intelligence instruments to identify and counteract deepfake content not only improve the sensed probity and translucence of their communications but also strengthen customer conviction (Fan et al., 2024; Gupta et al., 2024; Joshi et al., 2024), showing a resilient trust framework that protects trademark equity in the circumstances rife with digital manipulation and deceitful media tactics, thereby placing the brand as a vanguard of moral and technologically proficient market supervision (Sardana et al., 2024).
- The influence of brand trust on financial resilience is both climacteric and multifaceted, as the potency of customer conviction in a brand's genuineness and moral probity performs as a crucial protector against market volatility, encouraging maintained consumer commitment and encouraging remuneration continuity (Kunwar et al., 2024), which in turn improves a firm's capability to withstand economic stupefaction, optimise heap allocation, and guide financial upheavals, thus strengthening the organisation's general fiscal robustness and long-term operational equilibrium within a positively competitive and inconsistent industry terrain (Salam et al., 2024).

15.4 Research Gap

This analysis manages an essential space in the existent body of publications by systematically exploring the heretofore underexplored crossroad of deepfake technology, brand trust, and financial resilience, especially within the context of AI-driven commerce creations, thereby serving the apparent void in practical examinations that evaluate the palpable and supernatural effects of deepfake disturbances on corporate stability, customer confidence dynamics, and strategic acquisitions in AI-based detection tools, suggesting a book donation to the address on digital commerce standards and economic risk administration in an era of increasing AI (Khanna et al., 2023; R. Kumar, Lande, et al., 2023; R. Kumar, Malholtra, et al., 2023; R. Kumar, Malhotra, et al., 2023; R. Kumar & Khanna, 2023a, 2023b; Mary Joshitta et al., 2023).

15.5 Research Methodology

The present research is conducted with the objective of measuring the impact of the prevalence of deepfake incidents in marketing and investment in AI-based defect detection on brand trust and financial resilience. To meet the research objective, a questionnaire was framed, which is shown in Table 15.1. Regarding the variables used in the research, the PLS-SEM technique was applied in Smart-PLS-4.

15.6 Data Analysis

The respondent profile in Table 15.2 illustrates a pronounced predominance of scholarly expertise in the intersecting fields of marketing, artificial intelligence, and business ethics, which far outweighs the representation of other critical cohorts such as advertising professionals, technology and IT specialists, as well as financial and marketing executives, thereby underscoring an intellectual bias that, while offering profound theoretical insights, may lack the pragmatic depth necessary to fully comprehend the operational complexities and real-world ramifications of deepfake technology on marketing innovation and financial resilience.

The intricate dynamics elucidated in the Figure 15.1, leveraging Partial Least Squares (PLS) algorithm, underscores a multifaceted interplay wherein the prevalence of deepfake incidents in marketing and investment in AI-based deepfake detection and prevention tools intricately modulate brand trust, with the latter exerting a bifurcated influence on financial resilience, specifically through the vectors of Confidence and Loyalty, as evidenced by robust path coefficients, thereby revealing the latent mediating role of Brand Trust as a pivotal determinant in enhancing Flexibility and Stability within the broader financial architecture, all while highlighting the profound significance of technological investment in countering deepfake proliferation.

The construct reliability and validity assessment, as presented in Table 15.3, indicates a robust internal consistency across the examined variables, including Brand Trust, Financial Resilience, Investment in AI-based

Table 15.1 Questionnaire.

Variable name	Item	Question statement	Scale
Financial Resilience	Stability	How stable do you feel your organisation is in terms of financial performance in the current market?	1 (Very Unstable)–7 (Very Stable)
	Flexibility	How flexible is your organisation in managing financial disruptions caused by external factors?	1 (Not Flexible at All)–7 (Very Flexible)
Brand Trust	Confidence	To what extent do you trust the marketing content delivered by brands, given the rise of deepfakes?	1 (No Trust at All)–7 (Complete Trust)
	Loyalty	How likely are you to remain loyal to a brand that uses AI-generated content, such as deepfakes, in its marketing?	1 (Not Likely at All)–7 (Extremely Likely)
Prevalence of Deepfake Incidents	Awareness	How aware are you of deepfake technology being used in marketing?	1 (Not Aware at All)– 7 (Very Aware)
	Concern	How concerned are you about the increasing use of deepfake technology in marketing campaigns?	1 (Not Concerned at All)– 7 (Very Concerned)
Investment in AI Detection Tools	Resources	How significant are your organisation's investments in AI tools to detect deepfakes?	1 (No Investment)– 7 (Very High Investment)
	Importance	How important do you believe AI tools are in maintaining the integrity of your marketing content?	1 (Not Important at All)– 7 (Very Important)

Source: Calculated by authors.

Deepfake Detection and Prevention Tools, and Prevalence of Deepfake Incidents in Marketing, with each construct demonstrating exceptional composite reliability and average variance extracted, thereby affirming the measurement model's soundness and ensuring that the latent variables are accurately captured with minimal error, fostering strong convergent validity while providing a solid foundation for subsequent structural equation modelling and hypothesis testing.

Table 15.2 Respondent profile.

Respondent type	Number of respondents	Percentage
Marketing Executives	17	6.72%
Financial Executives	11	4.35%
Technology and IT Executives	33	13.04%
Advertising and Media Professionals	56	22.13%
Scholars in Marketing, AI, and Business Ethics	136	53.75%
Total	253	100%

Source: Calculated by authors.

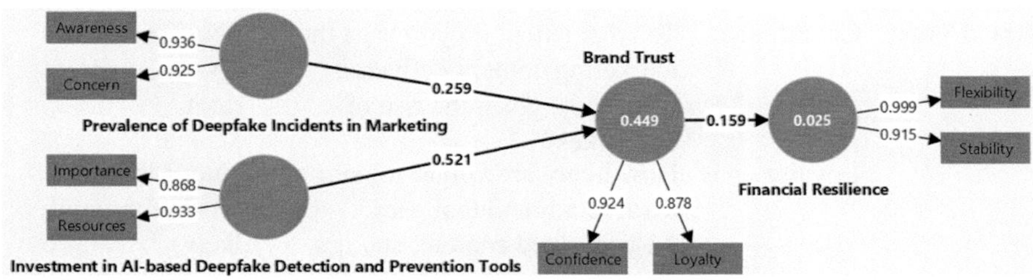

Figure 15.1 PLS Algorithm/conceptual model. Source: Calculated by authors.

The Heterotrait-Monotrait (HTMT) ratio of correlations presented in Table 15.4 reveals well-below-threshold inter-construct correlations, particularly between Brand Trust and Financial Resilience, as well as between Prevalence of Deepfake Incidents in Marketing and Financial Resilience, while demonstrating more substantial correlations between Brand Trust and Investment in AI-based Deepfake Detection and Prevention Tools, thereby indicating strong discriminant validity across the model's constructs, affirming that the constructs are sufficiently distinct from one another to ensure the theoretical robustness and empirical rigor of the proposed framework.

The Fornell-Larcker criterion results, as delineated in Table 15.5, demonstrate that the square roots of the average variance extracted for each construct exceed the inter-construct correlations, particularly highlighting the substantial distinction between Brand Trust, Financial Resilience, Investment in AI-based Deepfake Detection and Prevention Tools, and Prevalence of Deepfake Incidents in Marketing, thus reinforcing the model's discriminant validity by confirming that each latent variable shares more variance with its own indicators than with other constructs, thereby fortifying the integrity and theoretical precision of the structural model.

The outer weights presented in Table 15.6 and Figure 15.2 reveal a highly differentiated contribution of each indicator to its corresponding

Table 15.3 Construct reliability and validity.

	Cronbach's alpha	Composite reliability (rho_a)	Composite reliability (rho_c)	Average variance extracted (AVE)
Brand Trust	0.772	0.799	0.896	0.813
Financial Resilience	0.946	7.314	0.957	0.918
Investment in AI-based Deepfake Detection and Prevention Tools	0.775	0.831	0.896	0.813
Prevalence of Deepfake Incidents in Marketing	0.846	0.849	0.928	0.866

Source: Calculated by authors.

Table 15.4 HTMT.

	Brand Trust	Financial Resilience	Investment in AI-based Deepfake Detection and Prevention Tools	Prevalence of Deepfake Incidents in Marketing
Brand Trust				
Financial Resilience	0.118			
Investment in AI-based Deepfake Detection and Prevention Tools	0.774	0.175		
Prevalence of Deepfake Incidents in Marketing	0.590	0.090	0.514	

Source: Calculated by authors.

latent variable, with Awareness and Concern exhibiting substantial influence on Prevalence of Deepfake Incidents in Marketing, while Confidence and Loyalty heavily load onto Brand Trust, and Flexibility and Stability significantly impact Financial Resilience, concurrently underscoring the paramount role of Importance and Resources in shaping Investment in AI-based Deepfake Detection and Prevention Tools, thus confirming the multidimensional nature

Table 15.5 Fronell-Larcker criterion.

	Brand Trust	Financial Resilience	Investment in AI-based Deepfake Detection and Prevention Tools	Prevalence of Deepfake Incidents in Marketing
Brand Trust				
Financial Resilience	0.118			
Investment in AI-based Deepfake Detection and Prevention Tools	0.774	0.175		
Prevalence of Deepfake Incidents in Marketing	0.590	0.090	0.514	

Source: Calculated by authors.

Table 15.6 Outer weights.

	Brand Trust	Financial Resilience	Investment in AI-based Deepfake Detection and Prevention Tools	Prevalence of Deepfake Incidents in Marketing
Awareness	0.455	0.065	0.312	0.936
Concern	0.423	0.052	0.455	0.925
Confidence	0.924	0.117	0.671	0.397
Flexibility	0.172	0.999	0.183	0.077
Importance	0.466	0.145	0.868	0.391
Loyalty	0.878	0.177	0.437	0.464
Resources	0.643	0.173	0.933	0.356
Stability	0.018	0.915	0.114	–0.078

Source: Calculated by authors.

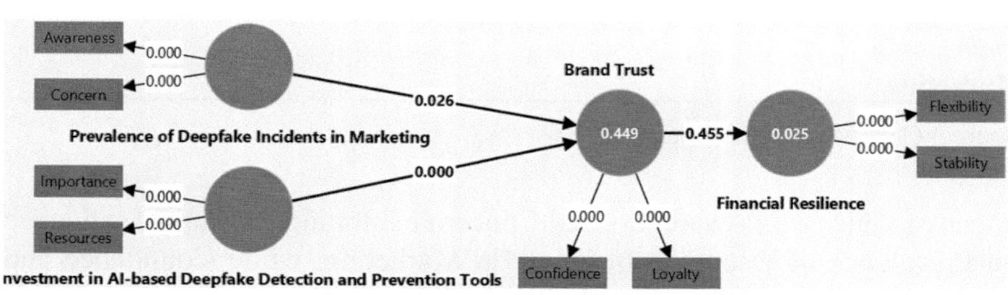

Figure 15.2 Bootstrapping. Source: Calculated by authors.

Table 15.7 Hypothesis testing.

	Original sample (O)	Sample mean (M)	Standard deviation (STDEV)	T statistics (|O/STDEV|)	P values
Brand Trust -> Financial Resilience	0.159	0.134	0.213	0.746	0.455
Investment in AI-based Deepfake Detection and Prevention Tools -> Brand Trust	0.521	0.522	0.116	4.496	0.000
Prevalence of Deepfake Incidents in Marketing -> Brand Trust	0.259	0.268	0.116	2.231	0.026

Source: Calculated by authors.

of these constructs and the nuanced interplay of their indicators in capturing the underlying theoretical framework with precision.

The hypothesis testing results in Table 15.7 reveal a non-significant relationship between Brand Trust and Financial Resilience, juxtaposed against a highly significant and positive effect of Investment in AI-based Deepfake Detection and Prevention Tools on Brand Trust, alongside a similarly significant but more moderate influence of Prevalence of Deepfake Incidents in Marketing on Brand Trust, thereby delineating the pivotal role of AI investments and deepfake occurrences in shaping brand perception, while financial resilience remains less directly influenced by brand trust in the context of deepfake disruption.

The outer loading analysis, as displayed in Table 15.8, illustrates exceptionally high loadings across all constructs, indicating strong indicator reliability, with Awareness and Concern significantly contributing to Prevalence of Deepfake Incidents in Marketing, Confidence and Loyalty heavily reinforcing Brand Trust, Flexibility and Stability anchoring Financial Resilience, and Importance and Resources strongly underpinning Investment in AI-based Deepfake Detection and Prevention Tools, thereby confirming the robustness and validity of the measurement model, where each latent variable is consistently and significantly represented by its corresponding indicators.

Table 15.8 Outer loading.

	Original sample (O)	Sample mean (M)	Standard deviation (STDEV)	T statistics (|O/STDEV|)	P values
Awareness <- Prevalence of Deepfake Incidents in Marketing	0.936	0.935	0.025	37.524	0.000
Concern <- Prevalence of Deepfake Incidents in Marketing	0.925	0.920	0.035	26.255	0.000
Confidence <- Brand Trust	0.924	0.920	0.026	35.960	0.000
Flexibility <- Financial Resilience	0.999	0.924	0.180	5.538	0.000
Importance <- Investment in AI-based Deepfake Detection and Prevention Tools	0.868	0.861	0.060	14.371	0.000
Loyalty <- Brand Trust	0.878	0.880	0.047	18.615	0.000
Resources <- Investment in AI-based Deepfake Detection and Prevention Tools	0.933	0.937	0.013	69.965	0.000
Stability <- Financial Resilience	0.915	0.889	0.189	4.850	0.000

Source: Calculated by authors.

15.7 Managerial Implications

The managerial implications drawn from the comprehensive analysis underscore the imperative for decision-makers to strategically prioritise substantial investments in AI-based deepfake detection and prevention tools (P. Kumar, Taneja, & Ozen, 2024; Taneja et al., 2023), given their profound impact on fortifying Brand Trust, which emerges as a critical mediator in navigating the complexities of consumer perception amidst escalating occurrences of deepfake-driven disruptions in marketing; moreover (Kumari et al., 2024; Sayeduzzaman et al., 2024), while Brand Trust serves as a vital intangible asset, its direct influence on Financial Resilience may be less pronounced (Cavaliere et al., 2024; Samantaray et al., 2024; R. Sharma, Kumar, et al., 2024), suggesting that firms must concurrently bolster operational flexibility and stability through integrated risk management frameworks, thereby cultivating a robust organisational architecture capable of withstanding financial shocks in an increasingly volatile digital ecosystem where the sophistication and pervasiveness of deepfake technologies continue to challenge traditional brand-consumer dynamics (Swain et al., 2024; Yashu et al., 2024).

15.8 Conclusion

The conclusion distilled from this extensive discourse underscores the indispensable need for organisations to strategically recalibrate their operational and marketing frameworks by placing significant emphasis on Investment in AI-based Deepfake Detection and Prevention Tools, which demonstrably fortifies Brand Trust – a pivotal mediator influencing consumer Confidence and Loyalty – while concurrently acknowledging that Financial Resilience in the face of escalating deepfake-induced disruptions requires not only brand perception management but also the cultivation of Operational Flexibility and Stability through robust risk mitigation strategies, as the intricate dynamics between Prevalence of Deepfake Incidents and organisational response mechanisms elucidate the exigent reality that firms must harmonise their technological investments with overarching resilience-building initiatives to thrive amidst the profound complexities of the digital ecosystem, wherein deepfakes challenge the very fabric of traditional marketing and financial paradigms.

References

Abhishek, N., Rahiman, H. U., Kodikal, R., Kulal, A., Kambali, U., & Kulal, M. (2024). Contribution of CSR for the Attainment of Sustainable Goals: A Study of a Developing Nation. *Technical and Vocational Education and Training*, *39*, 271–285. https://doi.org/10.1007/978-981-99-7798-7_23

Arora, M., Mishra, K. K., Singh, M., Singh, P., & Tripathi, R. (2024). Deepfake technology and its implications for influencer marketing. In *Navigating the World of Deepfake Technology*. IGI Global. https://doi.org/10.4018/979-8-3693-5298-4.ch005

Arya, A., Bachheti, A., Bachheti, R. K., Singh, M., & Chandel, A. K. (2024). Role of Artificial Intelligence in Minimizing Carbon Footprint: A Systematic Review of Recent Insights. *Green Energy and Technology*, *Part F2511*, 365–386. https://doi.org/10.1007/978-3-031-51601-6_14

Arya, P., Shreya, S., & Gupta, A. (2023). Amazing potential and the future of fungi: Applications and economic importance. In *Microbial Bioactive Compounds: Industrial and Agricultural Applications*. Springer Nature. https://doi.org/10.1007/978-3-031-40082-7_2

Bhatnagar, M., Kumar, P., Taneja, S., Sood, K., & Grima, S. (2024). From digital overload to trading Zen: The role of digital detox in enhancing intraday trading performance. In *Business Drivers in Promoting Digital Detoxification*. IGI Global. https://doi.org/10.4018/9798369311073.ch010

Bhatnagar, M., Rajaram, R., Taneja, S., & Kumar, P. (2024). Balancing acts: The Yin and Yang of debit and credit on the stage of financial well-being. In *Emerging Perspectives on Financial Well-Being*. IGI Global. https://doi.org/10.4018/979-8-3693-1750-1.ch002

Bhatnagar, M., Sharma, R., & Singh, M. (2024). Digital transformation of wealth management: Exploring the impact of robo-advisor adoption and regulatory environment on risk mitigation. In *Robo-Advisors in Management*. IGI Global. https://doi.org/10.4018/979-8-3693-2849-1.ch001

Bijalwan, P., Gupta, A., Mendiratta, A., Johri, A., & Asif, M. (2024). Predicting the Productivity of Municipality Workers: A Comparison of Six Machine Learning Algorithms. *Economies*, *12*(1). https://doi.org/10.3390/economies12010016

Cavaliere, L. P. L., Byloppilly, R., Khan, S. D., Othman, B. A., Muda, I., & Malhotra, R. K. (2024). Acceptance and effectiveness of Industry 4.0 internal and external organisational initiatives in Malaysian firms. *International Journal of Management and Enterprise Development*, *23*(1), 1–25. https://doi.org/10.1504/IJMED.2024.138422

Chandel, N. S., Tripathi, V., Singh, H. B., & Vaishnav, A. (2024). Breaking seed dormancy for sustainable food production: Revisiting seed priming techniques and prospects. *Biocatalysis and Agricultural Biotechnology*, *55*. https://doi.org/10.1016/j.bcab.2023.102976

Fan, L., Usman, M., Haseeb, M., & Kamal, M. (2024). The impact of financial development and energy consumption on ecological footprint in economic complexity-based EKC framework: New evidence from BRICS-T region. *Natural Resources Forum*. https://doi.org/10.1111/1477-8947.12448

Gupta, S., Gilotra, S., Rathi, S., Choudhury, T., & Kotecha, K. (2024). Plant Disease Recognition Using Different CNN Models. In T. S., G. R., S. A., K. S., K. S., A. R., & S. K. R. (Eds.), *Proceedings of the 14th International Conference on Cloud Computing, Data Science and Engineering, Confluence 2024* (pp. 787–792). Institute of Electrical and Electronics Engineers Inc. https://doi.org/10.1109/Confluence60223.2024.10463383

Joshi, M. N., Dixit, A. K., Saxena, S., Memoria, M., Choudhury, T., & Sar, A. (2024). A Study of the Application of AI & ML to Climate Variation, with Particular Attention to Legal & Ethical Concerns. *EAI Endorsed Transactions on Internet of Things, 10*. https://doi.org/10.4108/eetiot.5468

Kangotra, R., & Bhatnagar, M. (2024). Financial management and market dynamics: An empirical analysis of heteroscedasticity in India's communication sector. In *Recent Developments in Financial Management and Economics*. IGI Global. https://doi.org/10.4018/979-8-3693-2683-1.ch017

Kashif, M., Singhal, N., Goyal, S., & Singh, S. K. (2024). Foreign Exchange Reserves and Economic Growth of Brazil: A Nonlinear Approach. *Finance: Theory and Practice*, *28*(1), 145–154. https://doi.org/10.26794/2587-5671-2024-28-1-145-154

Kaur, A., Kukreja, V., Malhotra, S., Joshi, K., & Sharma, R. (2024). Rice Sheath Rot Disease Detection and Severity Classification: A Novel Framework Leveraging CNN-LSTM Models for Multi-Classification. *2024 IEEE International Conference on Interdisciplinary Approaches in Technology and Management for Social Innovation, IATMSI 2024*. https://doi.org/10.1109/IATMSI60426.2024.10502629

Khanna, R., Jindal, P., & Noja, G. G. (2023). Blockchain technologies, a catalyst for insurance sector. In *The Application of Emerging Technology and Blockchain in the Insurance Industry*.

Kumar, P., Taneja, S., Bhatnagar, M., & Kaur, A. K. (2024). Navigating the digital paradigm shift: Designing CBDCs for a transformative financial landscape. In *Exploring Central Bank Digital Currencies: Concepts, Frameworks, Models, and Challenges*. IGI Global. https://doi.org/10.4018/979-8-3693-1882-9.ch006

Kumar, P., Taneja, S., & Ozen, E. (2024). Exploring the influence of green bonds on sustainable development through low-carbon financing mobilization. *International Journal of Law and Management*. https://doi.org/10.1108/IJLMA-01-2024-0030

Kumar, R., & Khanna, R. (2023a). Role of Artificial Intelligence in Digital Currency and Future Applications. *Proceedings of the*

2023 2nd International Conference on Augmented Intelligence and Sustainable Systems, ICAISS 2023, 42–46. https://doi.org/10.1109/ICAISS58487.2023.10250480

Kumar, R., & Khanna, R. (2023b). RPA (Robotic Process Automation) in Finance & Accounting and Future Scope. *Proceedings of the 2023 2nd International Conference on Augmented Intelligence and Sustainable Systems, ICAISS 2023*, 1640–1645. https://doi.org/10.1109/ICAISS58487.2023.10250496

Kumar, R., Lande, A., Kumar, D., Malhotra, R. K., & Sharma, A. (2023). Technology Bridging -in Entrepreneurs and Consumers in Product Development. *ISED 2023 - International Conference on Intelligent Systems and Embedded Design*. https://doi.org/10.1109/ISED59382.2023.10444599

Kumar, R., Malholtra, R. K., Singh, R., Kathuria, S., Balyan, R., & Pal, P. (2023). Artificial Intelligence Role in Electronic Invoice Under Goods and Services Tax. *2023 International Conference on Computational Intelligence, Communication Technology and Networking, CICTN 2023*, 140–143. https://doi.org/10.1109/CICTN57981.2023.10140870

Kumar, R., Malhotra, R. K., Pandey, S., Gehlot, A., Gautam, I., & Chamola, S. (2023). Role of Artificial Intelligence in Input Tax Credit Reconciliation. *Proceedings - 2023 3rd International Conference on Pervasive Computing and Social Networking, ICPCSN 2023*, 497–501. https://doi.org/10.1109/ICPCSN58827.2023.00086

Kumari, J., Singh, P., Mishra, A. K., Singh Meena, B. P., Singh, A., & Ojha, M. (2024). Challenges Hindering Women's Involvement in the Hospitality Industry as Entrepreneurs in the Era of Digital Economy. In *Revolutionizing the AI-Digital Landscape: A Guide to Sustainable Emerging Technologies for Marketing Professionals*. Taylor and Francis. https://doi.org/10.4324/9781032688305-9

Kunwar, S., Pandey, N., Bhatnagar, P., Chadha, G., Rawat, N., Joshi, N. C., Tomar, M. S., Eyvaz, M., & Gururani, P. (2024). A concise review on wastewater treatment through microbial fuel cell: sustainable and holistic approach. *Environmental Science and Pollution Research*, *31*(5), 6723–6737. https://doi.org/10.1007/s11356-023-31696-x

Mary Joshitta, S., Sunil, M. P., Badriasulaimanalfurhood, Bodhankar, A., Ch.Sreedevi, & Khanna, R. (2023). The Integration of Machine Learning Technique with the Existing System to Predict the Flight Prices. *2023 3rd International Conference on Advance Computing and Innovative Technologies in Engineering, ICACITE 2023*, 398–402. https://doi.org/10.1109/ICACITE57410.2023.10182539

Miglani, M., Bhatnagar, M., & Singh, M. (2024). Enhancing employee financial wellness: Development of HR-integrated robo- advisory tools for comprehensive budgeting and investments. In *Robo-Advisors in Management*. IGI Global. https://doi.org/10.4018/979-8-3693-2849-1.ch022

Salam, M. A., Rayun, S. M. N., Islam, W., Hasan, R., Firmansyah, E. A., & Kalinaki, K. (2024). Consumer engagement: Exploring deepfake applications in consumer marketing communication. In *Navigating the World of Deepfake Technology*. IGI Global. https://doi.org/10.4018/979-8-3693-5298-4.ch020

Samantaray, A., Chattaraj, S., Mitra, D., Ganguly, A., Kumar, R., Gaur, A., Mohapatra, P. K. D., Santos-Villalobos, S. de los, Rani, A., & Thatoi, H. (2024). Advances in microbial based bio-inoculum for amelioration of soil health and sustainable crop production. *Current Research in Microbial Sciences*, *7*. https://doi.org/10.1016/j.crmicr.2024.100251

Sardana, F., Mishra, K. K., Singh, A., & Saini, N. (2024). Transforming social media marketing through deepfake technology. In *Navigating the World of Deepfake Technology*. IGI Global. https://doi.org/10.4018/979-8-3693-5298-4.ch022

Sayeduzzaman, M., Hasan, T., Nasser, A. A., & Negi, A. (2024). An Internet of Things-Integrated Home Automation with Smart Security System. In *Automated Secure Computing for Next-Generation Systems*. wiley.

Sharma, P., Hussain, S. S., Taneja, S., & Sheikh, R. (2023). Gig economy, workplace culture and talent crunch: A conceptual model for future work. In *Green Management - A New Paradigm in the World of Business*. Nova Science Publishers, Inc.

Sharma, R., Kumar, A., Kaur, H., Sharma, K., Verma, T., Chauhan, S., Lakhanpal, M., Choudhary, A., Singh, R. P., Reddy, D. M., Venkatapuram, A., Mehta, S., & Husen, A. (2024). Current understanding and application of biostimulants in plants: an overview. In *Biostimulants in Plant Protection and Performance*. Elsevier. https://doi.org/10.1016/B978-0-443-15884-1.00003-8

Sharma, R., Sharma, M., Singh, M., & Bhatnagar, M. (2024). Facades and fortunes: Intellectual capital's influence on firm dynamics in the deepfake epoch. In *Navigating the World of Deepfake Technology*. IGI Global. https://doi.org/10.4018/979-8-3693-5298-4.ch009

Swain, K. P., Ranjan Nayak, S., Ravi, V., Mishra, S., Alahmadi, T. J., Singh, P., & Diwakar, M. (2024). Empowering Crop Selection with Ensemble Learning and K-means Clustering: A Modern Agricultural Perspective. *Open Agriculture Journal*, *18*. https://doi.org/10.2174/0118743315291367240207093403

Taneja, S., Bansal, N., & Kumar, P. (2023). Tech-driven sustainability: Fintech innovations revolutionizing green banking. In *Green Management - A New Paradigm in the World of Business*. Nova Science Publishers, Inc.

Yashu, Kukreja, V., Srivastava, P., & Garg, A. (2024). TuberVision: Unveiling Potato Diversity through Advanced Classification Techniques. *2024 IEEE International Conference on Interdisciplinary Approaches in Technology and Management for Social Innovation, IATMSI 2024*. https://doi.org/10.1109/IATMSI60426.2024.10502772

16

Impact of Deepfake Technology on Job Satisfaction and Commitment: Case Analysis

Navjyoti Prasher[1], K. K. Mishra[1] and Zelhuda Shamsuddin[2]

[1]University School of Business, Chandigarh University, Punjab, India
[2]Universiti Sultan Zainal Abidin, Malaysia

Email: navjyotiprasher@gmail.com; kkmsitmbbk@gmail.com; zelhudasham@unisza.edu.my

Abstract

Deepfake technology, a potent force in digital manipulation, has permeated various forms of media, including audio, video, and images. Its influence on the workplace and broader society is a matter of concern. This study offers a comprehensive exploration of the evolution and implications of deepfake technology, covering its origins, techniques, applications, ethical dilemmas, and legal repercussions. It also delves into the connection between the level of training and resources allocated to combat deepfake threats and their impact on job satisfaction and organisational commitment. Drawing on case studies from diverse sectors, this chapter provides a thorough examination of how deepfake technology shapes organisational commitment and job satisfaction. An empirical study, employing statistical tools like correlation analysis, was conducted to establish the relationships between various factors. The study also discusses a range of mitigation strategies, from technological advancements to platform policies. The findings underscore a significant correlation between specific variables, as detailed in the research. Moreover, this chapter illuminates the risks and opportunities that deepfake technology presents for organisations striving to foster a positive work environment.

16.1 Introduction

The rapid advancement of artificial intelligence and machine learning has ushered in an era where digital media manipulation has become remarkably sophisticated (Banerjee, Kukreja, Verma, et al., 2023; Rao et al., 2023). One notable manifestation of this technological progress is deepfake technology, which enables the creation of convincingly realistic synthetic media content, often indistinguishable from authentic recordings. While deepfakes have gained prominence primarily in entertainment and politics (A. Kaur, Kukreja, Manwal, et al., 2023; Suryavanshi et al., 2023), their potential ramifications within the workplace have yet to receive comprehensive scrutiny.

This chapter explores the intricate impact of deepfake technology on two crucial aspects of organisational life: job satisfaction and organisational commitment. Job satisfaction refers to an individual's contentment with their job role and work environment , and organisational commitment, denoting an employee's loyalty and dedication towards their organisation , are integral components of employee well-being and organisational success (G. Kaur et al., 2023; Sharma et al., 2023).

As deepfake technology continues to evolve and increase it presents opportunities and challenges for employers and employees. On one hand, the ability to create highly realistic simulations could revolutionise training and development programs, enhance marketing efforts and streamline communication channels (Gill et al., 2023; Malik et al., 2023). On the other hand, the potential for misuse, such as creating deceptive content for malicious purposes , raises ethical concerns and threatens trust within organisations (Agarwal et al., 2023; Pillai, Sharma, Chauhan, et al., 2023).

Through a comprehensive analysis supplemented by real-world case studies, this chapter seeks to shed light on the nuanced implications of deepfake technology within the workplace context (Gupta et al., 2023). By examining its effects on employee morale, trust, and organisational dynamics across various industries, we aim to provide valuable insights for practitioners and scholars alike. Ultimately, this exploration underscores the imperative of fostering a discerning approach to adopting and managing deepfake technology in the modern workplace landscape.

16.2 Research Objectives

The objectives of the study are as follows:

- To examine the evolution and implications of deepfake technology, including its origins, techniques, applications, ethical considerations, and legal ramifications.

- To identify the relationship of training and resources provided to recognise and respond to deepfake threats on job satisfaction and organisational commitment within the workplace.
- To present case studies from diverse industries to illustrate the real-world implications of deepfake technology on job satisfaction and organisational commitment, offering insights into industry-specific challenges and opportunities.

16.3 Literature Review

16.3.1 Understanding deepfake technology

It is crucial to explore the fundamentals and origins of deepfake technology to provide a comprehensive understanding of it. Deepfakes utilise deep learning algorithms to manipulate audio, video, and images, seamlessly substituting faces and voices in digital content. Leveraging extensive datasets and sophisticated neural networks, these algorithms produce convincing replicas of individuals, blurring the boundary between reality and fabrication (Jindal, Kukreja, Mehta, Srivastava, et al., 2023).

16.3.1.1 Definition and origins of deepfake technology

"Deepfake technology" refers to the application of machine learning and artificial intelligence, profound learning algorithms, to create or alter audiovisual content to appear authentic. The term "deepfake" itself stems from the amalgamation of "deep learning" and "fake" (Kunwar et al., 2023).

The origins of deepfake technology can be traced to academic research in machine learning and computer vision, particularly advancements in generative adversarial networks (GANs) and deep neural networks. Early experiments focused on synthesising realistic facial expressions and speech, gradually evolving into the development of full-fledged deepfake videos (A. Kaur, Kukreja, Verma, et al., 2023).

16.3.1.2 Techniques used in creating deepfakes

Several techniques are employed in the creation of deepfake content, each leveraging advanced AI algorithms to manipulate digital media. These techniques include:

- **Facial reenactment:** This involves mapping facial expressions from a source actor onto a target actor's face in a video, creating a realistic portrayal of the target actor mimicking the source actor's expressions.

- **Face swapping:** This involves replacing the face of a target individual in a video with the face of another individual, seamlessly blending the replacement to match the facial movements and expressions of the original footage.
- **Voice synthesis:** Utilises machine learning algorithms to generate synthetic voice recordings that mimic the tone, pitch, and cadence of a target individual's voice, even if the individual has not provided any audio samples.

16.3.1.3 Applications of deepfake technology

Deepfake technology has found various applications across different domains [3], including:

- **Entertainment and media:** Used to create realistic visual effects in movies, television shows, and video games, as well as for impersonations and satire on social media platforms.
- **Politics and propaganda:** Deployed to create misleading or fabricated political speeches, interviews, and news segments, potentially influencing public opinion and election outcomes.
- **Security and surveillance:** Poses risks for identity theft, fraud, and blackmail, as deepfake videos can be used to impersonate individuals or manipulate surveillance footage.
- **Education and training:** Offers opportunities for immersive learning experiences, such as simulated role-playing scenarios or language learning exercises.

16.3.1.4 Ethical and legal considerations surrounding deepfakes

The proliferation of deepfake technology raises significant ethical and legal concerns, including:

- **Misinformation and deception:** Deepfake content can be used to spread false information, manipulate public discourse, and damage individuals' reputations.
- **Privacy and consent:** Raises questions about the unauthorised use of individuals' likeness and voice, potentially infringing upon their privacy rights and consent.

- **Manipulation and coercion:** This creates opportunities for malicious actors to blackmail, manipulate, or extort individuals by generating compromising or incriminating deepfake content.
- **Intellectual property rights:** Raises issues regarding the ownership and distribution of deepfake content, mainly when it involves the unauthorised use of copyrighted material or likeness.
- **Regulation and accountability:** Calls for the development of regulatory frameworks and technological safeguards to mitigate the risks posed by deepfake technology and hold accountable those who misuse it for malicious purposes.

Deepfake technology represents a double-edged sword, offering innovative opportunities for creative expression and immersive experiences while posing significant ethical, legal, and societal challenges. As its capabilities continue to evolve, addressing these concerns proactively and responsibly is crucial to ensuring the responsible deployment and use of deepfake technology in the digital age.

16.3.1.5 The link between deepfakes and job satisfaction

Deepfake technology poses significant challenges to job satisfaction within organisations. Trust erosion is crucial, as employees may find it difficult to trust the authenticity of communications from colleagues, superiors, or official company channels. This can lead to increased stress, decreased collaboration, and reduced job satisfaction. Identity threat is another significant issue, as deepfakes uniquely threaten individual identity and professional reputation (Jindal, Kukreja, Mehta, Yadav, et al., 2023). Employees may fear being misrepresented or exploited in deepfake content, increasing anxiety and decreasing job satisfaction. The ambiguity introduced by deepfakes can create a sense of uncertainty and disillusionment among employees as they struggle to discern what is real and what is not. To address these challenges, organisations must invest in robust cyber security measures, provide clear communication and transparency from leadership, and provide training and resources to help employees recognise and respond to deepfake threats. This will empower them to confidently navigate the evolving media landscape, ultimately safeguarding their job satisfaction and well-being (Shukla et al., 2023).

H1: The higher the level of training and resources provided to recognise and respond to deepfake threats, the higher the job satisfaction among employees.

16.3.1.6 Job satisfaction and organisational commitment

The level of contentment, fulfilment, and happiness employees have with their jobs and work environment is known as job satisfaction. It is essential because it directly affects retention, productivity, and employee engagement. Employee satisfaction increases the likelihood that they will be dedicated, driven, and ready to put in extra effort to meet company objectives. High job satisfaction levels influence a favourable work environment that promotes cooperation, creativity, and invention (Banerjee, Kukreja, Gupta, et al., 2023). The work environment, interactions with coworkers and managers, work-life balance, chances for professional progress, pay and perks, employment autonomy and control, and recognition and incentives all affect how satisfied one is with one's job. The degree to which workers feel emotionally involved in and connected to their organisation is known as organisational commitment. Affective commitment (emotional connection), continuation commitment (perceived cost of quitting), and normative commitment (feeling of responsibility) are its three constituent parts. Several factors can influence an individual's organisational commitment, including leadership effectiveness, organisational culture, opportunities for involvement and participation, perceived organisational support, job satisfaction, career development opportunities, and organisational reputation. Leadership effectiveness fosters employee trust, loyalty, and commitment. A positive and values-driven organisational culture promotes transparency, fairness, and employee well-being. Involving employees in decision-making processes and providing meaningful involvement in activities fosters a sense of ownership and commitment. Perceived organisational support also increases commitment among employees. Job satisfaction is closely linked to organisational commitment, as satisfied employees are likelier to feel committed to their organisation. Career development opportunities increase commitment to the organisation. A positive organisational reputation and perceived attractiveness as an employer can enhance organisational commitment among employees (Banerjee, Kukreja, Bordoloi, et al., 2023).

16.3.1.7 Importance of job satisfaction and organisational commitment

Dedication to the organisation and job happiness are essential for individuals and organisations. They support a positive workplace culture, employee retention, productivity, engagement, and well-being. A favourable correlation exists between job satisfaction, organisational commitment, and an employee's mental and emotional well-being. Their increased engagement at work results in increased productivity and creative ideas. Another critical factor influencing organisational commitment and work satisfaction is retention. Contented and dedicated workers are less inclined to look for work elsewhere, lowering expenses and employee turnover (Pillai, Sharma, Malhotra, et al., 2023). An organisation's reputation is improved, top talent is drawn to and retained, and customer satisfaction rises when there is a healthy organisational culture]. A supportive work environment that empowers people to voice their ideas and take measured risks fosters innovation and creativity. Organisations get a competitive edge from creating new goods, services, and procedures brought about by this environment. Satisfied and committed employees are strong advocates for their organisation, speaking positively about their workplace experiences to attract top talent and enhance the organisation's employer brand. By prioritising these factors, organisations can cultivate a motivated and engaged workforce that drives long-term success and sustainability (Tanwar et al., 2023).

16.3.1.8 Integration of deepfake technology into existing frameworks

Deepfake technology has the potential to revolutionise various industries and domains by enabling realistic digital manipulation of audiovisual content. It can be used in media production and entertainment, advertising and marketing, digital identity verification, education and training, healthcare and telemedicine, cyber security and defence, and healthcare and defence (Kumar et al., 2023). Media production and entertainment can use deepfake algorithms to integrate actors into scenes, resurrect deceased celebrities, or dub dialogue in multiple languages without re-shoots. This can streamline workflows, reduce costs, and expand creative possibilities. Advertising and marketing can create hyper-realistic advertisements featuring virtual brand ambassadors or superimpose products into user-generated content on social media. Digital identity verification can use deepfake detection algorithms to enhance security and prevent fraud. By integrating deepfake detection technology into identity verification processes, businesses and government agencies can mitigate risks associated with identity theft and impersonation. Education and training can use deepfake technology to create immersive and interactive learning environments, providing students with hands-on learning opportunities, personalised feedback, and real-world simulations. Healthcare and telemedicine can use deepfake algorithms to generate customised avatars for virtual consultations, simulate surgical procedures, or create lifelike prosthetics and orthotics. Cyber security and defence can also leverage deepfake detection algorithms to identify malicious content, detect cyber-attacks, and authenticate digital evidence in legal proceedings. By proactively addressing these challenges, organisations can harness the power of deepfake technology to drive innovation, enhance productivity, and improve quality of life (Jindal, Kukreja, Mehta, Chauhan, et al., 2023).

16.3.1.9 Impact on organisational commitment

Deepfake technology significantly impacts organisational commitment, causing distrust, communication breakdown, and reduced organisational resilience. Employees may become sceptical of the authenticity of leadership messages, leading to feelings of uncertainty and disengagement. This can result in a decline in commitment as employees struggle to align with an untrustworthy entity. The disruption of traditional communication channels by deepfakes can create barriers to effective information sharing and collaboration, hindering decision-making processes and weakening interpersonal relationships. This can result in a decline in organisational commitment. (Thakur et al., 2023). Failing to address the risks associated with deepfake technology can also lead to diminished organisational resilience in crises or reputational threats. Deepfakes can manipulate public perception, damage organisational reputation, and undermine trust in leadership. This perception can lead to decreased commitment and loyalty among employees seeking opportunities in more secure environments. To mitigate the negative impact of deepfakes on organisational commitment, organisations must implement robust cyber security measures, promote transparency and authenticity in communication, and foster a culture of trust and resilience. Prioritising the integrity of information and communication channels can help organisations maintain a loyal and engaged workforce (Yashu et al., 2023).

H2: The higher the level of training and resources provided to recognise and respond to deepfake threats, the higher the Organisational Commitment among employees.

16.4 Research Methodology and Analysis

This study employs a descriptive research approach. Primary data was collected through the distribution of surveys to get a deep understanding of the impact on working employees. This study is a part of quantitative research. Additionally, this study is based on a simple random sampling method. An empirical study with statistical analysis using tool correlation was conducted to ascertain the relationship between various variables – training level to recognise deepfake threats, job satisfaction, and Organisational Commitment. For data collection, Google Forms was used to create online questionnaires

Table 16.1 Correlation between training level to recognise deepfake threats and job satisfaction and Organisational Commitment.

		Training levels	Job satisfaction	Org. commitment
Training Levels	Pearson Correlation	1		
	Sig. (2-tailed)			
	N	100		
Job Satisfaction	Pearson Correlation	0.706**	1	
	Sig. (2-tailed)	0.000		
	N	100	100	
Org. Commitment	Pearson Correlation	0.621**	0.670**	1
	Sig. (2-tailed)	0.000	0.000	
	N	100	100	100

** Correlation is significant at the 0.01 level (2-tailed). Source: Calculated by authors.

distributed across social media platforms like Instagram, WhatsApp, and email for ease of use (Banerjee, Kukreja, Jain, et al., 2023). We chose to disassemble the questionnaires online and in person because, through online questionnaires, we could access a more substantial number of audiences in no time. Thus, the population comprises professional employees working within an organisation. One hundred respondents were selected from the Chandigarh tri-city, of which 58% were female and 42% were male. Additionally, the average age of the respondents lies between 25 and 40 years, which covers 87% of the respondents, and the data was gathered over two months, from March to April 2024, for data analysis. The analyses as per the objectives are given below:

The data provided offers an insightful correlation matrix (Table 16.1) that delineates the relationships between three pivotal variables: Training, Job Satisfaction, and Organisational Commitment. The Pearson Correlation Coefficient, a statistical measure, is employed to ascertain the strength and direction of the linear relationships between these variables.

A strong positive correlation of 0.706 is observed between Training and Job Satisfaction. This correlation, significant at the 0.01 level (2-tailed), suggests a direct relationship between the two variables. In essence, an increase in the level of training is likely to result in a corresponding increase in job satisfaction. Similarly, a positive correlation of 0.621 is noted between Training and Organisational Commitment. This correlation, also significant at the 0.01 level (2-tailed), implies that higher levels of training could potentially lead to an increase in organisational commitment. Furthermore, a strong positive correlation of 0.670 between Job Satisfaction and Organisational Commitment is found. This correlation, significant at the 0.01 level (2-tailed), indicates that an increase in job satisfaction is likely to result in a corresponding increase in organisational commitment. In conclusion, the data reveals a significant positive correlation between all three variables. This suggests that enhancements in one area, such as training, could improve job satisfaction and organisational commitment.

16.5 Case studies: Deepfakes in the workplace

16.5.1 Case study: IT sector

Company name: Google
In 2019, Google's security team uncovered a sophisticated deepfake audio attack aimed at its employees. Malicious actors leveraged AI-generated voices to impersonate company executives, attempting to deceive staff members into divulging sensitive information. The attackers exploited the trust and authority associated with high-ranking executives, underscoring the potential risks posed by deepfake technology in corporate environments.

The incident is a stark reminder of organisations' evolving threat landscape worldwide. Deepfake attacks have the potential to inflict substantial damage, including data breaches, financial losses, reputational harm, and legal ramifications. Moreover, traditional cyber security measures may prove inadequate in detecting and mitigating such threats, necessitating proactive strategies tailored to combat deepfake attacks effectively.

This case study underscores the critical importance of robust cyber security measures and employee awareness programmes to safeguard against deepfake threats in the workplace. Organisations must invest in advanced technologies capable of detecting and mitigating deepfake attacks in real time. Additionally, comprehensive training programmes should educate employees about deepfake technology and empower them to identify and respond to potential threats promptly.

16.5.2 Case study: Finance sector

Company name: JPMorgan Chase
In 2019, JPMorgan Chase took decisive steps to bolster its cyber security defenses by implementing a deepfake detection system. Recognising the potential risks posed by deepfake technology, the company leveraged AI

algorithms to analyze and detect fraudulent content, including deepfake videos, audio recordings, and text-based communications. By deploying cutting-edge technology, JPMorgan Chase aimed to protect its employees and customers from phishing attacks, identity theft, and other forms of cybercrime.

The deepfake detection system employed by JPMorgan Chase represents a proactive approach to mitigating the negative impact of deceptive content on organisational integrity and employee satisfaction. By identifying and intercepting fraudulent communications, the company sought to maintain the trust and confidence of its stakeholders while upholding the highest standards of security and compliance.

JPMorgan Chase's deepfake detection system underscores the importance of proactive cyber security measures and advanced technology in safeguarding against emerging threats. Organisations must invest in robust detection and prevention mechanisms to effectively detect and mitigate the risks posed by deepfake technology. Additionally, comprehensive cyber security training programmes are essential to educate employees about the dangers of deepfake attacks and empower them to recognise and report suspicious activities promptly.

16.5.3 Case study: Media and entertainment

Company name: Disney
In 2019, Disney used deepfake technology to de-age actor Kurt Russell in a movie. By leveraging deepfake algorithms, filmmakers digitally altered Russell's appearance to portray a younger version of his character, achieving a more realistic and seamless visual effect. While deepfake technology enabled Disney to enhance the film's aesthetic quality, it also sparked ethical debates regarding manipulating actors' likenesses without explicit consent.

The use of deepfake technology in "The Guardians of the Galaxy Vol. 2" exemplifies the ethical dilemmas inherent in its application in film production. While the technology offers creative possibilities and enhances filmmakers' artistic vision, it raises concerns about the authenticity and integrity of actors' performances. Moreover, the lack of explicit consent from actors regarding manipulating their appearances infringes upon their autonomy and raises questions about the ethical boundaries of digital manipulation in filmmaking.

Disney's utilisation of deepfake technology underscores the urgent need for ethical guidelines and industry standards to govern its responsible usage in film production. Filmmakers must prioritise transparency and consent, ensuring that actors are fully informed and consent to any digital alterations made to their appearances. Additionally, industry stakeholders should collaborate to develop ethical frameworks that balance artistic innovation with respect for actors' rights and integrity.

16.6 Mitigating the Impact of Deepfakes

Deepfake technology poses a significant threat to organisations, requiring a comprehensive approach that addresses both technological and human factors. To mitigate this, organisations should invest in advanced AI-driven detection tools, which use machine learning algorithms to analyse audiovisual content and detect anomalies indicative of deepfake manipulation. These tools can quickly identify and neutralise deepfake threats before they cause significant harm.

In addition to detection tools, organisations should implement enhanced cyber security measures, such as multifactor authentication, encryption, and other security protocols, to safeguard against deepfake-related threats. This will minimise the risk of attacks and data breaches.

Promoting media literacy and critical thinking skills is crucial for empowering individuals to recognise and respond effectively to manipulated content. Employee training programmes should educate employees about the techniques used to create deepfakes, highlight common red flags, and provide practical strategies for verifying digital media authenticity.

Transparent communication from organisational leadership is essential for building trust and resilience within the workforce. Regularly communicating with employees about the potential impact of deepfakes and providing guidance on staying vigilant and reporting suspicious content or incidents can strengthen employee trust and confidence in the organisation's ability to address emerging threats effectively.

16.7 Implications of Deepfake Technology on Job Satisfaction and Organisational Commitment

The implications of deepfake technology on job satisfaction and organisational commitment are profound. Deepfakes, which are AI-generated synthetic media, have been identified as potential disruptors within organisational contexts. Research suggests that the emergence of deepfakes poses multifaceted challenges to individual employees and the organisations they belong to.

Firstly, deepfakes can erode trust and confidence within organisations, affecting job satisfaction. The existence of deepfakes can lead to heightened anxiety among employees due to the risk of being misrepresented or exploited in manipulated media. This uncertainty regarding the authenticity of digital content can breed mistrust among colleagues and superiors, ultimately diminishing overall job satisfaction levels.

Furthermore, the threat of deepfakes impersonating employees or executives poses a significant risk to individual identity and professional reputation. Employees may fear the consequences of being falsely portrayed or manipulated by their words in digital media. Such concerns impact individual job satisfaction and can create a sense of vulnerability and insecurity within the organisation, thereby affecting organisational commitment.

Communication breakdowns resulting from deepfakes can further exacerbate the situation, fostering employee misunderstandings and alienation. In an environment where the authenticity of digital communications is called into question, employees may become hesitant to engage in open and transparent communication, leading to silos and fragmentation within the organisation.

Moreover, the ambiguity introduced by deepfakes blurs the line between genuine and fabricated content, making it challenging for employees to discern truth from fiction. This ambiguity can lead to disillusionment and disengagement among employees as they struggle to navigate an environment where the integrity of information cannot be easily verified.

Failure to address these risks may result in diminished organisational resilience, as employees perceive their organisation as vulnerable to manipulation. This perception of vulnerability can have far-reaching implications for organisational morale, effectiveness, and competitiveness. Therefore, it is imperative for organisations to proactively address the challenges posed by deepfake technology to safeguard employee job satisfaction and organisational commitment.

16.8 Recommendations for Organisations

To combat the dangers of deepfake technology, organisations should prioritise investments in robust cyber security measures, such as advanced detection tools, encryption techniques, and authentication protocols. Employee training programmes should be provided to educate employees about the risks and implications of deepfake technology, focusing on media literacy and critical thinking skills. Transparency and authenticity should be promoted within the organisation, encouraging employees to report suspicious content and provide guidance on verifying digital media authenticity.

Organisational resilience should be strengthened by developing contingency plans and response strategies to address deepfake-related threats. Collaborating with industry stakeholders, government agencies, and cyber security experts can share best practices and develop standards for responsible deepfake technology use. Staying informed about emerging trends and advancements in deepfake technology can help proactively anticipate and mitigate potential risks.

Fostering a culture of trust and support within the organisation can enhance employee morale and commitment. Open communication, feedback opportunities, and commitment to ethical practices and values can help foster a resilient and trustworthy workplace environment. By implementing these recommendations, organisations can effectively mitigate the impact of deepfake technology on job satisfaction and organisational commitment.

16.9 Conclusion

The rise of deepfake technology presents significant challenges to job satisfaction and organisational commitment within modern workplaces. The potential consequences of deepfakes extend beyond mere technological advancements, impacting the very fabric of trust, confidence, and engagement within organisations. As highlighted throughout this discussion, deepfakes can erode trust and confidence among employees, fostering disillusionment and disengagement, ultimately leading to diminished levels of job satisfaction and organisational commitment.

Moreover, the implications of deepfakes extend to reputational damage and vulnerability to cyber threats. The manipulation of digital content through deepfake technology can tarnish individual and organisational reputations, leading to lasting repercussions on employee morale and organisational effectiveness. Case studies from various industries provide empirical evidence of the detrimental impact of deepfakes on job satisfaction and commitment, emphasising the urgency for proactive interventions.

In response to these challenges, organisations must adopt proactive measures to mitigate the adverse effects of deepfakes and safeguard their workforce and reputation. This entails investing in robust cyber security infrastructure, providing comprehensive employee training programmes, promoting transparency in communication practices, and fostering a culture of trust and accountability. By implementing such measures, organisations can enhance their resilience against deepfake threats and cultivate a workplace environment that prioritises employee well-being and organisational integrity.

Furthermore, organisations must remain vigilant and adaptable in the rapidly evolving digital landscape by continuously monitoring emerging trends and advancements in deepfake technology. By staying abreast of technological developments and proactively addressing potential risks, organisations can effectively mitigate the impact of deepfake technology on job satisfaction and organisational commitment.

In summary, deepfake technology presents multifaceted challenges to job satisfaction and organisational commitment, necessitating a comprehensive and proactive approach from organisations. By adopting a holistic strategy that integrates technological solutions, organisational policies, and employee education, organisations can navigate the complexities of deepfake technology and cultivate a resilient and trustworthy workplace environment for their employees.

16.10 Acknowledgements

We express our heartfelt gratitude to all those who have helped in this research by providing their input directly or indirectly through their research work as references or direct input as respondents. We express our heartfelt indebtedness to the almighty God, who has given us the strength to complete the research work.

References

Agarwal, J., Vaswani, S., Sharma, A., Kaushik, D., & Bhardwaj, D. (2023). Optimization of Crop Yield Using Machine Learning. In C. N. (Ed.), *Proceedings - International Conference on Technological Advancements in Computational Sciences, ICTACS 2023* (pp. 469–474). Institute of Electrical and Electronics Engineers Inc. https://doi.org/10.1109/ICTACS59847.2023.10389927

Banerjee, D., Kukreja, V., Bordoloi, D., & Joshi, K. (2023). Hybrid CNN & Random Forest Model for Effective Turmeric Leaf Disease Diagnosis. *2023 3rd International Conference on Smart Generation Computing, Communication and Networking, SMART GENCON 2023*. https://doi.org/10.1109/SMARTGENCON60755.2023.10442441

Banerjee, D., Kukreja, V., Gupta, A., Singh, V., & Pal Singh Brar, T. (2023). Combining CNN and SVM for Accurate Identification of Ridge Gourd Leaf Diseases. *2023 3rd Asian Conference on Innovation in Technology, ASIANCON 2023*. https://doi.org/10.1109/ASIANCON58793.2023.10269834

Banerjee, D., Kukreja, V., Jain, A., Rawat, D., & Jain, V. (2023). Enhancing Tulsi Leaf Disease with CNN and SVM-Based Classification. *2023 1st International Conference on Optimization Techniques for Learning, ICOTL 2023 - Proceedings*. https://doi.org/10.1109/ICOTL59758.2023.10435248

Banerjee, D., Kukreja, V., Verma, A., Garg, N., & Hariharan, S. (2023). Hybrid CNN & Random Forest Model for Effective Guava Leaf

Disease Diagnosis. *2023 IEEE International Conference on Research Methodologies in Knowledge Management, Artificial Intelligence and Telecommunication Engineering, RMKMATE 2023*. https://doi.org/10.1109/RMKMATE59243.2023.10369898

Gill, K. S., Anand, V., Chauhan, R., Verma, G., & Gupta, R. (2023). Agricultural Pests Classification Using Deep Convolutional Neural Networks and Transfer Learning. *2023 2nd International Conference on Futuristic Technologies, INCOFT 2023*. https://doi.org/10.1109/INCOFT60753.2023.10425080

Gupta, P., Gopal, S., Sharma, M., Joshi, S., Sahani, C., & Ahalawat, K. (2023). Agriculture Informatics and Communication: Paradigm of E-Governance and Drone Technology for Crop Monitoring. *9th International Conference on Smart Computing and Communications: Intelligent Technologies and Applications, ICSCC 2023*, 113–118. https://doi.org/10.1109/ICSCC59169.2023.10335058

Jindal, V., Kukreja, V., Mehta, S., Chauhan, R., & Verma, G. (2023). Towards Sustainable Agriculture: Federated CNN Models for Cucurbit Leaf Disease Detection. *2023 10th IEEE Uttar Pradesh Section International Conference on Electrical, Electronics and Computer Engineering, UPCON 2023*, 561–566. https://doi.org/10.1109/UPCON59197.2023.10434321

Jindal, V., Kukreja, V., Mehta, S., Srivastava, P., & Garg, N. (2023). Adopting Federated Learning and CNN for Advanced Plant Pathology: A Case of Red Globe Grape Leaf Diseases Dissecting Severity. *2023 3rd Asian Conference on Innovation in Technology, ASIANCON 2023*. https://doi.org/10.1109/ASIANCON58793.2023.10270034

Jindal, V., Kukreja, V., Mehta, S., Yadav, R., & Garg, N. (2023). Improved Food Security of Bottle Gourd Leaf Disease by Federated Learning CNN: A Case Study. *2023 Annual International Conference on Emerging Research Areas: International Conference on Intelligent Systems, AICERA/ICIS 2023*. https://doi.org/10.1109/AICERA/ICIS59538.2023.10420151

Kaur, A., Kukreja, V., Manwal, M., Joshi, K., & Jain, V. (2023). Blending Forest with Neural Networks: An Insight into Marula Leaf Disease Prediction. In N. P., S. M., K. M., J. V., & G. K. (Eds.), *Proceedings - 4th IEEE 2023 International Conference on Computing, Communication, and Intelligent Systems, ICCCIS 2023* (pp. 255–260). Institute of Electrical and Electronics Engineers Inc. https://doi.org/10.1109/ICCCIS60361.2023.10425029

Kaur, A., Kukreja, V., Verma, A., Rawat, D., & Jain, V. (2023). Tales of the Rosehip: A Journey Through Neural Networks and Whispering Forests. In N. P., S. M., K. M., J. V., & G. K. (Eds.), *Proceedings - 4th IEEE 2023 International Conference on Computing, Communication, and Intelligent Systems, ICCCIS 2023* (pp. 212–217). Institute of Electrical and Electronics Engineers Inc. https://doi.org/10.1109/ICCCIS60361.2023.10425261

Kaur, G., Sharma, N., Chauhan, R., Pokhariya, H. S., & Gupta, R. (2023). Fruit and Vegetable Classification Using MobileNet V2 Transfer Learning Model. *2023 3rd International Conference on Smart Generation Computing, Communication and Networking, SMART GENCON 2023.* https://doi.org/10.1109/SMARTGENCON60755.2023.10442618

Kumar, V., Banerjee, D., Chauhan, R., Joshi, K., & Gill, K. S. (2023). Optimizing Mango Leaf Disease Evaluation: CNN and Random Forest Fusion. *2023 3rd International Conference on Smart Generation Computing, Communication and Networking, SMART GENCON 2023.* https://doi.org/10.1109/SMARTGENCON60755.2023.10442934

Kunwar, S., Joshi, A., Gururani, P., Pandey, D., & Pandey, N. (2023). Physiological and AI-based study of endophytes on medicina A mini review. *Plant Science Today*, *10*, 53–60. https://doi.org/10.14719/pst.2555

Malik, D., Kukreja, V., Mehta, S., Gupta, A., & Singh, V. (2023). Mitigating the Impact of Guava Leaf Diseases Using CNNs and Federated Learning. *2023 3rd Asian Conference on Innovation in Technology, ASIANCON 2023.* https://doi.org/10.1109/ASIANCON58793.2023.10270236

Pillai, R., Sharma, N., Chauhan, R., Rawat, D., & Gupta, R. (2023). CNN-based Approach for Classification of Rice Varieties. *2023 2nd International Conference on Futuristic Technologies, INCOFT 2023.* https://doi.org/10.1109/INCOFT60753.2023.10425548

Pillai, R., Sharma, N., Malhotra, S., Dangi, S., & Gupta, R. (2023). Detection and Classification of Plant Seedlings: Distinguishing Crop Seedlings from Weed Seedlings Using MobileNetV2 Transfer Learning Model with Fine-Tuning Layers. *2023 3rd International Conference on Smart Generation Computing, Communication and Networking, SMART GENCON 2023.* https://doi.org/10.1109/SMARTGENCON60755.2023.10442772

Rao, K. V. G., Kumar, M. K., Goud, B. S., Krishna, D., Bajaj, M., Saini, P., & Choudhury, S. (2023). IOT-Powered Crop Shield System for Surveillance and Auto Transversum. *2023 IEEE 3rd International*

Conference on Sustainable Energy and Future Electric Transportation, SeFet 2023. https://doi.org/10.1109/SeFeT57834.2023.10245773

Sharma, G., Anand, V., Malhotra, S., Kukreti, S., & Gupta, S. (2023). CNN-Based Intelligent Classification of Bell Pepper Plant Diseases: A Novel Approach for Precision Agriculture. *2023 3rd International Conference on Smart Generation Computing, Communication and Networking, SMART GENCON 2023*. https://doi.org/10.1109/SMARTGENCON60755.2023.10442079

Shukla, A., Sharma, M., Tiwari, K., Vani, V. D., Kumar, N., & Pooja. (2023). Predicting Rainfall Using an Artificial Neural Network-Based Model. *Proceedings of International Conference on Contemporary Computing and Informatics, IC3I 2023*, 2700–2704. https://doi.org/10.1109/IC3I59117.2023.10397714

Suryavanshi, A., Kukreja, V., Chamoli, S., Mehta, S., & Thapliyal, S. (2023). Enabling Precision Agriculture: A Federated Learning CNN Approach to Diagnosing Jackfruit Leaf Diseases. In D. R.K., S. A.Kr., S. R., B. S., & K. V. (Eds.), *Proceedings of the 2023 12th International Conference on System Modeling and Advancement in Research Trends, SMART 2023* (pp. 29–35). Institute of Electrical and Electronics Engineers Inc. https://doi.org/10.1109/SMART59791.2023.10428555

Tanwar, V., Anand, V., Chauhan, R., & Rawat, D. (2023). An Intelligent Deep-Learning Model CNN Used for Multi-Class Classification of Apple Leaf Disease. *2023 2nd International Conference on Futuristic Technologies, INCOFT 2023*. https://doi.org/10.1109/INCOFT60753.2023.10425539

Thakur, S., Malik, D., Kukreja, V., Sharma, R., Yadav, R., & Joshi, K. (2023). Multi-Stage Classification of Pomegranate Anthracnose Disease Severity Levels with CNN and SVM. *Proceedings of the 4th International Conference on Smart Electronics and Communication, ICOSEC 2023*, 1117–1121. https://doi.org/10.1109/ICOSEC58147.2023.10276047

Yashu, Kukreja, V., Chamoli, S., & Thapliyal, S. (2023). Severity Levels of Apple Disease Recognition Using CNN and Random Forest: An Integrated Approach. *2023 3rd International Conference on Smart Generation Computing, Communication and Networking, SMART GENCON 2023*. https://doi.org/10.1109/SMARTGENCON60755.2023.10441917

17

Navigating the Synthetic Media Conundrum: A Manager's Integrated Roadmap for Enhancing Religious Tourist Satisfaction and Attitude

Mayur Thakur[1], Shikha Sharma[1] and Timi Olubiyi[2]

[1]Department of Tourism, Chandigarh University, Mohali, India
[2]West Midlands Open University, Nigeria

Email: thakurmayur3333@gmail.com; shikhasharma.uithm@cumail.in; timi.olubiyi@westmidlands.university

Abstract

In this case, this study examines the deeper meaning of deepfake technologies on consumer trust, satisfaction and perceived authenticity in the religious tourism sector. In this realm, the holiness and credibility of experiences are highly critical. As artificial media expands to the next level with tremendous complexity for producing highly deceptive yet realistic fake content, religious tourism is highly vulnerable, given its core marketing proposition of authenticity, reliability, and openness. This research employs an understanding that combines quantitative and qualitative approaches to systematically investigate the effects of deepfake exposure on religious tourists' perceptions and behaviours to address the ethical issues and managerial solutions for controlling such harms. Self-administered questionnaires, employing a 7-point Likert scale, systematically assess tourist trust, satisfaction and attitudes towards tangible and intangible religious tourism. In contrast, interviews covering tourism managers and focus group discussions with religious tourists offer detailed and rich material for appreciating cultural norms of the operational, ethical and technological paradigms required to maintain religious tourism's purity from the growing trend of digital influence. The research also explores using AI-enabled deepfake detection tools, ethical communication, and consumer awareness to limit the harms of deepfakes. It offers a holistic managerial plan that outlines its moral aspects and novel technological tools, focusing on transparency as a critical strategic act. The conclusions highlight the necessity of the transdisciplinary effort to guarantee the sacredness of the religious experience and its integrity, considering the study's limitations, such as the constant development of deepfakes and geography focus. Using such an analysis, this study advances the existing knowledge regarding the imperative of ethical and operational reception of synthetic media in today's aggressively digital context that poses threats to the very trust of tourists, not to mention the spirituality of religious tourism.

17.1 Introduction

Those new to synthetic media, especially deepfakes, have triggered a change in content creation in the digital world, which has led to the manipulation of reality reaching its peak. As a result of the application of AI and neural networks, deepfake technology creates hyperrealistic images, audio and videos, blurring imitation and originality to a great extent. What was initially a fun quirk of entertainment and social media platforms has become systemic in the politics, journalism, finance, and advertising industries (Banerjee, Kukreja, Sharma, et al., 2023; S. Joshi et al., 2023; Mehta, Kukreja, Vats, et al., 2023; Pant et al., 2023), cracking open the vulnerable core of digital systems to manipulation, fraud, and disinformation. The normality of deepfakes is especially malicious because it destabilises one of the most valuable resources in the world of technology: trust, which, thanks to deepfakes, can no longer reliably rely on a face and voice. The growth of industries incorporating digital networks magnifies the instability of published content, and synthetic media impacts outreach beyond damage control for individuals and companies (Jindal, Kukreja, Mehta, Gupta, et al., 2023). However, in sectors such as finance and governance, deepfakes can have ripple effects that put a person's reputation, the company, the economy, and everyone else at risk. However, in the case of tourism, particularly religious and cultural tourism, this technological advance poses a significant threat to the quality of the heritage experience (Vishalli et al., 2023), thereby creating tonnes of consumer distrust amongst religious and cultural tourists who require nothing more than the real deal. These are logical. Therefore, the rapid diffusion of synthetic media necessitates an immediate rethinking of how businesses, particularly those built upon the foundations of credibility and trust, can develop sustainable approaches to dealing with the threats that this constantly evolving, high-stakes technological problem presents (Nishinari et al., 2023).

The sudden appearance of synthetic media technologies, primarily deepfakes, triggered a more and more heated discussion of the compassionate ethical questions and integrity problems that these tools create, primarily in such trusted industries as media and tourism (Gusain et al., 2023; Mehta, Kukreja, Sharma, et al., 2023; Rather et al., 2023). That is the sophistication and capability of misappropriating these technologies' advances in parallel, eroding the basis of knowledge at the organisational, industrial, and societal levels. The ability to produce representations in the form of text, graphics, audio, and video that are so realistic that they are almost indistinguishable from the real world is already here (Jindal, Kukreja, Mehta, Yadav, et al., 2023; Pokhariya et al., 2023). It produces doubts about the produced material's credibility, decency, and honesty. Where media reflects the distribution of information with trust, deepfakes subvert the possibility of journalistic integrity through disinformation, defamation, and the influence of public opinion. The prospect of a fake news creator using deepfakes in the engineering of a political disinformation campaign, news manipulation, or a smear campaign against political opponents poses an inherently dangerous threat to good journalism and democracy as well (Ganesan et al., 2023; N. C. Joshi & Gururani, 2023; Vashishth et al., 2023). Likewise, in the peripheral tourism industry, such as religious and cultural tourism, the experience's authenticity is crucial. Cultural consumers, especially tourists looking for enlightenment, as is typical with religious pilgrims, need to trust what is offered to their sight, hearing, and touch. The concept of synthetic media coupled in some way with such experiences threatens to contaminate them with fake news or distorted representations, undermining the very stand of the traveller representing engagement by turning the holy places/tourist attractions into virtual realities that can be commercialised as well as misrepresented (Gonfa et al., 2022; Kholiya et al., 2023). As they infiltrate our lives, the ethical dilemma escalates as these technologies become indiscernible from actuality; the issues of consent to the use and ownership and the ethics of synthetic media's application come to the fore, along with the responsibilities of those using them. The problem, hence, is as much ethical as it is technical, requiring a renewed appreciation of how subsequently regulatory policies, codes of ethics, and managerial strategies that preserve the credibility of both media and tourism can be developed in light of a synthetic media environment (Awasthi et al., 2023; Bhatnagar et al., 2022; Semwal et al., 2023).

Several factors define the tourism industry and its types: religion, culture, history, and trust; however, these, especially the religious tourism sector, are vulnerable to the influence of deepfake manipulation and fake news distribution (Parkash et al., 2022; Rawat et al., 2022). Experiential and emotional aspects represent the essence of religious tourism. Based on attributes of religious sites, rituals, and history, it is highly susceptible to the influence of synthetic media, which can deform or mimic the vital aspects of religious experience. By their potential to provide believable but entirely fake audio-visual content through artificial intelligence, deepfake technology poses a significant threat to religious experiences and the surrounding discourse by offering fake faces of holy personalities or impersonations of sacred sites or holy occasions (Chakravorty et al., 2022; Pokhariya et al., 2022). Pilgrims and tourists, who very often follow the program based on the beliefs and expectations regarding the receipt of the spirit and values, can become the spectators of fakes that skilfully manipulate the attributes of deepfakes to create the necessary scenario and visually transform holy places. Such manipulations cannot only undermine the sensual/religious bond that tourists look for, but they can also commodify and vulgarise spiritual tourism in the worst possible manner of mechanistic reductionism (Gusain et al., 2022). Furthermore, with the help of modern information technologies, digital promotion of tourism services and the appearance of new ways of attracting the attention of global visitors, such as social media, online advertising, and others, deepfake-related misinformation may also increase tourist blogs and advertised materials. Such channels can lead to post-travel disillusion for tourists or even completely repel them from choosing other similar experiences. Therefore, religious tourism, as an industry that relies on the authenticity of cultural and spiritual knowledge and which is affected by a fake representation of historical and sacred spaces, firstly becomes a target for deepfake technology applications; secondly, it requires an urgent managerial and ethical response to address the issue of protecting religious tourism experiences from the growing invasion of deepfake technology (Mudholkar et al., 2022; Ram et al., 2022).

17.2 Literature Review

17.2.1 The rise of synthetic media and deepfakes

The usage and production of synthetic media, primarily through deepfake technologies, have rapidly grown exponentially and, as such, have received considerable research attention. While deepfake technology was initially used in entertainment and on social media, it quickly crossed over to related areas of sensitivity, such as politics, journalism, and tourism. Analysed the consequences of deepfakes to propose that they can negatively ingrain the concept of trust in interpersonal, organisational, and industrial relations owing to their disagreements with the fundamental principles of credibility (Jain et al., 2022; Shashikala et al., 2022). Through the use of neural networks and AI algorithms, deepfakes look as accurate as they are fake and completely bogus. While appropriate for arts, entertainment, and leisure, such technology presents a profound ethical dilemma for industries that require public trust. They explained in their work that the increase in AI-generated content is a threat to the epistemological quality of media, provoking a global discourse on the options for regulation and solutions. However, as much as deepfake technology has the potential to disrupt political realms, few researchers have investigated the subject's connection to the tourism industry, especially its religious sector (Adow et al., 2022; Kamal et al., 2022; Sajitha et al., 2022).

17.2.2 Ethical implications of deepfake technologies

The ethical implications of deepfake technologies have sparked an intense global discourse, as the capacity for these AI-driven tools to create hyper-realistic yet entirely fabricated audio-visual content fundamentally challenges the principles of authenticity, autonomy, and accountability in digital spaces, leading to profound concerns about consent, privacy, and the erosion of trust, particularly in industries reliant on credibility, such as media and tourism (A. Kaur, Kukreja, Gopal, Verma, et al., 2023); deepfakes not only raise questions about the ownership of digital identities, as individuals may find their likenesses manipulated without consent for malicious purposes, but also threaten to commodify and distort cultural and religious experiences, especially in sensitive sectors like religious tourism where the integrity of sacred narratives and cultural artifacts is paramount, creating a scenario where digital manipulation undermines the very essence of spiritual and heritage engagements, further exacerbating the ethical dilemmas of deepfakes as they blur the line between truth and fabrication, necessitating an urgent re-evaluation of moral frameworks, industry standards, and regulatory mechanisms to prevent the exploitation of synthetic media for manipulative or fraudulent purposes, while also safeguarding the integrity of individual rights and cultural heritage in an increasingly digitalised world (A. Kaur, Kukreja, Manwal, Garg, et al., 2023; Kumar, Banerjee, Chauhan, Rawat, et al., 2023).

17.2.3 Impact of deepfakes on consumer trust and integrity in tourism

The proliferation of deepfake technologies poses a significant threat to consumer trust and integrity within the tourism sector, as the ability of artificial intelligence to produce convincingly fabricated media challenges the authenticity and reliability of digital representations that tourists rely on when making travel decisions, particularly in niche segments like religious tourism where the experience is deeply rooted in cultural, spiritual, and historical authenticity; the manipulation of images (G. Kaur, Sharma, Chauhan, Joshi, et al., 2023; V. Sharma et al., 2023), videos, or promotional content through deepfakes can lead to disillusionment and mistrust among tourists who find that the reality of their travel experience does not match the expectations set by artificially enhanced or entirely fabricated depictions, eroding consumer confidence and damaging the reputations of destinations or organisations that unwittingly or deliberately propagate such content, thus exacerbating the broader issue of integrity in tourism marketing and operations, where the alignment between perceived and actual experiences is crucial for maintaining long-term customer satisfaction and loyalty, ultimately raising profound concerns about the commodification of authenticity and the ethical obligations of tourism operators to ensure that their digital content remains truthful and aligned with the genuine experiences they aim to offer (Banerjee, Kukreja, Bordoloi, et al., 2023; Kumar, Banerjee, Chauhan, Joshi, et al., 2023), as well as highlighting the urgent need for managerial strategies and technological safeguards that can help mitigate the risks of deepfake-induced misinformation, preserve the trustworthiness of tourism brands, and uphold the integrity of the sector in an era increasingly influenced by synthetic media and digital manipulation (Pillai et al., 2023; G. Sharma et al., 2023).

17.2.4 Managerial strategies for combating deepfakes in tourism

Managerial strategies for effectively combating deepfakes in the tourism industry, particularly in highly sensitive areas such as religious tourism where the authenticity and integrity of sacred experiences are integral to consumer satisfaction, require a profoundly complex, multi-layered approach that not only incorporates advanced AI-based detection tools to identify and prevent the dissemination of synthetic media but also emphasises the need for a robust ethical framework that governs digital content creation and marketing (Gill et al., 2023), ensuring that all promotional materials and online representations reflect the genuine, unaltered experiences offered by destinations; this strategy must be supported by an unwavering commitment to transparency in communication, coupled with proactive measures such as the education of tourists on the risks and recognition of deepfakes, fostering a more informed, critical audience capable of navigating the digital landscape with discernment (G. Kaur, Sharma, Chauhan, Pokhariya, et al., 2023;

Yashu et al., 2023), while simultaneously engaging in collaborative efforts with technologists, regulators, and industry stakeholders to establish comprehensive industry-wide standards and regulations that can mitigate the reputational risks posed by deepfakes, thereby preserving the trust and credibility of the tourism sector as a whole, as failure to address this growing threat could lead to irreparable damage to consumer trust and the commodification of authenticity itself in an era where artificial, manipulated content increasingly permeates the digital fabric of tourism marketing and operations (Banerjee, Kukreja, Jain, et al., 2023; Suryavanshi et al., 2023).

17.3 Research Gap

The research gap identified in this study lies in the insufficient exploration of the intricate interplay between deepfake-driven synthetic media and its nuanced effects on religious tourist satisfaction, particularly in how the psychological, emotional, and cultural dimensions of religious tourism – where authenticity is paramount – are influenced by manipulated digital content, with existing literature focusing predominantly on broader sectors such as political disinformation or general tourism without delving into the specific vulnerabilities of religious tourism; furthermore, there remains a lack of comprehensive, empirically driven models that integrate technological solutions, ethical communication practices, and managerial strategies into a cohesive framework capable of mitigating the complex challenges posed by deepfakes, thus calling for a deeper investigation into the effectiveness of organisational interventions in safeguarding the authenticity and integrity of religious tourism experiences in an increasingly digitalised and manipulated media landscape.

17.3.1 Research questions

- How do deepfakes impact the trust and satisfaction of religious tourists?
- What are the primary ethical challenges posed by deepfakes in the tourism industry, particularly in religious tourism?
- How can tourism managers ensure the integrity and authenticity of digital content in the age of deepfakes?
- What strategies can be implemented to detect and prevent the spread of manipulated media in religious tourism marketing?
- What role does transparency in communication play in maintaining consumer trust when deepfake technologies are prevalent?

17.3.2 Objectives

- To examine the impact of deepfake technologies on consumer trust and satisfaction in the religious tourism sector.
- To explore the ethical challenges deepfakes present in the tourism industry, particularly in the context of authenticity and integrity in religious tourism.
- To identify the strategies tourism managers can implement to detect, prevent, and mitigate the spread of deepfake-driven misinformation in marketing and digital operations.
- To analyse how manipulated digital content influences tourist perceptions, attitudes, and expectations toward religious destinations.
- To assess the effectiveness of AI-based detection tools and technological solutions in combating deepfakes within the tourism sector.

17.4 Methodology

The research methodology for this study encompasses a comprehensive, mixed-methods approach, designed to intricately blend both quantitative and qualitative paradigms, thereby facilitating a robust investigation into the multifaceted impact of deepfake technologies on consumer trust, satisfaction, and integrity within the religious tourism sector, with the quantitative arm involving the deployment of structured surveys utilising a 7-point Likert scale to elicit measurable data on critical variables such as tourist perceptions, trust, satisfaction, and attitudes toward authenticity, while simultaneously employing advanced statistical techniques, including correlation and regression analyses via SPSS, to quantitatively assess the influence of deepfakes on consumer behaviour; this quantitative analysis is complemented by an in-depth qualitative exploration through semi-structured interviews with tourism managers and focus group discussions with religious tourists, employing thematic analysis to identify emerging patterns, ethical considerations, and managerial strategies to mitigate the risks associated with synthetic media, all while ensuring that the research rigorously adheres to ethical standards – such as informed consent, confidentiality, and sensitivity to cultural and religious contexts – thereby creating a holistic methodological framework that integrates technological, moral, and managerial perspectives to critically assess the existential threats posed by deepfakes in an era of increasing digital manipulation, while also acknowledging the limitations

Table 17.1 Respondents data.

Particulars	Number of respondents	Percentage
Academics and Researchers	55	28.95%
Tourism Industry Professionals	22	11.58%
Religious Organisations	37	19.47%
Tourists	76	40.00%
Total	190	100%

Source: Calculated by authors.

inherent in self-reported data, regional specificity, and the rapid evolution of deepfake technology, which necessitates continuous adaptation of the proposed solutions and strategies to ensure their ongoing relevance in safeguarding the integrity and authenticity of religious tourism experiences.

17.5 Sampling

A purposive sampling technique will be employed to select participants who are either religious tourists or tourism managers within the religious tourism industry. The target population will include:

- Tourists who have visited religious sites, especially those with prior exposure to digital marketing or promotional content related to the destinations.
- Tourism managers responsible for marketing, operations, and management of religious tourism destinations.

The sample size will comprise approximately 190 respondents.

Table 17.1 shows the data that among a total of 190 respondents, 28.95% were Academics and Researchers (55 respondents), 11.58% were Tourism Industry Professionals (22 respondents), 19.47% were from Religious Organisations (37 respondents), and the majority, comprising 40.00%, were Tourists (76 respondents), collectively providing a well-distributed representation across various sectors in the study, with each group's proportion clearly outlined to emphasise their respective contributions to the overall respondent pool.

Figure 17.1 shows the diagram illustrating the relationship between the dependent and independent variables, with Religious Tourist Satisfaction as the dependent variable, influenced by four critical, independent variables. Manipulated Digital Content, which refers to the synthetic or altered media that may distort tourists' expectations; Managerial Strategies, encompassing

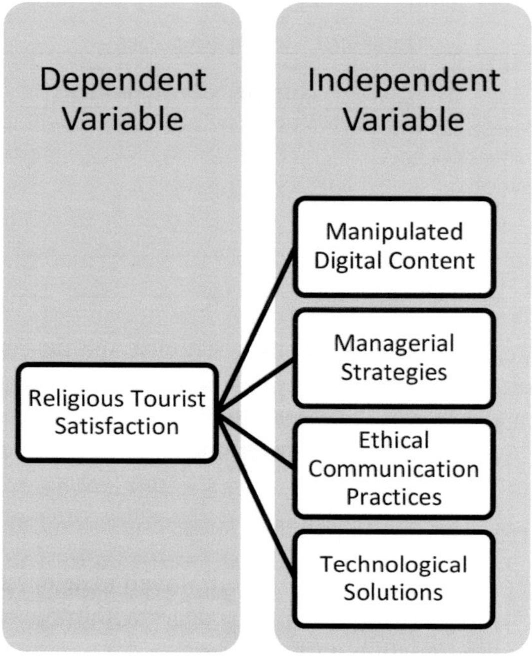

Figure 17.1 Conceptual model. Source: Designed by authors.

the tactical responses and policies tourism managers implement to counter the profound fake conundrum; Ethical Communication Practices, reflecting the transparency and honesty in conveying authentic experiences to tourists; and Technological Solutions, involving the deployment of AI-driven detection systems and tools to mitigate the risks of digital manipulation – all of which collectively determine the level of satisfaction religious tourists experience, thereby highlighting the intricate interplay of these elements in ensuring a trust-based and genuine tourism experience in an era of increasing synthetic media proliferation.

Figure 17.2 presents the image depicts a power analysis output using a linear multiple regression model with a fixed, single regression coefficient, aiming to compute the required sample size based on given parameters such as effect size ($f^2 = 0.14$), alpha error probability ($\alpha = 0.01$), power ($1\text{-}\beta = 0.99$), and a number of predictors (4), resulting in a critical t-value of 2.60489 and a total required sample size of 176 to achieve the desired statistical power, with the actual power calculated as 0.9903 and the non-centrality parameter δ as 4.9638695, represented visually through central and noncentral distributions, showing the region of rejection (α) and type II error (β) based on a two-tailed test.

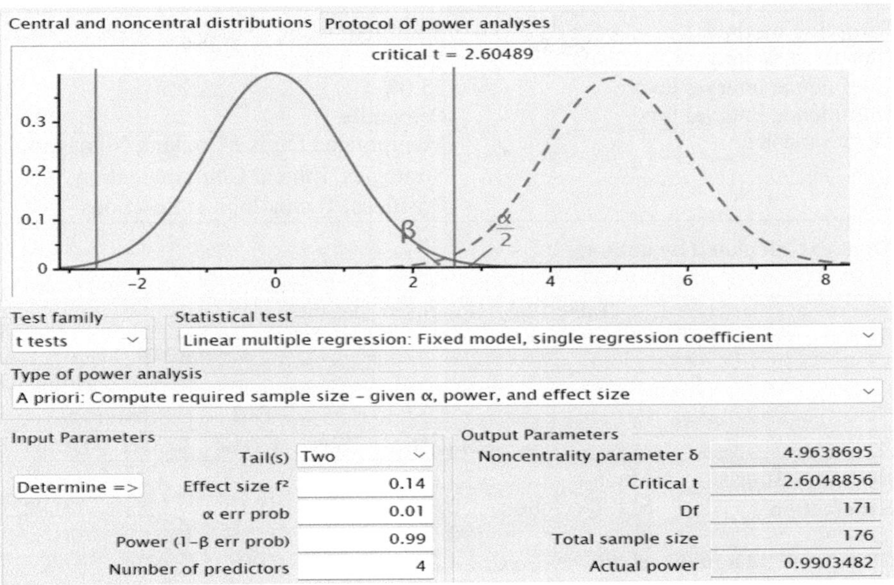

Figure 17.2 Power analysis. Source: Calculated by authors.

17.6 Analysis

In Table 17.2, the bootstrap specifications outline a stratified sampling method with 190 samples, utilising a 95.0% confidence interval level based on the percentile method, where the strata variables include Manipulated Digital Content, Managerial Strategies, Ethical Communication Practices, and Technological Solutions, ensuring that the resampling technique accounts for variations across these key independent variables while providing a robust estimate of the population's parameter distributions, thereby allowing for accurate inferences regarding the impact of these factors on religious tourist satisfaction in the face of profound fake challenges.

In Table 17.3 the descriptive statistics based on 190 stratified bootstrap samples reveal that the mean satisfaction of religious tourists is 4.06 with a standard deviation of 0.846, exhibiting negligible bias and a standard error of 0.02, while the 95% confidence interval ranges between 4.02 and 4.11, and similarly, the manipulated digital content variable shows a consistent mean of 4.24 with a fixed standard deviation of 0.863 across the same confidence interval bounds; managerial strategies and ethical communication practices demonstrate means of 4.16 and 4.76 respectively, with their standard deviations (0.827 and 1.381) reflecting their distribution patterns, while technological solutions exhibit the highest mean at 5.17 with a standard deviation of

Table 17.2 Bootstrap specifications.

Sampling method	Stratified
Number of samples	190
Confidence interval level	95.0%
Confidence interval type	Percentile
Strata variables	Manipulated Digital Content, Managerial Strategies, Ethical Communication Practices, Technological Solutions

Source: Calculated by authors.

Table 17.3 Descriptive statistics.

			Bootstrap			
					95% Confidence Interval	
		Statistic	**Bias**	**Std. Error**	**Lower**	**Upper**
Religious Tourist Satisfaction	Mean	4.06	0.00	0.02	4.02	4.11
	Std. Deviation	0.846	0.000	0.019	0.812	0.887
	N	190	0	0	190	190
Manipulated Digital Content	Mean	4.24	0.00	0.00	4.24	4.24
	Std. Deviation	0.863	0.000	0.000	0.863	0.863
	N	190	0	0	190	190
Managerial Strategies	Mean	4.16	0.00	0.00	4.16	4.16
	Std. Deviation	0.827	0.000	0.000	0.827	0.827
	N	190	0	0	190	190
Ethical Communication Practices	Mean	4.76	0.00	0.00	4.76	4.76
	Std. Deviation	1.381	0.000	0.000	1.381	1.381
	N	190	0	0	190	190
Technological Solutions	Mean	5.17	0.00	0.00	5.17	5.17
	Std. Deviation	1.298	0.000	0.000	1.298	1.298
	N	190	0	0	190	190

a. Unless otherwise noted, bootstrap results are based on 190 stratified bootstrap samples

Source: Calculated by authors.

1.298, all maintaining precision in the bootstrap estimates by demonstrating zero bias and consistent values across the confidence intervals, thus ensuring robust and reliable insights into the respective influences of these independent variables on the satisfaction and behaviour of religious tourists within the study's defined parameters.

Table 17.4, the model summary, indicates a strong correlation ($R=0.713$) between the predictors – Technological Solutions, Managerial Strategies, Ethical Communication Practices, and Manipulated Digital Content – and

Table 17.4 Model summary.

Model summary									
				Std. error	Change statistics				
Model	R	R Square	Adjusted R Square	of the estimate	R Square Change	F Change	df1	df2	Sig. F Change
1	0.713[a]	0.508	0.498	0.599	0.508	47.826	4	185	0.000

a. Predictors: (Constant), Technological Solutions, Managerial Strategies, Ethical Communication Practices, Manipulated Digital Content
b. Dependent Variable: Religious Tourist Satisfaction
Source: Calculated by authors.

the dependent variable, Religious Tourist Satisfaction. The R Square value of 0.508 signifies that approximately 50.8% of the variance in religious tourist satisfaction is explained by these independent variables. The adjusted R Square (0.498) accounts for potential model overfitting, and the standard error of the estimate (0.599) provides a measure of the model's accuracy. The model exhibits a significant R Square change of 0.508 with an F-statistic of 47.826 across 4 and 185 degrees of freedom, confirming that the inclusion of the predictors significantly improves the model's explanatory power. This underscores the critical role these variables play in influencing religious tourist satisfaction within the specified parameters, providing practical insights for tourism managers on how to improve tourist satisfaction.

Table 17.5, the ANOVA table, reveals that the regression model, which includes the predictors of Technological Solutions, Managerial Strategies, Ethical Communication Practices, and Manipulated Digital Content, accounts for a significant portion of the variance in Religious Tourist Satisfaction. The robustness of the model is evident in the regression sum of squares of 68.754 with 4 degrees of freedom and a mean square of 17.188, resulting in a highly significant F-value of 47.826 ($p = 0.000$). The residual sum of squares (66.488 with 185 degrees of freedom) reflects the unexplained variance, confirming that the model significantly predicts religious tourist satisfaction. The predictors jointly explain the outcome variable beyond what could be expected by chance, further reinforcing the robustness of the model.

In Table 17.6 the coefficients table reveals that among the predictors, Manipulated Digital Content exerts the most significant influence on Religious Tourist Satisfaction with an unstandardised coefficient (B) of 0.552, a standardised coefficient (Beta) of 0.563, and a highly considerable t-value of 8.858 ($p = 0.000$). Managerial Strategies, which has a positive effect with a B value of 0.222, Beta of 0.217, and a significant t-value of 3.468 ($p = 0.001$), is another key predictor. However, Ethical Communication

Table 17.5 ANOVA.

	Model	Sum of squares	df	Mean square	F	Sig.
1	Regression	68.754	4	17.188	47.826	0.000[b]
	Residual	66.488	185	0.359		
	Total	135.242	189			

a. Dependent Variable: Religious Tourist Satisfaction
b. Predictors: (Constant), Technological Solutions, Managerial Strategies, Ethical Communication Practices, Manipulated Digital Content
Source: Calculated by authors.

Practices and Technological Solutions show no statistically significant effect, with t-values of 0.838 (p = 0.403) and 0.012 (p = 0.991) respectively, highlighting their negligible contribution to the dependent variable. This reiterates the limitations of the study and the need for further research in these areas.

Table 17.7 shows the bootstrap results, based on 190 stratified samples, reveal that the coefficients for Manipulated Digital Content and Managerial Strategies remain highly significant with respective bias-corrected estimates of 0.552 (bias = –0.002, standard error = 0.028, 95% CI: 0.492 to 0.609) and 0.222 (bias = 0.002, standard error = 0.029, 95% CI: 0.172 to 0.285), reinforcing their strong positive impact on Religious Tourist Satisfaction, whereas Ethical Communication Practices exhibits a smaller yet borderline significant coefficient (B = 0.029, bias = –0.002, standard error = 0.013, 95% CI: 0.002 to 0.052), and Technological Solutions remains statistically insignificant (B = 0.000, bias = 0.001, standard error = 0.016, 95% CI: –0.026 to 0.036), with all predictors demonstrating minimal bias in the bootstrapping process, thereby confirming the robustness of the model's primary predictors – Manipulated Digital Content and Managerial Strategies – in explaining variations in religious tourist satisfaction within the specified confidence intervals.

Table 17.8 shows the collinearity diagnostics table, which assesses the potential multicollinearity among the predictors for Religious Tourist Satisfaction, shows that the first dimension has an eigenvalue of 4.855 and a condition index of 1.000, indicating no collinearity, while the second dimension, with an eigenvalue of 0.073 and a condition index of 8.129, reflects relatively low variance proportions across the predictors; however, in the third dimension (eigenvalue = 0.039, condition index = 11.178), Ethical Communication Practices (0.40) and Technological Solutions (0.89) exhibit higher variance proportions, potentially indicating mild collinearity issues, which become more evident in the fourth dimension (eigenvalue = 0.018, condition index = 16.608) where Manipulated Digital Content (0.77) and

Table 17.6 Coefficients.

Model		Unstandardised Coefficients		Standardised Coefficients			Correlations			Collinearity Statistics	
		B	Std. Error	Beta	t	Sig.	Zero-order	Partial	Part	Tolerance	VIF
1	(Constant)	0.659	0.300		2.199	0.029					
	Manipulated Digital Content	0.552	0.062	0.563	8.858	0.000	0.689	0.546	0.457	0.657	1.521
	Managerial Strategies	0.222	0.064	0.217	3.468	0.001	0.538	0.247	0.179	0.676	1.480
	Ethical Communication Practices	0.029	0.034	0.047	0.838	0.403	0.072	0.061	0.043	0.856	1.168
	Technological Solutions	0.000	0.037	0.001	0.012	0.991	0.159	0.001	0.001	0.823	1.215

a. Dependent Variable: Religious Tourist Satisfaction
Source: Calculated by authors.

Table 17.7 Bootstrap for Coefficients.

Model		B	Bootstrap				
						95% Confidence Interval	
			Bias	Std. error	Sig. (2-tailed)	Lower	Upper
1	(Constant)	0.659	0.002	0.128	0.005	0.381	0.909
	Manipulated Digital Content	0.552	–0.002	0.028	0.005	0.492	0.609
	Managerial Strategies	0.222	0.002	0.029	0.005	0.172	0.285
	Ethical Communication Practices	0.029	–0.002	0.013	0.021	0.002	0.052
	Technological Solutions	0.000	0.001	0.016	0.984	–0.026	0.036

a. Unless otherwise noted, bootstrap results are based on 190 stratified bootstrap samples
Source: Calculated by authors.

Table 17.8 Collinearity diagnostics.

Model	Dimension	Eigen value	Condition Index	Variance proportions				
				(Constant)	Manipul ated Digital Content	Managerial Strategies	Ethical Communication Practices	Technological Solutions
1	1	4.855	1.000	0.00	0.00	0.00	0.00	0.00
	2	0.073	8.129	0.00	0.06	0.07	0.49	0.04
	3	0.039	11.178	0.00	0.01	0.03	0.40	0.89
	4	0.018	16.608	0.46	0.77	0.10	0.06	0.00
	5	0.016	17.676	0.53	0.16	0.80	0.05	0.06

a. Dependent Variable: Religious Tourist Satisfaction

Source: Calculated by authors.

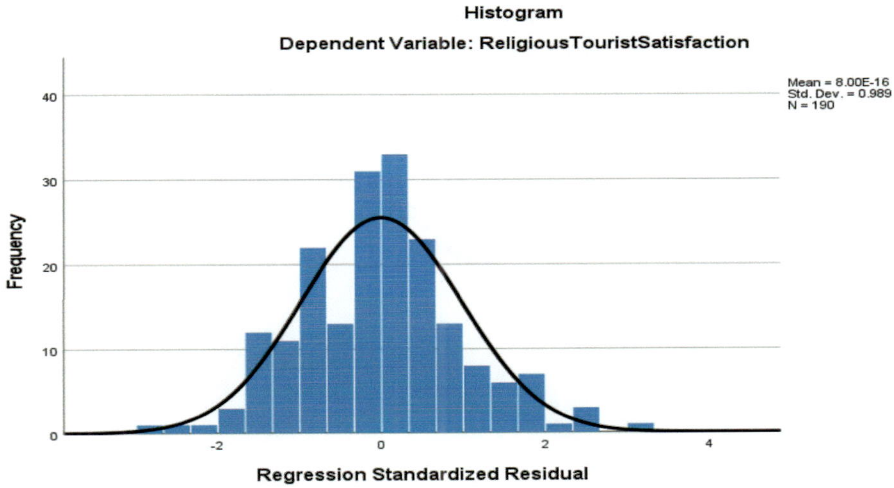

Figure 17.3 Histogram. Source: Designed by authors.

Managerial Strategies (0.46) contribute a larger share, while the fifth dimension (eigenvalue = 0.016, condition index = 17.676) presents high variance proportions for Managerial Strategies (0.80) and Manipulated Digital Content (0.16), suggesting that although the model exhibits some multicollinearity in the later dimensions, particularly between Managerial Strategies and Manipulated Digital Content, the condition indices remain within acceptable thresholds, indicating that multicollinearity is present but not severe enough to distort the model's predictive accuracy or reliability.

Figure 17.2 presents the histogram of regression standardised residuals for the dependent variable Religious Tourist Satisfaction displays a roughly normal distribution, with the residuals concentrated around a mean of approximately 0 (8.00E-16) and a standard deviation of 0.989, indicating that the residuals are symmetrically distributed around zero, with no significant skewness or kurtosis, which supports the assumption of normally distributed errors in the regression model, further validating the model's accuracy and robustness in predicting religious tourist satisfaction for the sample size of 190 participants.

Figure 17.3 presents the standard P-P plot of regression standardised residuals for the dependent variable, Religious Tourist Satisfaction; shows that the observed cumulative probabilities closely align with the expected cumulative probabilities along the diagonal reference line, indicating that the residuals follow a near-normal distribution, as the data points cluster tightly around the line with minimal deviation, which further supports the assumption of normality in the residuals and validates the reliability of the regression

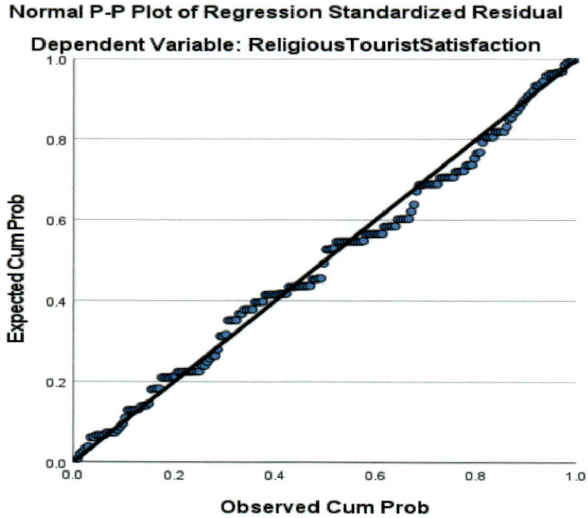

Figure 17.4 Normal P-P plot of regression standardised residual. Source: Designed by authors.

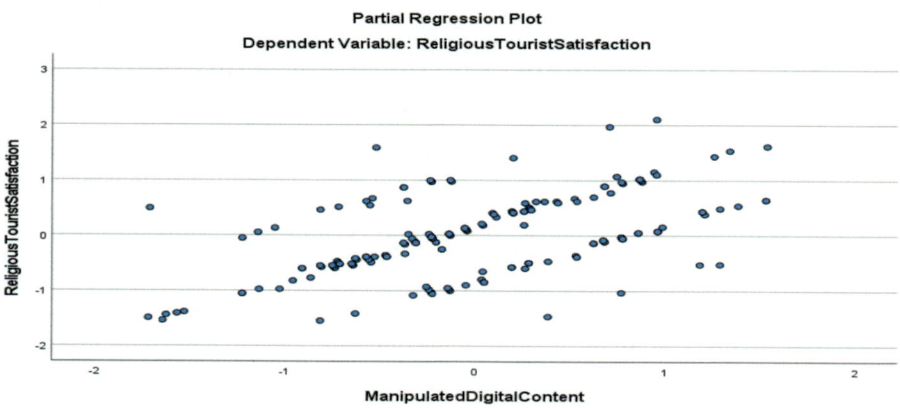

Figure 17.5 Partial regression plot. Source: Designed by authors.

model in predicting religious tourist satisfaction within the sample, thereby confirming the appropriateness of the model for inferential purposes.

Figure 17.4 presents the partial regression plot for the dependent variable, Religious Tourist Satisfaction and the predictor, Manipulated Digital Content; it demonstrates a positive linear relationship, where the points generally follow an upward trend, indicating that as manipulated digital content increases, religious tourist satisfaction tends to increase correspondingly, with a visible clustering of points around the fitted regression line, reinforcing the significant positive influence of manipulated digital content on tourist satisfaction. At the same time, some degree of dispersion suggests the presence of other contributing factors or variability in the relationship. Still, the overall pattern supports the robustness of the predictor in the regression model.

17.7 Finding and Suggestions

The findings of this study indicate that Manipulated Digital Content and Managerial Strategies are the most significant predictors of Religious Tourist Satisfaction, as evidenced by their strong positive correlations and significant coefficients in the regression analysis, highlighting that tourists' perceptions of authenticity and managerial responsiveness in mitigating deepfake-related issues are paramount to enhancing satisfaction, whereas Ethical Communication Practices and Technological Solutions demonstrated comparatively weaker or insignificant effects, suggesting that while transparency and technological interventions are crucial, they may need to be further integrated into comprehensive strategies that emphasise authenticity and managerial trust-building; thus, it is recommended that tourism managers focus on developing more robust mechanisms for detecting and countering digital manipulation, ensuring that marketing content is both authentic and verifiable, while simultaneously investing in strategic training for managers to handle crises related to digital misrepresentation, promoting ethical communication, and fostering consumer education on the risks of deepfakes, thereby safeguarding the integrity of the tourist experience in the increasingly digitalised landscape of religious tourism.

17.8 Conclusion

In conclusion, this study underscores the profound impact of Manipulated Digital Content and Managerial Strategies on Religious Tourist Satisfaction, revealing that while advanced technological solutions and ethical communication practices play essential roles, they are not sufficient in isolation, and therefore, a more integrative approach is required – one that not only strengthens the detection and prevention of deepfake-related digital manipulations but also places greater emphasis on fostering trust, authenticity, and managerial accountability within the broader context of religious tourism, where tourists' emotional and spiritual engagement with sacred experiences is particularly sensitive to the authenticity of digital representations; thus, the findings suggest that tourism managers must proactively develop and implement multifaceted strategies that ensure the alignment of digital content with the actual experiences offered, while also enhancing transparency, consumer education, and crisis management, thereby securing long-term trust and satisfaction in an era increasingly influenced by synthetic media technologies, thus preserving the sanctity and cultural significance of religious tourism in the face of rapidly evolving digital manipulation threats.

References

Adow, A. H., Shrivas, M. K., Mahdi, H. F., Zahra, M. M. A., Verma, D., Doohan, N. V., & Jalali, A. (2022). Analysis of Agriculture and Food Supply Chain through Blockchain and IoT with Light Weight Cluster Head. *Computational Intelligence and Neuroscience*, *2022*. https://doi.org/10.1155/2022/1296993

Awasthi, M. K., Verma, M., & Ram, M. (2023). Advances in Mathematical and Computational Modeling of Engineering Systems. In *Advances in Mathematical and Computational Modeling of Engineering Systems*. CRC Press. https://doi.org/10.1201/9781003367420

Banerjee, D., Kukreja, V., Bordoloi, D., & Joshi, K. (2023). Hybrid CNN & Random Forest Model for Effective Turmeric Leaf Disease Diagnosis. *2023 3rd International Conference on Smart Generation Computing, Communication and Networking, SMART GENCON 2023*. https://doi.org/10.1109/SMARTGENCON60755.2023.10442441

Banerjee, D., Kukreja, V., Jain, A., Rawat, D., & Jain, V. (2023). Enhancing Tulsi Leaf Disease with CNN and SVM-Based Classification. *2023 1st International Conference on Optimization Techniques for Learning, ICOTL 2023-Proceedings*. https://doi.org/10.1109/ICOTL59758.2023.10435248

Banerjee, D., Kukreja, V., Sharma, V., Manwal, M., & Jindal, V. (2023). An Ensemble Approach of CNN and SVM for Precise Classification of Sweet Corn Leaf Diseases. *2023 14th International Conference on Computing Communication and Networking Technologies, ICCCNT 2023*. https://doi.org/10.1109/ICCCNT56998.2023.10306754

Bhatnagar, P., Gururani, P., Bisht, B., Kumar, V., Kumar, N., Joshi, R., & Vlaskin, M. S. (2022). Impact of irradiation on physico-chemical and nutritional properties of fruits and vegetables: A mini review. *Heliyon*, *8*(10). https://doi.org/10.1016/j.heliyon.2022.e10918

Chakravorty, M., Nanda, M., Arora, N., Singh, S., Kumar, V., & Deshwal, S. (2022). CRISPR-Cas9 mediated genome tailoring to improve nutritional quality and shelf life in crops: A review. *Plant Gene*, *31*. https://doi.org/10.1016/j.plgene.2022.100369

Ganesan, R., Manjula, G., Chandan, M., Thamarai, I., Rajavelu, S., Bhatt, U. M., & Sarkar, S. (2023). Application of Deep Neural Networks for Weed Detection and Classification. *Proceedings of the 2nd International Conference on Applied Artificial Intelligence and Computing, ICAAIC 2023*, 1014–1024. https://doi.org/10.1109/ICAAIC56838.2023.10140235

Gill, K. S., Anand, V., Chauhan, R., Verma, G., & Gupta, R. (2023). Agricultural Pests Classification Using Deep Convolutional Neural Networks and Transfer Learning. *2023 2nd International Conference on Futuristic Technologies, INCOFT 2023*. https://doi.org/10.1109/INCOFT60753.2023.10425080

Gonfa, Y. H., Tessema, F. B., Bachheti, A., Tadesse, M. G., Eid, E. M., Abou Fayssal, S., Adelodun, B., Choi, K. S., Širić, I., Kumar, P., & Bachheti, R. K. (2022). Essential Oil Composition of Aerial Part of Pluchea ovalis (Pers.) DC., Silver Nanoparticles Synthesis, and Larvicidal Activities against Fall Armyworm. *Sustainability (Switzerland)*, *14*(23). https://doi.org/10.3390/su142315785

Gusain, R., Vidyarthi, A., Prakash, R., & Shukla, A. K. (2022). Statistical Analysis of Positional Variations of NavIc Receiver. In S. S. & J. T. (Eds.), *2022 International Conference on Advances in Computing, Communication and Materials, ICACCM 2022*. Institute of Electrical and Electronics Engineers Inc. https://doi.org/10.1109/ICACCM56405.2022.10009498

Gusain, R., Vidyarthi, A., Prakash, R., & Shukla, A. K. (2023). Assessing Seasonal Variations in CEP for NavIC Positioning in Dehradun Region. *5th International Conference on Energy, Power, and Environment: Towards Flexible Green Energy Technologies, ICEPE 2023*. https://doi.org/10.1109/ICEPE57949.2023.10201493

Jain, S., Verma, I., & Sharma, S. (2022). E-Agriculture Integration with Cloud Computing. In R. H.S., B. R., G. P.K., & S. V.K. (Eds.), *PDGC 2022 - 2022 7th International Conference on Parallel, Distributed and Grid Computing* (pp. 298–303). Institute of Electrical and Electronics Engineers Inc. https://doi.org/10.1109/PDGC56933.2022.10053302

Jindal, V., Kukreja, V., Mehta, S., Gupta, A., & Sharma, M. (2023). Tackling Agricultural Challenges of Red Globe Grapes Leaf Diseases: A Federated Learning CNN Approach. *2023 3rd Asian Conference on Innovation in Technology, ASIANCON 2023*. https://doi.org/10.1109/ASIANCON58793.2023.10270032

Jindal, V., Kukreja, V., Mehta, S., Yadav, R., & Mohd, N. (2023). Evolving Agritech: Implementing Federated Learning & CNN for

Parsley Leaf Disease Detection. *2023 3rd Asian Conference on Innovation in Technology, ASIANCON 2023*. https://doi.org/10.1109/ASIANCON58793.2023.10270228

Joshi, N. C., & Gururani, P. (2023). A mini review on heavy metal contamination in vegetable crops. *International Journal of Environmental Analytical Chemistry*. https://doi.org/10.1080/03067319.2023.2210058

Joshi, S., Sharma, M., Kaushal, D., Misra, A., Gupta, P., & Gopal, S. (2023). Optimizing Productivity and Efficiency in Agriculture through the Integration of Digital Technologies: A Smart Agriculture Perspective. *9th International Conference on Smart Computing and Communications: Intelligent Technologies and Applications, ICSCC 2023*, 119–125. https://doi.org/10.1109/ICSCC59169.2023.10335086

Kamal, S., Shende, V. G., Swaroopa, K., Bindhu Madhavi, P., Akram, P. S., Pant, K., Patil, S. D., & Sahile, K. (2022). FCN Network-Based Weed and Crop Segmentation for IoT-Aided Agriculture Applications. *Wireless Communications and Mobile Computing*, *2022*. https://doi.org/10.1155/2022/2770706

Kaur, A., Kukreja, V., Gopal, L., Verma, G., & Sharma, R. (2023). Cultivating Precision: A Multi-Layer Perceptron Approach for Accurate Classification of Maize Rust Disease Intensity in Precision Agriculture. In G. R., H. K., P. R., G. S., T. A. J.V., V. R., M. R., & K. T. (Eds.), *Proceedings of the 2023 6th International Conference on Recent Trends in Advance Computing, ICRTAC 2023* (pp. 267–270). Institute of Electrical and Electronics Engineers Inc. https://doi.org/10.1109/ICRTAC59277.2023.10480724

Kaur, A., Kukreja, V., Manwal, M., Garg, N., & Hariharan, S. (2023). Harnessing Deep Learning for Tea Tree Leaf Disease Management: A CNN-SVM Perspective. *2023 IEEE Pune Section International Conference, PuneCon 2023*. https://doi.org/10.1109/PuneCon58714.2023.10450005

Kaur, G., Sharma, N., Chauhan, R., Joshi, K., & Gupta, R. (2023). Rice Leaf Disease Detection Using InceptionV3 Transfer Learning Model. *2023 3rd International Conference on Smart Generation Computing, Communication and Networking, SMART GENCON 2023*. https://doi.org/10.1109/SMARTGENCON60755.2023.10442321

Kaur, G., Sharma, N., Chauhan, R., Pokhariya, H. S., & Gupta, R. (2023). Fruit and Vegetable Classification Using MobileNet V2 Transfer Learning Model. *2023 3rd International Conference on Smart Generation Computing, Communication and Networking, SMART GENCON 2023*. https://doi.org/10.1109/SMARTGENCON60755.2023.10442618

Kholiya, D., Bagla, P., Mishra, A. K., Tripathi, N., & Pandey, N. K. (2023). Sustainable Development of Smart Farming and Agriculture Business using Data Mining. *ICSCCC 2023 - 3rd International Conference on Secure Cyber Computing and Communications*, 75–80. https://doi.org/10.1109/ICSCCC58608.2023.10176431

Kumar, V., Banerjee, D., Chauhan, R., Joshi, K., & Gill, K. S. (2023). Optimizing Mango Leaf Disease Evaluation: CNN and Random Forest Fusion. *2023 3rd International Conference on Smart Generation Computing, Communication and Networking, SMART GENCON 2023*. https://doi.org/10.1109/SMARTGENCON60755.2023.10442934

Kumar, V., Banerjee, D., Chauhan, R., Rawat, R. S., & Gill, K. S. (2023). Revolutionizing Pear Tree Disease Detection: An In-Depth Investigation into CNN-Based Approaches. *2023 Global Conference on Information Technologies and Communications, GCITC 2023*. https://doi.org/10.1109/GCITC60406.2023.10426553

Mehta, S., Kukreja, V., Sharma, V., & Manwal, M. (2023). Exploring a Novel Methodologies for Beetroot Leaf Disease Severity Prediction: Federated Learning and CNN. *Proceedings of the 4th International Conference on Smart Electronics and Communication, ICOSEC 2023*, 980–985. https://doi.org/10.1109/ICOSEC58147.2023.10276191

Mehta, S., Kukreja, V., Vats, S., & Verma, A. (2023). A Paradigm Shift in Pomegranate Leaf Disease Detection with Federated Learning and CNN. *2023 14th International Conference on Computing Communication and Networking Technologies, ICCCNT 2023*. https://doi.org/10.1109/ICCCNT56998.2023.10308132

Mudholkar, M., Mudholkar, P., Dornadula, V. H. R., Sreenivasulu, K., Joshi, K., & Pant, B. (2022). A Novel Approach to IoT based Plant Health Monitoring System in Smart Agriculture. *Proceedings of 5th International Conference on Contemporary Computing and Informatics, IC3I 2022*, 113–116. https://doi.org/10.1109/IC3I56241.2022.10072603

Nishinari, K., Zhang, K., Yang, N., Gao, Z., Gamonpilas, C., Turcanu, M., Peyron, M.-A., Fang, Y., Nitta, Y., Yao, X., Zhao, M., Ishihara, S., Nakauma, M., Funami, T., Kohyama, K., Moritaka, H., Yoshimura, M., Takemasa, M., Hori, K., … Meng, A. G. S. (2023). Rheology for Safe Swallowing 1. *Nihon Reoroji Gakkaishi*, *51*(4), 219–248. https://doi.org/10.1678/rheology.51.219

Pant, B., Obaidat, M. S., Singh, S., Pant, M., Wazid, M., Das, A. K., & Hsiao, K.-F. (2023). SLA-SCA: Secure and Lightweight Authentication and Key Agreement Mechanism for Smart City Applications. In O. M.S., N. Z., H. K.-F., N. P., & G. Y. (Eds.), *Proceedings of the 2023 IEEE International Conference on Communications, Computing, Cybersecurity and Informatics, CCCI 2023*. Institute of Electrical and Electronics Engineers Inc. https://doi.org/10.1109/CCCI58712.2023.10290729

Parkash, V., Chauhan, A., Gaur, A., & Rai, N. (2022). Advances in bionic approaches for agriculture and forestry development. In *The Digital Agricultural Revolution: Innovations and Challenges in Agriculture through Technology Disruptions*. wiley. https://doi.org/10.1002/9781119823469.ch9

Pillai, R., Sharma, N., Malhotra, S., Dangi, S., & Gupta, R. (2023). Detection and Classification of Plant Seedlings: Distinguishing Crop Seedlings from Weed Seedlings Using MobileNetV2 Transfer Learning Model with Fine-Tuning Layers. *2023 3rd International Conference on Smart Generation Computing, Communication and Networking, SMART GENCON 2023*. https://doi.org/10.1109/SMARTGENCON60755.2023.10442772

Pokhariya, H. S., Singh, D. P., & Prakash, R. (2022). Investigating the impacts of urbanization on different land cover classes and land surface temperature using GIS and RS techniques. *International Journal of System Assurance Engineering and Management*, *13*, 961–969. https://doi.org/10.1007/s13198-021-01512-1

Pokhariya, H. S., Singh, D. P., & Prakash, R. (2023). Investigating the Effect of Urbanization on Environmental Quality Using RS and GIS. In S. J., S. P., C. Y., A. K.U., A. P.K., M. N., B. S. Universiti Kebangsaan Malaysia 43600 UKM, T. G., & S. S. (Eds.), *14th International Conference on Advances in Computing, Control, and Telecommunication Technologies, ACT 2023* (Vols. 2023-June, pp. 1459–1466). Grenze Scientific Society.

Ram, M., Bisht, D. C. S., Goyal, N., Kazancoglu, Y., & Mathirajan, M. (2022). Newly developed mathematical methodologies and advancements in a variety of engineering and management domains. *Mathematics in Engineering, Science and Aerospace*, *13*(3), 559 – 562.

Rather, M. A., Thakur, R., Hoque, M., Das, R. S., Lima Miki, K. S., Teixeira-Costa, B. E., Mishra, P., & Gupta, A. K. (2023). Sorghum (Sorghum bicolor): Phytochemical Composition, Bio- Functional, and Technological Characteristics. In *Nutri-Cereals: Nutraceutical and Techno-Functional Potential*. CRC Press. https://doi.org/10.1201/9781003251279-3

Rawat, K. S., Sehgal, V. K., Singh, S. K., & Ray, S. S. (2022). Soil moisture estimation using triangular method at higher resolution from

MODIS products. *Physics and Chemistry of the Earth, 126.* https://doi.org/10.1016/j.pce.2021.103051

Sajitha, N., Nema, S., Bhavya, K. R., Seethapathy, P., & Pant, K. (2022). The Plant Disease Detection Using CNN and Deep Learning Techniques Merged with the Concepts of Machine Learning. *2022 2nd International Conference on Advance Computing and Innovative Technologies in Engineering, ICACITE 2022*, 1547–1551. https://doi.org/10.1109/ICACITE53722.2022.9823921

Semwal, P., Painuli, S., Jamloki, A., Rauf, A., Rahman, M. M., Olatunde, A., Hemeg, H. A., Abu-Izneid, T., Naz, S., Punia Bangar, S., Lorenzo, J. M., & Simal-Gandara, J. (2023). Himalayan Wild Fruits as a Strong Source of Nutraceuticals, Therapeutics, Food and Nutrition Security. *Food Reviews International*, *39*(9), 6500–6536. https://doi.org/10.1080/87559129.2022.2121407

Sharma, G., Anand, V., Malhotra, S., Kukreti, S., & Gupta, S. (2023). CNN-Based Intelligent Classification of Bell Pepper Plant Diseases: A Novel Approach for Precision Agriculture. *2023 3rd International Conference on Smart Generation Computing, Communication and Networking, SMART GENCON 2023*. https://doi.org/10.1109/SMARTGENCON60755.2023.10442079

Sharma, V., Kukreja, V., Mehta, S., & Choudhary, A. (2023). Severity Stratification of Brinjal Leaf Diseases: A Federated Learning CNNs Approach. In H. V.R., S. S., M. D., & K. S. H. (Eds.), *Proceedings of the 4th IEEE International Conference on Smart Technologies in Computing, Electrical and Electronics, ICSTCEE 2023*. Institute of Electrical and Electronics Engineers Inc. https://doi.org/10.1109/ICSTCEE60504.2023.10584836

Shashikala, R., Singh, B. P., Azam, M., Magesh, C. R., Rajat, & Singh, D. P. (2022). IoT Engineering Nanomaterial's Approach To Sustainable Advance Crop Production Management. *2022 2nd International Conference on Advance Computing and Innovative Technologies in Engineering, ICACITE 2022*, 2284–2288. https://doi.org/10.1109/ICACITE53722.2022.9823573

Suryavanshi, A., Kukreja, V., Chamoli, S., Mehta, S., & Thapliyal, S. (2023). Enabling Precision Agriculture: A Federated Learning CNN Approach to Diagnosing Jackfruit Leaf Diseases. In D. R.K., S. A.Kr., S. R., B. S., & K. V. (Eds.), *Proceedings of the 2023 12th International Conference on System Modeling and Advancement in Research Trends, SMART 2023* (pp. 29–35). Institute of Electrical and Electronics Engineers Inc. https://doi.org/10.1109/SMART59791.2023.10428555

Vashishth, D. S., Bachheti, A., Bachheti, R. K., & Husen, A. (2023). Allelopathic effect of Callistemon viminalis's leaves extract on weeds, soil features, and growth performance of wheat and chickpea plants. *Journal of Plant Interactions*, *18*(1). https://doi.org/10.1080/17429145.2023.2248172

Vishalli, Kukreja, V., Mehta, S., Das, P., & Singh, V. (2023). Dissecting Parsley Leaf Disease Severity: A Federated Learning and CNN Perspective. *2023 3rd Asian Conference on Innovation in Technology, ASIANCON 2023*. https://doi.org/10.1109/ASIANCON58793.2023.10270195

Yashu, Kukreja, V., Chamoli, S., & Thapliyal, S. (2023). Severity Levels of Apple Disease Recognition Using CNN and Random Forest: An Integrated Approach. *2023 3rd International Conference on Smart Generation Computing, Communication and Networking, SMART GENCON 2023*. https://doi.org/10.1109/SMARTGENCON60755.2023.10441917

18

Ethical Implications of Deepfake Technology in User Interfaces

Muskan Singh[1], Sachin Ghai[1], Sanjay Taneja[1,2] and Zelhuda Shamsuddin[2]

[1]Graphic Era Deemed to be University, India
[2]Universiti Sultan Zainal Abidin, Malaysia

Email: muskansinghofficial1998@gmail.com; professorsachinghai@gmail.com; drsanjaytaneja1@gmail.com; zelhudasham@unisza.edu.my

Abstract

Deepfake technology has advanced tremendously, allowing for incredibly realistic synthetic visual and audio material. However, its growing capability presents ethical problems, especially for usage in user interfaces (UIs). This paper investigates the fundamental ethical problems surrounding deepfakes in user interfaces. One major problem is the increased danger of fraud. Deepfakes make creating a video or audio recording of a non-existent event simple. This raises questions about the integrity of information received through UIs and its potential damage to individuals and society. Another critical problem is the demand for more excellent user agency and autonomy. Deepfakes can trick consumers into believing they are engaging with a natural person when they are not. Manipulation can give users less control over their decisions, raising ethical questions regarding autonomy. Deepfakes may violate consent and privacy. Deepfakes can be developed without authorisation and utilised for harmful reasons. This potential raises serious ethical questions about privacy and consent. This article overviews deepfake technology, including its present capabilities and public perception. The article covers ethical and design considerations related to deepfakes, such as transparency, informed consent, and respect for user dignity. The essay argues that developing and deploying deepfake technology in UIs involves proactive ethical forethought to reduce risks and minimise damage. The study underlines the importance of industry-wide research and self-regulation in developing ethical standards and best practices for deepfakes in user interfaces, as collective action is crucial in addressing this complex issue. Establishing rules and regulations to enable ethical development and deployment of deepfakes in UIs while protecting user rights is critical.

18.1 Introduction

EnergyDeepfake technology, which employs AI to create realistic synthetic visual and audio information, has prompted ethical issues in several areas of society (Khan et al., 2022). Incorporating deepfakes into user interfaces (UIs) poses distinct hazards and problems requiring thorough ethical study. An increasing body of work explores the impact of deepfakes on human-computer interaction and user experience design. More multidisciplinary study is needed to understand the moral implications of deepfakes in UIs and establish responsible techniques for reducing hazards and boosting good uses (Agrawal, Bhagoria, et al., 2023; A. Kumar, Nirala, et al., 2023; Yadav, Alam, et al., 2022). This article addresses ethical concerns about deepfakes in user interfaces. It provides technical background on deepfakes and their potential and discusses public opinion studies on developing technology (Dash et al., 2022; R. Kumar, Dwivedi, et al., 2023; Yadav, Mishra, et al., 2022).

The article explains key ethical concepts from philosophy and UI/UX design, such as transparency, informed consent, privacy, autonomy, beneficence, and non-maleficence (Dewangan et al., 2020; Kumari et al., 2022; Prasad et al., 2023). After providing a conceptual foundation, the paper examines ethical concerns about deepfakes in user interfaces. Potential concerns include increasing deceit, loss of user agency and autonomy, abuses of privacy and consent, and harm to human dignity. We offer ethical options for tackling deepfakes in user interfaces, including technical interventions, industry self-regulation, and regulatory approaches. The essay emphasises the need for ongoing research and collaboration across ethics, design, and technology to integrate deepfakes into UI experiences in an ethical manner (Mahor, Bijrothiya, Mishra, Rawat, et al., 2022; Mahor, Pachlasiya, Garg, Chouhan, et al., 2022; Pithode et al., 2023).

Deepfake technology, with its capacity to generate hyper-realistic synthetic visual and audio content, has ignited ethical debates across various sectors of society. As these sophisticated manipulations increasingly find their way into user interfaces (UIs), unique challenges and risks emerge, demanding comprehensive ethical scrutiny (Chincholikar et al., 2023; A. Kumar, Singh, et al., 2023; Mahla et al., 2022). Scholars from diverse fields are delving into the ramifications of deepfakes on human-computer interaction and user experience design. However, a more profound, multidisciplinary investigation is warranted to fully grasp the ethical dimensions of deepfakes in UIs and devise responsible strategies to mitigate risks while harnessing their potential for beneficial applications. This article addresses the ethical quandaries posed by deepfakes in user interfaces, offering a nuanced exploration of pertinent issues and ethical considerations (V. P. Singh et al., 2023).

To lay the groundwork for this discourse, the article furnishes readers with a technical primer on deepfakes, elucidating their capabilities and potential implications. Moreover, insights from public opinion studies on this evolving technology are synthesised, providing valuable context for understanding societal attitudes and concerns surrounding deepfakes. Drawing from the rich reservoir of ethical theory, concepts such as transparency, informed consent, privacy, autonomy, beneficence, and non-maleficence are unpacked within the UI/UX design and philosophy context. With this conceptual foundation established, the article scrutinises the ethical quandaries of integrating deepfakes into user interfaces. Concerns range from the exacerbation of deceit and manipulation to the erosion of user agency and autonomy. Moreover, issues about privacy violations, consent abuses, and the potential harm to human dignity are meticulously examined.

In response to these ethical challenges, the article delineates a spectrum of ethical options for addressing deepfakes in user interfaces (Chauhan et al., 2018; Dihom et al., 2022; Guo et al., 2020). These options encompass technical interventions aimed at detection and mitigation, industry-led initiatives focused on self-regulation and ethical guidelines, and regulatory approaches to enforce accountability and safeguard user interests. Notably, the essay underscores the imperative of ongoing research and collaboration across disciplines – ethics, design, and technology – to responsibly navigate the ethical complexities inherent in integrating deepfakes into UI experiences (Barwar et al., 2021). By engaging in a robust discourse on the ethical dimensions of deepfakes in user interfaces, this article endeavours to foster greater awareness, dialogue, and proactive measures to uphold ethical standards and ensure the ethical integration of deepfake technology into the fabric of user experience design (A. Kumar, Maithani, et al., 2023; H. Sharma et al., 2023).

Deepfake technology, with its ability to generate convincing synthetic visual and audio content using artificial intelligence, has emerged as a significant ethical concern across various domains of society. One area where the ethical implications of deepfakes are particularly pronounced is user interfaces

(UIs). The integration of deepfakes into UIs presents unique challenges and risks that necessitate careful ethical scrutiny (Rawat et al., 2022). As deepfake technology advances, a growing body of research explores its impact on human-computer interaction (HCI) and user experience (UX) design. However, there remains a need for more multidisciplinary inquiry to grasp the ethical dimensions of deepfakes in UIs fully and to develop responsible strategies for mitigating risks and promoting beneficial uses (Mahor, Bijrothiya, Mishra, & Rawat, 2022; Mahor, Garg, Telang, Pachlasiya, et al., 2022).

This article addresses the ethical concerns surrounding deepfakes in user interfaces by providing technical background on deepfake technology and insights from public opinion studies. By examining critical ethical concepts from philosophy and UI/UX design, such as transparency, informed consent, privacy, autonomy, beneficence, and non-maleficence, we aim to establish a conceptual foundation for discussing the ethical implications of deepfakes in UIs. Building upon this foundation, the paper will explore potential ethical concerns associated with the proliferation of deepfakes in user interfaces, including increasing deception, erosion of user agency and autonomy (Kour et al., 2021; A. Singh et al., 2015, 2015; S. Singh et al., 2019), breaches of privacy and consent, and potential harm to human dignity. Furthermore, we will propose ethical strategies for addressing these concerns, ranging from technical interventions and industry self-regulation to regulatory approaches. Ultimately, this essay underscores the importance of ongoing research and collaboration across ethics, design, and technology domains to ensure that deepfakes are ethically integrated into UI experiences (Kaswan & Rathi, 2019; Patel, 2011; A. P. Singh et al., 2021). By fostering dialogue and cooperation among stakeholders, we can strive towards harnessing the potential of deepfake technology while safeguarding the values and rights of users in the digital age.

18.2 Literature Review

18.2.1 A synopsis of deepfake technologies

Artificial media produced by deep learning algorithms – especially convolutional neural networks (CNNs) – is called "deepfakes". Previous methods, such as Photoshop, made altering already-existing photos and films possible. Nevertheless, deep learning has made it possible to produce incredibly lifelike artificial visual and aural information representing speech or events that never occurred. Commonly employed techniques include speech synthesis, which replicates a person's voice, and facial re-enactment, which involves swapping one person's face onto another's body. While non-consensual pornography was the primary source of deepfakes' initial popularity in 2017–2018, its inventors have now expanded their use to encompass parody videos and the alteration of TV and movie material (Rathod et al., 2024).

Deepfake artwork has been disseminated via internet discussion boards such as Reddit. Although deepfakes are often associated with pornography and disinformation, researchers point out that they have significant potential across many fields of human-computer interaction. The need for ethical analysis is growing as AI tools advance (V. Kumar et al., 2019; Saxena, Prasad, Haldhar, et al., 2018; P. Sharma et al., 2010). Deepfake technology, broadly described as the alteration of audio or video to make it appear like someone is saying or doing something they are not, has significantly evolved with the advent of AI. However, equivalent outcomes may be obtained without sophisticated artificial intelligence (AI), primarily by traditional editing techniques (Kushwaha et al., 2023).

Video alteration was formerly accomplished with manual editing and compositing capabilities included in programmes like Adobe After Effects, Final Cut Pro, or even more basic video editing software before AI-enabled deepfakes. Editors can use these techniques to synchronise lip movements with dubbed audio, adjust facial expressions, and sew together video footage. The results frequently lacked the smooth realism of AI-generated deepfakes, and the method was laborious and required frame-by-frame correction. For years, these methods have been employed in the making of films and television shows to improve story points, fix mistakes, and provide spectacular effects (Agrawal, Yugbodh, et al., 2023).

Apart from human editing, additional non-artificial intelligence methods involve employing impersonators or lookalikes who replicate the target's appearance, movements, and speech patterns. This method, combined with deliberate makeup and meticulous camera work, can occasionally provide convincing results – but usually only for short video snippets instead of longer ones. The degree of verisimilitude attained with these techniques varies widely, and upon closer examination, it is frequently simple to discern from authentic film.

Even while non-AI techniques are still capable, deepfake technology has advanced significantly in terms of accessibility, efficiency, and realism thanks to the introduction of AI. Artificial intelligence (AI) techniques, especially those based on machine learning models such as generative adversarial networks (GANs), automate the very accurate synthesis of human likenesses, reducing the manual labour required and yielding more convincing results. The development of these technologies presents severe moral and legal issues, primarily about consent and the possibility of abuse leading to the creation of damaging or deceptive information (Alam et al., 2023).

The role of non-AI techniques is still essential, even if AI has taken centre stage in debates about deepfakes. This is particularly true when resources for advanced AI tools are few or when ethical and legal requirements constrain the use of AI-generated material. Comprehending the disparate approaches is imperative in formulating all-encompassing tactics to detect, govern, and alleviate the consequences of deepfakes in diverse industries (Shrivastava et al., 2022).

Further investigation into non-AI deepfake technology finds a long history of cinematic methods and tools that have aided in the development of video editing. Before the advent of digital technology, filmmakers could create the appearance of actors acting out scenes or existing in unreal locations by using analogue techniques like matte painting, back projection, and prosthetics (Haldhar et al., 2018; Khamparia et al., 2019; Poongodi et al., 2020). These techniques show early attempts at manipulating perceived reality in visual media, even if they are not "deepfakes" in the contemporary meaning. A key component of non-AI deepfake technology is straightforward software tools with robust editing capabilities but no machine learning capabilities. Morph software, for example, may softly alter features, mix faces, and alter emotions. The fundamental concepts of picture blending and interpolation underpin the operation of these technologies. For some applications, including producing transitional effects for television or movies, the results can still be highly effective, even if they are not as sophisticated as those produced by AI (Barwar et al., 2022).

Before artificial intelligence, audio manipulation techniques included pitch and tempo adjustments and layering effects to simulate human voices or noises. These methods are frequently applied to manufacture music but may also be used to make phoney audio samples. The audio engineer's competence and the source material's calibre significantly impact how effective these non-AI methods are from the perspective of security and verification; the emergence of non-AI deepfake techniques has spurred the creation of several detection approaches. These involve using digital watermarking, teaching people to recognise manipulation signals, and using forensic analysis to find audio or video footage discrepancies. While these techniques might be helpful, they frequently need specialised expertise and are rarely infallible – especially as editing technologies advance.

18.2.2 Social impressions on deepfakes

Public scepticism about deepfake technology and its ramifications is regularly seen in surveys. Over 68% of participants in worldwide research said that deepfakes posed a severe threat to society, and 63% were in favour of outright prohibitions. Privacy breaches and the dangers of misinformation were the primary concerns. On the other hand, people had more favourable opinions of the independent creation of safe entertainment material. According to research, permission, transparency, risk of damage, and usage context are essential elements that influence how acceptable deepfakes are seen. Applications intended for historical recreations, consenting creative works, and teaching often raised fewer red flags. Respondents did, however, stress the importance of watermarking deepfakes and identifying their artificial origins. Ethical methods of governance can benefit from ongoing public opinion research (Ahmadi et al., 2020; Prakash & Uddin, 2017).

Social perceptions of conventional media manipulation methods and non-AI deepfakes have been noticeably divided, impacted by their potential for abuse and entertainment usage. Special effects and hand editing are widely acknowledged and even praised in television and film because they improve storytelling and provide captivating visual narratives. The artistic merit of conventional effects like prosthetics and matte paintings, which have long contributed to the enchantment of filmmaking, is frequently recognised by audiences. However, the public's reaction is unfavourable mainly when comparable tactics are employed outside these contexts, such as malevolent hoaxes or political propaganda (G. Singh et al., 2018).

The fact that audio and video may be edited to propagate false information, harm people's reputations, or unjustly sway public opinion raises even more concerns in the absence of advanced artificial intelligence. As a result, consumers now view media material cautiously and are less convinced about its veracity, especially when it comes to easily shared news on social media. This mistrust is exacerbated by the ease with which audio and video may be altered and the challenge of identifying such manipulations (Dar et al., 2019).

Furthermore, suggestions have been made for improved media literacy instruction and more precise limits on using such technologies due to educational and regulatory agencies' inability to keep up with the quick development of AI and non-AI media manipulation techniques. More people realise that although innovative use of these methods can be enjoyable and valuable, strict regulations must be implemented to avoid negative uses. Society faces the difficulty of balancing ethical norms, the need for openness to preserve public confidence in the media, and innovation in online media (Anand et al., 2017).

The ethical ramifications of these technologies are being more widely discussed in public as the effects of non-AI deepfakes and conventional media manipulation on society increase. This conversation has sparked a more thorough investigation into the impact that altered media – even those produced without advanced artificial intelligence – can have on people and societies. The possibility that these methods might encourage cyberbullying, character assassination, and even sway court decisions by fabricating evidence is a common source of worry. When victims see the manipulation of their voices and pictures, the psychological impact can be severe, causing distress and a sense of violation (Panda et al., 2021).

The ramifications are significant in the political sphere. Videos that misrepresent a person's words or behaviour can be made using even the most straightforward video editing software, possibly distorting public opinion and impacting election procedures. More robust systems to confirm and certify material as authentic are being sought after as these capabilities become more widely available and accessible, particularly in delicate settings like courtrooms and journalism. Conversely, there is a rising curiosity among the public about the possibilities presented by these technologies. Non-AI manipulations are being investigated as instruments for creativity and involvement in fields like education and the arts. While educators could use these approaches to produce engaging reconstructions or re-enactments for history lectures, artists are employing them to question perceptions and explore new forms of expression (Yuvaraj et al., 2021).

Notwithstanding these advantageous uses, a thorough understanding of digital literacy is still essential to reducing the hazards of media manipulation. To provide viewers with the tools they need to assess the content they consume critically, public education campaigns and workshops on how to identify doctored films are becoming increasingly widespread. Together with this, legal frameworks are continuing to evolve and are starting to make a more apparent distinction between what is considered harmful intent and reasonable use of digital manipulation (Bashir et al., 2020; Kalkal et al., 2021).

Society generally has a complicated and multifaceted perception of non-AI deepfakes and related manipulations. Although the technical expertise required and the potential for valuable applications are admired, there is also great concern about how easily these approaches may be abused. The way we comprehend the effects of technology is changing along with it, which leads to constant discussions on how to use and manage these potent instruments moving ahead. (Vaid et al., 2014).

18.2.3 Essential ethical guidelines

Key ideas from design theory and moral philosophy are used to examine developing technologies ethically. Basic ideas related to deepfakes in user interfaces are as follows:

Transparency: The extent to which users may easily access and comprehend a system's capabilities, limitations, and decision-making processes. Deceit may be made more accessible by a lack of openness on deepfakes. Transparency is crucial in the ethical implications of deepfake technology in user interfaces (UIs). By definition, deepfakes produce a misleading environment in which users find it difficult to discern between real-time interaction and artificially enhanced images. This lack of openness encourages manipulation and erodes user freedom of choice. Consider a situation where a deepfake customer support agent uses your browser history to tailor their sales presentation, gently urging you to buy a particular product without making it evident that they are phoney (Bordoloi et al., 2018).

This confidentiality might erode trust and lead to biased decision-making. To alleviate these concerns, developers need to prioritise transparency. One way to do this is by giving consumers clear and upfront disclosures about interacting with simulated content inside the user interface. Visual cues such as subtle badges or insignia might help reinforce this transparency. It is also the responsibility of developers to give consumers control mechanisms. This can include providing the option to switch between deepfake and face-to-face contact or having complete access to information about the deepfake technology in use. Ultimately, promoting transparency is essential. It boosts self-assurance, enables individuals to make informed judgments, and reduces the moral difficulties caused by user deepfakes (Saggu et al., 2014).

Autonomy: The ability of people to freely and intelligently choose what they do and how they utilise technology. Deepfakes may violate user autonomy through manipulation or forced usage. Deepfakes in user interfaces (UIs) are so common that they pose serious risks to user autonomy. Because of deepfakes' hyper-realistic capabilities, it cannot be easy to distinguish between modified material and actual interaction. Users are vulnerable to manipulation due to this lack of differentiation, which may unconsciously impact their choices. Consider a social media network where influencers that are deepfakes advertise things that seem natural or support particular political viewpoints. Unaware of the falsity, users could be influenced by these fake recommendations, impairing their capacity to make free and responsible decisions. This loss of autonomy makes it more difficult for people to make their own decisions and creates mistrust in the digital environment (Saxena, Prasad, & Haldhar, 2018).

Developers need to prioritise informed consent-enabling features to protect user autonomy in UIs with deepfake capabilities. Implementing a tiered authentication system that expressly indicates the degree of "realness" people are engaging with might be one strategy. This might be anything from allowing people to confirm the origin and legitimacy of the material they come across to clearly labelling deepfakes with disclaimers. Furthermore, promoting user control by implementing opt-in and opt-out procedures is essential. It should be up to the users to decide whether to interact with deepfakes or stick with a conventional, unaltered interface (Alharbi et al., 2021).

Developers can ensure that deepfakes improve user experience rather than harm it by putting user autonomy first. Fostering transparency and giving users the means to manoeuvre through the intricacies of UIs imbued with a deepfake can help achieve this. Ultimately, giving consumers the ability to give informed consent protects their freedom to make their own decisions online (Ansari et al., 2015).

Informed consent: It strongly relates to autonomy and suggests that users must explicitly disclose the ramifications of technology before approving its usage. It is not easy to get valid permission for deepfakes. User interfaces (UIs) using deepfakes pose severe concerns with informed consent. Deepfakes, in contrast to typical interactions, have the potential to mask the actual nature of the experience, making it challenging for users to comprehend the content they are engaging with or consuming. Users may unintentionally contribute to data gathering, be influenced by altered material, or even become the target of bad actors due to this lack of informed permission. Consider a virtual assistant that advertises items by deepfaking a famous person. Customers may buy products without fully understanding the source of the suggestion because the familiar face draws them in (Masud et al., 2021).

Developers need to put transparency first to guarantee informed consent. The usage of deepfakes should be made clear through succinct and unambiguous disclaimers in the user interface. Users should also be able to get comprehensive information on the data being gathered and its intended use through deepfake interactions. This gives people the ability to choose their involvement with awareness. Moreover, it is imperative to incorporate opt-in processes. Users should be given the clear choice to accept deepfake interactions, with the opportunity to switch to a conventional, unaltered interface if they would like. Developers may establish confidence and guarantee that users are actively engaging with profound fake-driven experiences within user interfaces (UIs) instead of being unintentionally exposed to them by placing a high priority on informed permission (Kapoor et al., 2021).

Beneficence: It is the idea that technology ought to benefit society and its users. Deepfakes have potential advantages in culture, entertainment, and design. The notion of beneficence is crucial when examining the ethical ramifications of deepfakes in user interfaces (UIs). The duty to behave in the user's best interests is beneficence. Deepfakes have the potential to improve accessibility and provide personalised experiences, but when misused, they can have negative consequences (Garg et al., 2017).

Consider an app for learning languages using deepfake teachers customised to the user's preferences. This might be helpful, providing a more exciting and productive learning environment. Deepfakes, however, may also be used to trick users. For example, a news app may utilise deepfake anchors to disseminate false content, hindering consumers' access to factual information (S. Singh et al., 2020).

The welfare of users must be the top priority for developers to maintain beneficence. Careful design selections can help achieve this. Deepfakes ought to improve the user experience, including offering interactions appropriate for the user's culture or customising interfaces for accessibility. Furthermore, developers have to prioritise measures that prevent abuse. This might entail identifying potential biases in the deepfake creation process or putting fact-checking procedures for deepfake material in place. Developers may ultimately ensure that deepfakes are used as a tool for user empowerment rather than as a means of manipulation or damage inside user interfaces by putting benevolence first (Bhushan et al., 2021).

Non-maleficence: The requirement to refrain from using technology to hurt people. The hazards of physical, psychological, social, and dignity harm from deepfakes are many. The non-maleficence criterion is crucial regarding deepfakes in user interfaces (UIs). According to this idea, one should refrain from harming others. Although deepfakes provide intriguing opportunities, users may experience psychological and emotional suffering due to their false nature (Bhushan et al., 2021).

Consider a social media platform where users may create personalised "roasts" that, thanks to deepfakes, seem like compliments. While some might find this humorous, others might get insecure or experience social anxiety as a result. Deepfakes may also be employed maliciously as weapons. For instance, someone may use a deepfake movie depicting a vulnerable person to damage someone's reputation or engage in cyberbullying (H. Kumar et al., 2020).

To maintain non-maleficence, developers have to prioritise protection against possible damage. Putting in place user reporting tools for content that has been recognised as deepfake might be one strategy. Furthermore, it is imperative to set unambiguous norms and content control procedures that hinder the harmful usage of deepfakes. Encouraging digital literacy and teaching people how to spot deepfakes is also critical. By emphasising non-maleficence, developers may ensure that deepfakes are not utilised in user interfaces to cause emotional or psychological harm (G. Singh & Arya, 2019).

Privacy: Users' right to manage who has access to their data and maintain certain levels of confidentiality. Deepfakes need to gather much personal information. Deepfakes seriously threaten user privacy in user interfaces (UIs). Deepfakes can function in a grey region, obfuscating the distinction between data gathering and user input in contrast to conventional interfaces. This lack of openness raises concerns concerning the collection, usage, and possible misuse of user data (Raza et al., 2015).

Consider a virtual assistant that adjusts suggestions for each user based on deepfake avatars' subtle emotional indications. This circumstance presents privacy concerns even though it is handy. Users may not be aware that their speech inflexions or facial expressions are being used to gather data when engaging in a deepfake engagement. Without the user's express knowledge or consent, this data may be sold to unaffiliated companies or used for specific marketing purposes (Manzoor et al., 2019).

To protect user privacy, developers need to put control and openness first. Deepfake user interfaces should clarify what information is collected during user interaction and how it will be used. Users should also have fine-grained control over their privacy settings, allowing them to reject particular data-collecting methods or, if they want, engage with a non-deepfake interface. Strong security measures are also necessary to stop illegal access to user data obtained by deepfakes. Developers can ensure that deepfakes do not open the door for data exploitation inside user interfaces by putting user privacy first (R. Sharma et al., 2020).

These core principles deeply inform ethical assessments of human-computer interaction. However, novel technologies like deepfakes complicate their application and introduce new tensions requiring context-specific analysis.

18.2.4 Hazards associated with deception

A significant worry is the potential for lifelike deepfakes to trick and control people. UIs may use deepfakes in ways that compromise user autonomy and transparency if appropriate protections and disclosures are not in place. Think about personalised marketing that uses deepfakes to replace influencers or celebrities in advertisements, addressing users by name and promoting goods without their knowledge or agreement. While hiding the commercial persuasion attempt, such personally customised information may evoke more significant emotional responses and apparent endorsements. Deepfakes may be used to produce interactive guides or companions for augmented or virtual reality (AR/VR) experiences that are more immersive, even when they do not reveal their artificial origins. Previous surveys suggest the public would be wary and distrustful of fraud involving digital entities posing as actual people. As such, gaining informed consent from users and adhering to transparency norms are essential for adequately integrating deepfakes into user interfaces. As with current procedures for declaring sponsored sponsorships on social media, any usage of deepfake avatars, virtual representations, or synthetic product endorsements must be explicit. In addition to enabling user customisation about the degrees of deepfake exposure, explicit watermarking and other technological safeguards may also assist in protecting transparency. In general, staying honest is consistent with research on developing reliable AI systems. However, context is vital since light-hearted usage of fictitious deepfake avatars in entertainment or gaming may call for different guidelines than those used in informative user interfaces. Further investigation on the optimal transparency threshold is required.

The act of deceiving or hiding the truth, or deception, presents several serious risks in social, professional, and personal spheres. In interpersonal interactions, lying may seriously undermine trust, the cornerstone of any connection. When trust is lost, it may be tough to rebuild, and the emotional damage can result in long-term problems, including anxiety, sadness, and a reduced ability to trust others in the future. Lying may damage someone's ethics and reputation in the workplace. Organisations may face severe legal and financial consequences due to dishonest employee behaviour, fraudulent methods, and years-long reputational harm. On a larger social scale, deceit in the form of false information may diminish public confidence in essential institutions like the government, the media, and science, leaving the populace ill-informed and undermining democratic processes. False information may also cause fear, exacerbate social tensions, and result in poor judgment in vital areas like health and safety. The risks connected to lying emphasise the importance of openness, responsibility, and moral behaviour to preserve the well-being and operations of any group or society.

The risks of lying go beyond these immediate effects, including the deterioration of social standards and community ethics. When lying becomes regular, dishonesty may become accepted as the standard in politics, commerce, or interpersonal relationships. This weakens society's moral fabric. Due to this societal change towards tolerating or anticipating dishonesty, people may find it more difficult to perceive the truth and make moral judgments, which can feed a vicious cycle of distrust and false information (Bharany et al., 2022).

Lying may have serious detrimental effects on the economy. For example, dishonest corporate practices have the potential to skew market dynamics, resulting in bottlenecks and asymmetries in the economy. Unfair business practices that mislead consumers and other enterprises into making bad financial decisions may cause them to suffer financial losses and a decline in economic activity. Furthermore, sectors rife with dishonesty could need more regulation and monitoring, adding to the expenses for corporations and taxpayers. Not to be overlooked is the psychological cost of being in a society where dishonesty is the norm. People may become generally uneasy and suspicious since they find it difficult to know who to trust. This environment may hamper collaboration and creativity as people and organisations are increasingly reticent to share information and cooperate (Bhyan et al., 2011).

Moreover, the quick spread of false information in the digital era can greatly magnify these impacts. Misformation can spread extensively before remedial measures or fact-checking occur, causing widespread panic and confusion. For instance, misleading information on treatments or preventative measures during medical emergencies may cause people to act in ways that worsen the situation. Lying has serious and varied risks that impact everything from interpersonal relationships to international economic and social systems. Enforcing regulatory requirements, fostering an ethical culture that values and encourages honesty, promoting media literacy, and maintaining openness are all necessary to mitigate these dangers (Jilte et al., 2019).

18.2.5 Insufficient agency and autonomy for users

Threats to user agency, or the ability to freely and thoughtfully choose how to utilise technology, are closely associated with deception hazards. Without permission or a way to opt out, deepfakes incorporated into user interfaces might jeopardise the agency. Think about AI personal assistants who steal the likeness of users' departed loved ones without their consent by creating deepfakes. Real-time, hyper-personalised deepfake marketing material modifications may trample upon user autonomy. Leading ethicists caution that the realism of deepfakes presents a more significant "agency hazard" than that of earlier media, such as text and pictures. Ethically deploying deepfakes should prioritise maintaining user agency. Acquiring explicit and informed consent before utilising deepfakes is a crucial prerequisite made possible by initial permission prompts and within-experience features that allow revocation (Ansari et al., 2016). In addition to initial disclosures, users should be routinely reminded that synthesised information respects their autonomy. Human responses to humanoid robots have been studied, and it has been shown that infrequent “state declarations” of artificiality can assist in avoiding unnecessary anthropomorphism. Agency inside UIs, such as adjusting personalisation levels, is also made possible by allowing user customisation about the kinds or intensities of deepfakes. Consent might be maintained throughout time using dynamic watermarking and adaptive transparency. Investigating technical interventions related to agency hazards is also worthwhile. Deepfake identification is becoming more accessible because of advancements in detection techniques, which may be combined with user alerts. Consent might become more relevant if gamification features that reward identifying synthetic material are included. Respecting the dignity and well-being of users instead of taking advantage of weaknesses will be the central focus of supporting agencies (Charbe et al., 2020).

Lack of agency and autonomy can lead to severe problems and disappointments for users of various systems and platforms. Losing control over one’s personal data, decisions, and interactions can have more severe consequences for privacy and individual freedoms than just having a detrimental effect on the user experience. Social media, e-commerce platforms, and service-oriented applications are primary digital spaces where users often feel insufficiently independent (Mahesh et al., 2014). These platforms often utilise algorithms to regulate what content users see, which advertisements appear, and how their private information is handled. Users who lack understanding and control over these processes may feel more like passive players than active controllers in their online relationships. People’s expectations and the truth of their interactions with the internet may differ due to this lack of control, which can occasionally result in the exposing of unwanted content or the inappropriate use of personal data.

When using surveillance technologies that track employees’ movements without their consent or awareness, workplaces are a significant source of inadequate agency. Such acts might infringe upon people’s right to privacy and foster a feeling of constant observation, both of which are detrimental to morale. A perception of lack of autonomy is inversely connected with employee engagement and productivity, which is contrary to the main goals of this type of monitoring. Household electronics and technology products with restricted ecosystems or non-customisable interfaces are less autonomous than others. Users are sometimes forced to utilise the preset configuration provided by the manufacturer and cannot customise the system to suit their needs better. This might reduce the use of devices for people with specific requirements or preferences and leave users feeling helpless and dependent on the technology supplier for updates and changes.

An increasing number of people are calling for more consumer control and transparency in digital and physical products to allay these worries. Efforts to enhance user agency include the right to repair and advocacy for digital rights, which call for laws and policies that give people more control over their devices and digital interactions. These programs highlight the importance of building goods and systems with user autonomy as the top priority, ensuring that technology is used to augment rather than limit human capabilities. Encouraging a healthy societal connection with technology is as essential as enhancing individual experiences to ensure appropriate user agency and autonomy. We can build more egalitarian, inclusive, and robust technology ecosystems by encouraging settings where people have significant authority and supervision.

The issue of inadequate agency and autonomy encompasses broader ethical and societal issues, particularly in healthcare and financial services, where individual autonomy is crucial. Patients in the healthcare industry may find themselves in situations where experts severely restrict or dictate their alternatives for treatment without giving the patient's preferences or comprehension any thought. This can affect patient outcomes and treatment effectiveness by causing a lack of empowerment and unhappiness with healthcare encounters. Enhancing informed consent procedures, providing patients with easily comprehensible information about available treatments, and actively involving patients in care decision-making are all necessary to promote patient autonomy.

Customers frequently have to traverse complicated processes in the financial industry with little transparency or control over how banks, loan agencies, and other financial organisations utilise their financial data. This might make customers feel helpless, especially when addressing problems like identity theft or credit reporting. Financial services prioritising user autonomy provide their clients with greater control over their data and alternatives and foster long-term relationships and trust.

The question of autonomy also pertains to public governance and urban planning since residents may feel powerless to influence choices that impact their everyday lives and local ecosystems. Insufficient involvement in planning procedures may lead to projects that do not satisfy community requirements or preferences, which can cause dissatisfaction and a rift between the populace and their urban environments. Increased community participation in these choices promotes a feeling of accountability and ownership, raising urban initiatives' standards and acceptability.

In education, inadequate agency is noted when systems enforce inflexible learning models that do not consider students' unique learning styles or requirements. This can discourage motivation and inventiveness, particularly in pupils who do not fit into the mould of conventional learning paradigms. Educational approaches that prioritise student choice, project-based learning, and customised lesson plans foster more involvement and autonomy. This improves learning results and increases student happiness.

18.2.6 Infringement of data permission and confidentiality

Privacy problems are associated with the large amounts of data needed to create convincing deepfakes. Detailed face and voice records can be used without the subject's consent to create customised deepfakes. This thus increases the potential of biometric data disclosure due to deepfake algorithms. Given the public's mistrust of corporate data activities, caution is necessary. Robust data governance will be necessary to integrate deepfakes into user interfaces in a way that respects human rights. Respecting user rights may be prevented by adhering to privacy and ethics by design principles. Data minimisation should be used by those who create deepfakes, limiting the amount of information collected and stored.

It is also critical to be transparent about the kinds of training data deepfake algorithms use; third-party authorisation should be sought whenever feasible. Cybersecurity and access restrictions will prevent biometrics from being used without authorisation. Granular permissions and on-demand deepfake creation are two ways that UI designers may empower user control over the collection of personal data instead of assuming consent. Synthetic media watermarking also restricts possible abuse and aids with identity protection. Proactive strategies that prioritise user privacy can foster trust. However, continued examination of the power disparity surrounding personal data is necessary.

Data authorisation and secrecy violations are serious problems that impact many industries, including e-commerce and healthcare, underscoring the urgent need for strict data protection regulations. The fundamental problem is that personal information cannot be disclosed or accessed without the individual's permission. Such breaches may result in detrimental outcomes that affect a person's life and well-being for a long time, such as identity theft, financial loss, and loss of privacy.

Consumer data is frequently gathered in the e-commerce industry for transactional and tailored marketing objectives. In this case, infringement may happen if businesses do not safely retain this data or utilise it for uses that do not have the customer's authorisation. In this industry, data breaches can result in direct cash theft and damage consumer confidence, leading to lower client retention and even legal action against the affected organisation. In the corporate world, trade secrets, financial records, and strategic plans are examples of sensitive company information that needs to be strictly protected to preserve operational security and competitive advantage. Unauthorised access to or disclosure of such data may result in significant financial losses and harm a company's reputation.

Various legal frameworks and technology solutions are available to organisations to prevent these violations. Legal frameworks worldwide, including the General Data Protection Regulation (GDPR) in the European Union, set strict requirements for data collection, storage, processing, and sharing. These regulations also give customers more control over their data through rights like data access, deletion, and faulty data repair. Technical data protection strategies include strong encryption, regular security audits, safe access controls, and comprehensive regulations that are rigorously followed within businesses. Employee training is also crucial to ensuring that all personnel of an organisation understand the importance of data confidentiality and are aware of the protocols to prevent breaches.

18.2.7 Detrimental effects on human dignity

The potential violation of human dignity by deepfakes is a deeper philosophical worry. Without permission, the power to alter or fabricate someone's identity runs the risk of objectifying or disregarding the inherent value of every human being. In UI/UX design, substituting artificial avatars for actual people undermines their agency and risks "dehumanising" interactions. Additionally, deepfakes run the danger of using computational distortions to reinforce or magnify social prejudices. It takes careful approaches to representation, personalisation, and bias mitigation to uphold dignity in design. Instead of treating consumers like data points, AI-generated content must cater to their interests. Narrowly technocratic viewpoints can be corrected via diverse participation in the production of deepfakes. Ongoing ethical inspections of UX innovations and procedures can find dignity damages. As was previously said, putting into practice rights-preserving data procedures also safeguards people's sovereignty. Acceptability ultimately rests on honouring people's innate values and respecting their right to self-determination rather than taking advantage of their weaknesses.

Many situations can harm human dignity, particularly when social, institutional, or interpersonal behaviours compromise individual rights, privacy, or intrinsic value. A fundamental tenet of human dignity is the belief in the inherent value of every person, regardless of their circumstances or characteristics. There are severe and wide-ranging repercussions when this dignity is violated, whether by prejudice, exploitation, or a disdain for individual liberty. For example, there may be a significant effect on an employee's self-esteem and mental health when they work in an environment where they are treated like machines for profit, with little regard for their welfare or rights. Similarly, privacy violations deprive people of their sense of security and agency, making them feel vulnerable and exploited. These violations can occur through unauthorised monitoring or data breaches. These incursions have the potential to be highly dehumanising as they turn people into objects of study or data. Systemic problems like racism, sexism, and economic inequality have a profound effect on human dignity on a more significant social level. They feed cycles of marginalisation and contempt that prevent people from fully realising and expressing their value. Recognising and dealing with these effects is essential to preserve human dignity and ensure everyone is respected and cherished in their communities.

Keeping with the subject of how violations of human dignity affect lives, medical facilities offer a powerful illustration. Patients may feel dehumanised and powerless if they are not respected or if their autonomy is not given priority while making medical decisions. Experiences like this affect people's psychological health as well as their faith in medical systems, which may discourage them from getting the care they need. Furthermore, students' intrinsic worth is compromised in educational settings when they are not valued or given a voice, which can hinder both academic success and personal growth.

Concerns about refugee treatment frequently draw attention to grave violations of human dignity on a worldwide basis. In addition to being deprived of their dignity, displaced people may experience incarceration, subpar housing, and a lack of fundamental respect from host nations. These circumstances not only compound their pain and suffering but also rob them of their dignity. In a similar vein, compulsion, exploitation, and the total denial of freedom and rights characterise modern slavery and human trafficking as some of the gravest breaches of human dignity.

These violations frequently cause social disintegration and a decline in fundamental human rights, which may pave the way for more pervasive violations. This vicious cycle means that societies that allow violations of human dignity risk sinking further into injustice and finding it increasingly difficult to recover equality and respect.

Human rights are protected by robust legal frameworks that must be upheld. Inclusive policies that value variety and individual worth and public education about these rights and their relevance are all examples of preventive and corrective measures that safeguard human dignity. To draw attention to abuses of human dignity and promote change, grassroots movements and international campaigning are equally essential.

18.3 Method Formulation

In this post, we will talk about ethical analysis utilising both conceptual and applied methods. We will examine the literature on UX design, ethics, and human-computer interaction pertinent to developing technologies to pinpoint the main moral dilemmas raised by deepfakes. We hope to clarify the ethical issues by examining possible applications of deepfakes in user interfaces and experiences. Technical details of deepfake techniques, including their advantages and disadvantages, will also be covered in this article. The outcomes of recent studies on public opinion on deepfakes and their regulation will also be considered. To put fundamental values and standards about deepfakes into context, we will now closely examine pertinent technological ethics rules and guidelines. The synthesis that results seeks to offer a thorough ethical analysis to direct appropriate deepfake usage in user interfaces.

Deepfake technology's ethical ramifications for user interfaces are complex, necessitating the development of thorough procedures to manage hazards and guarantee appropriate use. Several crucial actions would need to be taken to investigate these consequences thoroughly. Before implementing deepfake technology in user interfaces, a comprehensive risk assessment should be carried out to pinpoint any particular ethical concerns, such as the possibility of deceiving people, invading their privacy, or fostering prejudices. To guarantee a wide range of viewpoints, this review should engage stakeholders from various backgrounds, including ethicists, technological developers, legal experts, and intended users.

The creation of a solid ethical framework is crucial after the risk evaluation. Fundamental ideas like accountability, consent, and openness ought to serve as the foundation of this framework. Being transparent entails telling users when deepfake technology is being used and why. All parties whose data or likeness is utilised in the creation or interaction with the deepfake must provide their consent and guarantee that they are adequately informed about the use of their data. Accountability measures, such as channels for users to report issues and developers to take remedial action, must be implemented to address any exploitation of the technology or unintentionally detrimental outcomes.

Therefore, creating technical standards and guidelines that align with ethical principles is necessary for implementing this ethical framework. These rules should govern the design, development, and deployment processes to ensure that deepfake technology in user interfaces is created and utilised in ways that respect human rights and dignity. The influence of these technologies in real-world situations should also be continuously monitored and evaluated, and the ethical framework should be modified as needed in response to input and evolving conditions. Lastly, it is critical to maintain a continuous communication channel with the public, other technology developers, and regulators in the larger community. The goal of this discussion should be to increase awareness of the moral dilemmas and possible laws that may be required to protect rights and encourage the responsible application of deepfake technology.

18.4 Results and Discussion

This section examines the ethical implications of integrating deepfakes into user interfaces and experiences. The report summarises findings and makes suggestions for ethical behaviour. In examining the implications of deepfake technology for ethics in user interfaces (UIs), several pressing issues and potential harms emerge, necessitating careful consideration and ethical analysis. By applying critical ethical principles, such as transparency, informed consent, privacy, autonomy, beneficence, and non-maleficence, we can elucidate the ethical challenges associated with deepfake integration into UIs and devise strategies for ethically responsible practices. Transparency emerges as a crucial ethical principle in the context of deepfake technology in UIs. The deceptive nature of deepfakes, which can manipulate visual and audio information to create false impressions, raises concerns about user trust and integrity. Without clear disclosure of deepfakes in UIs, users may be misled or manipulated, undermining the principles of transparency and honesty. Therefore, ensuring transparency about using deepfake technology in UIs is essential to upholding ethical standards and maintaining user trust.

Informed consent is another fundamental ethical principle that must be addressed in the context of deepfake integration into UIs. Users have a right to be informed about how their data is being used and manipulated, particularly regarding sensitive personal information that may be altered or synthesised through deepfake technology. Without informed consent, users may unwittingly consent to interactions with UIs that employ deepfakes, compromising their autonomy and privacy. Therefore, UI designers and developers must prioritise obtaining informed consent from users regarding deepfake technology and its potential implications. Privacy concerns also loom large in the discussion of deepfake technology in UIs. The ability of deepfakes to generate realistic simulations of individuals' appearances and voices raises significant privacy risks, as personal data may be exploited or misrepresented without users' consent. Unauthorised use of individuals' likeness or voice for commercial or malicious purposes infringes upon their privacy rights and may result in reputational harm or identity theft. Therefore, robust privacy protections must be implemented to safeguard user data and prevent misuse in deepfake-enhanced UIs.

Furthermore, integrating deepfake technology into UIs raises questions about user autonomy and agency. By manipulating visual and audio stimuli, deepfakes can influence users' perceptions, emotions, and decision-making processes, diminishing their autonomy and free will. Users may unknowingly interact with UIs that employ deepfakes, leading to unintended consequences or behaviour manipulation. Therefore, ensuring users retain control over their interactions with deepfake-enhanced UIs is essential to uphold their autonomy and agency. Regarding beneficence and non-maleficence, ethical considerations must be made to mitigate potential harms and maximise benefits associated with deepfake integration into UIs. While deepfake technology offers exciting possibilities for enhancing user experiences and enabling novel forms of interaction, its misuse or abuse can significantly harm individuals and society. Therefore, ethical guidelines and best practices should be established to promote the responsible use of deepfake technology in UIs, prioritising the well-being and safety of users.

Applying vital ethical principles to examine deepfake technology's implications for ethics in user interfaces (UIs) reveals pressing issues and potential harms that necessitate careful consideration. We can derive concrete recommendations for ethically responsible practices in integrating deepfakes into UIs and user experiences by synthesising these analyses. Transparency emerges as a critical ethical principle when assessing the integration of deepfake technology into UIs. The deceptive nature of deepfakes, capable of creating highly realistic simulations of individuals' appearances and voices, poses significant risks to user trust and integrity. Users may be misled or manipulated without transparent disclosure of deepfakes in UIs, undermining their autonomy and decision-making processes. Therefore, ensuring transparency about using deepfake technology in UIs is essential to upholding ethical standards and maintaining user trust (Khamparia et al., 2020).

Informed consent is another fundamental ethical consideration in the context of deepfake integration into UIs. Users have a right to be informed about how their data is being used and manipulated, particularly when it involves synthesising or altering their personal information through deepfake technology. Without informed consent, users may unknowingly interact with UIs that employ deepfakes, compromising their privacy and agency. Therefore, obtaining informed consent from users regarding using deepfake technology in UIs is imperative to respect their autonomy and rights. Privacy concerns also loom large in discussing deepfake technology's implications for ethics in UIs. The ability of deepfakes to manipulate and simulate individuals' likeness or voice raises significant privacy risks, as personal data may be exploited or misrepresented without users' consent. Unauthorised use of individuals' images or voices for commercial or malicious purposes infringes their privacy rights and may result in reputational harm or identity theft. Therefore, robust privacy protections must be implemented to safeguard user data and prevent misuse in deepfake-enhanced UIs.

Moreover, integrating deepfake technology into UIs raises questions about user agency and autonomy. By manipulating visual and audio stimuli, deepfakes can influence users' perceptions, emotions, and decision-making processes, undermining their autonomy and free will. Users may unwittingly interact with UIs that employ deepfakes, leading to unintended consequences or behaviour manipulation. Therefore, ensuring users retain control over their interactions with deepfake-enhanced UIs is essential to uphold their autonomy and agency. Regarding beneficence and non-maleficence, ethical considerations must be made to mitigate potential harms and maximise benefits associated with deepfake integration into UIs. While deepfake technology offers exciting possibilities for enhancing user experiences and enabling novel forms of interaction, its misuse or abuse can significantly harm individuals and society. Therefore, ethical guidelines and best practices should be established to promote the responsible use of deepfake technology in UIs, prioritising the well-being and safety of users.

18.5 Conclusion

Deepfakes, a complex and rapidly expanding technology, have the potential to transform our lives in a wide range of ways. However, the abuse or reckless usage of this technology may be hazardous. IT competence is critical in this environment. They can support the ethical and responsible use of deepfakes, maximising their social benefits. Given the fast growth of deepfake technology, defining standards and best practices is an urgent issue. Establishing guidelines early on ensures that deepfakes uphold humanistic goals and serve society. As a result, engagement with technology professionals is essential in defining these guidelines and standards since they have the necessary expertise and abilities to navigate the complexities of this emerging technology. Policymakers, educators, and social scientists may help build ethical and responsible practices for deepfakes alongside technical specialists. Working cooperatively, we can employ deepfakes to help society while reducing possible threats. Deepfakes' success hinges on our capacity to use technology in ways that match our beliefs and promote humanity.

Deepfake technology is a complicated and quickly expanding area that can transform many parts of our lives. However, this technology's abuse or reckless use raises severe ethical considerations and possible damage. In addressing the ethical issues of deepfakes in user interfaces (UIs), technology professionals are essential in supporting ethical and responsible usage, maximising the technology's potential for social good. Given the fast growth of deepfake technology, forming conventions and best practices is urgently necessary. Early adoption of standards guarantees deepfakes are consistent with humanistic goals and contribute constructively to society. Collaboration with technology professionals is crucial in this attempt, as they have the essential knowledge and ability to manage the complexity of this expanding technology.

However, the duty to tackle the ethical concerns of deepfakes goes beyond technological professionals. Policymakers, educators, and social scientists all play essential roles in promoting ethical and responsible deepfakes. By collaborating across disciplines, we can maximise the benefits of deepfake technology while limiting any dangers and threats. Finally, the success of deepfakes depends on our collective ability to use technology in ways consistent with our beliefs and promote humanity. By adopting ethical principles and encouraging multidisciplinary cooperation, we can manage the moral challenges of deepfake technology in UIs and guarantee that its use benefits society.

18.6 Limitations

Analysing ethical notions that included high-level ideals with damages was the main focus of the investigation. To support responsible governance, further study may be done to understand better how the public feels about deepfakes in various user interface scenarios. Examples of deepfake user interfaces might be used to illustrate some ethical issues and their solutions. Furthermore, although the main focus of this essay was on Western ethical concepts, including views from other cultures would improve the study. The need to reevaluate ethical consequences over time arises from the evolution of technical capabilities for creating, identifying, and engaging with deepfakes.

Continual multidisciplinary cooperation and recurring ethical evaluations of procedures and guidelines will be necessary to stay current with these new technologies.

Several restrictions may affect the efficacy and scope of investigating the ethical implications of deepfake technology in user interfaces. The fast advancement of deepfake technology, which frequently surpasses the creation of appropriate moral standards and legal frameworks, is one of its main drawbacks. Because of this, it is challenging for ethicists and decision-makers to foresee the gamut of possible problems completely or to put preventative precautions into place. Furthermore, the efficiency of ethical solutions that have been suggested is limited because of the absence of thorough empirical evidence on the societal impact of deepfakes.

The variety of legal and cultural situations in which these technologies are used is another major problem. The development of global ethical standards may be hampered by regional variations in norms and laws about digital rights, consent, and privacy. Furthermore, there is frequently a conflict between ethical restraints and technical progress since strict laws may hinder the latter. The comprehensive resolution of these concerns, encompassing technology, ethics, law, and social sciences, necessitates an interdisciplinary approach that may result in disparate methods without a cohesive plan. These constraints make it necessary to do continuous research, collaborate internationally, and develop flexible policies to successfully handle the moral dilemmas that deepfake technology in user interfaces provides.

Beyond these initial restrictions, the intrinsic complexity of deepfake material presents a considerable obstacle to addressing the ethical implications of deepfake technology in user interfaces. Due to their remarkable resemblance, users may struggle to distinguish modified information from genuine deepfakes. This reality can potentially erode public confidence in digital media, making setting user expectations and ethical standards more challenging. Not only does this undermine public trust, but it also makes regulatory compliance more difficult because effective identification and mitigation of misuse need advanced technology and knowledge.

Another complex constraint is the consent problem. People whose voices or photos are utilised to make deepfakes frequently do not know that their likenesses are being altered digitally are unable to provide informed permission or do not completely understand the implications of their likenesses being used this way. The ethical handling of permission in this situation presents many challenges related to individual autonomy and the right to one's voice and image. Moreover, a significant drawback of deepfake technology is the possibility of bias. Algorithms trained on data that may unintentionally reinforce social prejudices can produce deepfakes. This can result in unjust treatment and uneven representation of particular groups, which, when repeated in user interfaces, can further ingrain these prejudices into societal structures.

References

Agrawal, Y., Bhagoria, J. L., Gautam, A., Sharma, A., Yadav, A. S., Alam, T., Kumar, R., Goga, G., Chakroborty, S., & Kumar, R. (2023). Investigation of thermal performance of a ribbed solar air heater for sustainable built environment. *Sustainable Energy Technologies and Assessments*, *57*. https://doi.org/10.1016/j.seta.2023.103288

Agrawal, Y., Yugbodh, K., Ayachit, B., Tenguria, N., Kumar Nigam, P., Gautam, A., Singh yadav, A., Sharma, A., & Alam, T. (2023). Experimental investigation on thermal efficiency augmentation of solar air heater using copper wire for discrete roughened absorber plate. *Materials Today: Proceedings*. https://doi.org/10.1016/j.matpr.2022.12.244

Ahmadi, A., El Haj Assad, M., Jamali, D. H., Kumar, R., Li, Z. X., Salameh, T., Al-Shabi, M., & Ehyaei, M. A. (2020). Applications of geothermal organic Rankine Cycle for electricity production. *Journal of Cleaner Production*, *274*. https://doi.org/10.1016/j.jclepro.2020.122950

Alam, M. A., Kumar, R., Banoriya, D., Yadav, A. S., Goga, G., Saxena, K. K., Buddhi, D., & Mohan, R. (2023). Design and development of thermal comfort analysis for air-conditioned compartment. *International Journal on Interactive Design and Manufacturing*, *17*(5), 2777–2787. https://doi.org/10.1007/s12008-022-01015-8

Alharbi, K. S., Fuloria, N. K., Fuloria, S., Rahman, S. B., Al-Malki, W. H., Javed Shaikh, M. A., Thangavelu, L., Singh, S. K., Rama Raju Allam, V. S., Jha, N. K., Chellappan, D. K., Dua, K., & Gupta, G. (2021). Nuclear factor-kappa B and its role in inflammatory lung disease. *Chemico-Biological Interactions*, *345*. https://doi.org/10.1016/j.cbi.2021.109568

Anand, A., Patience, A. A., Sharma, N., & Khurana, N. (2017). The present and future of pharmacotherapy of Alzheimer's disease: A comprehensive review. *European Journal of Pharmacology*, *815*, 364–375. https://doi.org/10.1016/j.ejphar.2017.09.043

Ansari, K. R., Quraishi, M. A., & Singh, A. (2015). Isatin derivatives as a non-toxic corrosion inhibitor for mild steel in 20% H2SO4. *Corrosion Science*, *95*, 62–70. https://doi.org/10.1016/j.corsci.2015.02.010

Ansari, K. R., Quraishi, M. A., Singh, A., Ramkumar, S., & Obote, I. B. (2016). Corrosion inhibition of N80 steel in 15% HCl by pyrazolone derivatives: Electrochemical, surface and quantum chemical studies. *RSC Advances*, *6*(29), 24130–24141. https://doi.org/10.1039/c5ra25441h

Barwar, M. K., Sahu, L. K., Bhatnagar, P., Gupta, K. K., & Chander, A. H. (2021). A flicker-free decoupled ripple cancellation technique for LED driver circuits. *Optik*, *247*. https://doi.org/10.1016/j.ijleo.2021.168029

Barwar, M. K., Sahu, L. K., Bhatnagar, P., Gupta, K. K., & Chander, A. H. (2022). Performance analysis and reliability estimation of five-level rectifier. *International Journal of Circuit Theory and Applications*, *50*(3), 926–943. https://doi.org/10.1002/cta.3187

Bashir, S., Thakur, A., Lgaz, H., Chung, I.-M., & Kumar, A. (2020). Corrosion inhibition efficiency of bronopol on aluminium in 0.5 M HCl solution: Insights from experimental and quantum chemical studies. *Surfaces and Interfaces*, *20*. https://doi.org/10.1016/j.surfin.2020.100542

Bharany, S., Badotra, S., Sharma, S., Rani, S., Alazab, M., Jhaveri, R. H., & Reddy Gadekallu, T. (2022). Energy efficient fault tolerance techniques in green cloud computing: A systematic survey and taxonomy. *Sustainable Energy Technologies and Assessments*, *53*. https://doi.org/10.1016/j.seta.2022.102613

Bhushan, B., Sahoo, C., Sinha, P., & Khamparia, A. (2021). Unification of Blockchain and Internet of Things (BIoT): requirements, working model, challenges and future directions. *Wireless Networks*, *27*(1), 55–90. https://doi.org/10.1007/s11276-020-02445-6

Bhyan, B., Jangra, S., Kaur, M., & Singh, H. (2011). Orally fast dissolving films: Innovations in formulation and technology. *International Journal of Pharmaceutical Sciences Review and Research*, *9*(2), 50–57.

Bordoloi, N., Sharma, A., Nautiyal, H., & Goel, V. (2018). An intense review on the latest advancements of Earth Air Heat Exchangers. *Renewable and Sustainable Energy Reviews*, *89*, 261–280. https://doi.org/10.1016/j.rser.2018.03.056

Charbe, N. B., Amnerkar, N. D., Ramesh, B., Tambuwala, M. M., Bakshi, H. A., Aljabali, A. A. A., Khadse, S. C., Satheeshkumar, R., Satija, S., Metha, M., Chellappan, D. K., Shrivastava, G., Gupta, G., Negi, P., Dua, K., & Zacconi, F. C. (2020). Small interfering RNA for cancer treatment: overcoming hurdles in delivery. *Acta Pharmaceutica Sinica B*, *10*(11), 2075–2109. https://doi.org/10.1016/j.apsb.2020.10.005

Chauhan, C. C., Kagdi, A. R., Jotania, R. B., Upadhyay, A., Sandhu, C. S., Shirsath, S. E., & Meena, S. S. (2018). Structural, magnetic and dielectric properties of Co-Zr substituted M-type calcium hexagonal ferrite nanoparticles in the presence of α-Fe2O3 phase. *Ceramics International, 44*(15), 17812–17823. https://doi.org/10.1016/j.ceramint.2018.06.249

Chincholikar, P., Singh, K. R. B., Natarajan, A., Kerry, R. G., Singh, J., Malviya, J., & Singh, R. P. (2023). Green nanobiopolymers for ecological applications: a step towards a sustainable environment. *RSC Advances, 13*(18), 12411–12429. https://doi.org/10.1039/d2ra07707h

Dar, S. A., Sharma, R., Srivastava, V., & Sakalle, U. K. (2019). Investigation on the electronic structure, optical, elastic, mechanical, thermodynamic and thermoelectric properties of wide band gap semiconductor double perovskite Ba2InTaO6. *RSC Advances, 9*(17), 9522–9532. https://doi.org/10.1039/c9ra00313d

Dash, A. P., Alam, T., Siddiqui, M. I. H., Blecich, P., Kumar, M., Gupta, N. K., Ali, M. A., & Yadav, A. S. (2022). Impact on Heat Transfer Rate Due to an Extended Surface on the Passage of Microchannel Using Cylindrical Ribs with Varying Sector Angle. *Energies, 15*(21). https://doi.org/10.3390/en15218191

Dewangan, N. K., Gupta, K. K., & Bhatnagar, P. (2020). Modified reduced device multilevel inverter structures with open circuit fault-tolerance capabilities. *International Transactions on Electrical Energy Systems, 30*(1). https://doi.org/10.1002/2050-7038.12142

Dihom, H. R., Al-Shaibani, M. M., Radin Mohamed, R. M. S., Al-Gheethi, A. A., Sharma, A., & Khamidun, M. H. Bin. (2022). Photocatalytic degradation of disperse azo dyes in textile wastewater using green zinc oxide nanoparticles synthesized in plant extract: A critical review. *Journal of Water Process Engineering, 47*. https://doi.org/10.1016/j.jwpe.2022.102705

Garg, V., Singh, H., Bhatia, A., Raza, K., Singh, S. K., Singh, B., & Beg, S. (2017). Systematic Development of Transethosomal Gel System of Piroxicam: Formulation Optimization, In Vitro Evaluation, and Ex Vivo Assessment. *AAPS PharmSciTech, 18*(1), 58–71. https://doi.org/10.1208/s12249-016-0489-z

Guo, H.-H., Zhou, D., Du, C., Wang, P.-J., Liu, W.-F., Pang, L.-X., Wang, Q.-P., Su, J.-Z., Singh, C., & Trukhanov, S. (2020). Temperature stable Li2Ti0.75(Mg1/3Nb2/3)0.25O3-based microwave dielectric ceramics with low sintering temperature and ultra-low dielectric loss for dielectric resonator antenna applications. *Journal of Materials Chemistry C, 8*(14), 4690–4700. https://doi.org/10.1039/d0tc00326c

Haldhar, R., Prasad, D., & Saxena, A. (2018). Myristica fragrans extract as an eco-friendly corrosion inhibitor for mild steel in 0.5 M H2SO4 solution.

Journal of Environmental Chemical Engineering, *6*(2), 2290 – 2301. https://doi.org/10.1016/j.jece.2018.03.023

Jilte, R. D., Kumar, R., & Ahmadi, M. H. (2019). Cooling performance of nanofluid submerged vs. nanofluid circulated battery thermal management systems. *Journal of Cleaner Production*, *240*. https://doi.org/10.1016/j.jclepro.2019.118131

Kalkal, A., Kumar, S., Kumar, P., Pradhan, R., Willander, M., Packirisamy, G., Kumar, S., & Malhotra, B. D. (2021). Recent advances in 3D printing technologies for wearable (bio)sensors. *Additive Manufacturing*, *46*. https://doi.org/10.1016/j.addma.2021.102088

Kapoor, B., Kapoor, D., Gautam, S., Singh, R., & Bhardwaj, S. (2021). Dietary Polyunsaturated Fatty Acids (PUFAs): Uses and Potential Health Benefits. *Current Nutrition Reports*, *10*(3), 232–242. https://doi.org/10.1007/s13668-021-00363-3

Kaswan, M. S., & Rathi, R. (2019). Analysis and modeling the enablers of Green Lean Six Sigma implementation using Interpretive Structural Modeling. *Journal of Cleaner Production*, *231*, 1182–1191. https://doi.org/10.1016/j.jclepro.2019.05.253

Khamparia, A., Gupta, D., Nguyen, N. G., Khanna, A., Pandey, B., & Tiwari, P. (2019). Sound classification using convolutional neural network and tensor deep stacking network. *IEEE Access*, *7*, 7717–7727. https://doi.org/10.1109/ACCESS.2018.2888882

Khamparia, A., Saini, G., Gupta, D., Khanna, A., Tiwari, S., & de Albuquerque, V. H. C. (2020). Seasonal Crops Disease Prediction and Classification Using Deep Convolutional Encoder Network. *Circuits, Systems, and Signal Processing*, *39*(2), 818–836. https://doi.org/10.1007/s00034-019-01041-0

Khan, S. A., Alam, T., Khan, M. S., Blecich, P., Kamal, M. A., Gupta, N. K., & Yadav, A. S. (2022). Life Cycle Assessment of Embodied Carbon in Buildings: Background, Approaches and Advancements. *Buildings*, *12*(11). https://doi.org/10.3390/buildings12111944

Kour, D., Kaur, T., Devi, R., Yadav, A., Singh, M., Joshi, D., Singh, J., Suyal, D. C., Kumar, A., Rajput, V. D., Yadav, A. N., Singh, K., Singh, J., Sayyed, R. Z., Arora, N. K., & Saxena, A. K. (2021). Beneficial microbiomes for bioremediation of diverse contaminated environments for environmental sustainability: present status and future challenges. *Environmental Science and Pollution Research*, *28*(20), 24917–24939. https://doi.org/10.1007/s11356-021-13252-7

Kumar, A., Maithani, R., Ali, M. A., Gupta, N. K., Sharma, S., Alam, T., Majdi, H. S., Khan, T. M. Y., Yadav, A. S., & Eldin, S. M. (2023).

Enhancement of heat transfer utilizing small height twisted tape flat plate solar heat collector: A numerical study. *Case Studies in Thermal Engineering*, *48*. https://doi.org/10.1016/j.csite.2023.103123

Kumar, A., Nirala, A., Singh, V. P., Sahoo, B. K., Singh, R. C., Chaudhary, R., Dewangan, A. K., Gaurav, G. K., Klemeš, J. J., & Liu, X. (2023). The utilisation of coconut shell ash in production of hybrid composite: Microstructural characterisation and performance analysis. *Journal of Cleaner Production*, *398*. https://doi.org/10.1016/j.jclepro.2023.136494

Kumar, A., Singh, V. P., Nirala, A., Singh, R. C., Chaudhary, R., Mourad, A.-H. I., Sahoo, B. K., & Kumar, D. (2023). Influence of tool rotational speed on mechanical and corrosion behaviour of friction stir processed AZ31/Al2O3 nanocomposite. *Journal of Magnesium and Alloys*, *11*(7), 2585 – 2599. https://doi.org/10.1016/j.jma.2023.06.012

Kumar, H., Bhardwaj, K., Sharma, R., Nepovimova, E., Kuča, K., Dhanjal, D. S., Verma, R., Bhardwaj, P., Sharma, S., & Kumar, D. (2020). Fruit and Vegetable Peels: Utilization of High Value Horticultural Waste in Novel Industrial Applications. *Molecules*, *25*(12). https://doi.org/10.3390/molecules25122812

Kumar, R., Dwivedi, R. K., Arya, R. K., Sonia, P., Yadav, A. S., Saxena, K. K., Khan, M. I., & Moussa, S. Ben. (2023). Current development of carbide free bainitic and retained austenite on wear resistance in high silicon steel. *Journal of Materials Research and Technology*, *24*, 9171–9202. https://doi.org/10.1016/j.jmrt.2023.05.067

Kumar, V., Singh, S., Srivastava, B., Bhadouria, R., & Singh, R. (2019). Green synthesis of silver nanoparticles using leaf extract of Holoptelea integrifolia and preliminary investigation of its antioxidant, anti-inflammatory, antidiabetic and antibacterial activities. *Journal of Environmental Chemical Engineering*, *7*(3). https://doi.org/10.1016/j.jece.2019.103094

Kumari, N., Alam, T., Ali, M. A., Yadav, A. S., Gupta, N. K., Siddiqui, M. I. H., Dobrotă, D., Rotaru, I. M., & Sharma, A. (2022). A Numerical Investigation on Hydrothermal Performance of Micro Channel Heat Sink with Periodic Spatial Modification on Sidewalls. *Micromachines*, *13*(11). https://doi.org/10.3390/mi13111986

Kushwaha, A. D., Patel, B., Khan, I. A., & Agrawal, A. (2023). Fabrication and characterization of hexagonal boron nitride/polyester composites to study the effect of filler loading and surface modification for microelectronic applications. *Polymer Composites*, *44*(8), 4579–4593. https://doi.org/10.1002/pc.27421

Mahesh, K. V., Singh, S. K., & Gulati, M. (2014). A comparative study of top-down and bottom-up approaches for the preparation of nanosuspensions of glipizide. *Powder Technology*, *256*, 436–449. https://doi.org/10.1016/j.powtec.2014.02.011

Mahla, S. K., Goyal, T., Goyal, D., Sharma, H., Dhir, A., & Goga, G. (2022). Optimization of engine operating variables on performance and emissions characteristics of biogas fuelled CI engine by the design of experiments: Taguchi approach. *Environmental Progress and Sustainable Energy*, *41*(2). https://doi.org/10.1002/ep.13736

Mahor, V., Bijrothiya, S., Mishra, R., & Rawat, R. (2022). ML techniques for attack and anomaly detection in internet of things networks. In *Autonomous Vehicles* (Vol. 1). wiley. https://doi.org/10.1002/9781119871989.ch13

Mahor, V., Bijrothiya, S., Mishra, R., Rawat, R., & Soni, A. (2022). The smart city based on AI and infrastructure: A new mobility concepts and realities. In *Autonomous Vehicles* (Vol. 1). wiley. https://doi.org/10.1002/9781119871989.ch15

Mahor, V., Garg, B., Telang, S., Pachlasiya, K., Chouhan, M., & Rawat, R. (2022). Cyber Threat Phylogeny Assessment and Vulnerabilities Representation at Thermal Power Station. *Lecture Notes in Networks and Systems*, *481 LNNS*, 28–39. https://doi.org/10.1007/978-981-19-3182-6_3

Mahor, V., Pachlasiya, K., Garg, B., Chouhan, M., Telang, S., & Rawat, R. (2022). Mobile Operating System (Android) Vulnerability Analysis Using Machine Learning. *Lecture Notes in Networks and Systems*, *481 LNNS*, 159–169. https://doi.org/10.1007/978-981-19-3182-6_13

Manzoor, S. I., Singla, J., & Nikita. (2019). Fake news detection using machine learning approaches: A systematic review. *Proceedings of the International Conference on Trends in Electronics and Informatics, ICOEI 2019*, 230–234. https://doi.org/10.1109/ICOEI.2019.8862770

Masud, M., Gaba, G. S., Alqahtani, S., Muhammad, G., Gupta, B. B., Kumar, P., & Ghoneim, A. (2021). A Lightweight and Robust Secure Key Establishment Protocol for Internet of Medical Things in COVID-19 Patients Care. *IEEE Internet of Things Journal*, *8*(21), 15694–15703. https://doi.org/10.1109/JIOT.2020.3047662

Panda, S. K., Aggarwal, I., Kumar, H., Prasad, L., Kumar, A., Sharma, A., Vo, D.-V. N., Van Thuan, D., & Mishra, V. (2021). Magnetite nanoparticles as sorbents for dye removal: a review. *Environmental Chemistry Letters*, *19*(3), 2487–2525. https://doi.org/10.1007/s10311-020-01173-9

Patel, S. (2011). Harmful and beneficial aspects of Parthenium hysterophorus: An update. *3 Biotech*, *1*(1), 1–9. https://doi.org/10.1007/s13205-011-0007-7

Pithode, K., Singh, D., Chaturvedi, R., Goyal, B., Dogra, A., Hasoon, A., & Lepcha, D. C. (2023). Evaluation of the Solar Heat Pipe with Aluminium Tube Collector in different Environmental Conditions. *2023 3rd Asian Conference on Innovation in Technology, ASIANCON 2023*. https://doi.org/10.1109/ASIANCON58793.2023.10269867

Poongodi, M., Sharma, A., Vijayakumar, V., Bhardwaj, V., Sharma, A. P., Iqbal, R., & Kumar, R. (2020). Prediction of the price of Ethereum blockchain cryptocurrency in an industrial finance system. *Computers and Electrical Engineering*, *81*. https://doi.org/10.1016/j.compeleceng.2019.106527

Prakash, C., & Uddin, M. S. (2017). Surface modification of β-phase Ti implant by hydroaxyapatite mixed electric discharge machining to enhance the corrosion resistance and in-vitro bioactivity. *Surface and Coatings Technology*, *326*, 134–145. https://doi.org/10.1016/j.surfcoat.2017.07.040

Prasad, A. O., Mishra, P., Jain, U., Pandey, A., Sinha, A., Yadav, A. S., Kumar, R., Sharma, A., Kumar, G., Hazim Salem, K., Sharma, A., & Dixit, A. K. (2023). Design and development of software stack of an autonomous vehicle using robot operating system. *Robotics and Autonomous Systems*, *161*. https://doi.org/10.1016/j.robot.2022.104340

Rathod, N. J., Chopra, M. K., Shelke, S. N., Chaurasiya, P. K., Kumar, R., Saxena, K. K., & Prakash, C. (2024). Investigations on hard turning using SS304 sheet metal component grey based Taguchi and regression methodology. *International Journal on Interactive Design and Manufacturing*, *18*(5), 2653–2664. https://doi.org/10.1007/s12008-023-01244-5

Rawat, R., Mahor, V., Chouhan, M., Pachlasiya, K., Telang, S., & Garg, B. (2022). Systematic Literature Review (SLR) on Social Media and the Digital Transformation of Drug Trafficking on Darkweb. *Lecture Notes in Networks and Systems*, *481 LNNS*, 181–205. https://doi.org/10.1007/978-981-19-3182-6_15

Raza, K., Thotakura, N., Kumar, P., Joshi, M., Bhushan, S., Bhatia, A., Kumar, V., Malik, R., Sharma, G., Guru, S. K., & Katare, O. P. (2015). C60-fullerenes for delivery of docetaxel to breast cancer cells: A promising approach for enhanced efficacy and better pharmacokinetic profile. *International Journal of Pharmaceutics*, *495*(1), 551–559. https://doi.org/10.1016/j.ijpharm.2015.09.016

Saggu, S., Sakeran, M. I., Zidan, N., Tousson, E., Mohan, A., & Rehman, H. (2014). Ameliorating effect of chicory (Chichorium intybus L.) fruit extract against 4-tert-octylphenol induced liver injury and oxidative stress in male rats. *Food and Chemical Toxicology*, *72*, 138–146. https://doi.org/10.1016/j.fct.2014.06.029

Saxena, A., Prasad, D., & Haldhar, R. (2018). Investigation of corrosion inhibition effect and adsorption activities of Cuscuta reflexa extract for mild steel in 0.5 M H2SO4. *Bioelectrochemistry*, *124*, 156–164. https://doi.org/10.1016/j.bioelechem.2018.07.006

Saxena, A., Prasad, D., Haldhar, R., Singh, G., & Kumar, A. (2018). Use of Sida cordifolia extract as green corrosion inhibitor for mild steel in 0.5 M H2SO4. *Journal of Environmental Chemical Engineering*, *6*(1), 694–700. https://doi.org/10.1016/j.jece.2017.12.064

Sharma, H., Rana, A., Singh, R. P., Goyal, B., Dogra, A., & Lepcha, D. C. (2023). Improving Efficiency of Panel Using Solar Tracker Controlled Through Fuzzy Logic. *2023 International Conference on Sustainable Emerging Innovations in Engineering and Technology, ICSEIET 2023*, 286–289. https://doi.org/10.1109/ICSEIET58677.2023.10303639

Sharma, P., Kaur, R., Baskar, C., & Chung, W.-J. (2010). Removal of methylene blue from aqueous waste using rice husk and rice husk ash. *Desalination*, *259*(1–3), 249–257. https://doi.org/10.1016/j.desal.2010.03.044

Sharma, R., Jasrotia, K., Singh, N., Ghosh, P., srivastava, S., Sharma, N. R., Singh, J., Kanwar, R., & Kumar, A. (2020). A Comprehensive Review on Hydrothermal Carbonization of Biomass and its Applications. *Chemistry Africa*, *3*(1). https://doi.org/10.1007/s42250-019-00098-3

Shrivastava, V., Yadav, A. S., Sharma, A. K., Singh, P., Alam, T., & Sharma, A. (2022). Performance Comparison of Solar Air Heater with Extended Surfaces and Iron Filling. *International Journal of Vehicle Structures and Systems*, *14*(5), 607–610. https://doi.org/10.4273/ijvss.14.5.10

Singh, A., Lin, Y., Ebenso, E. E., Liu, W., Pan, J., & Huang, B. (2015). Gingko biloba fruit extract as an eco-friendly corrosion inhibitor for J55 steel in CO2 saturated 3.5% NaCl solution. *Journal of Industrial and Engineering Chemistry*, *24*, 219–228. https://doi.org/10.1016/j.jiec.2014.09.034

Singh, A. P., Pradhan, N. R., Luhach, A. K., Agnihotri, S., Jhanjhi, N. Z., Verma, S., Kavita, Ghosh, U., & Roy, D. S. (2021). A Novel Patient-Centric Architectural Framework for Blockchain-Enabled Healthcare Applications. *IEEE Transactions on Industrial Informatics*, *17*(8), 5779–5789. https://doi.org/10.1109/TII.2020.3037889

Singh, G., & Arya, S. K. (2019). Utility of laccase in pulp and paper industry: A progressive step towards the green technology. *International*

Journal of Biological Macromolecules, *134*, 1070–1084. https://doi.org/10.1016/j.ijbiomac.2019.05.168

Singh, G., Gupta, M. K., Mia, M., & Sharma, V. S. (2018). Modeling and optimization of tool wear in MQL-assisted milling of Inconel 718 superalloy using evolutionary techniques. *International Journal of Advanced Manufacturing Technology*, *97*(1–4), 481–494. https://doi.org/10.1007/s00170-018-1911-3

Singh, S., Kumar, V., Datta, S., Wani, A. B., Dhanjal, D. S., Romero, R., & Singh, J. (2020). Glyphosate uptake, translocation, resistance emergence in crops, analytical monitoring, toxicity and degradation: a review. *Environmental Chemistry Letters*, *18*(3), 663–702. https://doi.org/10.1007/s10311-020-00969-z

Singh, S., Prakash, C., & Ramakrishna, S. (2019). 3D printing of polyether-ether-ketone for biomedical applications. *European Polymer Journal*,*114*,234–248.https://doi.org/10.1016/j.eurpolymj.2019.02.035

Singh, V. P., Kumar, R., Kumar, A., & Dewangan, A. K. (2023). Automotive light weight multi-materials sheets joining through friction stir welding technique: An overview. *Materials Today: Proceedings*. https://doi.org/10.1016/j.matpr.2023.02.171

Vaid, S. K., Kumar, B., Sharma, A., Shukla, A. K., & Srivastava, P. C. (2014). Effect of zinc solubilizing bacteria on growth promotion and zinc nutrition of rice. *Journal of Soil Science and Plant Nutrition*, *14*(4), 889–910.

Yadav, A. S., Alam, T., Gupta, G., Saxena, R., Gupta, N. K., Allamraju, K. V., Kumar, R., Sharma, N., Sharma, A., Pandey, U., & Agrawal, Y. (2022). A Numerical Investigation of an Artificially Roughened Solar Air Heater. *Energies*, *15*(21). https://doi.org/10.3390/en15218045

Yadav, A. S., Mishra, A., Dwivedi, K., Agrawal, A., Galphat, A., & Sharma, N. (2022). Investigation on performance enhancement due to rib roughened solar air heater. *Materials Today: Proceedings*, *63*, 726 – 730. https://doi.org/10.1016/j.matpr.2022.05.071

Yuvaraj, N., Srihari, K., Dhiman, G., Somasundaram, K., Sharma, A., Rajeskannan, S., Soni, M., Gaba, G. S., Alzain, M. A., & Masud, M. (2021). Nature-Inspired-Based Approach for Automated Cyberbullying Classification on Multimedia Social Networking. *Mathematical Problems in Engineering*, *2021*. https://doi.org/10.1155/2021/6644652

Index

About the Editors

Dr. Sanjay Taneja is an Associate Professor in the Department of Management Studies at Graphic Era Deemed-to-be University, India. His research expertise spans accounting and finance (FinTech, green finance), risk and insurance management, green economics, and innovation in insurance. He holds dual master's degrees (MBA and M.Com.) with specializations in finance and marketing, earning a gold medal from Chaudhary Devi University, Sirsa, India, in 2012. Dr. Taneja completed his Ph.D. (ICSSR-sponsored) on the financial performance of Indian banks in 2016 and his post-doctoral research on the European Green Deal's impact on Turkey's CO_2 emissions in 2023. He has over 50 publications in reputed journals (Scopus/ABDC/Web of Science), 2 e-books, 1 textbook, 20 edited books, and 4 Scopus-indexed book chapters. His scholarly impact includes 938 Google Scholar citations (h-index: 17, i10-index: 31) and 1023 Scopus citations (h-index: 21). He has presented at 50+ conferences, organized 40+ FDPs, and published case studies. A frequent keynote speaker, session chair, and guest lecturer globally, Dr. Taneja has also filed five patents (three published). Known for his dynamic approach and commitment to growth, he inspires excellence in academics and research.

Swati Gupta, A dynamic individual with a doctoral degree and over nine years of professional experience across various educational institutions and universities in diverse locations. She specialises in teaching subjects such as Management and Technology. Known for her energy and dedication, she possesses excellent analytical, problem-solving and decision-making skills. Having served as the editor for four books under renowned publishing houses including NOVA, Emerald, IGI Global, and AAP, she has contributed significantly to the academic field. Additionally, she has undertaken the role of a reviewer for IGI Global and has chapters indexed in Scopus covering topics in marketing, Digital Marketing, Green Business Management, Consumer Behavior among others. Furthermore, she holds a patent for The Role of Blockchain Technology in Crypto Currency Transaction with the Indian Patent, Application no. 202211041663, and the Date of Publication being 29/07/2022

Mohit Kukreti holds a Ph.D. in Human Resource Development (HRD), with over 25 years of international expertise in roles such as higher education administration, academic quality assurance, and strategic planning for higher education institutions (HEIs). With a rich career, he has held academic leadership positions in Nepal, Ethiopia, and Sultanate of Oman. He had served as the head of departments, program director for the IBA Program at the Directorate General of 6 CAS Colleges in the Ministry of Higher Education in the Sultanate of Oman. He is presently associated with the recently established government's University of Technology and Applied Sciences (College of Economics and Business Administration – Ibri). Dr. Kukreti's academic contributions extend to numerous articles and chapters published in peer-reviewed, ABDC and Scopus-indexed international Q1 journals and international books. His has participated and presented at conferences in the various countries. He has conducted various workshops, served as a session chair in conferences, undertaken editorial roles, and presently working as a reviewer for esteemed journals publishers such as Emerald, Routledge, IGI, and Inderscience. He has delivered talks at various universities, colleges and to the Ministry of Tourism officials, Government of India. His expertise extends to HEI quality assurance, HEI strategic Management, curriculum and courses designing at both undergraduate and postgraduate levels. He has lent his expertise as a Ph.D. examiner at several universities in India. His research areas span HRD, Business Management, HEI's strategy development and quality assurance, entrepreneurship, and tourism.

Abhishek Singh Chauhan is associated with Graphic Era Deemed to be University as a Professor in department of Management studies and an esteemed editor with a commendable 17-year track record in research and academia within the realms of International Business and Marketing. His depth of expertise is evidenced by his profound understanding of global market dynamics and strategic marketing principles. Through meticulous editorial oversight, he ensures scholarly publications meet the highest standards of accuracy and relevance. Chauhan's extensive experience enables him to provide invaluable insights, guiding authors towards impactful contributions in their respective fields. With a commitment to excellence and a keen eye for detail, he plays a pivotal role in shaping discourse and advancing knowledge in the domains of International Business and Marketing.

For Product Safety Concerns and Information please contact our EU representative GPSR@taylorandfrancis.com Taylor & Francis Verlag GmbH, Kaufingerstraße 24, 80331 München, Germany